The 'Liber de Diversis Medicinis.'

Early English Text Society.
Original Series, No. 207.
revised reprint 1969

Price 42s.

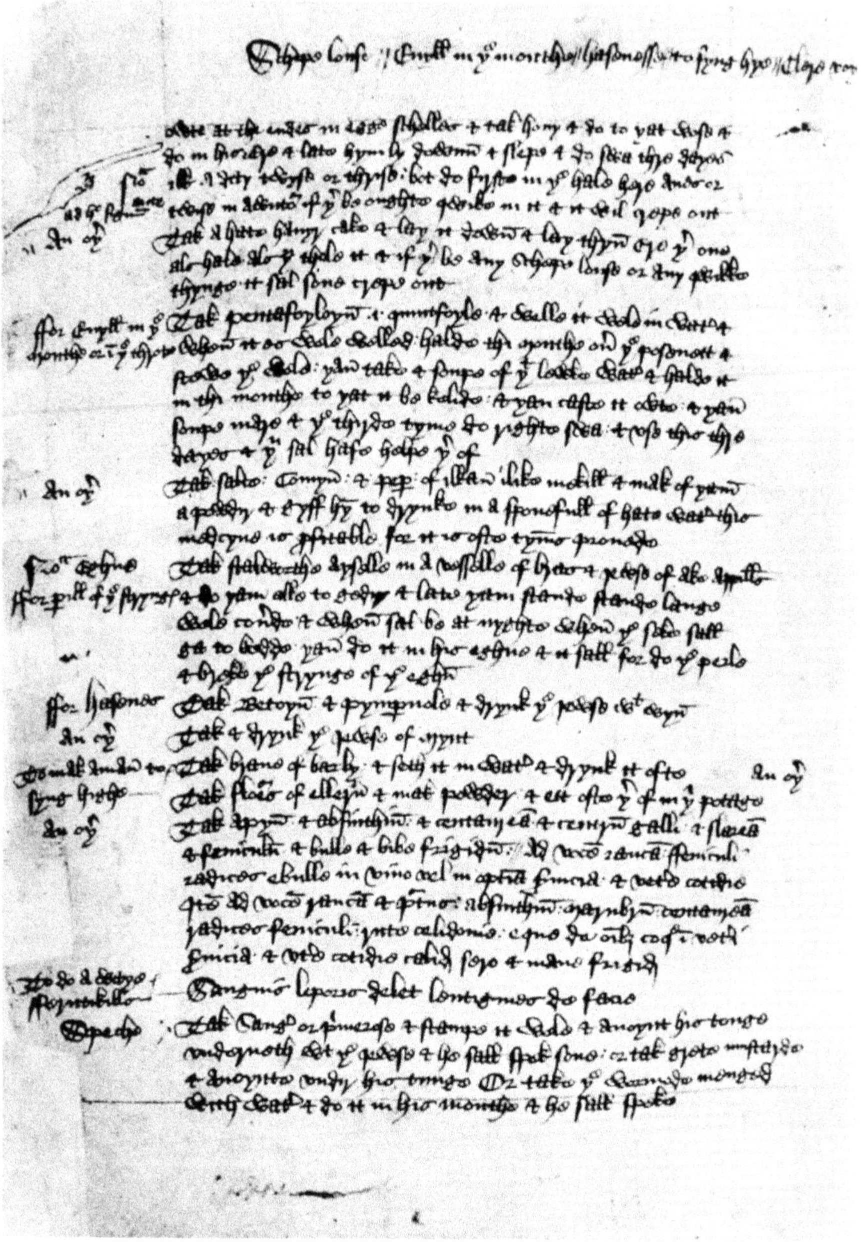

Lincoln Cathedral MS. A 1.17 (A 5.2), fol. 285 v

The 'Liber de Diversis Medicinis'

IN THE THORNTON MANUSCRIPT (MS. LINCOLN CATHEDRAL A.5.2)

EDITED BY

MARGARET SINCLAIR OGDEN

Published by
THE EARLY ENGLISH TEXT SOCIETY
by the
OXFORD UNIVERSITY PRESS
LONDON   NEW YORK   TORONTO

OXFORD
UNIVERSITY PRESS

Great Clarendon Street, Oxford OX2 6DP
United Kingdom

Oxford University Press is a department of the University of Oxford.
It furthers the University's objective of excellence in research, scholarship,
and education by publishing worldwide. Oxford is a registered trade mark of
Oxford University Press in the UK and in certain other countries

© The Early English Text Society 1938

The moral rights of the authors have been asserted
Database right Oxford University Press (maker)

First Edition published in 1938
Revised Reprint 1969

All rights reserved. No part of this publication may be reproduced,
stored in a retrieval system, or transmitted, in any form or by any means,
without the prior permission in writing of Oxford University Press,
or as expressly permitted by law, or under terms agreed with the appropriate
reprographics rights organization. Enquiries concerning reproduction
outside the scope of the above should be sent to the Rights Department,
Oxford University Press, at the address above

You must not circulate this book in any other form
and you must impose this same condition on any acquirer

Published in the United States of America by Oxford University Press
198 Madison Avenue, New York, NY 10016, United States of America

British Library Cataloguing in Publication Data
Data available

Library of Congress Cataloging in Publication Data
Data available

Original Series, 207

ISBN 978-0-19-722207-2

PREFACE

DURING the preparation of this edition, originally a dissertation submitted to the faculty of the University of Chicago in candidacy for the degree of doctor of philosophy, I have received much kind assistance. My chief debt of gratitude is to Sir William Craigie and Professor James Hulbert, who first suggested that I should study the Thornton manuscripts and whose advice and suggestions have been invaluable. Professor Edith Rickert has generously allowed me to study and quote from her rotographs of medical manuscripts. I owe a special debt of gratitude to the editors of the *Middle English Dictionary*, the late Professor Samuel Moore and Professor Thomas Knott, who have allowed me free use of the facilities of the dictionary and whose encouragement and advice have been of the greatest aid. The Assistant Editors have also contributed many useful suggestions, especially Professor Sanford Meech, who has been able to draw upon his wide experience with fifteenth-century manuscripts for the solution of several cruces in the transcription. Miss Hope Allen of the *Early Modern English Dictionary* has also offered helpful suggestions, especially concerning the identification of Robert Thornton. Mrs. Singer and Mr. Salzman have kindly answered queries with regard to English documents; and recently Miss Mabel Day has examined the edition thoroughly and offered a considerable number of valuable suggestions.

In the winter of 1935, I received a letter from Miss Virginia Everett, of the University of Chicago, indicating that she was preparing a paper on the identification of Robert Thornton, and asking what conclusions I had reached. I wrote that I had not yet made a systematic study of the subject, but enclosed the scattered bits of material which I had come upon with a statement of the general procedure I intended to follow in establishing the identification. As Miss Everett's reply indicated that she had already followed substantially this procedure, I asked if I might use the results of her work in my dissertation. To this she very generously consented. I have not duplicated her search through the records for references to Robert Thornton. I have, however, checked each reference which

I have taken from her work. I have also added a few facts of my own finding and have evaluated her evidence, discarding some points as too doubtful or not pertinent and re-interpreting others. However, in the main, I have agreed with Miss Everett, and wish to acknowledge the substantial contribution which her work has made to the first section of the introduction.

ERRATA

Delete: p. 12 fn. 2, p. 13 fn. 2, p. 37 fn. 2, p. 52 fn. 1.
p. 22 l. 26 peþir: *read* pepir
p. 33 Add fn. to l. 14 oftesones: ? *read* eftesones
p. 45 side-n. 2 pe: *read* þe
p. 73 side-n. 3 oper: *read* oþer
p. 92 l. 25 yuels: *read* yueles
    l. 26 stomach: *read* stomake
p. 95 l. 8 on: *read* of
    l. 24 ysid: *read* Ysider
p. 106 l. 8 Kotham: *read* Ketham
p. 109 l. 18 Unguentum vocatur Popileon sic debus: *read* Vnguentum vocatum Popilioun sic debet
    l. 26 quatron: *read* quartron
    l. 27 gronden: *read* grounden
    l. 34 oþer: *read* oþur
p. 111 col. 4 l. 21 664: *read* 644
p. 113 l. 31 dede: *read* dede nettel
p. 114 col. 1 ll. 8, 43 tay: *read* taþ [*read* tay]
    ll. 17–18 bultyde: *read* bustyde [*read* bultyde]
    l. 28 another: *read* anoþer
    l. 32 til: *read* till
    l. 46 if: *read* is
    l. 49 provyd: *read* þervyd [*read* provyd]
   col. 3 ll. 21, 31 oþer, water: *read* oþur, watur
    l. 22 als: *read* als as
    l. 40 Þen: *read* þen
    l. 43 noÞur: *read* noþur
    l. 44 Þat: *read* þat
    l. 47 hed: *read* ⟨hed⟩ [*cancelled*]
p. 115 col. 1 l. 4 noþer: *read* noþur
    l. 14 well: *read* wele
p. 115 l. 49 *entruce*: read *encruce*

Errata.

p. 117 l. 10 seemeþ : *read* semeþ
p. 120 col. 1 l. 9 *ande* : read *andi*
p. 121 col. 2 l. 57 *brand-reid* : read *brand-reið*
    l. 60 *Caesalpina* : read *Caesalpinia*
p. 125 col. 1 l. 23 *daeʒes eage* : read *dæges ēage*
    l. 59 *lionis* : read *leonis*
    col. 2 l. 17 *dille* : read *dile*
p. 131 col. 1 l. 26 *hasnes* : read *hāsnes*
p. 132 col. 1 l. 51 *hoste* : read *hósti*
    col. 2 l. 59 *kyli* : read *kýli*
p. 133 col. 1 l. 59 *laece* : read *lǣce*
p. 136 col. 2 l. 11 *fneosung* : read *fnēosung*
p. 146 col. 1 ll. 14–15 OF. *tyrdel* : read OE. *tyrdelu* (pl.)
p. 148 col. 2 l. 3 *altea* : read *alcea*
p. 149 col. 2 l. 7 Shöffler : *read* Schöffler

CONTENTS

	PAGE
PREFACE	v
INTRODUCTION	viii
The Manuscript and the Scribe	viii
The Medical Background of the Text	xv
The Language of the *Liber*	xxvi
TEXT	1
NOTES	83
GLOSSARY	119
BIBLIOGRAPHY	151
APPENDIX	159

INTRODUCTION

The Manuscript and the Scribe

THE Thornton manuscript (MS. Lincoln Cathedral A.5.2) is a paper volume of 314 leaves, measuring 11·5 by 8·5 inches. It is written in a cursive hand which is carelessly formed and which exhibits considerable variation.[1] The final folios contain a collection of medical prescriptions and charms. Beginning at folio 280r with the heading *Hic incipit liber de diversis medicinis*, the collection breaks off with the manuscript at folio 314v. There are, in addition, seven small fragments of later pages containing medical material.[2] Besides the medical text, the manuscript contains various romances, sermons, mystical writings, and religious lyrics.[3]

On several of the folios there are notations, apparently in the hand of the scribe, which indicate that the scribe was named Robert Thornton. One of the most explicit of the notations is the following which occurs on folio 213r : *R Thornton dictus qui scripsit sit benedictus Amen.*[4] The names of other members of the Thornton family,

---

[1] New Palæographical Society, *Facsimiles of ancient manuscripts*, Series II (London, 1913–1914), plate 45.

[2] These seven fragments vary in size from small marginal scraps which contain nothing or only three or four letters, up to marginal strips the length of the page and two inches wide at the broadest point. Being next to the binding, even the largest strips are mostly blank margins. Four marginal headings have been preserved in this way. See below, p. xvi, n. 4 and p. xvi, n. 9. Of the text itself, in only a few cases are there as many as fifteen letters of a line preserved. Many of the lines contain only the initial or final letter or a fragment of one. Upon careful examination of the rotographs of these fragments, it was decided that they contributed too few complete words to be worth reproducing in this edition.
  Sir William Craigie has recently called my attention to the following incomplete recipe on folio 279v : "For the scyatica. Tak a gowpyn full of sawge & als mekyll of rewe and choppe þam smalle."

[3] The contents of this manuscript are described in detail in *The Thornton romances*, ed. J. O. Halliwell (Camden Society; London, 1844), pp. xxv–xxxvi.

[4] The notations which may be in the hand of the scribe are : folio 53r, at the bottom of the page : *Espoyez*
  ygl En espyrance may;
  Thornton ;
folio 93v, in a scroll upon which an eagle is standing, the eagle and scroll being in the margin beside a capital K : *Robart Thornton*; folio 98v, at the end of the *Morte Arthure*, possibly not in the hand of the scribe: *Here endes Morte*

Wylliam, Edward, Ellinor, and Dorythy Thornton, are scribbled in the margins of the manuscript in later hands.[1] At the top of folio 49v, which also contains the words *Wylliam Thornton his Boke* in a similar hand, there occurs the following note concerning the birth of a Robert Thornton, obviously not the scribe of the manuscript : *Isto die natus fuit . . . Robertus Thornton in Ridayll anno Domini Mcccliij*.[2] The names of a few other persons have been scribbled in the margins : *Jhon Rokeby, Robert louson*, and *Roger blande*.[3]

Another manuscript, British Museum Additional 31042, is generally believed to have been written by the same scribe. The hands of the two manuscripts are very similar, although the hand of the Additional MS. varies even more than that of the Lincoln MS. At the end of the *Northern Passion* there occurs the name *R. Thornton* partially erased and disfigured. *The Siege of Jerusalem* ends with the colophon : *Explicit la sege de Ierusalem. R. Thornton* [written over and changed to another surname] *dictus qui scripsit sit benedictus. Amen.* In a mid-sixteenth-century hand there is scribbled in the margin of folio 49 *John Nettletons boke* and four times in the margin of folio 139v

---

Arthure writen by Robert of Thornton, and on the next line : *R Thornton dictus qui Scripsit Sit benedictus Amen*; folio 129v, at the end of the *Life of St. Christopher* : *Explicit vita sancti christofori Th* [the rest of the word has been erased]; folio 211v, at the end of a *Poetical address to Christ* : *Explicit Tractatus Explicit Amen Thornton Amen*; folio 213r, at the end of a meditation on the Cross : *P Thornton dictus qui scripsit sit benedictus Amen*; folio 278v, at the top of the page : *Thornton Misereatur mei dei.*

In the *Alexander*, within a capital A, there is a picture of a barrel drawn on its side with a tree springing from it *(The prose life of Alexander,* ed. J. S. Westlake [Early English Text Society, Original Series, No. 143; London, 1913], p. 60). Miss Everett in " Some notes on the identity of Robert Thornton," an unpublished term paper presented in partial fulfilment of the requirements of English 342, University of Chicago, 1935, suggests that this may be a rebus on the Thornton name. She cites an instance of a similar rebus : William Page, *The Victoria history of the county of York, North Riding* (London, 1914), I, 256. She also suggests that a dragon over the letter T in the *Alexander (The prose) . . . Alexander,* ed. Westlake, p. 90) may be a reference to the Thornton family crest (cf. A. C. Fox-Davies, *Armorial families* [Edinburgh, 1895], p. 90).

[1] The name *Edward Thornton* appears on folios 75v, 137r, and 194r ; *Ellinor Thornton* on folio 135v ; and *Dorythy Thornton* on folios 265r and 266r.

[2] Folio 49v is blank except for the following scribbles which seem to be in the same hand :

" Isto die natus ffuit sancta maria ante domini nostri Ihesu christi Robertus Thornton in Ridayll anno domini Mcccliij/Isto die natus ffuit Robertus/Isto die natus ffuit Roober/a a a In ye nam of owr lorde/b b b In domino confido quomo/c c c In domino confido/d d d d/e e/f ff/g g g g/h h/i i/k k/L ll L/M N en m m/N N N/O o o o/Wylliam thornton his Boke." The name *Wylliam Thornton* appears on folio 144v.

[3] On a margin of folio 220v the following appears : " Oft craving maikes sone forgittinge Ihon Rokeby." The name *Robert louson* appears on folio 29r, *Roger blande* on folio 265r.

xii   *Introduction.*

Nettleton.[1] These notations suggest that the Additional MS. passed out of the hands of the family early, probably before the middle of the sixteenth century. Nothing else is known of the history of the manuscript before the nineteenth century.[2] On the other hand, the Lincoln MS. may have remained in the family considerably longer.[3] Some of the Thornton names are written in hands of the late sixteenth century, and there is no positive record that the manuscript was at Lincoln Cathedral before the nineteenth century.[4]

Both the manuscripts are written in a characteristically mid-fifteenth-century hand. The inclusion of several poems by Lydgate (*d.* 1449) in the Additional MS. suggests that it was probably not written until the second quarter, and perhaps not until after the middle of the fifteenth century.[5] The Lincoln MS. seems to have been written some time after 1422, the date assigned to a holy woman's visions of purgatory in one of the prose pieces,[6] and before 1453–1454,

[1] MS. British Museum Additional 31042 is a paper manuscript consisting of 179 leaves, bound in two vellum leaves from a Latin breviary of the fifteenth century. It is described in: *The quatrefoil of love*, ed. I. Gollancz (Early English Text Society, No. 195; London, 1935), pp. vii–viii. *The sege of Melayne*, ed. Sidney Herrtage (Early English Text Society, Extra Series, No. XXXIV, Part 2; London, 1879), p. viii; and Karl Brunner, " Hs Brit. Mus. Additional 31042," *Archiv*, CXXXII (1914), 316–327. Miss Everett takes the following statement in a seventeenth-century hand on the fly-leaf of a copy of the *Pricke of conscience* to indicate that the scribe may have written a third manuscript containing all of the *Pricke of conscience* : " Ye book is complete tis wrote in the stile and maner of (Occ) leve Chaucer's scholar tho in my Coppy tis said to be ' Mr. Thorntone one of the grooms of the Princes Chamber ' which I understand of Hen. 5 " (H. E. Allen, *Writings ascribed to Richard Rolle* [New York and London, 1927], pp. 382–383). It should not be overlooked that the Lincoln MS. contains ll. 438–551 of the *Pricke of conscience* on folios 276v and following (Halliwell, *The Thornton romances*, p. xxxv). In the court records, Miss Everett has found a John Thornton and a Thomas Thornton in the reigns of Edward III and Richard II (R. E. Kirk, *Life records of Chaucer, Part IV* [Chaucer Society Publications, No. 47; London, 1900], pp. 173, 179, and Sir Thomas Hardy, *Syllabus of Rymer's Foedera* [London, 1873], II, 482). She has been unable to find record of any Thorntons at the court of Henry V.

[2] The Additional MS. was sent from America to Mr. J. Pearson for sale in 1879, in which year it was purchased by the British Museum (*The sege of Melayne*, ed. Herrtage, p. viii). [3] See below, p. xi, n. 5.

[4] In spite of Woolley's surmise that the manuscript came to Lincoln Cathedral between 1511 and 1527, there is no record of it in the catalogues before the nineteenth century. Cf. Reginald Woolley, *Catalogue of the manuscripts of Lincoln Cathedral Chapter Library* (London, 1927), pp. v–xx, 51–61.

[5] Poems in the Additional MS. probably by Lydgate are : No. 8, *Passionis Christi*; No. 9, *Memorial verses on the kings of England*; No. 10, *Dietary*; Nos. 14, 15, and 16, *The virtues of the mass* (*Archiv*, CXXXII [1914], 317–318).

[6] Cf. *Yorkshire writers*, ed, Carl Horstman (New York, 1895), I, 385–386 : " Lystonys and heris howe a womane was trauelde in hir slepe with a speryte of purgatorye, and how þat scho made hir compleynte to hir gastely ffadir and said on this wyse : Fadir, I do ȝow to wiete how grete trybulacyone I had in my slepe appone saynt Lowrence day at nyghte, þe ȝere of oure lorde a thowsande fowre hundrethe twenty and two."

Introduction. xiii

the date given in the note recording the birth of Robert Thornton at Ryedale.[1] This dating is confirmed by the water-marks on the paper of the manuscript. Documentary material dated as early as 1413 and as late as 1461 has been found bearing the same watermarks as those in the paper of which the Lincoln MS. is composed.[2] Certain facts point to the localization of the Lincoln MS. in the North Riding of Yorkshire. Ryedale, mentioned as the birthplace of the later Robert Thornton, is the name of a wapentake in the south-eastern part of the North Riding. A number of the medical prescriptions begin or end with the phrase: *Secundum Rectorem de Oswaldkirk*.[3] Oswaldkirk is a parish in the wapentake of Ryedale. This positive evidence for the localization of the manuscript in Yorkshire stands out the more prominently because of the lack of any record as to the presence of the manuscript in the Lincoln Cathedral library before the nineteenth century.[4]

If the manuscript is to be localized in Yorkshire, the most likely Thorntons to be connected with the manuscript are the Thorntons of East Newton in the wapentake of Ryedale. In the late seventeenth century, the family seems to have recognized some connection with the manuscript. On the fly-leaf of a genealogy of the Thorntons of East Newton which he compiled, Thomas Comber, Dean of Durham (*d.* 1699), mentions a note concerning the family on a leaf of the Thornton MS. Although he makes no statement as to the location of our manuscript, his note implies that he had access to it and that he regarded the Thorntons mentioned in it as belonging to his family.[5] In Jackson's edition of the *Autobiography of Mrs. Alice Thornton*, the mother-in-law of Dean Comber, there is a pedigree of the family of Thornton of East Newton based on the pedigree of Dean Comber, verified, and, in some points, corrected by the pedigrees of the family in the "York visitations" of 1563, 1584, 1612, and 1665 and various other documents.[6]

According to this pedigree, Robert Thornton, who became lord of East Newton on the death of his father in 1418, was probably the

[1] See above, p. ix, n. 2, where this is quoted.
[2] New Palæographical Society, *Facsimiles*, Series II, plate 45.
[3] See below, p. xvi, n. 5.
[4] See above, p. x, n. 4.
[5] *The autobiography of Mrs. Alice Thornton of East Newton*, ed. Charles Jackson (Surtees Society Publications, No. 62; London, 1875), p. viii. It is possible that the book passed out of the hands of the family in 1692 when East Newton and its furnishings were sold (*Victoria history, Yorkshire North Riding*, I, 562–563).
[6] This pedigree appears on an unnumbered sheet at the end of the volume.

scribe of the Lincoln MS. It is probably this Robert Thornton who is recorded twice in 1428 as holding lands with others in the wapentake of Ryedale [1] and is named in 1441 as one of the executors of the will of a *Ricardus Pikeryng de Oswaldkirk miles*.[2] Jackson's pedigree states that the scribe's son William was living at Thirkleby in 1456, apparently not yet having succeeded to East Newton by the death of his father. By 1465 Robert Thornton must have been dead, as his wife Isabel is recorded in the pedigree as having been married in that year to a John Mekylfeld. Both the location and the date of this Robert Thornton seem to fit the location and date which we have already selected as most probable for the composition of the manuscripts.

The identification is to some extent confirmed by the fact that the other Thornton names in the manuscript might have belonged to persons directly descended from the scribe. William Thornton, whose name appears on folios 49v and 144v, may have been the son of the scribe.[3] Robert Thornton, whose birth in 1453-1454, is recorded on folio 49v, probably was the grandson of the scribe.[4] The name *William Thornton* and the note regarding Robert Thornton on folio 49v seem to be in the same hand. It is possible, then, that William Thornton, the son of the scribe, wrote his name at the foot of the blank page at the top of which he had announced the birth of his son Robert. The family pedigree states that this William Thornton was living at Thirkleby in 1456 and that his will, dated 1487, was proved in 1489. Perhaps, however, the name refers to William Thornton, the great-grandson of the scribe, who died in 1545.[4]

Edward Thornton appears on folios 75v. 137r, and 194r. The only Edward Thornton in the family pedigree is a younger son of William

---

[1] *Inquisitions and assessments relating to feudal aids, 1284-1431* (London, 1920), VI, 314, 316. Miss Everett, *op. cit.* has also found references in Yorkshire documents from 1391 to 1414 to Robert Thornton, including one in 1398 to *Robert de Thornton of Neuton* (*Calendar of the Patent Rolls, 1396-1399* [London, 1909], p. 365). As the pedigree states that both the scribe's father (*d.* 1418) and his grandfather (*d.* 1402) were named Robert Thornton, it seems probable that these references are to earlier members of the family.

[2] Cf. *Testamenta eboracensia*, ed. James Raine (Surtees Society Publications, No. 30; Durham, 1854), II, 82 : [Will dated September 1, 1441] " Ego Ricardus Pikeryng, de Oswaldkirk, miles—sep. in ecclesia parochiali de Oswaldkirk, ante altare Beatae Mariae in australi parte in eadem ecclesia . . . Roberto Thornton meam nigram togam furratam cum foynes. Residuum margaretae uxori meae, quam facio executorem et sibi Robertum Thornton et Edmundum Pikeringe."

[3] " Pedigree of the family of Thornton of East Newton," *Autobiography of Mrs. Alice Thornton*, unnumbered final sheet.

[4] *Ibid.*

Introduction. xv

Thornton, the great-grandson of the scribe. Edward is recorded in the pedigree as still living in 1586, the year of the death of his wife Margery.

Ellinor Thornton is written on folio 135v. According to the pedigree, the wife of William Thornton, the grandson of William Thornton, great-grandson of the scribe, was an Eleanor, eldest daughter of Thomas Grimston of Grimston Garth. She was married before 1571 and still living in 1575.[1]

The name *Dorythy Thornton* is written on folios 265r and 266r in a decidedly late hand. The most likely person to whom this name may refer is Dorothy, daughter of Thomas Metham and wife of Robert Thornton, the eldest son of the Eleanor Thornton mentioned above. This Dorothy Thornton was buried at Stonegrave in 1619.[2] It is possible, however, that the signature refers not to the wife of this Robert Thornton, but to his sister Dorothy, who was married to William Askwith in 1591.[3] While Robert, William, Edward, Eleanor, and Dorothy are among the commonest English names, it is perhaps significant that among the Lincolnshire Thorntons of this period Miss Everett has been able to find Robert and William Thorntons, but no Edward, Eleanor, or Dorothy Thornton.[4]

The names of persons not belonging to the Thornton family which appear in the margins of these manuscripts are more difficult to identify. However, a few of these names suggest connection with Yorkshire. Miss Everett has found that there were families living near East Newton in the sixteenth century named Rokeby, Lowson, and Blande.[5]

In the medical text, individual prescriptions are attributed to

---

[1] "Pedigree of the family of Thornton of East Newton," *Autobiography of Mrs. Alice Thornton*, unnumbered final sheet.

[2] *Ibid.* On July 8, 1607, Dorothea, wife of Robert Thornton, of Stanegrave, was under charge for recusancy. Cf. *Quarter Sessions records*, ed. John Atkinson (The North Riding Record Society; London, 1884), p. 79.

[3] William Brown, "On the heraldry at Thirsk," *Yorkshire archæological journal*, XXII (1912–1913), 215: "William [Askwith] married, in 1590–1591, Dorothy, daughter of William Thornton, of East Newton, in Ryedale, and Eleanor, daughter of Thomas Grimston, of Grimston."

[4] A. R. Maddison, *Lincolnshire pedigrees* (Harleian Society, No. 52; London, 1904), p. 974 : William Thornton of Grantham (1627); p. 975 : Robert Thornton of Roughton (will dated 1612); p. 975 : William Thornton of Willoughby (1625).

[5] A *John Rhokebie* is recorded in 1577–1578 in the *Feet of fines of the Tudor period, Part II,* Yorkshire archæological and topographical association, Record Series, V (1888), 109, 114. A Robert Lowson is named in 1575 (*ibid.,* 67). Various members of a Blande family living near East Newton are mentioned in the same volume (pp. 22, 23, 60, 109, 128, and 144).

three persons, *Magistrum William de Excestre*,[1] the Rector of Oswaldkirk,[2] and *Ser Apilton*.[3] No information concerning *William de Excestre* has been found. The Rector of Oswaldkirk was thought by Halliwell to be the *Ricardus Pikeryng*, who in 1441 named Robert Thornton an executor of his will. Miss Everett has pointed out that Halliwell is wrong in identifying this person, who is styled *miles* in his will, as the Rector of Oswaldkirk.[4] William Appleton, a Minorite friar, is recorded as having been a physician in the employ of John of Gaunt, who paid him an annual stipend from 1373 until the friar's death in 1381.[5] While it is not likely that Thornton was old enough at the time of his death to have known him personally, it is possible that Thornton is quoting a recipe traditionally attributed to him. Pickering, one of the castles of John of Gaunt, was only about fifteen miles from East Newton.[6] The one recipe attributed to *Ser Apilton* lists rare unguents that a physician to royalty would have been most likely to prescribe.[7]

Everything that we know about Robert Thornton of East Newton agrees with what we know about the manuscripts more closely than what we know of any other Robert Thornton in the fifteenth century. If Robert Thornton of East Newton did not write the manuscripts, the most probable person becomes Robert Thornton, archdeacon of Bedford (*d.* 1450). Perry's undocumented statement that Robert Thornton, archdeacon of Bedford, was born either at East Newton or at Oswaldkirk seems to be without foundation.[8] As nothing is known of the archdeacon's family, no connection with the manuscript can be established in that way.[9] No positive evidence has been found connecting the Lincoln cathedral MS. with Lincolnshire

---

[1] See below, p. xvi, n. 7.
[2] See below, p. xvi, n. 5.
[3] See below, p. xvi, n. 6.
[4] See above, p. xii, n. 2.
[5] *John of Gaunt's register*, ed. Sydney Armitage-Smith (Camden Society, 3rd Series, Vol. 20; London, 1911), p. 335; Sydney Armitage-Smith, *John of Gaunt* (London, 1904), p. 248 note. In considering this identification, it should not be overlooked that the name may refer to some person connected with the parish or manor of Appleton in Ryedale (now Appleton-le-Street), which were east of Oswaldkirk and East Newton in the wapentake of Ryedale. Cf. *Victoria history, Yorkshire North Riding*, I, 451.
[6] Armitage-Smith, *John of Gaunt*, p. 218; *Victoria history, Yorkshire North Riding*, I, supplementary maps V and VI.
[7] See the note to p. 47/6–11.
[8] *English prose treatises of Richard Rolle*, ed. George Perry (Early English Text Society, Original Series, No. 20; London, 1866), p. vi.
[9] Miss Everett, who has made a careful study of the archdeacon's life, has been unable to find any information about his family.

Introduction. xvii

before modern times, nor has any Lincolnshire family of Thorntons been found bearing the given names written in the margins of the Lincoln MS.[1]

Moreover, the manuscripts themselves are in some respects more like the product of a gentleman amateur than of a cleric, licentiate in both laws.[2] The ornamentation and the hand of the manuscripts appear to be the work of an amateur.[3] The Latin is far more corrupt than the Latin in the samples of the archdeacon's official reports which have been preserved.[4] Although the manuscripts contain many religious pieces, their contents are by no means predominantly religious. Two-thirds of the folios of the Lincoln MS. and half of the folios of the Additional MS. contain secular material, chiefly romances.[5] Both from the closer agreement of the facts of localization, and the general character of the manuscripts themselves, the identification of the scribe as Robert Thornton of East Newton seems to be the most likely one which has so far been presented.

The Medical Background of the Text

The *Liber de diversis medicinis* is a compendium of remedies for various ailments. The remedies are arranged according to the part of the body affected, proceeding roughly from head to foot. They are for the most part in the form of recipes or prescriptions, varying in length from a single line to more than half a page. The simplest prescribe a specific medicine, especially part of an herb or an animal, for a given disease. The most complex list the ingredients and give directions for the preparation of elaborate medicaments, compound unguents, potions, and the like. Occasionally fairly long passages appear which are not in the regular form of a prescription or recipe. Among these are a list of the signs of death,[6] a set of somewhat garbled

---

[1] See above, p. x, n. 4 and p. xiii, n. 4.
[2] Miss Everett has pointed out several instances when the archdeacon served on legal commissions in London, and the following in which he is referred to as licentiate in both laws: *Calendar of the Patent Rolls, 1436–1441* (Publications of the Public Record Office of Great Britain; London, 1911), p. 28.
[3] New Palæographical Society, *Facsimiles*, Series II, plate 45; Karl Brunner, *Die mittelenglische Versroman über Richard Löwenherz* (Vienna, 1913), pp. 4–5.
[4] Samples of the archdeacon's Latin writings are to be found in: *Visitations of religious houses in the diocese of Lincoln*, ed. A. Hamilton Thompson (Horncastle, 1914), I, 82–86.
[5] The Lincoln MS. has 198 folios of secular material, 116 of religious. The Additional MS. has 90 folios of religious and 86 of secular material.
[6] P. 58/28–38.

directions for a simple surgical treatment in the case of headwounds,[1] and a three-page discussion of the symptoms and treatment of the pestilence.[2] Scattered through the English material there are a number of Latin recipes and charms, including three lines of verse and a long Latin passage giving directions for the mass of exorcism in the treatment of epilepsy.[3] Apparently, from the marginal headings preserved in the fragments of leaves after folio 314, the treatise originally continued with recipes arranged according to their chief herbal ingredient.[4]

Thornton gives certain of his recipes upon the authority of others. A score of his English and one of his Latin recipes are ascribed to the Rector of Oswaldkirk.[5] One recipe is attributed to Sir *Apilton*[6] and another to Master *William of Excestre*.[7] Two others are supported upon the authority of the famous Greek *Ypocras*.[8] The names of both *Ypocras* and *Plinius* also appear in the fragmentary leaves at the end of the manuscript.[9]

Many similar medical works have survived from the Middle Ages, some in Latin, some in French, and some, especially from the fifteenth century, in English.[10] They are composed of much the same kind of recipes as the Thornton *Liber de diversis medicinis*. Recipes in these other collections are occasionally attributed to one or another of the great medical authorities of antiquity, especially Hippocrates, Pliny, and Galen.[11] Their indebtedness to antiquity is by no means

---

[1] Pp. 69/14-70/19.
[2] Pp. 51/14-54/7.
[3] Pp. 4/15-16; 5/11-12; 14/7-14; 18/13-30; 19/32-33; 27/16-18, 29-30; 29/20-21; 33/37-38; 34/34-36; 35/15-17; 37/6; 42/18-23; 43/20-26, 34-36; 45/13-15; 51/3-4, 26-28; 56/29-37; 57/5, 8-15, 17, 24-25; 63/11-20. The three lines of Latin verse: p. 11/33-35; the Latin mass of exorcism: pp. 39/19-20, 22-41/25.
[4] The names of the herbs, *Dok, Betoyn id sunt,*
 Vetoyn
Haryue, and *Pympernolle* appear in the margins of the fragmentary pages. See above p. viii, n. 2.
[5] Pp. 20/17-22; 22/35-37; 27/31-34; 28/1-5, 30-31; 29/32-34; 30/15-17, 32-33; 31/9-10; 35/27-36/6, 24-28; 37/4-5; 38/4-7, 21-22; 44/31-33; 45/4-5, 16-37; 47/12-18; 76/12-15.
[6] P. 47/6-11.   [7] Pp. 6/37-7/4.
[8] Pp. 11/28-32; 56/24-28.
[9] On the fragment of folio 316r, there appears: *dronk.* . . ./*Plinius* . . ./ *& dryn* . . ./; on folio 320r: *and kepid clene with* . . ./*als sais Maister Ypocra* . . ./*þat coueres þe fallande* . . ./.
[10] Dorothea Singer, "A survey of medical MSS. in the British Isles dating from before the sixteenth century," *Proceedings of the Royal Society of Medicine*, XII (1919), 96-107.
[11] See, for example: *A leechbook*, ed. Warren Dawson (London, 1934), Nos. 485, 496, and 1064.

Introduction. xix

limited to a score of recipes. In fact, the fifteenth-century collections like Thornton's are to a considerable extent composed of ancient materials transmitted to them through a long line of similar compilations, each composed of whatever material had seemed best to its eclectic and often uncritical compiler. Certain unifying elements gave to these heterogeneous compilations a homogeneity which grew as the tradition advanced.

One of the most important unifying elements in the tradition was the general acceptance of the medical theory which Galen set forth in his works. Founding his system upon the Hippocratic theory of the humours and upon the idea of treatment by opposites, Galen classified diseases according to the particular humour or humours which he believed to be deficient. The materials which could be used to affect the body he divided into three classes : first, those which operated directly through the elementary qualities of hot, cold, moist, and dry, corresponding to the humours in the body; second, those which in addition had secondary attributes, such as sourness, bitterness, sharpness, and so forth; and finally, those which had besides these two some further quality, such as a purgative effect. Maintaining that these qualities were present in substances in varying degrees of intensity, he marked off four such degrees; in the first, the quality was barely perceptible; in the second, its effect was apparent; in the third, the effect was drastic; and in the fourth, complete and destructive.[1] From these general principles he elaborated a complicated system of cures. This he presented by quoting a large number of recipes from his contemporaries and predecessors, praising those which were in accord with his system, criticizing those which were contrary to it, and adding successful remedies of his own.

The system was variously interpreted by Galen's followers, but the fundamental body of principles remained in general much as Galen conceived it and became one of the most powerful influences upon medieval medicine. In the fifteenth-century recipe literature these principles are tacitly assumed rather than consciously expounded. It is only in the treatise on the pestilence, which we shall see was of entirely separate origin, that we find explicit discussion of the humours.[2] In the recipes themselves we find here and there a refer-

[1] "Ton Apton Pharmakon," *Claudii Galeni opera omnia*, ed. Carolus G. Kühn (Leipzig, 1826), XI.
[2] Pp. 51/14–54/7. See below, p. xxii.

xx   *Introduction.*

ence to the *dry coghe*,¹ to palsy as one of the cold passions,² to hot and cold dropsy.³ Occasionally the quality or, more rarely, the degree of a herb is mentioned.⁴ The long list of hot gums, spices, roots, herbs, and seeds appearing in a recipe for the palsy is unparalleled in English recipe literature.⁵ Yet the general principles of the Galenic system are often implied in the kind of remedy prescribed. It is obvious that cold remedies are prescribed for hot diseases and vice versa,⁶ that ingredients are prescribed for their secondary as well as their primary qualities,⁷ and that the degree of ingredients is implied more often than it is stated.⁸ The whole body of recipe literature is shot through with evidence of this theory, which the compilers consciously or unconsciously took for granted.

The medical tradition behind the Thornton recipes was further unified by the large body of recipes which had persisted in an unbroken succession of compilations from antiquity. This body of material contained much that originated before the time of Galen. The traditional arrangement and presentation of material in the recipes seem to be as old as Egyptian medicine.⁹ Some preparations and prognostic recipes owe their origin to the medical works of Hippocrates (*d*. 377 B.C.), though it is clear that many of them have been considerably modified in becoming part of the recipe tradition.¹⁰ An occasional recipe in the *Liber* is paralleled in the works of Aristotle (*d*. 322 B.C.),¹¹ Celsus (*d*. 50 A.D.),¹² Scribonius Largus (*d*. 47),¹³ and Dioscurides

---

¹ P. 20/ side-notes 11, 12. Cf. *Galeni opera omnia*, ed. Kühn, XIII, 63, 64 and, for the moist cough, *ibid*., 68.
² P. 66/8–9. Cf. *Galeni opera omnia*, ed. Kühn, XV, 369.
³ Pp. 32/side-note 7; 33/side-note 3. Galen mentions dropsy as a cold disease (*Galeni opera omnia*, ed. Kühn, VII, 609), as dry (*ibid*., XVII, 669), and as cold and moist (*ibid*., I, 522).
⁴ P. 2/27.
⁵ P. 66/8–39. Systematic lists of the qualities and degrees of materia medica are common enough in the more sophisticated medical works of the Middle Ages, *e.g*., " Des degres des médicaments," *La grande chirurgie de Guy de Chauliac*, ed. E. Nicaise (Paris, 1890), pp. 628–658.
⁶ See Table I, in the notes to p. 66/8–39.
⁷ For example, the recommendation of vinegar as an alternative for cold water (p. 48/36–37) implies that its dual properties of coldness and sourness had been assumed.
⁸ For example, the recommendation of hot water and lukewarm ale as alternatives (p. 20/35–36) implies that ale is considered hotter than water.
⁹ See *A leechbook*, ed. Dawson, p. 15, and Warren Dawson, *Magician and leech* (London, 1929), pp. 110, 133, 141–147.
¹⁰ See the notes to pp. 56/24–28; 58/28–38; 62/31–63/4.
¹¹ See the notes to pp. 29/24–25; 32/28–32.
¹² See the notes to p. 11/1–2.
¹³ See the notes to pp. 13/22–28; 17/11–18, 19–21.

Introduction. xxi

(*d.* 90).[1] The works of Pliny (*d.* 79) contain an unusually large number of simple prescriptions which are paralleled in the Thornton collection.[2] The bulk of the Egyptian, Greek, and Roman material was gathered together in the works of Galen (*d.* 200). While Galen's medical theory dominated the whole medieval medical tradition, there are but few recipes in Thornton's collection which represent Galen's recipes unmodified by later tradition.[3]

Starting from the nucleus of material afforded them by the collections of Galen and his predecessors, a number of influential writers of the fifth, sixth, and seventh centuries made similar compilations of recipes. These men tended to be less critically selective than Galen had been. Some augmented their collections with simple remedies composed of common ingredients, while others added elaborate recipes containing rare and exotic drugs. Many included magical cures of various kinds. Besides adding new recipes to their collections, they often combined and modified many of the original recipes. On the whole, they did much to establish the conventional features of medieval recipe compilations. Among the best known of the post-Galenic compilers are: Oribasios Pergamenos (*d.* 403), Apuleius Barbarus (*fl.* 400), Sextus Placitus (*fl.* 370), Marcellus Empiricus (*fl.* 425), Alexander of Tralles (*d.* 605), and Paul of Aegina (*d.* 690). Their compilations all include recipes which are paralleled in the Thornton collection.[4]

The early medieval compilers who followed the post-Galenic writers inherited the medical tradition of antiquity, either directly or through the medium of their post-Galenic predecessors. They continued the process of addition and modification. A significant development was the gradual Christianization of the pagan charms and magical cures. Such works as the London *Antidotarium*, the Anglo-Saxon *Leechbooks*, the Cambridge and Glasgow *Antidotaria*, and the medical section of the encyclopedia in MS. 17 St. John's

[1] See the notes to pp. 13/22–28; 27/17–18; 28/38–29/3, 22–23; 30/12–14 etc.
[2] See the notes to pp. 1/12–14; 2/3–5, 33–34; 3/20–24; 5/9–10, 11–12; 6/23–30, 31–32, 33–34, 35–36; 7/12–13, etc.
[3] See the notes to pp. 1/12–14; 2/6–7, 33–34; 4/15–16; 5/9–10, 11–12, 29–30, etc.
[4] For parallels to recipes in the works of Oribasios, see the notes to pp. 16/32–35; 80/23–27; Apuleius Barbarus, the notes to pp. 21/35–36; 26/1–2, 3–13, 24–27; 29/22–23, etc.; Sextus Placitus, the notes to pp. 11/26–27; 14/14; 18/1–2; 22/17–18; 28/19–21, etc.; Marcellus Empiricus, the notes to pp. 1/15–17; 6/23–30; 8/10–11; 17/11–18; 32/22–23, etc.; Alexander of Tralles, the notes to pp. 5/9–10, 29–30; 6/23–30, 35–36; 7/26–28; 8/3–5, etc.; Paul of Aegina, the notes to pp. 2/27–28; 4/26–29; 5/29–30; 6/35–36; 7, 26–28, etc.

c

College, Oxford, probably represent the early medieval recipe tradition before the advent of Arabian influence. The Thornton collection has parallels with recipes in all of these works except the London *Antidotarium*.[1]

With the translation of the medical works of the Arabians into Latin, a new and important source of recipes was made available. Starting from a Hippocratic and Galenic origin, the Arabian medical tradition had progressed independently of the western European. Partly because of the Mohammedan prohibitions against drunkenness, a large number of recipes to prevent and overcome intoxication appear in the Arabian medical works, and seem to have come into medieval recipe collections through Arabian influence. The Arabians were also very active in the use of materia medica of Eastern origin and in the preparation of elaborate syrups, *cyroyns*, and electuaries. Among the Arabian medical writings, of which the Latin translations contain parallels to the recipes in the Thornton *Liber*, are the works of Mesue the elder (d. 857),[2] Rhazes (d. 923),[3] Haly Abbas (d. 994),[4] Avicenna (d. 1037),[5] Averrhoes (d. 1198),[6] and Najm ad-din Mahmud (13th cent.).[7]

The Arabian influence was introduced into Europe by a group of writers who practised and taught their art at Salernum. Combining the European and Arabian medical theories, they continued the development of the recipe tradition. Although the Salernitans showed themselves progressive thinkers in the fields of anatomy and surgery, their attitude toward the recipe tradition was thoroughly conservative. The recipes in the *Antidotarium* of Nicolaus, for example, exhibit the tendency of the Salernitans to multiply the

---

[1] For parallels in the Anglo-Saxon *Leechbooks*, see the notes to pp. 1/20-21; 5/21-23; 6/23-30, 31-32, 35-36; 7/26-28, etc.; the Cambridge *Antidotarium*, the notes to pp. 1/12-14, 22-24, 27-28; 6/23-30; 7/12-13, 18-19; 13/29-32, etc., the Glasgow *Antidotarium*, the notes to pp. 5/21-23; 6/35-36; 14/14, etc.; MS. 17, St. John's College, Oxford, the notes to pp. 8/3-5, 10-11; 10/32-34; 13/22-28; 44/5-6; 58/28-38.

[2] See the notes to pp. 28/38-29/3; 65/10-11.

[3] See the notes to pp. 5/11-12; 7/12-13; 37/9, 10-11, 12-13, 16-17; 47/8-9; 65/10-11.

[4] See the notes to pp. 8/3-5; 11/1-2; 28/8-12; 31/31-32; 42/19-20; 61/20-23.

[5] See the notes to pp. 2/27-28; 5/11-12, 29-30; 7/5-7; 8/10-11; 9/5-6; 10/15-25, 35-39; 11/1-2, 28-32, 36-37; 13/22-28; 16/30-31, 32-35; 17/5-6; 18/1-2; 27/16-17, 17-18, 22-24; 28/19-21, 38-29/3; 30/30-31; 31/20-24; 33/9; 37/11, 12-13, 16-17; 42/19-20; 49/1-2; 57/3-4; 58/28-38; 66/8-39; 70/4, 6.

[6] See the notes to pp. 11/28-32; 58/28-38.

[7] See the notes to pp. 5/29-30; 11/28-32, 36-37; 47/8-9; 60/14-17; 61/20-23.

Introduction. xxiii

number of the ingredients and complicate their mixture, but not to change the kind of ingredients, nor the theory of the proposed cures. There are parallels in the Thornton collection to recipes in the works of Constantinus Africanus (*d.* 1087),[1] and other Salernitans.[2] Several of the preparations in the *Antidotarium* of Nicolaus (*ca.* 1140) are mentioned in the *Liber*.[3] Echoes of the *Regimen sanitatis Salernitanum* are also to be found.

The medical writings of the thirteenth and fourteenth centuries contribute little that is new to the recipe tradition. The writings of John of Gaddesden (*d.* 1361) and Bernard de Gordon (*fl.* 1300) contain comparatively few new recipes and no important new types of recipes. This is also true of the writings of the great surgeons of this period, Lanfranc (*fl.* 1315), Henri de Mondeville (*d.* 1320), Guy of Chauliac (*d.* 1368), and John of Arderne (*d.* 1380). There are a few parallels to Thornton recipes in the works of each of these men.[4]

In addition to the works of famous men, there were in these centuries and the fifteenth a large number of anonymous compilations. In the thirteenth century, numerous anonymous Anglo-French collections of recipes were made. Parallels in the *Liber* have been found to a number of the recipes in the material included in Paul Meyer's descriptions of unedited Anglo-French manuscripts.[5] Whether in French, in Latin, or in English, these works were almost entirely collections of recipes which had already been in existence for a long time. We may look upon the anonymous collections from the thirteenth century onwards as representing the beginning of the decadence of the recipe tradition. Older recipes are frequently garbled, run together, and fragmentarily recorded, while no genuinely new recipes appear.

The immediate channels through which the recipes of this long

---

[1] See the notes to pp. 5/11-12; 7/26-28; 11/1-2; 14/14; 22/17-18, etc.
[2] See the notes to pp. 1/8-11; 2/3-5; 3/20-24; 7/9-11, 26-28; 8/16-17, 18-19, etc.
[3] See the notes to pp. 45/4-5; 47/6-11; 60/14-17; 61/15, 19, 33; 62/31-63/4; 79/15.
[4] For parallels in the works of John of Gaddesden see the notes to pp. 18/13-30; 33/37-38; 34/29; 39/19-41/25; 42/19-20; 57/1-2, 3-4, 20-22, 26-29; Bernard de Gordon, the notes to pp. 37/12-13; 39/19-41/25; 42/9-12, 19-20; Lanfranc, the notes to pp. 5/29-30; 79/15; Henri de Mondeville, the notes to p. 47/6-11; Guy of Chauliac, the notes to pp. 33/9; 47/6-11; 66/27; John of Arderne, the notes to pp. 28/13-15, 32-37; 45/4-5; 48/36-37, 49/3-4; 50/23-25; 65/10-11; 75/22-23; 76/34.
[5] See the notes to pp. 1/12-14; 3/13-19; 14/15-19, 25-26; 26/17-18; 38/25-28; 48/31-37; 58/26-28; 59/15-16, 20-25; 67/15-16; 71/4-6, 7-8; 81/27-31.

tradition reached the Thornton compilation are difficult or impossible to determine. Obviously with a continuous tradition of compilation, the mere existence of parallels does not imply direct source relationship. It is unlikely that the works of most of his great predecessors were available to Thornton directly, and the fact that there are recipes in the Thornton collection parallel to recipes in all the major works of the recipe tradition does not indicate that Thornton had access to any of the more famous recipe collections. The echoes of the *Regimen*, found in a couplet and a single line, well may have reached the compiler by tradition. The couplet is altered by the addition of a new and otherwise unknown line, and the single line occurs in a charm.[1] Thus, even here, the evidence points rather to transmission through oral or learned channels than to direct knowledge of the *Regimen*. A few Latin recipes, which reproduce recipes from known medical works verbatim, may possibly have been obtained directly, although they probably were obtained through the medium of other compilations.[2]

One small fourteenth-century work is incorporated as a whole into the compilation. It is the smaller of the two treatises on the pestilence commonly attributed to John of Burgundy.[3] Thornton introduces it and concludes it without mention of the authorship. However, it is clear that he is translating the Latin treatise or giving a transcript of one of the many English translations. A comparison of Thornton's text with that of the one Latin manuscript which has been edited shows that it follows the Latin original closely.[4] It is certainly not a transcript of either of the two manuscripts of English translations which have been edited.[5]

As the *Liber* includes a number of Latin recipes, we may infer that Thornton was probably acquainted with some collection which was all or partly in Latin. This work was probably a contemporary

---

[1] See the notes to pp. 11/33-35 and 42/9-12.
[2] The recipe on p. 5/11-12 appears in the works of Rhazes, see note; for parallels to other Latin recipes see the notes to pp. 37/4-6; 39/19-41/25; 51/3-4.
[3] Pp. 51/14-54/7. Cf. David Murray, *John de Burdens or John de Burgundia . . . and the pestilence* (London, 1891), and Karl Sudhoff, "Pestschriften aus den ersten 150 Jahren nach der Epidemie des 'Schwarzen Todes' 1348 : 27 and 28, Die Pestschriften des Johann von Burgund und Johann von Bordeaux," *Archiv für Geschichte der Medizin*, V (1912), 58-75.
[4] British Museum, Royal MSS., 13 E. x, folio 24v : D. Murray, *John de Burdens*, pp. 24-29.
[5] Register of the Abbey of Kelso : *ibid.*, pp. 30-33, and British Museum, Sloane MSS., 2320, folios 13v-16 : K. Sudhoff, "Pestschriften," *Archiv für Geschichte der Medizin*, V (1912), 73-75.

Introduction.

one, more like that of Ketham (*fl.* 1480) from the late fifteenth century than like the Latin *Antidotaria* from the early Middle Ages.[1] It is also likely that Thornton was familiar with one or more contemporary English recipe collections. The parallels from all edited Old and Middle English medical works and from a few others accessible in rotograph throw some light on the nature of Thornton's indebtedness to this kind of material.[2]

The parallels range from those which have a few prominent ingredients or some striking procedure in common, to those in which the details of wording are identical.[3] Sometimes one version is more specific in its designations and directions than another.[4] Sometimes the subject-matter is alike but the expression widely different.[5] Some recipes are so short that the similarities are not of great significance, while others are so long that the cumulation of similarities makes a common original certain.[6] Among the recipes which are closely parallel in wording, the differences are sometimes chiefly dialectal in character.[7] Some recipes represent more corrupt versions of the original recipe than others.[8] In other cases all versions are obviously garbled, and the correct reading is difficult or impossible to determine.[9] Sometimes a single recipe in one collection appears as two separate but adjacent recipes in another collection.[10] Probably the most common kind of parallel is that in which the subject-matter and the pattern of expression are substantially identical, with the occasional omission, addition, or substitution of a single, unimportant ingredient and with slight variations in wording.[11]

The closest verbatim parallels to the Thornton recipes occur in the short selection of fourteenth-century recipes edited in *Reliquiae*

---

[1] Parallels to Latin recipes from well known works are given in the notes to pp. 5/11–12; 37/4–6; 39/19–41/25; 51/3–4. Parallels to recipes in the works of Ketham are given in the notes to pp. 27/27–28; 44/36–39; 56/11–18; 57/18–19; 68/13–30; 79/15.
[2] References to all close Middle English parallels are given in the notes to the text and, where necessary, accompanied by explanatory discussions.
[3] See p. xxiv, n. 1 and notes to p. 2/11–13.
[4] See the notes to pp. 6/23–30; 9/25–29; and 11/7–14.
[5] See the note to p. 7/9–11.
[6] For parallels of very simple recipes, see the notes to pp. 1/1–3; 3/1–2, and 14/15–16; of fairly long recipes, the notes to pp. 8/20–28; 9/25–29; 45/6–8.
[7] See the notes to pp. 8/20–28; 17/11–18; 31/20–27; 63/30–35, 64/4–8.
[8] See the notes to pp. 8/20–28; 26/17–18; 44/22–25; 58/3–5.
[9] See the note to p. 25/3–17.
[10] See the notes to pp. 6/23–30; 7/5–8.
[11] See the notes to pp. 6/23–30, and 44/22–25.

Antiquae.[1] Close parallels are especially frequent in the following texts : MS. British Museum Harleian 2378, edited by Henslow (Henslow B);[2] the *Practica Edwardia Universitatis Oxoniensis* in MS. British Museum Royal 12 G iv;[3] and MS. Medical Society of London 136 edited by Dawson.[4] The Medical Society MS. and the *Practica Edwardia* begin with the heading : " Here bygynnes goode medicines þat goode leches haue fonden & drawen owte of bokes of galiene & esclepius & ypocras for þey were þe best leches of þe world."[5] The Harleian MS. has the same heading in the middle of the collection.[6] In each case the heading is followed by a recipe prescribing the washing of the head with a *lye* (or *lee*) of betony, vervain, and wormwood as a cure for the headache. This is the recipe with which the Thornton collection begins. There are parallels between the next five to seven recipes. The only other recipe which occurs in all four collections is one prescribing mustard seed and rue as a local application. In two collections it is to be applied for headache, and in the other two for earache.[7] One recipe which does not occur in the Thornton collection occurs shortly after the heading in the three other collections.[8] Five of the recipes appear shortly after the heading in at least two of the manuscripts.[9] These facts suggest strongly that all four compilations go back to some original with a

---

[1] See notes to pp. 36/32-38; 48/25-27; 49/12-16; 54/33-40; 57/37-58/2; 60/31-61/2; 64/16-30.
[2] *Medical works of the fourteenth century* (London, 1899), pp. 76-122.
[3] Folios 188v and ff.
[4] *A leechbook* (London, 1934).
[5] MS. Royal 12 G iv, folio 188v. The version in the Medical Society MS. is longer : " Here begynneþe gode medycyns for al maner yvellis that euery man hath that gode lechys drawen owt off þe bokys that men clepe Archippus & Ypocras ffor thiese ware þe best lechis off the world in her tyme and þer for who so will do as thys boke wyll tech hyme he may be sekyr to have help off all yvellys and woundys and oþer desesys and sekeness both with in and eke wyth owt." (*A leechbook*, ed. Dawson, p. 18, No. 1.)
[6] *Medical works*, ed. Henslow, p. 105, l. 21 to p. 106, l. 2. MS. Sloane 521, *ibid.*, p. 139 also contains this heading, but as Henslow has edited only selections, omitting especially recipes which have already appeared in his book, it is impossible to tell whether or not the same recipes follow.
[7] See the note to p. 1/15-17.
[8] This recipe appears in MS. Royal 12 G iv, folio 188v as follows : " A goode drynk for þe bed take betayne & veruayne & wermot & celydone & weybrede & rewe & walworte & sawge, & .v. cornes of peper & stampe hem & sethe hem to gidere in water & drynk hit fastyng." See also *A leechbook*, ed. Dawson, p. 19 and *Medical works*, ed. Henslow, p. 106, ll. 6-9.
[9] References to parallels in the Thornton recipes and the collection edited by Dawson are given in the notes to p. 1/4-7, 8-11, 12-14; one parallel occurs in MS. Royal 12 G iv, folio 188v and *A leechbook*, ed. Dawson, p. 18, No. 6 and another in MS. Royal 12 G iv, folio 188v and *Medical works*, ed. Henslow, p. 106, ll. 10-13.

similar heading followed by at least some of the recipes which occur shortly thereafter. This suggestion is given some confirmation from Henslow's statement that in Volume 101 of the *Class Catalogue of the British Museum* there are at least eight entries with this heading.[1] As both vernacular and Latin recipe literature have been little studied, it is not strange that no famous earlier compilation with this heading has been found. A special search for the work from which these collections have derived this material, perhaps at considerable distance, might bring to light one or perhaps several important sources, intermediate between the earlier more famous works, which have already been mentioned, and the late vernacular compilations. At present, we must limit ourselves to some general conclusions derived from a study of the Thornton parallels.

The material contained in these late vernacular collections is more stereotyped than has usually been recognized. It has sometimes, for example, been argued that the recipes represent the setting down of the details of folk procedure in a kind of spontaneous language which does not appear in ordinary literary prose. But the relationship of Thornton's text to other similar collections is too close and the wording is too often identical to admit the conclusion that the scribe was putting down from memory a miscellaneous collection of recipes which he had heard during the course of his life. The recipes which he attributed to the Rector of Oswaldkirk, Master William of Excestre, and Sir *Apilton* were probably not home remedies. Sir *Apilton's* recipe and one of those attributed to the Rector prescribe highly complicated preparations mentioned by names which these or similar compounds had born since the early Middle Ages.[2] One of the Rector's recipes is in Latin, and there are parallels to three of his English recipes.[3] While some of the recipes in the *Liber* may have been put down from memory, it is clear that the pattern of content and expression of the individual recipe was conventional and considered of sufficient importance to be retained as accurately as possible. Few instances of probable errors of the ear have been found, but there are many possible miscopyings.[4] We know that

---

[1] *Medical works*, p. 74. See also Dawson's discussion of the heading, in which a similar heading in MS. Sloane 610 is mentioned (*A leechbook*, pp. 8–9).
[2] See the notes to pp. 45/4–5 and 47/6–11.
[3] See the notes to pp. 37/4–6; 44/31–33, and 47/12–15.
[4] Possible errors of the ear are *dede tonge*, p. 79/21; *rede diptonge*, p. 66/24–25; *tonge of dragon*, p. 75/28; probable errors of the eye are *flexigines*, p. 32/28; *pitory*, p. 66/30; *playlster*, p. 2/21–22; *rois*, p. 54/19; and *skafiʒagre*, p. 2/27; see notes.

the treatise of the pestilence probably had a written source. It is even possible that the whole *Liber* was a copy of a collection in another manuscript. One similar fifteenth-century collection has survived in five different manuscripts.[1] However, instances of this practice seem to be somewhat uncommon. On the whole, it seems likely that Thornton had access to several manuscripts containing recipe material of this sort, which he gathered together in an arrangement which had been conventional for centuries.

The Language of the *Liber*

The language in which the *Liber de diversis medicinis* is written shows strongly marked dialectal features. The most striking and significant feature is the regular occurrence of *a*- spellings for Old English *ā*.[2] Occasional instances of *o*- spellings occur.[3] As these are grouped in a few recipes, and as there are closely parallel recipes in which Midland and Southern forms appear throughout, it is probable that all of the *o*- spellings occur in passages in which the scribe was copying a non-Northern original.[4] According to the *Middle English Dictionary* Staff's "Middle English dialect characteristics and dialect boundaries," localized texts with regular *a*- spellings are not found south of a line running from the mouth of the River Lune, in Lancashire, to the mouth of the Humber.[5] On the basis of this dialect criterion the text was probably not written farther south than the northern part of the East and West Ridings of Yorkshire.[6]

The text contains no dialect features which would place it in another dialect than Northern. It contains none of the Southern

[1] British Museum, Sloane MSS., 405 and 3153, Royal MSS., 17 A. iii and 19, 674, and Harleian MS., 1600: *Ein mittelenglisches Medizinbuch*, ed. Fritz Heinrich (Halle, 1896).

[2] Among the frequent occurrences of *a*- spellings unaccompanied by *o*- variants are: *ake, ane, bare, clathe, hale, haly, sape, sare, taa, taken*, etc. For references, see the Glossary.

[3] The *o*- spellings are: *also, bone, bothe, fro, go*(*o*), *hote, more, no, none, whoso so, stone, þose, two*. For references see the Glossary.

[4] See the notes to pp. 17/11–18; 31/20–24, and 63/30–35.

[5] Samuel Moore, Sanford Meech, and Harold Whitehall, "Middle English dialect characteristics and dialect boundaries," *Essays and studies in English and comparative literature* (University of Michigan Publications, Language and Literature, Vol. XIII; Ann Arbor, 1935), pp. 8–9, 33–34.

[6] This treatment disregards the fact that the Thornton text was used as evidence for establishing this dialect line. It is possible so to disregard this fact because the Thornton text was added to the survey of Middle English dialects at the last moment, when line A had already been established by more than ample documentary evidence.

Introduction. xxix

or Western features for which dialect boundaries have been established. For example, there are no instances of the Southern initial *v-* for *f-*, nor of Western *o* for *a* before intervocalic or final nasals; there are no *eo-, o-, oe-, u-, ue-* spellings for either OE *y, ȳ*, or OE *ēo, eo*.[1] On the other hand, it contains non-Southern features which the Northern dialect has in common with the Northeast-Midland and the Central East-Midland. The present indicative plural as well as the present indicative third person singular regularly ends in *-s(e, -es,* or *-is, (-ys)*.[2] The third person plural pronoun is *þai (þay), þaire,* and *thaym (theym, þam, þem)*.[3] The third person singular feminine pronoun is *scho* throughout.[3] *Sal(l* occurs frequently, although there are also instances of *schal(l* and *scholde, schuld(e, shuld*.[3]

The *Liber* also contains a number of features which appear frequently in Northern texts, but which have not been established as dialect criteria with definite boundaries. The plural of *this* is frequently *thir*.[3] The preposition *at* is often used with the infinitive.[3] The present plural of *be* is *are* or *er*.[3] Old Northumbrian *a* before *ld* appears as *a* throughout.[4] OE and early ME *ō* appears frequently as *u*.[5] There are also frequent *gh-* spellings for OE ȝ, indicating that the guttural consonant probably was strongly pronounced.[6] In many cases in which an OE medial *v* has become final through the loss of following sounds, *f-* and *ff-* spellings occur.[7] In this text, the ME reflex of OE *hw-* is normally spelled *wh-*. However, it is once spelled *qw-*. While many Northern texts have *qw-* spellings entirely, there are, among the localized texts of which analyses were

[1] The consistent Northern forms are especially noticeable in contrast with the non-Northern forms in closely parallel recipes, *e.g.* Thornton : *fire,* Parallel : *fure*; Thornton : *fox*; Parallel : *vox.* See notes to pp. 31/20–24 and 64/4–8.

[2] Indicative third person singular : No instances of endings in *-eth, -th,* etc. occur. Illustrative verbs : *byhoues, comes, distourbes, febles, festres, gyffes, latis, dredis, fedis, swellis, sowdis,* etc. ; *gase, dose, hase,* etc. For references, see the Glossary.

Indicative present plural : No instances of endings in *-eth, -th,* etc. occur. Illustrative verbs : *bygynnes, calles, caldes, failes, makes, hides,* etc. ; *callis, ettis, ledis,* etc. ; *hase, opynns, folous, dose, suffers,* etc. For references, see the Glossary.

[3] For references, see the Glossary.

[4] Illustrative words in -ald- : *halde, scalde, walde, alde, calde. Holde* occurs once. For references, see the Glossary.

[5] The *u-* spellings are : *fute, gude, luke, blude, bludy, rute.* The spelling *touthe* occurs. *O-* spellings also occur, as in *gode, blode, rote, tothe, sothe.*

[6] Illustrative words in *-gh-* : *merghe, talghe (taughe), wilghe (wylken), weghte, weghe, eghe,* etc. Non-Northern spellings occur occasionally as in *swalowe, wey, ȝalowe, ȝarow, welowe,* etc. For references, see the Glossary.

[7] Illustrative words : *gif, lefe, schafe, knafe, lofage, olife, hafe, safe, clefe, dryfe.* For references, see the Glossary. Cf. also R. Jordan, *Handbuch der mittelenglischen Grammatik* (Heidelberg, 1925), p. 228, section 263, n. 1.

Introduction.

made for the Middle English Dialect Survey, Northern texts with few or no *qw-* spellings.¹

Considering the strong probability that many of the recipes may have been copied from versions in various other dialects and spelling traditions, the language of the *Liber* appears surprisingly uniform and consistent.² Altogether the dialect evidence points strongly to a localization in the southern part of the area in which the Northern dialect was spoken. This agrees with the localization of the manuscript and the scribe on the basis of non-linguistic evidence.

The vocabulary of the *Liber de diversis medicinis* is quite as interesting as its dialect. The words which it contains constitute in some cases a real contribution to our knowledge of words referring to household affairs as well as of botanical and medical terms. There are a fair number of rare words and a few entirely new words. As Halliwell printed occasional recipes from this collection in his *Dictionary of archaisms and provincialisms*,³ a number, though by no means a majority, of the most interesting occurrences are already recorded in the *Oxford Dictionary*. Among the interesting words which do not appear in the *Oxford Dictionary* are : *brynt, sb.* ' burnt matter,' *coyle, vb.* probably ' strain,' the plant names *epworte* and *laverwort*, and the names of the preparations *Agrippa*, *Diatarascos*, and *Benedicta*.⁴ Among the words the appearance of which antedates the recorded occurrences are *hauyrmele* (NED 1785), the names of the preparations *Catholicon* (NED 1611) and *Marciaton* (NED 1550), and many plant names, as *red kne* (NED 1597) and *dentdelyon* (NED 1513).⁴

There are a fair number of Scandinavian loan words. In many cases a word or phrase of Scandinavian origin appears where parallel recipes have a word or phrase of native origin. Among these parallel expressions are *scharthe* for *scherd*, *gare boyle it* for *let it boyle*, *galte* for *borw swyne*, and *garthe cresse sede* for *town cresse sed*.⁵ Other interest-

¹ The one *qw-* spelling is *qwete* 'wheat.' Illustrative *wh-* spellings : *while*, *whetstane*, *where*, *whelis*, *what*, *white*, etc. One *wh-* spelling of OE *w-* occurs (*whilde* [sauge] ' wild ') and one *w-* spelling of OE *wh-* (*wilk* ' which ').

² Possibly of dialectal significance is the frequent appearance of double consonants. The double spellings occur especially after a long stressed vowel, e.g. *droppe* (OE *dropa*), *whitte* (OE *hwīt*), *throtte* (OE *þrotu*), *wynne* (OE *win*), *souppe* (OF *souper*). Double spellings of this sort also appear in Old Northumbrian.

³ (London, 1860) s. *Allerone*, *Ampulle*, *Ana*, *Anenst*, *Aymers*, *Bere*, etc. A few articles refer to the Thornton medical text without quoting. Cf., for example, *Areges* and *Thocknedils*.

⁴ For references and discussion, see the Glossary.

⁵ See notes to pp. 30/34–31/2 ; 33/16–21 ; 64/4–8 ; 77/5–14.

Introduction. xxxi

ing Scandinavian loans are *gopen* 'a double handful,' *kile* 'ulcer,' and *alme* 'elm.'[1]

Even more striking is the number of French loan words. Plant names of French origin appear frequently, even in designating plants which have also a name of native origin, as *maroȝl* for *harhone, herb Wauter* for *wodrofe, burtre* for *ellern, longedeboef* for *oxtonge, lange de cheyn* for *hondistonge,* and *longe de cerf* for *hertis tonge.*[1] Some rare French words occur as *allerone, founce, artetik, refraide, remoile,* and many plant names, among which are *cucurd, crope de cambre, herb saunce crop, ypocone, rouge vrtice,* and *rouge runcebrere.*[2]

These facts about the loan words in the text are in general agreement with the localization of the manuscript and identification of the scribe. It is not surprising to find in a text from the North Riding of Yorkshire a larger number of Scandinavian loans than are found in other texts of the same sort. Moreover, the larger number of direct French borrowings tends to corroborate the identification of the scribe as a gentleman, since a knowledge of French was still an esteemed accomplishment among the nobility and gentry.

[1] For references, see the Glossary.
[2] For references and discussion, see the Glossary.

TEXT

f. 280r. HIC INCIPIT LIBER DE DIUERSIS MEDICINIS
& PRIMO PRO CAPITE

For werke and vanytee in þe hede

Take veruayne or vetoyn or filles of wormod and make lee þer-of and wasche þi heued þer-with thrys in a weke.

Take þe rote of [1] wormode & yven terrestre, ache & **An oþer.**
5 wax & rykils & stampe þam to-gedir with þe white of a negge & do it one lyn clathe & bynde it abowte þe heuede.

Take sauyne & stampe it and menge it with oyle of **An oþer.**
roses & anes late it welle wele & syne anoynte thi heued
10 þer-with agayne þe sonne or þe fyre in wynter. Do so ofte and it sall for-doo þe werke.

Tak puliole & sethe it in vynacre & drynke it & halde **An oþer.**
thi heued ouer þe substance & after emplaster it on thi heuede all þe nyghte.

15 Take mustarde seede & rewe & stampe þam & temper **An oþer.**
þam with water þat it be thikke and do it one thi heued, for it is righte gude.

Take þe wyse of tormentile & bray it & make lee of **An oþer.**
askes & wesche þi heuede þer-with.

20 Take puliol ryall and seeth it in oyle & anoynte thi **An oþer.**
fronte & thi thonnwanges.

Take puliole with þe [2] jeuse of þe floure & braye it in a **An oþer for**
þe herenes.
mortere & drynke it fastande with hate water & ete noghte or none.

25 Take rewe & stampe it wele & do it in strange vynagre **An oþer.**
and anoynte thi heuede þer-with a-bowne.

Take aueroyne & braye it with hony & vyneacre & **An oþer.**
drynke it.

Take a handefull of wormode & sethe it in vyneacre **An oþer.**
30 or in lee & wesche þi heuede þer-with hate & laye þe

---

[1] MS. *adds* word *crossed out.* [2] MS. *adds* je *crossed out.*

Liber de Diversis Medicinis.

wormode[1] / to þe heuede alle hate when þou gase to bedde f. 280v.
or to slepe, *etc.*

An oþer. Take þe jeuse of rewe, vyneacre & oyle of roses & beres
of lorell & laye þam to thi heuede. It helpes wonderfully. 5

An oþer. Take puliol reall & braye it with hony & emplaster it
to þi hede.

An oþer. Take sauyn, wormod, aueroyne, tansay, yven terrestre,
vetoyne, egremoyne & boyle þam wele with a handfull
of salte & morn & euen enoynte thi heued per-with. 10

A drynke for þe heued werke. Tak vetoyne & veruayne, wormode & celidoyne,
wayebrede, rewe, walworthe & ix cornes of pepir & hony
& sethe þam in water and drynke þam fastande.

For clen-synge of þe heuede. Take vetoyne & boile it wele in water & wasche þi
heuede per-with. 15

An oþer. Take vetoyne & stampe it & temper it with water and
drynke it fastande, and, if þu drynke venyme or puyson
þat day, þu sall spewe it owte sone, & it is gude powder
to ete.

If a man thynke þat his hede be tome a-boune. If þe thynk þat thi heuede be tome a-bouen, take and 20
sethe þe leues of egrymoyne with hony and make a play-
ster[2] and laye to þe heuede.

A gud oynement for fantome in þe heuede. Take rose, walworte, salt, hony, waxe, rycles and welle
þam to-gedir ouer þe fire & enoynte þi hede þer-with, &
it is gude also for flewme & reme in þe hede & for to sla 25
lyes & scalles.

An oþer þat helpes for dis-tourbance of tonge & euyll in þe mouthe & for flewme & remme in þe hede & for to sla lyes & scalles. Tak skafiȝagre, þat is hate & dry in þe thirde degre.
It is þe seede of a wilde vyne.

Take mastyke & chew it in thi mouthe. It helpes þe
tonge þat distourbes it when it is sare. 30

& [s]oke[3] a sothen henne or chapone or cheken in
vyneacre. Þat dose a man grete ese.

To sla lyes & scalles. Tak stafiȝagre, or-pyment & oyle mengede to-gedir and
anoynte the ther-with.

For trauel-lyng in slepe. Take vetoyne and hynge it a-bowte his nekke þat hase 35
trauellyng in his slepe.

Also for þe same. Take sauge & aueroyne & temper it with a littill pepir
in wyne & drynke it morne and euen. /

---

[1] MS. *repeats* and laye þe wormode.
[2] MS. playlster.   [3] MS. loke.

Liber de Diversis Medicinis. 3

f. 281r. Take aueroyne and temper it with wyne & drynk it   For hym
morne & euen.   þat spekes
                                                               in his slepe.
Take bulles pyssynge & do þer-to vertgrese & coperose   For hed
& sayme de-voyr ana, & do all to-gedir & anoynte thi hede   werke of
                                                              lange tyme.
5 þer-with ilke a daye morne & euen & wasche thi heuede
ofte with rynnand water & þu sal be all hale.
For hede stopped with reme : Take comyn, carui &   For hede
annys & stampe þam & ett þam or drynke þam.   [s]toppid
                                                             with
                                                             [r]eme.[1]
Take a handeful of sauge & stampe it and temper it   For to
10 with hate ale and sythen syle it thorowe a hate clathe & delyuer þe
drynke þer-of at morne a saucerfull calde and at euen als   [h]ede, þe
                                                             stomak [o]f
mekil hate iij dayes to-gedir.   reme.

First byhoues gere schafe þe scallede hede and þan   For to do
take virgyn wax and pyke, of aþer ilyke mekill, & boyle   a-way
                                                             scalles.
15 þam to-gedir and sprede a lyn clowte on a [2] bord & þis
plaster þer-on and mak it thyn with a sklisce and do it on
þe heuede all hate so þat it couer þe scalles & do it
noghte ix dayes & efterwarde anoynte it with hony ilke
a day & it sall hele it sekirly.

20 Take a cloue of garleke and stampe it wele and do hony   An oþer.
þer-to & do it on a clathe & lay it one þe heued & late it
lygge a daye & a nyghte. Þan wasche it with gude
strange lee & sape & lay thi plaster þer-to agayne & so do
ofte & it sall hele.

25 Take gose grese, ambros, spourge, redkne, sperworte,   An oþer.
littill burnett, of celidoyne als mekill als of all þe oþer,
sawnder, coperose & vertegrese, of ilkane an vnce, & make
a playster & lay þer-to.

Take horsell, þat some men calles elena campana, þe   An oþer.
30 rede d[o]ke [3] rote, twa parties of bromstane, May buttre
& qwik siluer, & þat is righte gude.

Take vertgrese & þe blaunke alome & menge to-gedir &   An oþer.
strewe it on þe heuede ofte.

Take sifull þat grewes one howses & bray it with grese   An oþer.
35 & anoynte þe scalles þer-with.

Take pik, rosyn, virgyn wax & bromstane, & resolue   An oþer.

---
[1] s and r worn away at edge of MS. The margin is often defective
and the emendations, where sufficiently obvious, will be put into
square brackets without comment.
[2] MS. adds bo crossed out.
[3] MS. deke.

þam ouer þe fire and anoynte þe heued þer-with ix dayes & ylke daye schafe it wele & wasche it in calde water. /

Skalles

Ane oyntement for all manere of scalles & to gare hare waxe & vocatur Vnguentum Aristotilis.

Tak sute, pixliquid, oyle de olyue, grete salt, of ilkane of þir foure euen porcioun, *id est* quartron, whit wax an vnce. Stampe þe sute & salt. Þan take þe pixliquid & þe oyle & þe white wax & do to þe fire in a panne and, when al is molten & scommede, do in powder of sute & salt & stirre it with a sclyce &, when it is wele boylede, tak it down & powre it thorow a lyn clathe & do it in boystes and, when þou wil anoynte þe scalled hede, gare clyppe it or schaue it bi-fore and anoynte it after and, when þe heued schall be waschen, make lee of haye ysels þat was mawen by-for myssomer day.

An oþer.

Farina siliginis cum aceto et melle mixta supponitur. Optime sanat caput tenosum.[1]

Item.

Take doke rotes & lefes of celydoyne, avance, wayebrede & braye þam with alde grese & salte & distemper þam with wyne & anoynte þe heuede þer-with twyse one a daye & þat helis wonderfully.

To make hare growe & waxe.

Wesche thi heued with þe white of an egge & hony & with þat lee twyse in þe woke & it sall hele it wele & faire & make þe hare to waxe.

An oþer.

Take welowe lefes & sethe þam in oyle & anoynt þe hede þer-with & it sal gare þe hare grewe & waxe.

An oþer.

Take þe skynne of a fox, þe heuede with þe lyppis, & brynne it to powdere.

Take egremoyne & stampe it & temper it with gayte mylke & anoynte þe heuede.

An oþer.

Take a chepes hert & bryne it to powdre & stampe it & temper it vp with oyle & schaue þe hede & anoynte it þer-with.

An oþer.

Take pelleter & make it in powder & temper it with grese of a bare & anoynte it with alle.

An oþer.

Take rede nettills, herbe benett, & homloke, waybrede, loueache, ryb, & þe rote of þe rede doke. Bray þam all in a mortere & drawe þe jeuse thorowe a clathe & frye it with fresche buttre of May & þan take powder of sawndyuer, vertgrese & qwyk siluer & do it in þat oynement

---
[1] tenenosum.

Liber de Diversis Medicinis.

f. 282r. whils it is hate & sithen do it in boystes & anoynt þe heued þer-with ylk daye / til[1] he be hale. Bot schafe þe hede at þe begynnynge & gare it blede and powdere þe scalles with sawndeuere.

5 Take þe beries of junyper & dry þam & make of þem *An oþer.* as þu dose of nuttes and [2] . . .

Take herte merghe & anoynte þer nede es & it sall[3] þe heuede. *An oþer.*

Take[4] malues with all þe rotes & sethe þam in water *A gud medcyn*
10 & wasche þi heuede þer-with. *to festen þe hare & lett to falle.*

Viaticum dicit quod, si capud fuerit lotum cum aqua mirte, confirmat capillos & eorum casum prohibet.

Take & make lee of hauyre straa & wasche þe hede *To do awaye hare.* þer-with ofte & sall do hare a-waye.

15 Take þe jeuse of yven leues &, when þe hare es pullede *An oþer.* a-waye, anoynte þe place.

Take askes of almebarke & vnslekked lyme, orpiment *For contrarius hare* & welle water & do þer-on.

Tak leues of woddbynde & stampe þam wele & *An oþer*
20 temper vp with vynecre & do it one þe heuede.

Take moure egges & þe blode of a bak & þe gvmme of *An oþer.* yven, orpyment, ayselle & stampe þam in a morter of lede with vnslekked lyme & frete it[5] þer-on ofte.

Tak nettill sedez & stampe it with vynacre & efter *An oþer.*
25 a grete hete anoynt it þer-with.

Tak & do awaye þe hare firste & take þe blode of a *An oþer.* bakke & þe galle of a gayte & anoynte it ofte þer-with & it will noghte suffre þe hare to growe.

Take & wasche þe heuede ofte in water þat luppines *To make hare*
30 hase bene sothen in. *lyk golde.*

Tak sawge & menge it with ashe when þu makes þi *For blake hare.* lee. Or make powdere of sawge and menge it with May buttre or henne grese & anoynte þe hare þer-with.

Tak gencyane sede & rewe & gyffe hym to drynke with *For a man þat es wode.*
35 vyneacre & schafe his hede.

---

[1] MS. *repeats* ilk daye *at the beginning of the line, before* til.
[2] *Recipe incomplete.*
[3] MS. *leaves space for a word after* sall.
[4] MS. *repeats* festyn þe hare *at the beginning of the line, before* take.
[5] MS. *repeats* it.

6 *Liber de Diversis Medicinis.*

Ane oþer. Take a blake cok & cleue hym in twa & lay it on þe hede al hate & bynd it faste & late it lygge a nyghte & a daye & þe thirde daye late blede in þe forheuede, for it is prouede sothe dyuerse tymms in dyuerse place.

An oþer. Take & gyffe hym at drynke þe jeuse of boxe & he sall hafe hele. 5

An oþer. Tak & gyffe hym to drynke þe jeuse of pympernoll tempered with wyne. /

Wodnes   To make hare lik gold   Heryng Defenes   f. 282v.
Wormes Schepelouse   Qwik thyng in þe ere   10

An oþer. Tak his handis & bynde þam bi-hynde hym faste. Þan take flour of affadill & do it in his righte hande & his bandes sall bryste. Or gif it hym at drynke & he sall passe owt[e] [1] of þe euyll faire & wele.

An oþer. Tak epworte & grynde it smalle & schafe his hede & 15 laye it appon þe schedde of his hede all þe nyghte.

An oþer. Tak aueroyne, marygolde & sawge & stamp it & temper it vp with wyne & drynke it fyve dayes.

Ane oþer. Take þe jeuse of walworte, hony & salt & swyn grese and boyle þam ouer þe fire til it be thikke & do a littill 20 encense þer-in and anoynte his heued þer-with ofte & he sal mende.

[Fo]r hym þat may [no]t wele here. Tak þe grene bowes of an asche & bryne þam & kepe þe jeuse þat commes owte at þe endis, a negschel full, and þe jeuse of senegrene, twa egschelfull, of hony an 25 eg-schelfull, of oyle of olyue a neg-schelfull, of þe woyse of þe pore leeke heued with þe faces þer-of, a neg-schelfull, & menge þam to-gedir & helle þer-of in þe hale here & lay þe on þe toþer syde at slepe & þe sall mende with schort tymm, & þu vse it. 30

An oþer. Tak þe jeuse of rewe & þe jeuse of moure egges & do in þi nere.

An oþer. Tak henne grese & þe jeuse of [gre]ne wormode with oyl & do in þi nere.

An oþer. Tak þe galle of a wedir with þe vryn or þe mylke of a 35 woman mengid to-gedir & do it in thi nere.

For harde herand men. Secundum Magistrum William de Excestre: Tak lorell leues, sedes of cermoyntayne, comyn, annys and

---
[1] MS. owto.

caruy, of ilkan ylike porcyon, and welle þam wele in faire water &, when þay are wele wellide, take and do þat water in a clene vesselle & do of þat water in þe¹ ere & he sal here wele with-in scorte tymm.

5 Take þe ȝerdis of hawthorne & kepe þe jeuse þat comes fro þe ȝerdis endis & menge oyle þer-with & putt it in þe hale ere & lay þe one þe toþer ere. Sepe probatum est per diuersos. *For defenes & men þat may not wele here.*

Take þe fattnes of a blake ele & þe jeuse of synegrene, 10 elike porcyon, & putt it ofte in þe hale ere & lay þe on þe toþer. *An oþer.*

Tak þe jeuse of² mentastrum & vynacre & mak it lewke & do it in þi nere & it dose þe same. *To slaa wormes in þe eres.*

Tak sperwort & stampe it & droppe þe jeuse lewke 15 in þe ere & it sall sla it or gare it come owte qwyke. / *[For] schepe louse or [a]ny qwik þynge [in] a mans erre.*

f. 283r. **Wormes Schepelouse Qwik thynge in þe ere Kyles in eres Sare eghne**

Take þe jeuse of mynt & mak it lewke & do it in þe eres. *To slaa wormes in þe eres.*

20 Or take þe jeuse of fenelle lewke & do it in þe eres & it sall sla þam.

Tak of rewe a grete qwantite & sawge halfe als mekill & rose maryn þe same quanttitee & stamp þam & wrynge owte þe jeuse & poure it in þe ere thre tymes, for þis 25 es oft prouede. *For schepelouse.*

If a schepe louse or any oþer qwik thynge be cropyn in-to thyn ere, tak þe jeuse of rewe or of wormod or of horshoue & do in þe ere & it sall sla it.

Tak grene ȝerdis of esche & lay þam ouer a brandrethe 30 & make a fire vnder þam & kepe þe woyse þat comes owt at þe endis in egges schelles & tak hony & do to þat woyse & do it in his ere & lat hym ly doun & slepe & do swa thre dayes, ilk a day twyse or thryse, bot do it firste in þe hale anes or twys, in auentour if þer be 35 oughte qwike in it, & it will sone crepe owte. *An oþer.*

Tak a hate hauyre cake & lay it down & lay thyn ere þer-on als hate als þu thole it &, if þer be schepe louse or any oþer qwik thynge in it, it sall sone crepe owte. *An oþer.*

¹ MS. *adds* he *crossed out.*   ² MS. *adds* mynt *crossed out.*

For kiles in þe eres.	Tak wormode & women mylke with þe jeuse of grene colyandre & do it in thyn eres.
An oþer.	Tak a childes [vryn]¹ & make it lewke with wyne & do it in thyn eres & it ² dryes þe humours & fordose werke & heles wonderfully. 5
Ane oþer.	An oþer: Take þe galle of a schepe with womans mylke & do it in thyn ere.
An oþer.	Tak wormod or harofe or wodebynde & stampe it & wrynge owt þe jeuse & do it lewke in thyn ere.
An oþer.	Tak þe merghe of a fresche calfe & braye it & do it in 10 thyn ere.
For eghn þat are waterand.	Tak a rede cale lefe & anoynte it with þe white of an egge & lay it to þe eghe, when þu gase to bedde, & late it lygge to þe morne & do it ofte, for it is proued for gude medcyn. 15
An oþer.	To make þe clere syghte: Ete ofte & drynke ofte puliolle rialle & fenkell sedis.
	Drynke ofte ewefrase, for it helpis ofte souereynly þe syghte.
Who so may not wele see & his eghne be [r]ede.	Tak white gynger & rub it on a whetstane or on a 20 basyn & tak als mekill salte as þu hase powdir & stampe þam & grynde þam wele to-gedir & temper þam with white wyne & late it stande in þat bacyne a daye & a nyghte & do þan þat oþer þat standis abouen in a ampull of glase or coper & anoynte / 25

Eghne Sare eghne f. 283v.

thyn ³ eghne þer-with a littill when þu gase to þi bedde with a fethir & do so ofte & dowteles þu sall be hale.

An oþer.	Take þe woyse of hondestonge or of centorye or of solsekill and do þe woyse in thyn eghne & it sal helpe 30 þe wele.
For perel or webe in þe eghe.	Tak pympernoll & stampe it & take þe jeuse þer-of & do þer-to þe grese of þe allerone of þe gose wenge & drope it in thyn eghne.
For hurte eghne.	For hurte eghne: Tak þe jeuse of egremone stamped 35

¹ MS. *omits* vryn; *see note.*
² MS. *adds* sal.
³ MS. *repeats* and anoynte *at the beginning of the line, before* thyn.

Liber de Diversis Medicinis.

    & egge whitt & menge þam to-gedir & take cotom &
wete *per*-in & lay it to þe sare eghe to it be hale.
    Late þe blode þe vij daye of Maye on þe righte arme,   An oþ*er*.
þe laste day of Aueryll on þe lefte arme.
5   Stampe þe leues of white thornes & do þe jeuse *per*-of   An oþ*er*.
in thyn eghe.
    Take Maye butt*re* & hony & þe white of an eggc &   To hafe clene eghne.
menge to-gedir and anoynte thyn eghne with all.
    Take wodbynde, rib and waybrede & stampe þam wele   An oþ*er*.
10 & smalle & take a gude porcyoun of fresche May butt*re*
& sethe þam to-gedir wele to þay be wele wellede, þan
wrynge þam thorow a clene clathe & do it in thi boystes
& ilk a nyghte take þe montenance of a fiche & do it in
thyn eghne by-fore þu laye the doune & it sall mend
15 the.
    Take waybrede & bayneworte & powdir of gyng*er*, a   An oþ*er*.
porcyon, & powdir of alom glase, als mekil porcion als
of thise, & make wat*er* for thyn eghne of þam.
    Tak powdir of alom glase & temp*er* it wi*th* womans   An oþ*er*.
20 mylke þat hase a knaue childe & do it in thyn eghne.
    Take rose flo*ures* and fenkell & filage, pymp*er*nolle,   An oþ*er*.
celidone, ewfrace. Stampe þam & temp*er* þam al
sammen wi*th* hony & þe grese of þe blake snyles & þe
whitt of an egge & anoynte thyn eghne þ*er*-with.
25   Tak arenement, hony and þe white of an egge, of   A gude oyneme*n*t for blered eghne and gundy. Opti*m*e.
ilkan elike mekill, & temp*er* þam to-gedir & tak herdes
& wete þam in wat*er* & wrynge it owte & do þ*ir* thynges
one þe herdes as a playst*er* &, if euyl*l* blode or whett*our*
be þare, it sall drawe it owte.
30   Tak calamynt & bryne it in þe fire till þat it glowe &   To slaa wormes þat ettis þe eghne.
sloken it in white wyne & efte bryn it & efte sloken it and
do so ix tymes. Þan may þu halde it alle þe ȝere &,
when /

Sare eghne   Colorye   An oynement

35 Þu hase to do þ*er*-with, tak als littill als a bene & grynde
it wele appon a borde & temp*er* it vpe wi*th* an egge schelle
ful of white wyne & late it sattill and wete a fethir in
þe clere abouuen, & þan wasche thyn eghne þ*er*-with,
when þu gose to bedde, & do so thre nyghtis & wi*th*-

10 Liber de Diversis Medicinis.

owtten faile it sall slaa þe wormes & clense þe eghne of many euylles, what euyll so es in þam.

An oþer. Tak salte & bryn it & do hony per-too & temper it to-gedir & doo it in thyn eghne.

And after all medcyns for eghne, wasche thyn eghne 5 with water þat fenell is sothen in.

Ane oþer. Tak tormentill, rewe, celidon, fenell & ryb, & anoynte thyn eghne with þe jeuse a littill, when þu gase to þi bedde.

An oþer. Tak þe rede snyle þat crepis houseles & sethe it in 10 water & gedir þe fatt þat comes of þam & anoynte thyn eghne ther-with or bryn it to powdere on iren or in a pott scarthe & do a [1] littill of þat powdir to thyn eghne when þu gase to slepe.

An oþer þat thies leches calles colorye. It is a gud oynement. Tak a bacyn & scoure it wele & anoynte þe sydis wele 15 with-in with þe larde of a galte & on þe larde anoynte it with hony þat it gange ouer þe larde all abowte a nynch. Tak þan a newe pott full of pys & whelme þe bacyn ouer þe pott & latte it stande thre dayes & thre nyghtis. Þe fourte day take þe bacyn &, what þu 20 fyndis per-in, do it of clene & gedir it in an ampull of glas or in a cle vrynall & tak a littill & anoynte thyn

Nota. eghne per-with, when þu gose to thi bedde. After this medcyn, ne after non oþer, wasche not thyn eghne bot with water þat fenell is sothen in. 25

An oþer. Tak celidon & do it in hardes & sythen do it in hate askes & late it sethe per-in & þan draw it owte & [2] wrynge þe jeuse in a bacyn & do it in þe sonne to drye and, when þu hase to do per-with, tak a littill per-of & distemper it with ayselle & do a littill in thyn eghne 30 per-of.

An oþer. Tak vetoyne & stampe it with water & drynke it ix dayes & it sall dryfe a-waye all þe wikkede humours of þe heued & of þe eghne.

An oþer. Tak May buttre & comyn & stampe þam samen & 35 laye it on lyne & þan laye it on þe eghe & ofte anewe it and, when þe bolnynge es swagede, þan tak safron & womans mylke þat fedis a knaue childe, if it be to a man, & grynde þam & droppe in þe sare eghne.

[1] MS. *repeats* a.   [2] MS. *adds* drynk þe jeuse *crossed out.*

Liber de Diversis Medicinis.

Tak þe blode of swalow birdis & anoynte thyn eghne *An oþer.*
þer-with & euer mare þay sall be þe bryghttere./

Tak strange vynegre or aysell & do it in a vessell of *Who so hase webe or perel in his eghne.*
bras, & þe blak slaes of þe wode & wormode do þer-with
5 & lat it stand langer couerde and, when nede es, take it
to thyn eghne & it sall brek þe web & do a-way þe euyll.

Tak ewfrace, a gude porcion, & stampe it wele & *An oþer.*
wrynge owte þe jewse thorow a clathe. Þan tak galte
grese & als mekill of gose grese & als mekill of henne
10 grese & menge it to-gedir in a panne of bras or in a pott
of bras & do þe jewse þer-to & boyle it wele & stir þe
bothome with a rownde staffe & lat it kele & do it in
boystes &, when þu hase nede, do it in thyn eghne a
littill, when þu gase to slepe, to þu be hale.

15 Tak comyn, pepir, hempsede, of rewe sede, of fenell *An oþer.*
sede, of ache þat growes ouer yven, & sal maritimum,
of ilkan ylike mekill, & stamp þam all to powdir & do
in thyn eghne þer-of when þou gase to thi bedde.

Tak bawme & þe jeuse of ewe & hony, of ilkan elyke *An oþer for þe maille in þe eghen.*
20 mekill, & coyle þam thorowe a clathe & do it in a fyall
of glase & with a fethir do it in thyn eghne.

Tak þe jeuse of rede wortes & of hesill, elike mekill, *An oþer.*
& do in a pot of bras & couer it wele & sett it in þe erthe
ix dayes & þan do it in thyn eghne.

25 Tak powdir of brynte pepir & do it in thyn eghne. *An oþer.*

Tak þe galle of an hare & twa sa mekill hony & *Nota optime pro oculis.*
temper it to-gedir & anoynte thyn eghne.

Ypocras sayse þat their thynges will gare a man see
þe sternes abowte myddaye, þat is, þe galle of a hare,
30 þe galle of a coke, þe galle of an owle & a littill jewse of
fenell & aloe cicotrine þat suffice & camfire, & mak
colore.

Feniculus, veruena, rosa, celidonia, ruta, *Versus notabilis.*
Si pimpernela ditis ewfrasia iuncta,
35 Ex istis fit aqua que reddat lumina acuta.

Tak powdir of aloes & do þer-in a littill. Bot firste *For charbocle grond in þe end of þe eghe.*
wasche it with whit wyne.

Tak leues of henebayne sothen in wyne & bray þam *An oþer.*
& laye þam ther-to.

Liber de Diversis Medicinis.

An oþer. Tak mynt & grynde it & lay þer-to.

For rede eghne. Tak þe galle of an ele & temper it with hony & do it in þin eghne. /

Sare eghne Schepe louse

f. 285r.

Gundy eghnen. Tak þe rute of fenkell & vetoyne & sethe þam in water & wasche thyn eghne þer-with.

An oþer. Tak daysies & þe whitt of an egge & braye þam & do it in thyn eghne.

For eghne þat are sare agayn þe euyn tide Tak ewfrase & stampe it in grese of a gose or of a henne & frye ewfrase & do in a vessell & anoynte thyn eghne. Or tak þe sede of centory & ett it fastande & þou sall mow at þe nonne to see þe sternes.

An oþer. Tak ewfrase & glair ana, & wete thorgh a lyn clathe & lay it on thyn eghne all nyghte, for it wil draw owt wikkide humours.

For blered eghne. Tak þe jewse of tansay or of vetoyne, & wryng thorow a clathe & do þer-of in thyn eghne.

An oþer. Tak a bryghte bacyn and anoynte [1] it with mylke reme, & whelm it ouer a preue iij dayes & sythen clens it & anoynt thyn eghne þer-with.

For þe haw in þe eghe. Tak pepir and bryn it in a clout & stamp it al to powdir & blende it with the merghe of a gose wenge & do þer-of in thyn eghene.

For eghne lamede. Tak pure glare of an egge & hony & arnement wele grownden & te[m]pered [2] to-gedir & do to thyn eghne with hardes or lyne.

An oþer. Tak þe jewse of egremon with þe whitt of an egge & blende to-gedir wele & laye to thyn eghne with cotome or clathe.

For myrknes of eghne. Tak þe rotes of fenell, vetoyne & yven terrestre, & sethe þam wele in water & do hony in þer-to & sythen coyl it thorow a clathe & anoynte thyn eghne þer-with.

An oþer. Tak ewfrase, pympernoll, veruayne, rede fenell, euen porcyon, & halfe þe porcion of rew & celidon, & braye þam wele in a mortere & welle þam wele with May buttre clarifiede & do þam in an erthe pott & couer þam wele & late þam rote to þay be white harede. Þan

---

[1] MS. *adds* thyn eghne *crossed out.*
[2] MS. tepered.

Liber de Diversis Medicinis.

do þat to þe fire & boile it wele & afterwardes drawe
it owte thurgh a clathe clene or a canvase & þan do it to
þe fire to it be wele claryfied & þan do it in boystes.
When þou hase nede to do þer-with, do it in thyn eghne
5 the montenance of a perle at morne & as mekill at
euen.
 Take þe jewse of rewe or of wormode or of horshoue *If a schepe*
& do in þe ere & it sall slaa it.   *louse or any qwikke*
 Tak þe grene ȝerdis of asche & ley þam ouer a brand- *thyng be cropyn*
10 reth & mak a fire vnder theym & kepe þe wose þat *in to thyn ere.*
rynnes /   *An oþer medcyn als.*

f. 285 v. **Schepe-louse Euyll in þe mouthe Hasenesse To syng hye Clere voyce**

owte at the endes in egge schelles & tak hony & do to
15 þat wose & do in his ere & late hym ly downn & slepe & *Nota ante ad hoc signum.*
do swa thre dayes ilk a day twyse or thrise. Bot do
firste in þe hale here anes or twise, in awntour if þer
be oughte qwike in it, & it wil crepe out.
 Tak a hate hauyr cake & lay it down & lay thyn ere *An oþer.*
20 þer one als ha[t]e [1] als þu thole it &, if þer be any schepelouse or any qwikke thynge, it sal sone crepe out.
 Tak pentafoyloyn, i*d est* quintfoyle, & welle it wele in *For euyll in þe*
water &, when it es wele welled, halde thi mouthe ouer *mouthe or in þe throte.*
þe posenett & stewe þe wele. Þan take & soupe of þat
25 lewke water & halde it in thi mouthe to þat it be kelide &
þan caste it owte & þan soupe mare & þe thirde tyme do
righte swa & vse this thre dayes & þu sal hafe [2] helpe
þer-of.
 Tak salte, comyn & pepir, of ilkan ilike mekill, & mak *An oþer.*
30 of þam a powdir & gyff hym to drynke in a sponefull
of hate water. This medcyne is profitable, for it is ofte
tymms prouede.
 Tak stalworthe ayselle in a vesselle of bras & jewse of *Nota.*
ake appills & do þam alle to-gedir & late þam stande [3] *Eghne : for perill of þe strynges.*
35 lange wele couerde &, when sal be at nyghte, when þe
seke sall ga to bedde, þan do it in his eghne & it sall
for-do þe perle & breke þe strynge of þe eghn.

  [1] MS. hale; *see note to* p. 7, ll. 36–38.
  [2] MS. *repeats* hafe.   [3] MS. *repeats* stande.

For hasenes.	Tak betoyn & pympernole & drynk þe jewse with wyn.
An oper.	Tak & drynk þe jewse of mynt.
To mak a man to syng highe.	Tak brane of barly & seth it in water & drynk it ofte.
An oper.	Tak floures of ellern & mak powder & ett ofte þer-of in þi potage.
An oper.	Tak apyum & absinthium & centauream & centrum galli, id est slaream, & feniculum, & bulle & bibe frigidum.
Ad vocem raucam	Feniculi radices ebulle in vino vel in optima seruicia & vtere [1] cotidie. Absinthium, marubrum, centauream, radices feniculi, rute celidonie, eque de omnibus, coque in veteri seruicia & vtere cotidie calida sero & mane frigida.
Item ad vocem raucam & pectus.	
To do awaye ferntikills.	Sanguis leporis delet lentigines de facie.
Speche.	Tak sauge or primerose & stampe it wele & anoynt his tonge vnderneth with þe jewse & he sall spek sone. Or tak grete mustarde & anoynte vndir his tunge. Or take þe wormode menged with water & do it in his mouthe & he sall speke. /

For speche
f. 286r.

An oper.	Tak pelleter & sethe in water & gyff it hym to drynke.
An oper.	Tak dytoyne & stampe it & temper it with wyn & water & drynke it.
An oper.	Tak archangelica & gyff it hym & it sal helpe.
An oper.	Tak pilial reall & stamp it with vynacre & caufe it & gyf hym to drynke & he sall speke.
For hym þat spittis blode.	Tak ache, mynt, rew & votoyn & welle þam wele in gayttes mylke & drynk it morne & euen.
An oper.	Tak piliol & vetoyne & mak powder þer-of & do þer-of in an egge & ete it & do so iij dayes & it sal helpe þe.
An oper.	Tak thre vnces of vetoyne and swete mylke of a gayte & temper þam to-gedir & drynk þat thris.
For hym þat spewes and haldis noghte.	Tak horshelme, þe rote, or mylfoil & temper it with water & drynk it. Or take rew & stamp it with white wyne & vse it lewke.
An oper.	Tak twa parties of þe jewse of fenell & a partie of hony & sethe þam thikke & drynk þer-of morn & euen,

[1] MS. vetere.

for it is gude for þe splene & for þe leuer & dose awaye
þe glett.

Tak þe skynn of a gyssarn of a capon or of a hen & roste it on þe coles & ette it. An oþer.

5 Tak mylfoil & stamp it & drynk it with lewke wyn. An oþer.

Tak at þe morne & ette iij lefes of rew fastand & iij lefes of sauge at þe euen. An oþer.

Or tak mynt & stamp it & wrynge out þe jewse & wete a lyn clathe þer-in & bynd it to his stomake.

10 Tak laureall & make powdir þer-of & do þat ilke weghte of hony þer-to & ette a sponefull or twa þer-of. To gare a man spewe.

Tak þe myddes barke of þe burtre & anete & areges sede & ix or x graynes of spourge & sethe þam & do a littill hony þer-to & drynk. An oþer.

15 Tak gomme araby ij vnce, of safron orientale iiij vnce, of sperwort a pond & hony þat suffice þer-to. An oþer.

Tak þe barke of þe walnot tre rute & do a-way þe vtter barke & stamp it & lay it in ale or water & lat it stand a nyghte & couer it & on þe morne drynke & An oþer.
20 þu sall cast. Or tak þe jus of spourges.

Tak þe rute of celidoyn, maluestri, spourge sede, & stampe þam & temper þam with ale & late þam stande al a nyghte, & at þe morne drynk þer-of a coupfull & þou sall caste abown & of þe menyson by-nethe. &, An oþer.
25 when þu arte clene purgede, /

f. 286v.   **Stynkand ande Touthewerke**

þan drynke annys & fenell sothen in hony & ette after-warde of a tendir henne sothen in mynt & malues. Syne do þer-to mylke and buttre & sethe all to-gedir &
30 ete [1] of þat wele.

Tak blak mynt and þe jewse of rew, elik porcyon, & do in þi nese thirlles. Stynkand ande.

Or tak an herbe þat es called thros nedils & drynk it ix mornes with stale ale.

35 Tak piliol & temper it with vynacre or with wyn & drynk it at euen. An oþer.

Or tak þe rote of sperwort & boil it in hony & vynagre & drynk when þu gose to thi bedde. An oþer. Nota.

[1] MS. *adds* re *crossed out.*

An oþer.	Tak þe jewse of gladyn & temper it with gud alde wyne & wasche thi mouthe þer-with ofte & halde it lange in thi mouthe with vynagre when þu gase to þi bedde.
An oþer.	Tak a littill of a lorell lefe & a littill mylke & laye vnder thi townge & it schal for-do the stynke.
Touthewerke.	For hym[1] þat hase þe touthewerke: Take hauyrmele[2] & sethe it in gud wyne to it be thikke and do it on a lyn clathe as it were a playster, & all warme bynd it to thi cheke & it schal for-do þe werke.
An oþer.	Tak straberye wyse & frote þam in thi handes & lay þam to thi touthe & it sall swage.
An oþer.	Tak xv pepir cornes & vij rede nettills croppes & a littill salte & stamp all to-gedir & bryn þam in a lyn clathe & halde it in thi mouthe by-twene þi tethe to þe werke be a-waye.
An oþer.	Tak þe jewse of baynewort or of segge rutes & do thre droppes in thi nose thirlles, bot noghte ouer þat syde þat werkes.
An oþer.	Tak þe merghe or þe grese of a horse & anoynt þi cheke or thi touthe þer-with.
An oþer.	Tak þe rute of henbayne & roste it wele & lay it to thi tethe.
An oþer.	Tak þe jewse of rede nettills & þe whitte of an egge & frankencens & whete mele & make a playster & laye þer-too.
An oþer.	Tak date stanes & mak powdir of þam and tak als so mekill weghte of poudir of pepir & temper with a littill hony & frote thi tethe þer-with & thi gommes.
An oþer.	Tak þe jewse of lekis & halde it lange in thi mouthe & þan spitt it owte and do so ofte.
An oþer.	Tak powdir of pepir & stampe it with lewke wyn & halde it in thi mouthe to it be calde & þan do it owte & ofte do so & wasche thi tethe þer-with & it sall do þam gude. /

Tothwerke

An oþer. Nota bene.	Tak brokes filth and do it in þe hole of þe tothe & it sall brek þe tothe & sese þe werkynge.

[1] MS. *adds* þat b *crossed out.*
[2] MS. *adds* grotis *crossed out.*

Liber de Diversis Medicinis.

Tak þe flour of pepills & do þer-in & it will helpe it
sone.   *An oþer.*

Tak & drynk þe jewse of veruayne & egrimoyne
fastand, & it dose awaye werke.   *An oþer.*

5 Tak erthe yven & stampe it & helle a littill jus in þe
ere appon þe þat side.   *An oþer.*

Tak yven and salte & stampe to-gedir & mak a playster
& laye to þe cheke, for þat hales wele.   *An oþer.*

Tak aueroyne & sauyn & alde grese & stampe wele &
10 bynde to þe cheke & it sall swage þe werke.   *Nota optime.*

Tak þe sedes of henbayne & þe sede of lekes & frankencense & laye all thies on a glowande tile stane & make a
pype þat hase a wyde ende & an narowe ende & sett þe
narowe end to þi tothe & laye þe sedis & þe frankencense
15 appon the hote tile stone & sett þe wyde ende of þe pipe
appon þam and late þe stewe of þam strike vp thorow
þe pype in-till thi tothe & it sall sla þe wormes & for-do
þe werke.   *An oþer to sla wormes in þe tethe.*

Tak þe rute of henbayne & schere a thyn schyfe þer-of
20 & lay it to thi tothe thrise & it sal sla þe worme & for-do
þe werke.   *An oþer.*

Tak playntayn, *id est* waybred, & þe taughe of a tupe,
& stampe þam wele to-gedir & anoynte thi cheke þer-with
& þe worme sal fall owte sone.   *An oþer.*

25 Tak an egge & mak an hole þer-in & do owte all þe
whitt & fill it full of smalle salte & stir all to-gedir & lay it
to þe fire & late it roste to it be harde. Þan tak it owte
& pille it & schere it in peces. Syne take hate syndirs of
yryn at a smythe & putt þam in an newe erthen potte.
30 Syene take an of þe peces of þe foresaide egge & putt it
emange þi tethe & halde thi heued ouer þe pott ay to thi
tethe water, & thurgh þe water þat falles fra þi tethe, þat
is þe tothewerke calde falles a-waye.[1] Bot this is harde
for to thole.   *An oþer Nota.*

35 Tak smalache & stampe it & þe white of an egge
to-gedir & whete flour & temper all to-gedir in a plaster
& lay to þe cheke with-owtten & with-in thrise. It
sall be hale, with þe grace of God, and þe tothe be
louse.   *An oþer.*

[1] MS. *adds* þe waye þe werke.

An oþer	Tak an hertis horne & bryn it & do þe askes in a lyn clathe & lay to þe tothe. /

Tothewerk Nesyng Talent of mete

f. 287 v.

An oþer for wo[r]mes[1] in the tethe þat ettes þe tethe.	Tak henbell & pympernoll, smalache, virgyn waxe, stor, & mak a candill of & halde thi mouthe ouer it & þu 5 sall see þe wormes come oute of þe tethe, & do so ofte & þu sall be hale.
An oþer.	Tak þe rute of henbelle, kerif & clefe it & lay it to thi tethe & þe wormes sall ga awaye with-in thre nyghtis. 10
An oþer.	Smere thi cheke and thi tothe with horse grese, & þat is proued gode.
A charme for the tethe.[2]	Destruens est larowe, pax in Christo Filio, & dices isti:[3] Adiuro te, gutta migranea, per Dominum nostrum Ihesum Christum, per Patrem & Filium & Spiritum sanctum, 15 vt non habeas potestatem in capite isto stare nec in dentibus nocere nec in pedibus[4] nec in manibus nec in aliquo loco morari. Virgo martir agregia, pro nobis, Appollonia, funde preces ad Dominum ne pro reatu creminum nostrum dolore vexemur dentium, & in-iunges 20 dicere iij Pater noster & iij Aue Maria. Et dicat Et ne nos & postea, virgo serenissima beata Apollonia, ora pro nobis ad Dominum, ora pro nobis, beata Appollonia, vt Deus dolorem a dentibus ab hoc famulo Dei : N : expellat. Oremus : Deus qui beatam Appolloniam de 25 manibus inimicorum eripuisti & eius oracionem exaudisti, te queso, Domine, per eius intercessionem & beati Laurencij martiris tui, vt dolorem a dentibus ab hoc famulo dei erepias & eum sanum & incolumem facias per Christum Dominum nostrum. Amen. 30
An oþer þat is a spice for þe tothwerke.	To make a spyce for þe tothewerke : Tak lij leues of sawge gedirde on a foure sqwarede bedde on crose from on cornere to an oþer, and saye at þe pullynge of euer ilk a lefe a Pater noster and Aue Maria, and þan tak two tyle stones and hete þam in the fire, and 35 þan tak als mekill salte als þe montenaunce of a ʒolke of an egge and laye it on þe stone on brede and tak an

[1] MS. womes.
[2] MS. repeats the.
[3] MS. issi.
[4] MS. pestibus.

halpeny worthe of powder of pepir and laye on brede
appon þe salte and þan laye þe leues abown appon ilkan
by oþer ay two & two to-gedir and þan laye þe toþer
stone abown als hate als it may be. Bot sett on foure
5 cobills stanes þat it ne touche not þe leues, and when þe
leues are dryede ynowghe & baken ymelle þe stones, tak
þan & braye þe leues all to powder and þe same pepir with
þe salte þat was baken and þan tak þer-to an halpeny-
worthe of powdir of licoresse and blende all foure to-gedir
10 and putt it in a bleddir, and þan late hym þat hase þe
tothwerke tak als mekill als a bene and lay to þe tothe þat
werkes on nyghte when he gose to bedde and lye down on
þat sam syde þat werkes and holde þe powder to þe
tothe als wele als he may & he sall hele. /

f. 288r. **Tothwerk þat may no ette ʒhiskyng Hoste Coghe**
16 Tak an hote tile stone, als hote als it may be made, and An oþer for to gare wormes com owte of a mans tethe.
leye it one a stole and sett þer-by a vessell with water
and þan take þe sedis of henbayne and leye appon þe
stone and halde thyn heuede ouer þe sedis þat lyes on þe
20 hote stone and gape als wyde als þu may and late close
in thyn heued with a schete þat none ayere goo owte
bi-syde thyn heued. Bot be-ware þat þu drawe nott
thyn ande for strikynge of þe sauoire of þe sedis in-to
thi throtte and, euer als thi mouthe waters, halde thyn
25 heuede ouer þe vessell with water þat standis by & it
walde be sett with-in þe schete by þe tile stone and, when
þe thynkes thi tethe & þi mouthe es stewed ynowghe,
þan tak a-waye þe schete &, if þu be stewede ynoghe,
þu sall see [1] þe wormes in þe water, some schortere & some
30 lengare, & þus may þou do to þu be stewede ynoghe & þu
sall slaa þe wormes & amend.

Puluieris piperis nigri iniectus naribus sternutacionem Ad sternuta-cionem pro-uocandam.
prouocat & cerebrum a superfluitate mundificat.

Tak centory & sethe it in water wele & drynk iij dayes For thaym þat may not ete.
35 lewke & it purges þe breste & the stomake.

Tak centorye & waybrede & pepir, & stampe thaym & An oþer.
sethe þam in wyne & drynk it lewke when þu gase to þi
bedde.

[1] see *in margin*.

Liber de Diversis Medicinis.

An oþer. A letuarye. Tak þe jewse of fenell, twa partise, & of hony, þe third partye, and sethe þam to-gedir to þe thiknes of hony & do pepir þer-to & ette ilke a daye iij sponefull & it will helpe mekill.

For thriste. Tak þe rute of louache & stampe it & temper it with wyne or with water & drynk it iij nyghtis when þu gase to thi bedde & it will for-do thi thriste.

For hym þat ȝiskes. Tak bathe thyn handis and halde theym in hate water ouer the wristes & it will lett þe ȝhiskynge.

An oþer. Tak & souppe thre sopes of vynacre or of water or of ale & it will for-do it.

An oþer. Say kyriel, kyriel, kyriel, & hald thyn heued vpwarde.

An oþer. Tak sawge & stampe it & temper it with vynacre & drynke it & hald þi handes by-for¹ thi throte & hald swa thyn ande in als lange als þu may & it wil lette þe ȝhiskynge to com on þe.

For þe hoste, per Rector de Oswaldkirke. Tak a gud porcyon of water cresse & sethe þam in a galon of water & þan wrynge it thorow a clathe & þan tak þat jewse & sethe it efte with a gude porcyon of hony & a gude / porcione of ȝucre caffatine & drynk þer-of at euen hate & at morne calde. Þis is prouede gud & medcynable for certayne.

An oþer. Tak horsehoue & ysope & stampe þam & sethe þam wele in white wyne or stale ale & fresche buttre & clens it & drynke it fastande to þu be hale.

An oþer. Tak lauerwort, hyndestong & mayden hare, of ilkan ylik mekill, & stampe þam wele & stope þam in alde ale & drynke of þat ale ix mornes fastande & als many euenys & it sal hele þe.

A lectuarie for þe host. A lectuarie for þe hoste or þe breste or for sare in þe syde or for þe mylte or for þe stomake : Tak horshoue, gronswall, ysope, centorye, ache, fenell, rew, solsekill, puliol & nepte, of ylkan ylik mekill, & do pepir þer-to & hony, and ette þer-of morn and euen.

An oþer for þe dry hoste. Tak sawge & stampe it & drynk it with hate water or lewke ale.

An oþer for þe dry coghe. Tak horshelme and comfery & ett with hony iij dayes.

An oþer for þe same. Tak waybrede & stamp it with hony & vynagre & drynk it and it sall hele the.

¹ MS. *adds* þie *crossed out.*

Liber de Diversis Medicinis.

  Tak pulyol & comyn, of ayther ylik mekill, & pepir & welle it in alde ale & drynk at euen hate & at morne calde. *An oþer for þe same.*

  Tak þe rute of fynkell and stamp it & drynk it thre
5 dayes with ald wyn & it sal helpe the mekill & hele þe. *An oþer for þe same.*

  Tak halfe an vnce of [1] liquorice & halfe an vnce of licorice of ynde & halfe an vnce of gome arabike & do away þe barke of licorise & sythen parte thi licorise in þi gome in ij parties. Do halfe in a pot & þe toþer halfe in
10 a oþer pot & do ij galons of water in þe ta pot & als mekil in þe toþer and sethe wele þe tane & þe toþer als þay were beefe & vse þer-of a copfull at morne with lew [2] water & at euen with skaldand water & kepe þe wele fra salte metis & mekill drynk. *An oþer for þe same.*

15 Tak sawge, rew, comyn & pepir, & sethe þam to-gedir in a panne with hony & at morne ette a sponeful & an oþer a[t] [3] euen. *For þe perilous coghe.*

  Tak vetoyne & dry it & mak powdir þer-of & tak als mekill of þat powdir als þu may tak in thi thre fyngers &
20 welle it to þe ij parties be wastede, þan drynk it lewke fastande & þu sall son[e] [4] be delyuerde. *For many euyllis in þe body.*

  Tak rosemaryn, lauandre, puliol rialle, puliol de montayne, mynt, sawge, rew, persell, ysoppe, dytoyn, betoyne, centorie, rede fenkell & auance, twa handefull, & þe toþer by-fore bot ane / and [5] tak alle thies & wasche
26 þam clene & drie þam wele & bake þam with brede & tak a pott of foure galouns of alde ale & drawe it in-til an oþer pott. And þan tak þe paste als hate als þou may and breke it into þe pott with alde ale and stoppe it wele
30 with claye & with a clene clathe, þat non ayer come owte, & drawe it at þe spigot & drynk fastand at [morne] [6] & at euen. Þis is proued right gude. *[F]or any sekeness in [þ]e body.*

  Tak feuelef & stampe it and tak ij sponfull of þe jewse & drynk it & it sall do a-waye þe werke & þe euyll. *For werke in a mans body.*

35 Tak þe jewse of waybrede & mak it lewke & drynk it, for it is gude. *An oþer.*

---

[1] MS. *adds* licerece *crossed out.*
[2] MS. rew.   [3] MS. a.
[4] MS. son *followed by a blurred letter, possibly* e.
[5] MS. *repeats* bot ane *at the beginning of the line, before* and.
[6] MS. *omits.*

An oþer.	Tak puliol & chewe it & bynd it to thi nauyll & it sal for-do þe euyll.
For thryng-yng in þe wambe.	Tak & stampe item & drynk þe jewse with stale ale or with water & do so ofte, for it sall do þe gude.
An oþer.	Tak carwy & stamp it & temper it with hate wyne & drynke it. Or tak mynt & nepte & do þe same.
For bolnyng of wambe.	Tak xij lefes of rewe & ix cornes of pepir & als mekill of dile as þu may tak vp with thi thre fyngers, & stampe it al to-gedir with hate water & drynke it. Or drynk rew stampid with wyne or with alde ale ofte & it sall mende the.
For to do away frekles.	Tak þe rute of loueache & þe rute of lely & sethe þam to-gedir in water & stampe þe rutes & anoynte thi face & wasche þe water & do so ofte & vse it & þay fall a-waye.
An oþer.	Tak þe blode of a bulle or of an hare & anoynte þi vesage.
An oþer.	Tak mercury & sape of spayn & welle it in oyle & anoynt þe þer-with.
For to do away frekles or rede blaynes.	Tak þe rute of waybrede & þe rute of burre & vynagre & salt & stampe þam alle wele samen & þer-with anoynte þi vesage.
An oþer.	Tak þe jewse of bursa pastoris & anoynt þe þer-with & it dose it sone a-way.
For sawse-fleme.	Tak gynger, pepir & mercury, & stampe & temper with jewse of pympernol & anoynte þi vesage wele agayne þe fire & þe thirde day after wasche it wele with water þat lely was sothen in.
An oþer.	Take oile of item & anoynte þi face þer-with & it sal hele it sone.
For euyll in þe stomak.	Tak þe rutes of fenell & þe rute of ache & stamp þam to-gedir & temper þam with wite wyne & gif þe seke to drynke.
An oþer.	Tak þe jewse of walwort & drynk it with wyne a gude egge schellefull at anes & it sall ga þer-owte & clense þe stomake, per R. de O.
An em-plaister for þe stomake.	Tak wormod, mynt, calamynt, camamill, puliol reall, gynger, galynga, roses, puliol montayne, comyn ana, riebrede and vynagre, & of all thies mak a playster

Liber de Diversis Medicinis.

& lay to thi stomake and þou sall mend ryghte sone, &
þu vse it. /

Tak rew, ambrose & horshoue ana, & stampe þam & *For euyll at þe breste.*
temper þam with wyn & drynk þat thre dayes fastande
5 & it sal mende þe.

Tak ysop & centorie, of ayther ylik mekill, horshoue *Nota bene optime.*
& sclary, als mekill as of ysop, & ane vnce of licorise, &
sethe þam in water þat it be sothen to þe third parte &
gyf to þe seke to drynk at morne calde, at euen hate.
10 A galon of water is ynoghe to sethe it in.

Ysop is a mild grise & heles a mans brest. Stampe it *Nota bene de ysopo.*
& temper with stale ale or with water & drynk it fastand.

Tak wormod, mynt, calamynt, sawge & vynagre, & *For þe breste.*
stampe thies gresis wele & small. Tak white brede &
15 toste it till it be brown. Tak þan & mye it smalle & do
it all to-gedir & mak it in a playster & lay it one thi
breste anense thi hert.

Tak rewe & aueroyne & horshoue, of ilkan a handfull, *An oþer.*
and stampe þam wele & temper þam with wyne & drynk
20 it iij dayes.

Tak percell rutes, fynkell rutes, radik rutes, horshelme *For stoppyng at the brest.*
rutes, of ilkan a handefull, & schere þam in sondre, halfe
a pownde of licorise bryssede, and sethe alle to-gedir
in iij qwartis of barly brothe vntil [it]¹ be sothen in-to
25 a qwarte, & þan syle it in-til an oþer pott & drynk it at
morne hate & at euen calde, bot luke þat þe pott be wele
stoppid þat non ayere com in þer-to, for þis is proued.

Tak rew & sethe it in ayselle & gyff it to þe seke at *An oþer.*
drynk.

30 Tak þe jewse of rubarbe & porcalane ana, stamp þam *For þe brest & þe stomak.*
& menge þam with vergeous & wasche a clathe in þe
jewse & lay on þe breste & the stomake.

Tak saueraye & stampe it & tak halfe wyne & halfe *An oþer.*
water & boile it & do buttre þer-to & temper þe saueray
35 þer-with & clens it thurgh a clathe & drynk it when
þu gase to bedde oft, for it is gude.

Tak þe flour of roses, violet, malue, borage, burtre & *For to clense þe breste.*
licorese, of ilkan ilik mekill, & sethe þam in water to þe
third part and vse it at morne calde & at euen hate.

---

[1] MS. *omits.*

An oþer.	Tak þe rute of fenkell, percell, hondistonge, violet, liuerwort, maydenhare & licores, & make it & vse it as it is saide bi-fore.
An oþer.	Tak centorie & waybrede, sethe þam in water & drynk iij dayes þer-of lewke & it purges þe breste & þe stomak wele. 5
For þe brest. Nota bene.	Tak a halpenyworth of hony & a halpenyworth of grete groun mustarde & a qwarte of alde ale & a blew clowte & do thies to-gedir in a panne & welle þam samen to þay begynn to waxe thikke & also do þer-to 10 sex garleke / heddes grete stampede & þan tak vp þe *t. 290r.* clowte & wrynge it softely and laye it to thi breste als hate als þu may suffre it & with-in schorte tyme it will dryfe þe euyll a-waye.
An oþer.	Tak horsehelme & a quart of gud ale & a halpenyworth 15 of hony & boile þam all samen & drynk þat laste at euen & firste at morn.
For onkome.	Tak sygrym, waybrede, columbyne & sile þam thorow a clathe and qwete flour & temper till it be thikke & mak a plaster þer-of & lay it appon þe sare. Tak galte 20 grese and menge þer-with, if it wax ouer thikke.
for þe morfewe.	Tak bromstane & bray it smalle to powder and put it in a lyn clowte & stepe it þan in whyte wyn to it be thurgh stepide & rub it þan appon þe morfewe dyuerse tymes vn-till it passe awaye. Þis medcyn is prouede 25 trewe.
For euyll at þe hert.	Tak centorie & sethe it wele in stale ale or in wyne and, when it is wele sothen, tak & stampe it & do it agayne in þe pott & sethe it wele in þe same brothe & þan tak and clens it thorow a clathe & þan tak ij parties of 30 jewse & the third of hony & boile al samen & scom & welle to-gedir & afterwardes do it in boystes & gyffe it þe seke at ette ilk a day iij sponefull fastand to he be hale, for it sall do awaye þe glett fra þe hert & gyff hym talent to mete. 35
An oþer.	Tak horshoue, puliol & a littill salte, & sethe þam in a pott with water & gyff þe seke to drynke ilk day fastande.
	Or tak ache sedes & comyn & stampe þam to-gedir & gyff hym ilk a day to drynke fastande to he be hale. 40

Liber de Diversis Medicinis.

  Tak feuerfew, wyn & salt, & welle to-gedir & drynk   An oþer.
þe brothe.
  Tak þe rutes of fenkell, þe rutes of percell, þe rutes   An oþer.
of horsehelme, þe rutes of radik, þe lefes of longe de
5 cerfe, lyuerworte, centorie, mogworte, modirworte,
waybrede, puliol, nept, mynt, fifleues and saueray, of
ilkan a handfull, & do þer-to a littill sawge & wormode
& þe flour of violet or þe leues & þe flours of þe roses
& a vnce of licorece or mare & hony and, if he or scho
10 be feble, do þer-to þe mare hony to mak it swettere
þat þay may þe better drynk it. Tak alle thies thynges
& sethe þam in a pott with water to þe thirde parte
be sothen in & þan lat it stande in þe pott & clens it
in-to an oþer for to hafe it þe fynere & þane gyffe þe
15 seke ilk day at drynk bi a mesure þer-of at þe morn
calde & at þe euen hate. To þus many gresses do iij
galons of water. /

f. 290v.   Tak wormode & sethe it in water & drynk it.   For þe hert-
  Tak ambrose, puliol & centorie, anete, ache, origanum   bryne.
20 & rew. Sethe all thiese gresses wele in water & drynk
it & he sall be hale.
  Tak & ette vj or vij almondes, or ette a fewe rawe   An oþer.
pese & it sal ga awaye.
  Tak vetoyne, sawge, water of mynt & þe sedis of   To spourge
25 dille, of ilkan ilik mekill, & do þer-to pepir & hony,   a man of ill
& stampe þam wele & temper þam þan with white   humour.
wyne & gyf hym to drynke.
  Tak centorye or þe rute of louache & sethe it &   For hym þat
temper it with white wyne lewke or with water & drynk   thristes ay.
30 it iij nyghtis, when þu gase to bedde, & it will for-do
þe thriste.
  Tak centorye & stampe it & drynke þe jewse with   For thriste
lewke water & it will do awaye þe thriste & clense þe   in þe feuer
stomake & þe breste.   agewe.
35   Tak rye & sethe it & stampe it with whit wyne hate   For þe
& halfe with water & do buttre þer-to & stampe þe   stomak &
rye þer-with & clense it and drynke a draghte when   þe heued.
þu gase to þi bedde.
  Tak dragans & gladyn & mynt ana, & stampe þam &   For drynk-
40 temper þam vp with wyne & drynk it & it sal helpe the.   yng of
  poyson or
  venym.

An oþer.   Tak þe rute of dragans & temper it vp with wyne & drynk it lewke.

An oþer.   Tak betoyne & dry it & mak powdir þer-of & tak þat powdir, as mekill as þu may tak vp with thi thre fyngers at twise, and sethe it in twa pecherfull of wyne to þe twa parties be sothen in & drynk it lewke fastande al at anes & þu sal be al hale. And wete þu wele for sothe þat botoyne is a ful gud herbe & a haly & full of gud vertous. For þam þat is ful of fanteme & hase trauellyng in þaire slepe & þay drynke botoyne & hafe it appon þam or abowte þam, þat day it sal ga awaye and, if þu drynk ilk a daye venym, drynk botoyne & thorow the vertue þer-of þu sall be deliuerde.

[A]n oþer for hym þat [is] envenymede.   Tak and drynk rede mynt and arnement menged to-gedir & he sall deliuer it abown or bynethe. Or temper garleke with hony. It purges venym.

An oþer.   Tak gayte milke [&]¹ caraway & sethe it wele to-gedir. In þe worlde is ther no better medcyne.

An oþer.   Tak þe jewse of þe rede malue & alde wyn & do to-gedir & it sall caste owte þe venyme & hele þe wombe.

An oþer.   Tak gayt mylk & sethe it to þe thirde part & drynk it iij dayes. It is þe beste medcyne saue treacle. /

For women pappes Encostyfnesse

An oþer.   Tak harehone and aueroyne & stampe þam & temper þam vp with alde wyn & gyf þe seke at drynke. It castes al venyme, ne þat venym ne sall noghte noye in no mete nor drynke.

An oþer.   Tak lentes sede & stamp it & drynk it with water fastand. Or tak a nott & ette it fastand & it sal saue the.

For werkyng & swellyng in pappes.   Tak waybrede & þe lefes of synegle & ald gres & stampe it &² bynd it þer-to. Or tak mynt & stampe it smalle & lay it þer-to.

An oþer.   Tak horshoue & stampe it with alde gres & anoynt þi pappis þer-with.

An oþer.   Tak þe rute of walworthe, peple & veruayne, & stampe þam with alde gres & lay to þe pappes.

---

¹ MS. or; *see note.*
² MS. *adds* drynk it with water fastand *crossed out.*

Liber de Diversis Medicinis. 27

Tak þe croppe of þe rede dok & fald it in a lefe of þe   **For bolnyng of pappis.**
seluen & roulle it in þe aymers. Þan stampe it & lay
it to þe sare & it sal breke &, if it brek, gif hir at drynk
þe croppe of tansay & brere croppe, rede cale croppe
5 & madir, as mekill as of al þe oþer, & gif it at drynk
tempered with ald ale.
    Tak ake appills & stampe thaym with oyle of rose   **An oþer.**
& lay it on þe bolnynge.
    Or tak þe jewse of morelle & baynwort & dregges of
10 vynagre & a hard egge sothen with þe schelles & barly
mele & stampe þam & sethe þam all to-gedir & mak a
plaster & lay on it.
    Tak þe jewse of morell & þe white of an egge &   **An oþer.**
bene mele & mak þer-of a plaster & lay it calde to þe
15 sare.
    Si mulier vnxerit[1] mammas suas cum succo sicute   **Nota bene.**
a principio, semper erunt parue dure & stantes. Succus
iusquiamiadi idem.
    Tak asafetida & aromatica, of aþer elik mekill, &   **To mak maydyns pappis**
20 wax & oyl, as reson gyffes. Welle al samen. This   **harde & for clusteryng of pappes.**
oynement makes hardnesse of pappes & softnes.
    Tak homlokes & stampe þam & temper þam with   **To mak a woman with-**
ayselle & lay þam to þe pappes & do so ofte & þer schal   **owtten milke.**
be littil or noghte, & þe milk sal waste a[waye].
25   Tak þe triddils of an hare & stampe þam with wyne   **An oþer.**
& anoynte þe pappes þer-with.
    Tak þe jewse of veruayne or of fenkell & drynk it   **A medcyn for to gete**
ofte & þou sall hafe mylke ynoghe in thi breste.   **a woman mylke.**
    Secundum maiorem partem omnia dura constipantia   **For þe encosty-**
30 & desictatiora, sepe & porri[2] sunt dure & laxantia.   **fenesse.**
    Secundum Rectorem de Oswaldkirk, tak sedis of
fenkall, anys, rew, lofage, percell, comyn & salt, &
pouder þam & gyff hym þam ay a sponfull in his metis
& in his drynkes. /

f. 291 v.
Encostyfenesse

36   Tak malues, mercuryale, longedeboef, arage, borage,   **Mak cale for þe same.**
cale, violet, percell, croppis of lyn & nettill ana, & mak
potage of thies with fresche porke & buttre.

    [1] MS. vngexerit.   [2] MS. porriis.

An oþer, secundum R. de O.	Tak þe leues of spourge and a gud porcion of ȝucre, gynger & flour of whete mele, & mak paste & bake it in oble yryns & ett growell of porke & after ete þe obletes & þu sal haue deliuerance bathe abown & bynethe. Þis is called angell brede. 5
An oþer.	Tak þe jewse of spourge & mastike powdir & whete flour & mak paste & bake obles & ete þam.
An oþer.	Tak whitt turbit at spicers & als mekill gynger & twys als mekill suger & do alle to-gedir, þat is at say iij peny weghte of turbitt & iij of gynger & als mekill of suger 10 als is of bathe þe toþer, & þat will serue iij tymes to rescheyue. It is trew & prouede.
An oþer.	Tak malues & sethe þam wele in water & þan caste þer-to a coppe-full of new ale & ete þer-of wele & þi wambe sal be soluble. 15
An oþer.	Tak hauyrmele & stampe it wele & sethe it with fresche brothe & ete þer-of wele & it sal mak þi wambe soluble.
An oþer.	Tak þe galle of a bulle & breke it & wete a loke of wolle þer-in & lay it to þi nauyll & bynd it faste to & it sal 20 deliuer þe.
An oþer.	Tak lynsede & sethe it in water &, when it is wele sothen, do a-way þe water & tak þe lynsede & fry it in white grese & gare þe seke ete þer-of als hate als he or scho may thole it and it sal sone do hym gude. 25
An oþer.	Tak a rawe egge ȝolke & euen quanttite of salte & melle to-gedir & bynde þam faste in littill lyn cloute & with thyn awen hande putt it in thi fundement & walke a littill abowte & it sal do þe remedie.
R. de O. Clister.	Tak salte, hony & arenement, & welle al to-gedir & 30 put in his fundement.
An oþer.	Tak a pype of messynge or of tre or of horne as grete as a spyndill & do it in his fundement a handbred depe & do þe toþer ende of þe pipe with-in a net bleddir or a lether & fill þat bledder full of oyle & late it ryne in-to 35 his wambe. Þan walke a littill or welter on a bedde a while & he sall delyuer hym sone.
An oþer.	Tak euerfernie & polipodi þat waxes on þe ake & wasche it & stampe it & temper it with mylke & tak a henne & scalde hir & farse hir wele with þat grese þat 40

þou hase stamped & sethe it wele in wa*ter* & a gud partie of þat grese *per*-with and, when þe henne is wele sothen, wasche it wele w*ith*-in /

f. 292r.
For euyll & bolny*n*g of wambe For wormes For þe flux For þe menyson

& w*ith*-owte w*ith* þat brothe þat it is sothen in & sythen clense [1] þat brothe thorow a clathe & welle þat same broo w*ith* comyn wele & þat fatt and temp*er* wele þat broo & ette of þat hen w*ith* comyn stalworthly &
10 þou sal waresche þat it sal not greue the.

Tak þe jewse of wallworte ij sponefull, and of hony a sponefull, & gyf þe seke to drynke & he sall delyu*er* hym a-bown & be-nethe, q*uod* probat*ur*. *An oþer.*

Tak vj leues of spourge, mynt & cifoil or fethirfewe. *An oþer.*
15 Stamp þam & drynk þe jeuse & it sall delyu*er* the.

Tak þe rute of titimale & drye it with þe son*n*e & mak it i*n* powdir & drynk it, for it is gude. *An oþer.*

Or tak a morsell of lard als thi fyng*er* & powdir it w*ith* sall gem*m*e & do it in thi fundame*n*t. *An oþer.*

20 Oṁnia que secessu*m* prouoca*n*t vrina*m* minuu*n*t & e co*n*u*er*so. *Nota.*

Tak ij sponefull of quintfoil & drynk it & it sal do þe gude. *For hardenes & werke in the wambe.*

Or tak rede cale & vyneagre & menge to-gedir & drynk
25 it & it sall swage thi wambe & thi lyu*er*.

Tak & drynk gayte milk & it will mak þe solubill. *An oþer.*

Tak waybrede & stamp it with swynne gresse & mak a plast*er* þ*er*-of & lay all hate to þi wambe & it sal do a-way þe bolnynge & mak the solubill. *An oþer.*

30 Or tak þe galle of an oxe and anoynte þe towelle abowte & it sal helpe the mekill.

Tak þe jewse of dentdelyon & menge it with his vryn & drynk it & it will hele the for sothe, q*uod* probat*ur* *secundu*m R. de Oswaldkirk. *An oþer for euyll in þe body þat es growen*

35 Tak burnett & stampe it with wyn or mylke & do it to þe fire & suppe it als hate [2] als thou may suffre it. *For scheryng & gryndyng in þe body.*

Tak hau*yr* & p*ar*che it wele in a pan*n*e & strenkill it wele in þe p*ar*chynge w*ith* wa*ter* & do it in a pokett *An oþer.*

[1] MS. *adds* it *crossed out.*   [2] MS. *has* als hate *in margin.*

	& lay it als hate to whare þu felis þe gryndyng als þu may suffre it.
An oþer.	Tak veruayne & dry roses & mak powdir of þam abowte missomer & drynk of þat powdir & it will do a-way þe gryndyng.
For hardnes & bolnyng of þe wambe.	Tak fiuelefe & stampe it & tak ij sponefull of þe wose & drynke it & it sall do a-waye þe euylle.
An oþer.	Tak þe wose of waybrede & mak it lewke & drynke it & sall do þe gude.
An oþer.	Tak þe erbe puliol & chew it & bynde it to thi nauyll & it sal swage þe bolnynge.
For wormes.	Tak nept & stamp it & temper it with hate wyne & drynk it & it caste owt all þe wormes in þi body qwik & dede.
An oþer.	Tak askes of burtre & mak lee per-of & drynk it ofte & it sall sla þe wormes & dryfe þam owte, quod probatum est secundum R. de O. /

For þe flix   For fluxus sa[n]guinis [1]   For þe menyson   For þe flix

For þe flix.	Tak þe a hate lafe as it commes owt of þe owun. Mak soppes of þe crommes in gude rede wyne & ette wele per-of & it sall do þe gude.
For fluxus sanguinis.	For an oþer þat is callede fluxus sanguinis: Tak þe ruste of a claper of a belle & stampe it to powdir & drynk it with water.
An oþer.	Tak gomme of araby & sethe it to it be defiede & drynke it iij dayes.
An oþer.	Take þe kynd of hert & drynk it with rede wyne & it strenghes wonderfuly to stawnce menyson or flix.
Menyson or flix.	Tak fresche chese & welle it in wyne rede or ells ale & drynke it.
An oþer, secundum R. de O.	Tak þe jewse of quintfoile & menge it with swete mylke & drynk it.
Nota.	If þu will wete ȝif he þat hase þe menyson sall liffe or dy, tak a peny weghte of garthe cresse sede & gyff hym at ete and gare hym after [drink] [2] a draghte of gude rede wyne lewke or lewk water & do so iij dayes &, if he

[1] MS. saguinis.   [2] MS. omits.

stawnche, he may lyfe & hafe helpe &, if he stawnche
noghte, he sall dy.

Tak þe jewse of ȝarowe & knede it in a cake wit*h*   An oþer.
whete flo*ur* & bake it in þe aymers & ette it hate &
5 drynke noghte aft*er*.

Also take a handfull of tormentill & stampe it & boyle   Anoþer.
it with swete mylke of a cowe & drynk it hate ij mornes
& j euen & it sall hele hym.

Or tak p*er*celle sede & stamp it and temp*er* it wit*h*   An oþer.
10 gude rede wyn & drynk it hate, q*uod* probat*ur* p*er* R. de O.

Tak þe mylke of a cowe þat had na calfe a twelmonthe   An oþer.
bifore & tak als mekill of gud red wyne & menge þam
to-gedi*r* & drynke it ofte & wit*h*-owtten dowte it sall
strene thi wambe & it es gude for þam þat the blude
15 gase fra.

Tak clene whete & sethe it to it be clene broken. Tak   An oþer.
it þan and stampe it wat*er*les in a mort*er* & wrynge owte
þe jewse. Þan tak þe jewse & sethe it in a posenett &
do salte p*er*-to & ette it and it sall helpe the wele.

20 Tak a cok þat is a tweluemonethe alde or mare and   An oþer.
dight it faire & stoppe it full of virgyn waxe & do it on a
spete & torne it by-for þe fire to þe waxe be al molten
a-way & till it be almaste dry for rostynge & caste
þ*er*-to salt & ett it & it sall do þe gude. Bot eft*er* þis
25 medcyn to þis euyll, drynk littill or noghte.

Tak waybrede & sethe it in vynagre & drynk a   An oþer.
coppefull fastand & it sall helpe the mekill.

Tak a handfull of ȝarow & stamp it and temp*er* it   An oþer.
wit*h* a coppfull of gude rede wyne & drynk it & it sal
30 do þe gude.

Tak hert horne & bryn it & bete it to powdir & scarce   An oþer.
it thorow a scarce & vse it ilk daye to þu be hale. /

For þe menyson   For þe dropsy

Tak virgyn wax & sethe it in þe whit of an egg &   An oþer.
35 vse it all hate and it will restreyne thi fundament.

Tak a pott of erthe & do it full of whete flo*ur* & do   An oþer.
it in a hate owen & late it bake als lange as brede dose.
Þan tak of þat flo*ur* a mesure in a coppe & tak þe
ȝolkes of iij hen eggis & þe jewse of mynt, of bathe ilike

Liber de Diversis Medicinis.

mekill of þe jewse & of þe ȝolkes, & make a cake & bake it & ete þer-of, bot nott ouer mekill, & it sal helpe the.

For þe bludy menyson.
Tak ȝarow & waybrede ana, & stampe þam & temper þam with wyn or ale & giff it þe seke at drynke, at euen hate & at morne calde, to he be hale. 5

For þe dropsy.
Tak þe rute of fenkall & of percell, of aþer ilike mekil, & tak of þe rute of ache als mekill als of bathe þe oþer, & tak owte þe hardest of þe rute & a handfull of hauyr-mele grotis & stampe þam smalle & tak xx penyweghte 10 of fenkell rute & xx peny weghte of percell rute & xx peny weghte of ache rute & take a galon of water & do all in a pott ouer þe fire & late it sethe to þe halfe & tak þan & sile it thorow a clathe & do it in a vesselle. Þan tak þe jewse of fenkall, a gude dischefull, and 15 sethe it by it ane to þe halfe be sothen in & do þer-to þe toþer jewse & welle þam wele ouer þe fire & late it sethe wele & þan tak owte ix sponefull of þe firste confeccion & iij sponefull of þe jewse of þe fynkall & tak þan & do bathe to-gedir & drynk it at euen calde 20 & at morne hate & kepe hym fra oþer drynk.

An oþer.
Tak betoyne & sethe it in wyne or hony & gif hym it ofte at drynke þat is bolnynge in the dropsy.

An oþer.
Tak alisaundir, aȝarabackara, smalache, fawethistills & tyme, of ylkan elike mekill, & bray þam wele in a 25 morter & stepe þam in alde ale & drynk it alle dayes to þu be hale.

An oþer.
Tak þe flexigines þat men schawes of schepe tharmes and of nete hidis & sethe þam swalange in water till it be als thike als lyme or englewe. Þan tak a schete 30 or an oþer clathe & bynde it abowt thi body & þi wambe al hate, for this is a full sekir medcyne.

An oþer.
Tak walwort & birs it & mak a bedde þer-of & lay þe seke þer-on alle nakede & couer hym wele with walwort & gyfe hym to drynke þe jewse of walwort & 35 it sall draw owte mekill of his euyll and spourge hym wele.

Medcyn for þe calde dropsy.
Tak þe rute of fynkall & þe sedis of brome. Tak matfelon / and fawthistyll and percell, of ilkan ilyke mekill, and of smalle ache als mekill als of alle þe oþer. 40

f. 293v.

Liber de Diversis Medicinis. 33

Þan tak radik rute, ysop, betoyne and auance sede and
a handfull of hauyrmele grotis, & stamp þam smalle
and welle þam in a galoun of water till þay be wellid
intill a potell and clarify it with suger & wryng it thorow
5 a clathe & drynk it morne and euen.

Tak soure brede of whete, clowes, canelle, galynga *A enplaster for þe dropsy.*
& vynagre, & stamp all to-gedir & do þam in a pokett
& bynd it on his navill.

Tak cald mynt, fenell, lauandre & parytory ana, *An oþer schewyng for þe dropsy.*
10 hony als mekill als of alle þe oþer. Couch thyn erbes
& thi fenell a-bown, þan tak & hete ij rownde pepble
stones & cast þam in thyn herbis & sprenkill a-bown
salte & vynagre &, when he swetis, wype hym with a
cloute & hete þe stanes oftesones &, when he hase
15 swett twyse, do hym in his bedde & couer hym wele.

Tak þe ȝonge syons þat growes by þe erthe of þe *For þe dropsy hate or calde.*
ellere tree & schafe of þe ouer barke & schafe of þe
grene barke, þe montenaunce of twa handfull, and gare
boyle it in a galon of stale ale to þe halfe be boilled
20 in & gare þe seke man or woman drynk þerof morne
and euen & he sall be hale.

Tak welle cresse a grete porcyoun, & a porcyoun of *An oþer.*
vetoyne, a porcyoun of betoyne, a porcyoun of[1] saxifrage,
a porcyon of waybred, a porcyon of centorye & sethe
25 centorye by it ane. Tak a knyfe & schere it smal,
þe rute & alle, & sethe it in water. Tak þe broo of þat
& late it go thorow a clowte. All þise herbis safe
centorye sall be stampid & þe jewse wrongen owte.
Þan tak þat jewse & putt it in a brase pott with a
30 porcyon of ald ale. Sethe it ouer þe fire & boile it &
scome it. Tak a porcyon of hony & putt þer-in &
scum it efte & sett it bi-syde to it be halfe calde. Tak
an egge & breke it with þe schelles & alle & putt it
þer-in ane erthe pott & couer it with[2] a lyn clothe and take
35 þe mountenance of a sawcerfull & drynk bath euen and
morne, firste at morne and laste at euen.

Nota quod cerum caprinum potatum cum spicaray *Nota.*
curat omnem ydropicum in frigida causa.

---

[1] MS. *adds* saxagre *crossed out*.
[2] a *preceding* a lyn clothe *crossed out*.

34   *Liber de Diversis Medicinis.*

[No]*ta*
opti*m*e for
þe [d]ropsy.
  Tak a potelle of clere rynnande wate*r* and a potelle
of thyn awenn stalynge, a potell of lee made / of ashes *t.* 294r.
askes [1] and wormot, au*e*royn *vel* sowthrenwode, an rede
fenkell and sethe al to-gedir & lygge the naked a-bownn
it þat þe hete þ*er*-of may entre in-to thi body and happe 5
þe wele w*ith* schetis and clathes as þu were in a bathe
and, if þu sall lyffe, it sall falle down in-to thi legges on
warantise or ells þu sal dy.

For þe
p*ar*lsy.
  Tak a schepe hede & fla it & alle þe iiij fete & breke
all to duste & do a-way þe hernes & syn caste þam in 10
a pott & do þ*er*-to a potell of white wyne & ij galons
of swete milke & sethe þam in-to a qwarte or lesse &
sythen pure it thorow a clathe or a clene streynʒo*ur*
& do it in boystes & ix dayes anoynte þe seke þ*er*-
with bi þe fire & it sall hele hym. 15

An oþ*er*.
  Tak sawge & ett ofte & in alle metis & hald it i*n* thi
mouthe.

An oþ*er*.
  Tak a foxe & mak hym in sew & ette of hy*m* wele.

An oþ*er*.
  Tak iij sawge leues, iij vetoyne leues, iij wodbynd
leues, iij ambros leues, iij erthe yven leues, iij gra*y*nes 20
of junip*er*, iij cornes of pep*ir* & a handfull of moushere
& a handful of leke fases, fel gerie de quercu radices
iij. Stamp al to-gedir wele & smalle & temp*er* þam
w*ith* v soppes of wyn & iiij soppes of haly wat*er* and drynk
it ofte. 25

An oþ*er*.
  Tak þe rutes of pion, rutis of fenkall, rutes of p*er*cell
& anete sede ana, & do all hale in a newe pott w*ith*
wat*er* ou*er* þe fire & welle þam wele to þe third p*ar*t
be wellid in & make a clarett þ*er*-of & drynk it w*ith*-
owtten wyn. 30

An oþ*er*.
  Tak henbayne sedis & stampe þam wele & temp*er*
it with þe jewse of dragans & lewk it & helle it in his
mouthe & he sal not tyne.

Cura
p*ar*alisis
exp*er*ta.
  Recipe grana juniperi ij & grana pip*er*is ij & medie-
tate*m* vn[ius] bacce lauri prot*er*antur & distemp*er*entur 35
cu*m* aqua rute *vel* cu*m* succo & det*ur* ad potandum.

No*ta* No*ta*.
  For hym þat is smetyn with his awen blode & spredis
ou*er* alle his lymmes & waxes plowkky & brekes owte :

---

[1] MS. *has* of ashes askes *at top of f.* 294r, *apparently repeating
with slight variation* of ashes bowes, *which occurs at foot of f.* 293v.

Liber de Diversis Medicinis.

Tak mogewort & celydoyne & stamp þam & temper þam with wyn and drynke it. *Nota Nota.*

Tak [1] cheruell & salt & stamp it & temper with wyn or water. *For þe stake in þe syde.*

5 Tak littill balles of sothen rede wirtes & bryn þam in an newe pott & sythen grynde þam to powdir & blend it with hony & alde grese & welle alle samen and plaster it ther-to & it sall awaye./

f. 294v. Tak egremoyn and mogwort. Bake þe leues & þe 10 rutes & stamp þam wele with alde swyn gres and ayselle.[2] Plaster it þer-to on þe bak. *For werk of bak.*

Tak a gude dele of puliol & stampe it & do þer-to aysell & oyle de olife & do it on a clathe & bynde it on thi bak. *An oþer.*

15 Ad cognoscendum vtrum apostema vertetur interius vel exterius : Si aliqua rubicunditas appareat, vertetur in saniem & exiet foras, sin autem, vertetur interius. *For apostymms.*

Tak þe rute of malue & þe sede of femygreke & þe sede of lyne & [3] flour of barly. Thies thynges grynde 20 wele al to-gedir & lay vn-to þe appostym.

Tak moushere & bray it wele with whit wyne or ale & drynk it & lay þe draffe to þe appostym & it sall breke þe same nyghte. *An oþer.*

Tak þe rute of henbayne & þe rute of wilde malue & 25 þe ȝolkes of egges & alde gres, þe whilke sall be sothen & syn stamped all to-gedir, & lay it to þe appostym. *An oþer.*

Tak fymter, wormot, centory, and drynk þam, per R. de Os. *For apostym within or with-owtt.*

Tak wormot, mynt, camamyll, herbe benet, malues & 30 cerefoill, floures of roses, sawge, comyn & crommes of soure brede, and welle þam alle wele in white wyne or pyssyng clarifiede & mak þan a plaster of þam & lay to þe sare syde ay to it be hale. *For þe apostym in the syde, per R. de Os.*

Tak camamyll, wormot, harune, comyn, salt & ald 35 pysse, & welle þam alle samen till a galon of pisse com to a potelle & þan tak & anoynte wele thi syde with þat licour &, when it is wele dronken in, tak & gedir þe mater þat was sothen & mak a plaster þer-of with hony *An oþer R. de O.*

---

[1] MS. adds cheuerell crossed out.
[2] MS. adds per crossed out.   [3] MS. adds flor crossed out.

& powdir it wele with powdir of comyn & lay it to thi
syde & þay sal amend with-in iij plasters & hele faire
& wele & gyffe þam at drynk a porcyon of þe jewse
of wormot with his awen fastand stalynge wele clarified
ilk daye to þay be hale, for þis is verrely sothe & ofte- 5
tymes wele proued.

A] gud drynke [for] þe apostym. Tak ach, rew, pulioll, sawge, nept, harhone, cress,
fenkell, saueray, isope, waybrede and swyn gres & stamp
al to-gedir wele with an vnce of pepir & halfe an vnce of
pelleter & syn boile all wele with a porcyon of hony & 10
sythen coile it thorowe a clathe & drynk þe coilett
chawfede morne & euen to þu be hale.

[An] oþer. Tak a new egg & do a-waye þe white & tak þe ȝolke &
hony & oil de olife & þe jewse of harune, of ilkan ylike
mekill, & do in þe egge schell & menge it to-gedir & gif 15
it to þe seke at drynk iij dayes with wyn or ale fastande
& he sal mende. /

A maturatife for apostym. Tak hauyrmele grotes & sethe þam wele in water *f. 295r.*
to þay be brostyn & tak þam þan vppe & do þam in a
panne & do to þam a gud porcyon of schepe talghe & 20
fry þam wele samen & lay þat on a clathe als it were a
plaster & lay it to all hate & lat it lygg a nyghte & a day
& sythen new it eftesones till it be broken.

An oþer. Tak gronswell & sethe it wele & þan do it in a panne &
fry it wele with galte gres & lay it þan to als hate als he 25
may suffre it to it be brustyn & þan tak whete floure &
temper it with comon oile and mak a plaster & lay it all
warme to, per R. de O.

An oþer. Tak þe jewse of ach & oyneȝouns and ryse mele &
apostolion, dewte and egg ȝolkes & hony, & menge 30
to-gedir & al hate lay it ouer þe apostym.

Nota bene. An oþer maturatyfe for bolnyng vnder þe chole:
Tak a fatt catt & fla it wele & clene & draw owt þe
guttis & tak þe gres of an vrcheon & þe fatt of a bare &
raysynges & femygreke & sawge & gumme of wobbynde 35
& virgyn waxe, & alle thies mye smalle & farse þe cate
with-in als þou farses a gose. Roste it hale & gedir þe
gres & anoynte hym þat hase nede.

An oþer maturatif for þe apostym. An oþer for þe apostym: Tak wormot, hony & ry
mele, & stamp þam to-gedir & lay appon it. 40

Liber de Diversis Medicinis.

For þe swynacy : Tak a horse ryghte balloke & clefe   þe swynacy.
it in twa & anoynte þe swynacy þer-with & bynde it to
al hate & do it not away to þe iij day.
    Tak colombyne or þe sede þer-of, & stamp it & drynk   An oþer
5 it also. Or take ambrose & drynke it.   *secundum* R. de O.
    Succus anarisci tollit de fauce squinanciam.
    Tak almondes swete & buttre & ett þam.   For hym
    Or ette þe jewse of wortes with fat [1] flesche.   þat will not be dronken.
    Or strenkill hym ofte with calde water or laye his
10 hyngers in calde water.
    Or drynk vynagre, mylk & water.
    Or tak oil of roses menged with vynagre & anoynt his
heued.
    Or tak & wasche his handes & his ballokes in calde
15 water.
    Or tak calde thynges of grete sauoure & halde to his
nese, as caumfere or water of roses.
    Tak þe rute of horsehelme & sethe it lange in water &   For scabbes.
þan tak þe nescheste þer-of & stamp it with alde gres
20 & do it þan in a lyn clathe & hete it at þe fire & anoynte
þe scabbes þer-with and it sal hele þam sone.
    Tak þe rute of horslne & stamp it & fry it in a panne   An oþer.
with swyne sayme & wryng it owte & do it in boistes &
anoynte þe scabbe of man or of horse or of oþer besteȝ
& it will hele wele. /
26   Tak þe rede doke rute and do a-way þe leues & þe   [An] oþer for þe scalles.
stalke & stampe þe rutis with May buttre & sethe it
wele in alde wyne & clense it thorow a clathe and do it in
boystes and anoynte þe scabbes þer-with at þe fire.
30   Tak þe rute of þe rede dok & stamp it wele & welle   An oþer.
it with Maye buttre & clense it thorow a clathe in-to a
bacyn full of water & late it hardyn on þe water & þan
do it in boystes & anoynte þe scabbes at þe fire.
    Tak moreoles & þe rute of euerferne þat waxes on þe   An oþer.
35 ake, & stamp it wele & temper it with mylk and anoynte
þe scabbes þer-with.
    Tak bromstane & brek it al to powdir & menge it   An oþer.
with alde gres and warme it in a scarthe & anoynte þe
bestis þat er scabbid þer-with to þay be hale.

---

[1] MS. flat, *probably an error for* ffat.

An oþer.	Tak rede nettills, salt & pyssynge, & sethe þam wele & þan stampe þam wele & drawe þam thorow a clathe & anoynte þe scabbes.
An oþer secundum R. de O.	Tak þe rutes of rede dokes and of celidon & wormot, spourge leues & leues of lorell & bromstane, & welle alle 5 in buttre or in fresche gres and anoynte þe scabbes þer-with.
For to distroye lysse,[1] id est pediculos.	Tak horsehofe, herbe Robert, baynewort & qwik siluer, & fry þam to-gedir when þay are wele stamped & anoynte þe þer-with. 10
	Ad pediculos vitandos : Ruta cum melle circa tempus iungatur.
Contra pulices.	Ad pulices fugandos : Coliandrum sparge vbi sunt & fugient.
	Item recipe puluerem stafiȝagre cum oleo & vnge. 15
	For wormes with-in a mans body, if þay haue made any hole, tak at þe bygynnyng & anoynte þe hole with hony & þan tak þe powdir of a grisse þat men callis woderofe & do þer-to & it sall sla þe wormes & hele þe wonde. 20
An oþer secundum R. de O.	Tak þe rute of radik and stamp it & wrynge þe jewse in þe hole and he sall warische sone.
An oþer.	Tak nesche sape & radik & menge to-gedir & mak a plaster & lay to.
An oþer.	Tak þe bark of wilghe þat is bitwene þe tre & þe 25 vtter barke & þe entres of þe rute alswa. Do stamp þam wele & sethe þam in swete mylke and giffe þe seke to drynk & he sal warische.
An oþer.	Tak hert horne and bryn it to powdir & temper it with wynagre & drynk it ofte and it sall sla þe wormes. 30
An oþer.	Tak ȝarow & comyn and sethe þam in vynagre & enplaster it & lay it on þe navill als hate als it may be suffred & þay sall sone come owte, oþer qwik or dede.
An oþer.	Tak þe rute of playntayn with þe sede & stampe þam with stalworthe vynagre & drynk þe jewse & enplaster 35 þe drafe apon þe navill & it sall caste þam owte by-nethe.
An oþer.	Tak peleter & bryn it to powdir & sythen sethe þe powdir in ayselle and giffe þe seke to drynk with wyne. Or [tak][2] pelleter barke sothen in aysell and drynk it

[1] MS. *repeats* lysse *in variant spelling* lisse. [2] MS. *omits*.

Liber de Diversis Medicinis. 39

f. 296r. ofte [& it]¹ sall sla þe wormes. / . . . or mare, if it be
ruted, & þu sal be hale &, if þu hafe no sugo*ur*, drynk it
w*ith* wyn.²
  Tak an vnce of gyng*er*, halfe an vnce of horshelne, **An oþer.**
5 of licorice an vnce & an halfe & make a confeccion þ*er*-of
& vse it.
  Tak bare gres & þe jus of cresses & þe jus of nettills, **For hym**
of ilkan elike mekill, & blend all samen & do þ*er*-to   **þat is leper.**
quik silu*er* & temp*er* all to-gedir & anoynt þi face þ*er*-
10 with at þe euen & morn & wasche it to it be hale.
  Tak a fatt gose & sla it & draw it clene & brysse þe **An oþer.**
gose w*ith* þe banes & do in þe gose hony & þe third
p*artie* of virgyn waxe & halfe a pownd of frank encense
& alle þe grese of þe gose & sew it wele & do it to þe
15 fire to roste & kepe wele þe gres. Þan tak a hundreth
wylken leues & stamp þam & tak þe jus & boil al to-
gedir with halfe a pownde of white lede & twa vnces
of mercury & anoynte hy*m* ofte þ*er*-w*ith* to he be hale.
  Consiliu*m* contra morbu*m* caducum per cui*us*dam
20 sapi*entis* :³
  Tak þe flo*ur* of titmeus & stamp it w*ith* rosen & + **Morbum**
anoynte hym & it⁴ + ne sall not growe +. Set   **caducum.**
confugiat infirmus ad sa*cerdotem* & confiteatur om*n*ia   **+ Falland**
peccata sua. Deinde dicat sacerdos symbolu*m* super   **euyll +**
25 capud infirmi, *scilicet*, Quicumque vult, & postea absoluat
eum iniungendu*m* ei vt om*nibus* diebus vite sue dicat
nouies ora*cionem* Dom*i*nicam & totie*n*s ora*cionem*
ang[e]licam, *scilicet*, Aue Maria & Credo in Deu*m*. Deinde
habeat in*firmus* vij candelas cereas, *scilicet*, iij in manu
30 dextra & iiij in manu sinis*tra*, & celebretur prisbiter
missa. Officium : Salus p*opuli* ego su*m*. Dicit Domin*us*
de q*uacumque* tr*ibulacione* clamaueri*n*t ad me, exaudiam
eos & ero illor*um* Domin*us* imperpetuu*m*. Pr*isbiter* :
Attendite, popule me*us*. Collecta : Omnipotens sem-
35 piterne Deus, salus eterna credencium, exaudi nos

---

¹ MS. *omits.*
² *Between the bottom of f. 295v and the top of 296r there is an omission of material, including the beginning of this recipe.*
³ MS. *probably omits a word, e.g.* verba, *upon which* cuiusdam sapientis *depends.*
⁴ MS. *repeats it.*

pro famulo tuo, N., pro quo egrotante misericordie tue
imploramus auxilium vt reddita sibi sanitate graciarum
tibi in ecclesia tua referat accionem per Dominum
nostrum etc. Epistola : Leccio epistoli beati Iacobi
apostoli karissimi : Tristatur aliquis vestrum, oret equo   5
animo & psallat. Infirmatur quis ex uobis, in-ducat
prisbiteros ecclesie & orent super eum invngentes eum
oleo in nomine Domini & oracio fidei saluabitur infirmum,
et alleuabit eum Dominus &, si in peccatis sit, dimittentur
ei. Confitemini ergo alterutrum peccata vestra & orate 10
pro inuicem vt saluemini. Graduale : Miserere mei,
Domine, qui infirmus sum ; sana me, Domine. Versus :
Conturbata sunt omnia ossa mea & anima mea turbata
est valde. Alleluia : Qui sanat contritos corde &
alligat contriciones eorum. Ewangelium : Secundum 15
Marcum : In illo tempore respondens vnus de turba
dixit ad Ihesum : Magister, attuli filium meum ad te
habentem spiritum mutum, qui vbicumque eum appre-
henderit allidit eum & spumat / & stridit dentibus & f. 296v.
arescit. Et dixi discipulis tuis vt eicerent illum & non 20
potuerunt. Qui respondens ait : O generacio incredula,
quam diu apud vos ero ! Quam diu vos paciar ! Afferte
illum ad me. & attulerunt eum & cum vidisset eum,
statim spiritus conturbauit eum & elisus in terram
volutabatur spumans. Et interrogauit patrem eius : 25
Quantum temporis est ex quo ei accidit ? At ille ait :
Ab infancia & frequenter eum in ignem & aquas misit
vt eum perderet. Set si quid potes, adiuua nos misertus
nostri. Ihesus autem ait illi : Si potes credere, omnia
possibilia sunt credenti. Et continuo exclamans pater 30
pueri cum lacrimis aiebat : Credo, Domine. Adiuua
incredulitatem meam. Et cum videre[t] [1] Ihesus con-
currentes turbas, comminatus est spiritui inmundo
dicens illi : Surde & mute spiritus, ego precipio tibi : Exi
ab eo & amplius non introeas in eum, & clamans & 35
decerpens eum exijt ab eo & factus est sicut mortuus,
ita vt multi dicerent quod mortuus est. Ihesus autem
tenens manum eius eleuauit eum & surexit et, cum
introisset domum, discipuli eius secrete interrogabant

[1] MS. videres.

Liber de Diversis Medicinis.

eum : Quare nos non potuimus eicere eum ? Et dixit
illis Ihesus : Hoc genus in nullo potest exire nisi in
oracione & ieiunio. Nota : Hoc euangelium legatur
super capud infirmi & osculetur librum. Offertorium :
5 Domine, conuertere & eripe animam meam. Saluum
me fac proptter misericordiam tuam. Deinde offerat
infirmus candelas suas et postea recipiat istas quas
habuit in manu dextra & mittat in sinistram & e conuerso
& teneat usque in finem misse. Secretum : Deus
10 cuius nutu vite nostre momenta decurrunt, suscipe
preces & hostias famuli tui pro quo egrotantte misericordiam tuam imploramus vt de cuius periculo metuimus
de eius salute letemur per Dominum nostrum etc. Infirmus accipiat pacem a sacerdote. Communio : Redime Communio.
15 me, Deus Israeli, ex omnibus angustijs meis. Post
Communio : Deus infirmitatis humane singulare pre-
sidium, auxilij tui super infirmum nostrum ostende
virtutem vt ope misericordie tue adiutus ecclesie tue
sancte incolimis presentari mereatur per Dominum
20 nostrum etc. Post missam : Legat sacerdos euangelia
de diuersis euangelistis super capud eius & faciat
votum quod tota vita sua ieiuniet feria v/ta in pane
& aqua in nomine Dei. Hec sunt euangelia : Recum-
bentibus etc. Cum natus esset Ihesus etc. Pastores
25 loquebantur etc. In principio erat verbum etc.

Tak þe firste tyme þat it takes þe man þat þou may An oþer.
wiete it : Tak a bee & drawe owte þe tonge & gare þe
seke swalowe it all hale with some drynk þat he weit
it noghte and he sall be delyuerde for euer mare. /

f. 297r. **Contra morbum caducum**

31 Tak rybwort & euerferne þat waxes one þe ake, An oþer.
egremoyn, solsekill, ȝarow, rykills & pepir, of ilkan
elik mekill & be weghte. Stamp þam al to-gedir &
gyff hym to drynke with water.

35 Tak þe wormes as þou will & stamp þam & temper An oþer.
þam with water & drynk þam all at anes & þu sal be
delyuerde for euer & al þi lyf tym.

Tak on Sayn John day or þe son ryse a gryse with An oþer.
all þe rote þat men calles mercuriale &, þe whils þu

drawes it vp, say þi Pater noster & þin Aue Maria &
lay it appon an autre til ix messes be said per-one & þan
tak þe gryse & dry it & mak powdir per-of & gyf hym
to drynk þat hase nede þe weghte of iij penyes & he
sal be hale. 5

Nota. A man þat saw hym neuer falle shuld schere his belt
in twa, when he saw þe euyll tak hym, & graue it one
aper halfe hym & he sall be hale.

An oþer. Tak þe blode of þe littill fynger of hym þat is seke
and wryte thir thre names in his forehed of þe iij kynges 10
of Colayn, þat is to say : Iasper fert aurum, thus Melchior,
Attro pamirram. He þat beris þir names of þir iij
kyngis with hym, he sall be lesid thurgh þe petee of
God of þe falland euyll. Or write þam with þe sam
blode & hynge þam abowt his nek in a writ. 15

Take & gare a childe drynke wretyn or he be vij ȝere
alde & he sall neuer hafe it afterwarde.

An oþer. Ille qui compatit morbum caducum bibat aquilayam
cum aqua aut semen aquilaye. Sumat etiam puluerem
pireti & pionie. Et erit abstinencia eius; in vita sua 20
non commedet anguillam nec ancam nec anatem nec
auem qui habet pedem clasum nec capud alicuius animalis
& curabitur.

For þe nauyll þat waxis & wanes. Tak oyl & water, euen porcyon of bathe, & welle
to-gedir till it be thik & lay it on a lethyre & lay it to 25
þe navyll all warme & bynd it faste per-to & it sall
amende.

Cramp. Tak rew & stamp it with fresche buttre & do it in a
vessell ix dayes & couer it wele & syn boile it & draw
it thorow a clathe & þan do per-to wax & encense & 30
boile it & scome it & do it in boystes & anoynte þe per-
with and bathe the in warme water & drynk sawge in
warme wyne.

An oþer. Nota. Tak & gare gedir on Gude Fryday at v paresche
kirkes fyve of þe firste penys þat er offrede at þe cros 35
& say fyve Pater nosters in þe wirchip of þe v wondis
& bere þam ouer on þe fyve dayes & say on þe same
wyse ilk a day als mekill / & þan gare mak a rynge per-
of with-owtten any oþer metall & write with-in þe
rynge : Iasper, Baltaȝare, Attropa, & write with- 40

Liber de Diversis Medicinis. 43

owtten : Ihesus nazarenus, & sythen tak it fra þe goldsmyth appon a Fryday & say v Pater noster als þou did by-fore & vse it alway afterwarde, for it hase bene proued sothe.

5 Tak & mak a rynge of laton fyne & were for þe crampe.

Tak cale stokes & bryne þam to askes & blende þam with hony and anoynt þe þer-with to þu be hale. *For glaunders.*

Or take þe gres of a neddir & anoynte þe þer-with. *An oþer.*

10 Tak sourdokes & salt & grynde it with oyle & mak a cake & lay it to þe sare. *An oþer.*

Tak tele stones & hete þam to þay glow & slokyn þam in wyn & swa do thris & tak þe powdir þer-of & of a brynt felten hatt & strewe þer-ouer & it sall halde in. *For goyng owt of þe sete.*

15 Tak þe jewse of maythes & drynke it & lay þe draffe apon þe fundament. *An oþer.*

Tak senigle, violet, tansay, hemp, mugwort, & sethe þam in ale & do it in a newe pott & drynk it ay to he be hale. *An oþer for þe [f]undament þat is owte.*

20 Accipe picem, vitellum oui & fac emplastrum & superpone oleum & de calido frunito. Item sinsibrium, rutam, rubrum, maratrum, ouum i, tiniarum manipulum i, radicem filij domestici i, ales Ironorum albumen, aceti ciatum i, olei i. Predictas fortiter tere herbas & succum earum
25 cum predictis misce, fortiter cola & cum penna lota vrgencia in-vnge & mirabilis est. *Nota ignem sacrum qui ex calore nascitur.*

Tak auance, millefoile & stampe þam wele to-gedir & temper þam with stale ale & drynke euen & morne. *[F]or þe emerawdes.*

Tak vnslokynde lyme & do it in a pane & do water *An oþer.*
30 þer-to so þat it be couerde & couer it & late it stand iij dayes. Þan take þe lyme or þe water & do it in an oþer pane & do oyle þer-to & boyle it & anoynte þe sare þer-with. It is a gud metigatyfe.

Item capiatur melle, olium, þe maynflour, plumbum,
35 rubium, porrett, id est lekes. Emplastetur & apponatur super emerawdes.

Tak sute & menge with oyle de olyfe & mak it thikke & lay þer-to. *An oþer.*

Tak comyn ij vnce, anys, fawthistill I vnce, camelle, *Ventosite.*
40 fenkell sede, percelle sede I vnce, of gynger iij peny

Liber de Diversis Medicinis.

weghte, & mak all in powdir & vse of þat in þi mete ilk a daye.

Wartes. Tak egremoyn & stamp it & do vynagre þer-to so þat it be thik & bynd to þe wartis & þay sal waste a-waye.

An oþer. Tak marygoldes and salte & stamp to-gedir & lay to þe wartis.

An oþer. Tak doufe fen & do it in vynagre & anoynt þe wartes þer-with.

[An] oþer. Tak þe jewse of wodbynde & egremoyn & do hony & salt & ayselle þer-to.

Or bryn þe wartes with bromstane & þay will a-waye. /

For hym þat may noghte pys. Tak gromelle, rede nettills, percelle sede, a handefull of white pepir, & stamp it & temper it & boile it in wyne, & tak a hare skyn & bryn it to powdir in a new pott & boille alle to-gedir & vse þat drynk & it wil hele þe. [f. 298r.]

An oþer. Tak rewe & gromelle & percelle & stamp þam to-gedir wele & temper þe jus with¹ wyn & drynk it ofte.

An oþer. Tak cristallanus & stamp it & temper it with wyn & drynk it & it sall gare þe pys wele.

An oþer. Tak þe jus of percelle & oyle of olyue & boyle þam wele to-gedir and drynke it.

For hym þat may not hald pys. Tak gud clowes & bryn þam in a new pott all to powdir & ett þat powdir ilk a day fastande in thi potage or how als þu may beste ette it, for with-owtten faile it sal helpe þe, if þu vse it.

For sare ȝerde. Tak þe jewse of þe water of playntayne & lay þer-to or wasche it þer-with.

For hym þat pysses blode. Tak ambros a handfull & sangwynarie a handefull & percell or þe sede a handefull & stamp þam & temper þam with gayte mylke and late hym drynk it ofte.

An oþer. An oþer, secundum R. de O.: Tak garleke with þe rutes & sethe þam in water to þe thirde partye and drynk þat water & it sal hele the.

An oþer Nota bene. Tak wodrofe & stamp it & temper it with wyn or alde ale & drynk it ofte lewke.

For euyll and werk in þe body in þe bledder. Tak ache, percill & fenkalle, of ilkan ilike mekyll, & stamp þam wele & temper þam with water & drynk it & it sall hele thi bledder & mak þe wele to pys, & caste owte þe stane & hele þe stomake.

¹ MS. *adds* wyth *crossed out.*

Liber de Diversis Medicinis.

Tak an vnce of benedicta & halfe an vnce of þe jewse
of rose & menge to-gedir & vse þam thryse or iiij sythes
in þe weke & ilk a tym bot a sponefull at anes. *For þe chawdpys.*

Tak agrippa & lay it on thi ʒerde, for þat is gud, *For þe stane and for þam þat may not pys.*
5 secundum R. de O.

Tak gromelle, percill, rede nettill, violett, frankencense, *For þe stane.*
& cherestankirnells & stamp þam to-gedir with stale ale
& drynk it.

Tak ix yven¹ beries & stamp þam wele and gyff hym *An oþer.*
10 at drynk per-with ilk a day iij sponefull of wyn & late
hym pys thorow a lyn clathe & þu sall se þe stane broken
þer-in.

Puluis silicis bene tritoniʒatus sero & mane cum
seruicia calida potatus frangit lapidem. Certissimum
15 est.

A gud drynk for þe stane, secundum R. de Osswald- *A gud drynk for þe stane.*
kirk : Tak þe blomes of brome a porcyoun, of pelleter a
porcyoun, a porcyon of egrimoyn, a porcyon of tansay,
a porcyon of grene gromelle. Tak a porcyon of ilkan
20 & stamp þam & wrynge owt þe jus. Tak þe jus & putt
f. 298 v. it in a pott of bras. Þan tak a porcyon of alde ale / &
put to þam & sett it ouer þe fire & scomme it wele.
Tak a porcyoun of hony & putt per-in & welle it &
scomme it efte &, when it is welled, tak it & sett it by-side
25 þe fire to it be halfe calde. Þan tak a negge with þe
schelles & all & breke it & putt it in þe pott & it wil
clarify it & þan late it stande to it be calde. Tak it
þan & late it ryne thorow a clowte in-till an erthen pott
&, when he sall drynk it, late it ryne thorow a clowte
30 agayne. Þan tak þe mountenance of a sawcerfull at
anes & drynke it bathe at morne nexte thy herte & laste
at euen, when þu gose to bedde.

Tak alysandre, gromelle, cerfoil, sangrede, nettyll, *An oþer gud medcyn for þe stane, secundum R. de Oswald-kirk.*
percell, papwort, philipendula, & þe skyn of a hare
35 brynte to powdir in a new pott & fenkell sede & pepir,
& welle all to-gedir in gud wyne & drynke a porcyon
ilk a day, for it is gude for þe stane.

Tak cherestane kyrnells & stamp þam & sethe tham in *An oþer.*
water & drynke þam.

---
¹ MS. *adds* leues *crossed out*.

Liber de Diversis Medicinis.

An oþer. Tak percell, wellecresse, fenkell, papewort & mak potage of þam and ette þam & þay sall do þe mekill ese, & þu vse þam.

An oþer. Tak percell, wellecresse, papwort, fenkell, & sethe þam in alde ale till þe halfe be sothen in or þe thirde party & drynk þer-of ilk day fastand, at morn a porcion & at euen.

An oþer. Nota. Tak a quartron of gud tried licoresche & ette þer-of ilk a day a porcyon.

An oþer. Tak þe bayes of yven & stamp þam wele & temper þam with whit wyne & drynk þer-of fastande ilk a day a porcion & þan sile thyn vryne thorowe a clathe & þu sall se þe stanes in þe founce of þe vessell þat þu pysses in.

An oþer. Tak wormot & dry it with-owtten þe sonne & mak powder þer-of & welle it wele with gayte mylke and drynk þer-of ix dayes & it sall breke þe stane and dystroye [1] it.

An oþer. Tak papwort & þe rute of gromelle, burnett & centory, & stamp þam wele & do to þam alde ale & drynk þer-of ilk a day fastande & ett comonly percell, for it is gud for þe stane and helpes mekill and in many wyes þer-fore.

[For hym] þat is enve-[nome]d, whilk parti .. y þat it be. Tak sawge leues and stamp þam wele & smalle & laye þam to þe sare with þe jus & þe draffe & bynd it faste þer-to & chaunge it morne & euen and, if he be en-venomed with-in þe body, tak sawge & stamp it smalle & temper þe jus with wyn or ale or water & drynk it morne and euen. /

For to dryve owte [þor]ne or iryn or tree. Tak & drynk þe jewse of dytane & lay þe draffe on þe wonde & bynd it þer-to.

Or tak betoyne and pympernoll & drynk þe jus with wyn, for it is proued for sothe.

Or drynk þe jus of mynt is gude also.

For bolnynge of strakes in þe hede or on þe body or any lym of man or woman. Tak & mynce a rede vnyon & tak thikk dregges of ale & whete branne & schepe talghe & do þam all in a pott & sethe þam all samen to þay be wele wellid & tak þan a faire new lyn clathe & lay all thiese thynges by-fore said þer-on als it were a plaster & lay it on þe sare & it sall waresche faire & wele.

---

[1] MS. drystroye.

Liber de Diversis Medicinis.

Tak a new lyn clathe & wete it in þe water þat þe smythe slekkes his yryn in & lay it on þe bryssour. *For all maner bryssour.[1]*
Or tak a gud thikke plaster of clene lyne & wete it wele in þe same water ilk a day twyse & lay to þe
5 bryssour to it be drawen owt.

Tak halfe an vnce of Diatarascos, halfe I vnce of Catholicon, halfe an· vnce of Diacolon, & tewe þam in thi handes agayne þe fire with oile Marciaton or oil of lorell ay till it be wele tempered & þan spred it appon *For werkyng and gnawyng of arme or of schankes.[2]*
10 a faire lethir & lay it to where it werkes, secundum Ser Apilton.

Tak þe rute of hertis tonge, id est cerfoil, & mynce it smalle & þan tak ale dregges & whete bran vt supra for bolnyng of hed or of body, with-in þe body, bi *An oþer, secundum R. de O.*
15 fallyng or strakes or any maner of oþer brissour.

Tak scabious and comfery & stamp þam & wryng þam and drynk þe jus, ij sponefull at euen & ij at morne, and þe jus of nepta emange appon þe same wyse. *For brissyng secundum R. de O.*

The manere to be laten blode, þis is : Sanguyen & *The maner to be laten blode.*
20 þe fleumatik sall be laten blode at vndron of þe day and the coleryȝen at þe midday and þe malecolyn at þe nonne or sone after. Bot luk at þu kepe hym wele fra surfett & luk þat he ette none egges nor geese ne no fruyte nor slepe mekill nor hafe mekill thoghte & luk
25 he kepe hym fra fire & lyghte.

For bolnynge of vayne after blode latynge : Tak þe floure of whete & þe jus of ache & schepe talghe & emplaster þer-to. *For bolnyi[n]g[3] of vayn after bledyng.*

Or tak sawge & hertistonge & stamp it and gyffe it
30 hym or hir to drynke & he sall warische.

Tak & sethe rew in wyn & temper þer-with gareleke & anoynte þer-with þe arme or þe schanke þat is sare, and also do of þe same likour on a wollelok / and lay it a-bowenn the sare & it sall hele it. *For vayne þat is schorne in twa[4] of blode latynge or of bolnyng or whelynge of garsynge or ventousynge.*
35 Tak wormot and sethe it wele & wasche þe sare wele with-all & tak þan þe wormot & stamp it & do it in a frying pan & do þer-to a quanttite of hony & fry þam *An oþer.*

---

[1] MS. *repeats* bryssours.
[2] MS. *repeats* armes or schankes.   [3] MS. bolnyig.
[4] MS. *adds* for vayn þat is schorne in twa *crossed out.*

samen & tak þan a lyn clathe & lay it on alle hate &
tak þan powdir of comyn & strew þer-on wele thikke
& lay it appon þe sare als hate als he may suffre it &
late it lygge ay till he be hale.

[For] vayn brokyn.
An oþer for vayne broken in twa: Tak þe blode & 5
menge it with oyle & anoynte þe arme þer-with &
sythen bynd it to þe vayne þat is broken in twa.

An oþer.
Tak brynt lym & mak powdir þer-of & tak hony &
þe white of an egge & stamp þam to-gedir þat it be
wele menged & lay lyn on þe sare bot thyn, & on þe 10
lyn do þe playster & efte of þe lyn & efte of þe playster
& vn-do it noghte or þe thirde day &, when þu vn-dose
it, wete it wele with þe seke mans pys for to leese it,
for, if þu drawe it away with strenghe, perauentoure it
wil blede lyghtly efte souns. 15

For to staunce blode [1] of vayne or nese or wounde.
Tak þe schelles of geese egges or of hennes egges
þat birdis hase bene in, and bryn þam & mak powdir
of þam & do þat powdir on þe vayn & bynd it on þe
arme & it sall stanche it wele.

An oþer.
Tak a brome stalke & schafe of þe rynde with a knyfe 20
& mak balles þer-of & do it in þe wounde & bynd it
wele with a clathe.

An oþer.
Tak salt & bryn it firste in a scarthe & mak powdir
þer-of & do it in the wounde.

An oþer.
Tak glase & mak powdir þer-of and mak powdir of 25
þe nettill þat was getyn on myssomer euen & do of
aþer illyk mekill in þe wounde.

An oþer.
Tak and scrape þe brynt of a caldron or of a bras
pott & mak powdir þer-of and do it in the wounde &
drynk þe jus of ache & it sal stanche. 30

An oþer.
Tak wormes in þe erthe & bryn þam & mak powdir
of þam and do in þe wounde.

[F]or nosse bledyng.
For nosse bledyng, a remedy: Tak ele skynnes and
dry þam & bryn þam & blaw þe powdir in his nose
thirlles with a pipe. 35

An oþer.
Tak ayselle or calde water & lay thi ballokes in &
it sal stanche.

An oþer.
Tak pnyger & hald in þi mouthe whils men latis þe
blode & þer sall no blode come owte of þe vayn.

---

[1] MS. *repeats* blode.

Liber de Diversis Medicinis. 49

  Tak þe powdir of a spyce þat men calles sange dragon   An oþer.
 & with a pype blaw it in his nese.
  Tak a lyn cloute & bryn it & sythen fry it in ayselle   An oþer.
 & oyl & salt & lay it hate on þe wonde & bynd it to.
5 Tak a pece of a feltyn hatte & bryn it & all hate do   An oþer.
 it on þe wounde.
  Or tak þe blode of hym þat bledis & wryte in his   [An] oþer.
 fronte + a + g + l + a + & he sal sone stanche. /
f. 300r. Tak hauyrmele & seth it wele & syndegrefe & schepe   An oþer.
10 talghe, & do it on a clathe & bynde it a-bowte þe bolnyng
 & it sal hele sone.
  Tak white malue & bryn it & tak þe askes & bare   For schankes broken owt.
 gres & stamp to-gedir & anoynte þe þer-with & tak
 of þose askes & mak lee & wasche thi thees & thi schankes
15 þer-with are þu anoynt þe & afterwarde, when þu will,
 wasche a-waye þe gres.
  Tak ganers fen & aysell & hete to-gedir and lay it   For agnayls on mans fete or womans.
 þer-to.
  Tak pouder of saundeuer or coperose & pare thi nayle   An oþer.
20 depe & caste on þe pouder & it sal ete it to þe grounde
 & hele it.
  For onkome on arme or of werke & swellyng on oþer
 stede, & þu trow it be able to bryste: Tak lynsede &
 stamp it wele & tak holyoke & stamp it & do it in a
25 pan & do fresche schepe talghe þer-to & mak it righte
 hate & bynd it on a clathe and bynde it to þe sare & it
 sal do it away or garre it gedir to a kile.
  Tak fenygreke & sethe it wele in water to it be thikk   An enplayster for rankill or bolnyng.
 & þan tak als mekill of lynsede & stamp it wele in a
30 morter and temper it with water þat it grynd wele.
 &, when it is wele gron, tak þan þi femygreke & þi
 lynsede & fresche schepe talghe & do it in a pan & welle
 it to-gedir & do it on a clathe all on brade with a sclyce
 & do it all abowte þe sare & bynd it fast & lat it be
35 all nyghte þer-to &, if it be nede, do so twa nyghtis or
 iij & it sal away or it sall gare it gedir to a kyle, and tak
 þan gronswall & alde swyn gres & stamp þam to-gedir
 & lay þer¹ to & it sall rote & do it breke the [kyle]²
 thare. Neuer do oþer medcyn þer-to to þat it be hale,

¹ MS. *adds* to *crossed out*.   ² MS. *omits* kyle.

bot do a tent þer-to of dry lyne ilk a daye twys &, if
þu see any dede flesche þer-in, tak wodsoures & do in
a doke lefe & do þam in þe aymers to sethe. Þan do
þam þer-in.

Or tak alde swyn gres & askes of bene straa or of
grene wode & do in þe wounde.

Or tak alde nete flesche þat is salted & dryed forhyngrede & bryn þat to powdir & do it in þe wounde.

Or tak coprose & stamp it alle to powdir & do it one
þe dede flesche. It is an of þe beste, bot it is strange
payne to brynge owte þis powder, bot it tholes nouther
kankire ne gutt ne festre grewe in þe wounde. /

An oþer for rankill þat swellis with-owttyn. Tak virgyn waxe & swyn fen & pyk & þe jus of spourge, *f. 300v.*
boile þam all to-gedir to þe wax be molten & þan do it
on a white lethir & lay it on þe sare.

It þer be any wounde. Tak þe jus of charwelle & þe jus of ache & þe jus of
comfery ana & tak rye mele & þe white of an egge & a
littill hony & menge all to-gedir & do it on a clathe &
lay it to.

An oþer for bolnyng whare so it be. Tak schepe triddils or swyn mukke & sethe it in white
wyne & lay it all hate appon þe bolnyng, & it helpes for
all manere of bolnynges.

An oþer. Tak wormot and malues & sethe þam in water & lay
þam hate to be bolnynge & bynde to all abowte & it
will swage.

An oþer for þe stane. Tak bene mele & syfte it & menge it with þe whitte
of an egge & enplayster it on þe sare, for it dose awaye
all werkyng & bolnyng ouer all.

A gude dragy for grauele in þe bleddir. Tak annys sede, fenkell sede, percell sede, comyn,
careaway sede, gromelle sede, papworte, philipendula,
cherestane kyrnells, pyons, clensed radik, mynt sede,
fawthistyll sede ana, & lycoryse þat suffice & mak a
dragie þer-of & vse it.

For to sla þe ryng worme. Tak turmentyne & groune glase & blend to-gedir &
anoynt þe sare þer-with & it sall sone be hale.

An oþer. Tak mosse & bryn it to powdir & frote it ofte þer-with
& it sall hele it.

For brynyng or schal-dynge. Tak dok leues all hate & lay þam on þe brynnynge &,
when þu dose þam awaye, wy[p]e [1] a-way þe filthe &

[1] MS. wyse.

Liber de Diversis Medicinis. 51

do þer-on an oþer lefe & bynd it with a clowte. Do
þis morne & euen & do no more þer-to to it be hale.

Oleum ex vitellis ouorum cutem renouat in qualibet arsura.

5 Tak sape & anoynte it with iij firste dayes & after An oþer.
þe iij day anoynte it with þe jus of rubarbe & oyle of
roses menged to it be hale.

Tak alde chese & hony & stamp to-gedir to þay be An oþer.
nesche & anoynte þe sare with & lay þer-till a cale lefe
10 & do so ay to it be hale.

Tak þe brere lefe or þe rute & waybrede & columbyne, An oþer.
of ilkan ilyke mekill jus, & menge thaym wele to-gedir
and anoynte þe sare þer-with alle.

Here bygynnes medcynes for þe pestilence

15 Here bygynnes medcynes for þe pestilence noble &
fyne & are departede in foure chapiters. The firste
chapiter telles how a man sal kepe hym in tyme þer-of.
The secounde how þis sekenes commes. The thirde
what medcyne is a-gayne it. The ferthe how he sall
20 be kepid in it. /

f. 301r. For full many for defaute of gud gouernance in dietynge
falles in þis sekenes, thare-fore þat tyme vse none excesse
nor surfete in mete & drynke nor bathes nor swete
noghte gretly þan, for all thies opyns þe pores of þe
25 body & makes venemous ayere to entre & þat febles þe
body, et super omnia alia nocet coitus & accelerat ad
hunc morbum quod maxime aperit poros & destruit
spiritus vitales, also vse littill froyte or none & ett littill
or noghte of garleke or lekes and slyke þat brynges a
30 man in-to a vnkyndely hete, also thriste noghte gretly
þat tyme þat þe pestylence regnes &, if þu thriste, drynke
mesurabili and sloken thi hete, and þe best drynke ware
calde water mengede with vynagre or tysayn, for tysayn
profettes mekill to men þat are colorik of compleccion.

35 The seconde chapeter how this sekenes comes & what Nota bene.
is þe cause of it is þis : In a man are thre pryncypalle
parties & membres, þat er to say the hert, the lyuer,
the harnes, and ilkane of thies hase his place whare he
may put owt his superflueties and are called in phiseke

Nota optime.

emun*d*atoria eo*rum*. The clensynge place of þe hert is vnder þe armes, the clensy*n*g place of þe lyu*er* is by-twyx þe thee & þe body, and þe clensyng place of þe harnes es vnder þe ere & vndir þe throtte. Þan þe seknes comes thus, when þe pores are opyn for su*m* encheson byfore said, þan entres ayere þat es venemous & als fast it is menged wi*th* a mannes blode & þan rynnes it to þe hert þat is grounde of mannes kynde for to distroy it & sla a man. Þe hert kyndely flyes it þat is agayne it and þat venemous matere puttes to his clensy*n*g place and, for it fyndis it sperred & may noghte owt, it passes to þe nexte pryncypall p*ar*tie, þat is þe lyu*er*, for to distroy it, & he puttis it to his clensynge place &, for þat also is sperred þat it may not owt þare, it passes to þe thirde pryncypalle p*ar*tie, þat is þe hernes, & he puttis it to his clensy*n*g place & for þat also is sperrede þat it may norwhare owte and þus lange it is mouande or it riste in any place, þat is to say xij hours & mare and þan at þe laste wi*th* in xxiiij hours, if it passe nott owte bi blode latynge, it festres in some place & castes a man in-to an agewe & makes a boche or a kille / in some place bi-fore said.

The thirde chapit*er* of helpe agayne þis seknes & wi*th*-in what tyme helpe may be. Who so feles any prikky*n*g of blode or flakery*n*g, þat is takeny*n*ge to-warde þat sekenes, there-fore þu scholde blede & þat schuld be sone, if it may be at þe firste, or ells with in vj houres aft*er* &, if it may be hadde thus, drynk nott nor ett or it be done & tary not ou*er* xij houres, for all þat tyme þe matir is mouande for þe cause bifore saide and bledy*n*g [be]-tymes o[f] [1] vaynes þat I sall telle aft*er* sall helpe & hafe it a-waye. If it be passede xxiiij houres, þe matir is gedirde & hardynde & will nott passe of þe vayne, if it be streken. Neu*er*-þe-lesse, if a man blede, þan it sall noghte harme, bot it is nott sekir þat it sall helpe. Ther-fore, if þe matir be gedirde vndir þe armehole, it comes of þe hert & þan blede on þe hert vayne þat is callede cordiaca & on þe same syde, or ells folous twa harmes. On is, if þu blede on þe toþ*er* syde, þe gude

---

[1] MS. in tymes or.

Liber de Diversis Medicinis. 53

blode & clene þat is noghte corrupt ne envenomed sall
be drawen owt & þe euyll duell still & þan þe body is
febillere for fawte of gude blode. Þe second harme es
mare, for þe venom sall passe to þe hert & venom it &
5 so haste a man to his endynge. Also, if þe boche be
bi-twix þe thee & þe body, it commes of the lyuer. Þen, if
þe mater appere in þe inwarde syde bi þe preue thynge,
þan blede on þe fute on þe same syde & on þe veyne
þat is bi-twix þe thomell taa & þe nexte; for, if þe
10 boche be þare & þu blede on þe arme, þe matir will
draw vp agayn to þe pryncypalle parties of þe hert or
of þe lyuer & do harme; also, if þe boche be mare
owtwarde to þe sidde & ferrer fro þe preue thynge,
blede þan on þe vayn þat is bitwix þe ankill & þe hele
15 or ells be ventoused on þe thee with a boyste bi-side þe
boche. And, if þe matere be in þe clensynge place of þe
heuede or of þe hernes, blede þan on þe heued vayne
on þe same arme & on þe same syde & on þe vayne þat
is called cephalica & it is nexte abowen þe myd veyn
20 þat is called mediana. Or ells blede on þe veyne þat
is abown þe hande bitwixe þe thombe & þe nexte
fynger. Or ells be ventousede by-twix þe schuldres
f. 302r. with boystes to þe blode be drawen owte / and þe
pryncypalle membre clensede.
25 Than the hert schulde be comforthede be calde
letuaryse to temper þe grete hetis þerof. Þen is gude to
hafe water stilled of thiese foure herbis: detony,
pympernole, tormentill and scabyous, for thies are gud
medcyns bothe in sekenes and to kepe the ther-fra.
30 And also, whils a man is in this euyll, he schulde be
dietide mesurably. For þe feuer agew of sekenes he
schuld not ett gret flesche, bot chekyns sothen with
water or littill fisches of fresche water rostede & ete
þam with vynagre. Also it is gud þat tyme to ete potage
35 of almondes & drynk tysayn or ells in þe hete a littill
smale ale & clene and, if a seke man couait mekill to
drynk wyn, gyff hym þer-for vynagre menged mekill
with water and, if he wil nedis drynk wyn, white is
mekill better þan rede. Tak detony, philadelphia
40 lactifer, pympernell, bolo armonico & oþer like; ilkan of

G

thir thynges sal be brayed by hym seluen & dronken
with wyn or ale. And a man be venomed, it will putt
owt þe venom bi þe same place þat it entrede. & who
so dredis for this sekenes, kepe þam fro thynges sett in
þe firste chapiter and, who so is þerin, do be tym as 5
teches toþer and thurgh þe grace of God he sal be helpede
of þis sekenes.

To brek felon or kile. Tak baynewort jus a sawcerfull and als mekill of a rede
cowe newe mylke & flour of whete & make it in a plaster
& lay it alle warme þer-on & it sal brek it. 10
Or tak orpyn & stamp it & fry it with whit gres.
Or tak þe ʒolke of an egge with salte or violett.
Or tak wormot & smalache ana & swyn gres, als
mekill als of þe herbes, & bray all to-gedir & do it on a
clout & lay it on þe felon or to appostym & it sal drawe 15
owt þe felon or þe appostym & all þe filthe & hele it with-
owtten any entrete, bot new it euen & morne.

An oþer, a drynk for þe felon. Tak matefelon & þe floures of marygoldes & morelle
& lely rutes, of ilkane illike mekill rois blende with
water & gyff hym to drynke thryse on a daye. 20

For to breke kyle. Tak egrimoyn, syfull of howses & pentafilon, of ilkan
illike mekill, and welle þam in ayselle & lay on þe sare.
Or take lynsede & welle it in water righte wele &
sythen stampe it and fry it in schepe talghe & lay it to
þe kile, for it wil breke it. / 25

An oþer. Tak gronswalle, wymalue, pympernole & fresche grese *f. 302v.*
or grese of a broke & stampe alle samen & lay þer-to.

An oþer. Tak herbe Robert & celidon & stampe þam wele &
wryng þan owte þe jus & temper it with hony & barke
duste & rye mele & make a playster and lay to the kyle. 30
Or tak turmentyn & barly mele & mak a plaster & lay
to þe kile.

A gude oynement for kiles, wondes, broken bones, bolnynges, to felon & to gowte. Tak bugle, synagle, avance, violett, waybrede, lely &
henbayne & morell, gume of the sour plumtre, wax,
white pik þat þir spicers calles pik album & fresche grese 35
of a swyn or of a bare & fresche suete of an hert & fresch
talghe of a moton, of ilkan elike mekill. Do all thies
thynges in a pan & welle þam wele & do rekills þer-to
& wryng it thorow a clathe in-till a clene basyn &, when
it is calde, do it in boystes. 40

Liber de Diversis Medicinis.

Tak þe fatt bakon of an alde swyn flyk & melte it in a
pan & late it stande to þe salt be fallen to þe gronde.
Tak þan þe schire abownne & do it in a pan & tak halfe
als mekil virgyn wax as þer is gres & tak rekylls & do
5 þer-to & welle to-gedir, bot firste braye þe rekills all to
powder &, when mekill hete es ouer-gane, tak als
mekil powder of mastik als of rekills & do þer-to &
euer styre it wele, bot, when it is sa kelede þat þu may
hald thi fynger þer-in, þan do als mekill þer-in powder
10 of bromstane als þer is of rekills & mastyk & stirre ay
wele till it be als thikk as hony & do it þan in boystes
&, when þou hase nede, do it on a clout or on a whitte
lethir & lay it on þe wounde & it sall drawe owte þe
werke & what gowt & what euer þe man hase, & he
15 anoynte hym þer-with twyse on þe day, with-owtten
dowte it sall do hym gude.

A gude entret to kile or wonde or bryssynge, to drawe owte werke & bryssed blode.

Tak swete milke als it comes fra þe cowe pappes al
warme & caste it in þe dowble of white wyne. Þan
tak an vnce of swete nutte kirnells with-owtten barke
20 stamped wele and smalle. Þan sethe thies thre to-gedir
to þay wax thikke / als paste. Sythen caste þat paste in
a clene canvace & wrynge owte þe moyster & þu sall
fynde in þe clathe a paste te[m]pered¹ vp with clene hony
fresche in maner of a plaster & als warme als it may be
25 suffrede. Lay it on þe malady & suffre it to lygge
vn-to þe ȝokynge & swythynge be all passede a-waye.
Þan tak it softely a-waye & with-in þe paste wele
depe þou sall fynd þe worme couchede. Þan þu
sall hele vp þe wonde with this grene oynement
30 sanatyfe.

[Fo]r to sla þe worme.

Tak a gud porcyon of violett & twise als mekill of
avance & stamp wele þe grysses & wrynge owt þe jus &
temper vp þe jus with a quanttite of powdir of pepir &
alde ale & drynk ix dayes twyse one þe day calde, ayther
35 tyme a gude sponefull, & halde in thyn ande after þe
drynke & on the ix day wayte wele þe hole & halde it
warme & beke it bi þe fire or in þe son, for in certayn
it sall come owte owþer qwike or dede. Þan tak &
mak entrete in þe moneth of May with þe same herbes &

An oþer.

---

¹ MS. tepered.

May butt*re* gedird w*ith*-in þe firste ix dayes & hele it vp w*ith* þat entrete.

For to stroye lyes.
Tak oyle of olyue & bare gres & qwik silu*er* & stafiʒagre and þe flo*ur* of lupners & grynd all to-gedir¹ w*ith* vynagre & anoynte þam þ*er*-with.

Or tak qwik silu*er* slokened & of powdir of stafiʒagre & oile & vynag*re* & menge al to-gedir & anoynte þe þ*er*-wi*th*.

Or draw a threde of cotome thurghe it & anoynte þe þ*er*-with & it sall sla þam w*ith*-in sex houres.

For to wiete wheþ*er* it is defaute of man or woman þat scho beres noghte. No*ta* be*ne* hic.
Tak twa smale new pottes of erthe & do a littill bran in aþ*er* pott & late hym stale in þe tane and hir in þe toþ*er* & þan late þam stande vp ix days or xiiij days and, if defaut be in þe man, þan sall þu fynde in his pott lyke wormes & it sall stynk &, if þu fynde þe same in þe womans pott, þan is defaut in hir and, if [þu]² fynd na takynynges in noþ*er* wat*er*, þan may men helpe þam to hafe childre w*ith* medcyns af*ter* neuennede.

If a man will þat a woman conceyue a childe sone.
Tak nept & sethe it with wyne to the third part & gyf hy*m* to drynke fastande thre dayes. /

To wiete whethir a woman be [w*ith*]⁴ a knafe childe or a mayden childe.
Tak welle³ watyr and late þe woman þat is w*ith* childe mylke a droppe þ*er*-in &, if it synke to þe grounde, þan is it taken of a knafe childe &, if it flete a-bown, þan es taken of a mayden childe. Ipocrase says þat þe woman þat is w*ith* a knafe childe, scho es ruddy & hir ryghte tethe are coruen about, and, if scho be w*ith* a mayden childe, scho es blak & hir lefte tethe are coruen about.

Here bygynnes a charme for trauellyng of childe.
In no*mine* patris & filij & sp*iritus* sancti. Amen. Arcus forciu*m* sup*er* nos sedebit, virgo Maria natabit, lux & hora sedule sedebit rubus rebu*s* rarantibu*s* natus nator natoribu*s* saxo. Sic memor esto vt sit puer vt puella. Eiu*s* exijt foras mat*er*, qu*um* ch*ristu*s natus est, nullu*m* dolorem passa est. Venit homo, fugit dolor. Ch*ristu*s adiutor, adiuro te virga per Patrem & Filium & Sp*iritu*m Sanctu*m* vt h*abe*as potestatem coniugendi. Say this charme thris & scho sal sone bere childe, if it be hir tyme.

---

¹ powder *between* to *and* gedir *crossed out.*   ² MS. *omits.*
³ MS. *adds* water *crossed out.*   ⁴ MS. *omits.*

Tak polipodie & enplaster it vnder hir fete & scho sall
sone be delyuerde, wheþer it be qwik or dede.
Tak cassia fastula, iiij florence weghte, & stamp it & *An oþer.*
drynk it & scho sall sone be delyuerde, if it be hir tyme.
5 Occeanum age, surge, rumpe & explica moras. Write *A charme.*
this charme & bynde it to hir knee righte with-in &,
alsone als scho es delyuered, tak it a-waye.
Beata Anna genuit sanctam Mariam matrem Domini *An oþer*
nostri Ihesu Christi & sancta Maria genuit Christum *charme. Nota bene optime.*
10 filium Dei nunciante Gabriele arcangelo. Per ipsam
natiuitatem credo ego quia omnis christianus a morte
& ab omni periculo [1] potest esse liberatus. Sancta
Maria, Dei genitrix, & omnes apostoli & omnes martires
& omnes sancti confessores & omnes sancte virgines inter-
15 cedant pro famula Dei. N. Amen.
Tak & write thir wordis in buttre or in chese & gare
hir ett it : Sator arepo tenet opera rotas.
Or drynk buttre & hony with hate wyn & drynk
womans mylke with oile of olyfe.
20 Or tak veruayne & stamp it & temper it vp with water
or wyn & gyffe it hir to drynke, for it is a souerayn
medcyne.
Tak & write þis in parchemyn of velym & bynd it at
f. 304r. stomake : Sancta Maria / peperit & matrix eius no[n] [2]
25 doluit. Christum genuit qui nos sanguine suo redemit.
Tak þe blades of lekes & schalde þam wele in þe fire *For to delyuer a woman of a dede childe.*
& do þam to hir nauelle & all a-bout the wambe & it
sall caste out þe dede childe &, when scho is delyuerde,
do a-waye þe leke blades or þay will do hir scathe.
30 Tak mugworte & rew & stamp þam & drynk þe jus or *An oþer.*
drynk þe jus of veruayn or þe jus of [3] ysoppe with
warme water or þe jus of rewe, wodrofe & mogwort
tempered with warme water.
Tak þe rute of pion & dry it & mak poudir per-of & *For women þat purges*
35 temper it & gif it hir to drynke with wyn & [it] [4] sall *þam ouer mekill after childynge.*
purge hir in-to gude state.
Tak a stane þat is called a gagate & lay it on hir lefte *For to gare*
pape, when scho slepis, þat scho wiet not, and, if þe *a woman say what þu askes hir.*

[1] MS. adds poss crossed out.
[2] MS. no.
[3] MS. adds ysopp crossed out.
[4] MS. omits.

stane be gude, all þat þu askes hir sall scho say þe,
what euer scho hase done.

For to mak a woman white & softe. Tak fresche swyn gres & the white of an egge halfe rosted & do þer-to a littill cokille mele & anoynte hir þer-with ofte. 5

For to gif comforthe in mete & drynk to þe seke. Tak calamynt, herbe John, rew dubill, aristotill, cresses, dytoyn, rede cale, betoyn, veruayn, ispia maior.

For þe mormaile. Tak rib, germaunder, herbe yue, smalache, hayrefe, jubarbe, celidon, of ilkan euen a pounde, of jus of littill 10 morell halfe a pound, of ȝolkes & whittes of thre egges, floure of whete, schepe talghe þat may suffice. Sethe all togedir : ambre orientale, a peny weghte, of mastik, orbane,[1] arnement, ij peny weghte.

For to wiete if a seke man or a woman sall lyfe or dy. Tak celidon and lay it vndir his hede &, if he synge, 15 he sall dy &, if he grete, he sal lyfe.
Or tak mogwort & lay vndir his heuede &, if he slepe, he sal lyfe &, if he wak, he sal dy.
Tak þe seke mans pys & late a woman mylke þer-on &, if þe[2] / mylk falle to þe grou*n*de, he sall dy &, if it *f.*304v. flete, he sal lyfe. 21

An oþer. Tak þe larde of a swyne flyk & anoynte þe mannes fete þer-with vnder-neth & after caste it to a hunde &, if þe hound ete it, he sall lyfe & fare wele &, if þe hound will nott ete it, he sal dy sou*n*e. 25

An oþer. Tak his water & menge it with a womans mylke þat hase a knaue childe &, if þat gange to-gedir, he sal lyfe

Nota bene. &, if þay depart, he sall dy. When his browes heldes down, the lefte eghe es mare þan þe reghte eghe, the nose ende waxes scharpe, his eres waxes calde, his eghne 30 waxes holle, the chyn falles, his eghne & his mouthe are opyn when he slepes bot he be wonut þer-to, his ere lappes waxes hethy, his fete waxes calde, þe wambe falles a-waye, if he pull þe strase or þe clathes, if he pyk at his nose thirlles, his forheuede waxes rede, ȝong man 35 ay wakande, alde man ay slepande, his ij membres caldes agaynes kynde & hides þam, if he rotell, thiese are þe takynynges of dede.

[1] MS. *adds a crossed out.*
[2] MS. *repeats & if before þe.*

Liber de Diversis Medicinis.

  Tak betoyn, vetoyn, matefelon, madir & stampe þam   **For to wiete**
wele & drynk þe jus with alde ale &, if he caste it owte at   **if a wondede**
þe mouthe, he sal dy.   **man sall lyfe or dy.**
  Tak baynwort & bugle & stamp þam wele & temper   **An oþer.**
5 þam with wyn or ale & gare hym drynk it &, if he caste it,
he sall dy &, if he halde it, he sal lyfe.
  Tak pympernole & stampe it & drynke þe jus menged   **An oþer.**
with water &, if it ga owte at þe wonde, he sal dy &, if he
hald it, he sal lyf.
10 Or gyff hym to drynk þe jus of letuceȝ &, if he delyuer
it at þe mouthe sone, he sal dy &, if he hald it, he sal lyfe.
  Or gyf hym to drynk þe jus of trayfoil &, if he hald it,
he sal dy.
  Or, if he fele sare or werke in his ache, he sall dy.
15 Or drynk þe jus of cerfoil & cheruell with water &, if   .
he cast it, he sal dy.
  Or gyf hym at drynke þe jus of peruynge or lange de
beefe or dytoyn menged with wyn & a littill pepir &/or[1]
hony &, if he caste it, he sal dy.
20 Or gyf hym at drynke hond tonge &, if he noghte caste
it, he sal hele. And sythen gyffe hym ilk a day to drynke
f. 305r. þise thre grisses tempered to-gedir / with a littill ale, þat is
to say, pympernoll, bugle & synegle, &, when he hase
dronken þe grisses, þay sall com out at þe wonde & make
25 hym clene with-in & hele þam with-owtten.
  Tak a drame of þe sede of ache & stamp it wele &   **For þe feuer**
temper it with iij sponfull of calde water & gyfe þe seke   **cotidiane.**
man at drynk righte as þu wates þat it takes hym.
  Tak horshoue þat is called vngula caballi þat grewes in
30 þe water &, when þu gedirs it, say þi Pater noster. Stamp
it & drynk þe jus by-fore þe axes take the, when þu will,
for it is wele prouede.
  Tak rubarbe & schafe it in a copefull of calde water &   **For þe feuer**
late it stande al a nyghte þer-in & on þe morne gyffe it   **tercyane þat**
35 hym at drynke or þe passion tak hym. Bot luke þat he   **takes man & women**
schake iij dayes or iiij or he tak it.   **ilk oþer day.**
  Tak þe jus of solsekill & preste crown & madir, of aper   **An oþer.**
illik mekill, & drynk it fastand. It helpes þe feuer
tercyane.

---

[1] MS. *has & above* or.

An oþer.	Tak iij planttes of waybrede als hale als þu may fynde þam, þat all þe leues be with-owtten wemme & þe rotes. Þan wasche þam wele & schak þe water of & stampe þam wele & menge þam with iij sponefull of wyn & iij sponfull of water & clence it thurgh a clathe & gyffe hym to drynk or þe euyll tak hym. & late hym blede of þe veyne of þe forhede &, if his lyuer is oghte hate, mak hym a playster of jubarbe & lay it on his righte syde.
Syrop for þe feuer tercyane & duble tercyane þat men calles omni rapacete.	Tak a party spik & a party jubarbe & schafe þam in ayselle & seth it to þe twa parties be sothen in. Þan clence it thurgh a clathe & do þan suger þer-to & sethe it to it be thik as hony. Gyf hym a sponfull or ij þer-of with hate water at morn.
Syrop þat es [ca]lled þe Rose.	Tak an vnce or twa of roses & sethe þam in water to þe ij partis be sothen in. Þan clence it thurgh clathe & do suger þer-to & sethe it to it be thikk as hony & vse as þu dose þe toþer.
An oþer.	Tak rew & pympernoll, jubarb, coliandre sede, xxv cornes of pepir. Stamp þam & drynk þam with hate water [1] ane houre bi-for þe axes. /
þe feuer þat is called þe quartane.	Þe feuer þat is callede þe quartane takes a man or a woman ilk thirde day. If þu will vse medcyn þer-fore, tak & mak a lafe of clene barly & gyff hym to ette þer-of all hate with hony, als mekill als he may ete, & gyf hym to drynk gude wyn, ynowghe plente, or it tak hym. & þan tak iiij plantis of waybrede with all þe leues & þe rutes &, when þay are wele waschen & stampede, þan temper vp þe jus with iiij sponefull of wyn & iiij of water & gyf þe seke man at drynke or þe euyll tak hym, & do hym at lygge & slepe, & couer hym wele.
An oþer.	Tak on myssomer euen efter þe sonn sett or one þe morn or þe sonn ryse & gedir pulioll royalle with þe rutes, as mekill als þe likes, & dry it and kepe it to ȝole and lay þat pulioll on ȝole nyghte appon þe awtre & late it lygge to iij messes be songen ouer it & þu sall see it floresche alle newe & new flores brynge forthe. Þan tak it a-waye & kepe it &, when þu will, gif it hym þat hase þe feuer quartane on þis wise: Stampe þe flour & temper it with warm wyn & gyf it hym to drynk & þer-whills þu & he

[1] MS. *adds* before.

Liber de Diversis Medicinis. 61

bothe says ȝour Pater noster with Credo in Deum & Aue
Maria.
    Tak þe gesarn of a hare & stampe it & temper it with   An oþer.
water & gyf it to þe seke man or woman at drynke & it
5 dose a-waye þe feuer quartane.
    Tak wormot & aueron & þe mydwarde barke of þe   An oþer.
scho asche & þe alme & sethe in gud wyn & gyf þe seke
to drynke be-fore mete and aftir & do suger þer-to for
swetenes. With-owtten doute it sal hele hym.
10 Who so hase þe feuer agewe þat men calles lente euyll,   For þe feuer lente.
[i]f [1] þe seke man heued werke þat he may not slepe :
Tak euerfern þat waxes on þe ake with þe rute & sethe it
wele & tak mynt, of aper ilike mekill, & stamp þam wele
& make a playster & lay on þe forhede & on þe thon-
15 wanges. Bot anoynte hym firste with popilion, if he hafe
anger in his lyuer.
    Tak & mak hym a plaster on his righte side of barly   An oþer.
mele & of jubarb & of morell & of ayselle, bot anoynte þe
firste with popilion & if he be encostyfe mak hym a
20 syrop on þis wyse : Tak ane vnce of flours of violet and   A Sirop.
sethe þam in a galon of water to þe ij partise be sothen
in & clence it þan thorow a clathe. Do þan to þat jus
a pounde of suger & sethe it to it be thikke as hony &
gyf hym to drynk vmwhile ij sponefull of þe syrop in a
25 littill copfull of calde water. & tak braunches of sawge &
þe smedes of barly and malues & henbayn & sethe þam
all to-gedir in a caldron with water & in þat water bathe
hym & wasche his fete & his schankes abouen his knees
& schafe his fete vndir-nethe & it sall do hym gude. &,
30 if he fall in þe fransie, late schafe his hede & tak a whelpe
or a ȝonge coke & clefe it in myddis bi þe bake & alle
hate with all þe guttes do it on his hede. Bot firste
anoynte his hede with popilion and, if he falle in þe
litage, schafe his heuede / & tak mustard sede & stamp it &
35 do ayselle þer-to & couer his hede þer-with & his foreheued
and bynd it þer-to with a clathe & late it be sa all a
nyghte & tak þe jus of oyneons & caste his nose thirlles full
with a pipe of a gose fethir or fill a pipe full of þe jus &
blawe it in his nose & do a man or a woman to kis ofte on

[1] MS. of.

his heuede & lay hym in þe lighte agayn þe son & lat
ryng & blawe & mak mekill dyn about hym & lat prik
hym with prikkes alwaye for slepynge.

[A m]edcyn for alle feuers. Tak vetoyn, ambrose, herbe John, solsikill, tansay, mogwort, wormot, rew and sauyn and of alle thies grisses ana. 5
Sethe thise grysses in wyn & water till þe thirde part
water. Gif þe sek at drynk þer-of a copfull or þe euyll
tak hym & an oþer after þat it hase taken hym. And,
if þu wene þat þe feuer sall tak þe man on þe morne,
tak on þe euen by-fore a gude fatt ele & do it all qwik in 10
a littill possenet full of gud wyn & couer it wele with
a tele stane þat it ga not out & lat it be sa all nyghte, &
on þe morne, or þe euyll tak hym, vn-do þe ele & mak it
clene & sethe it wele with þe skynne & giff þe seke to ette
of þis ele or alle, if he may, & þe wyn þat it is sothen in, 15
gare hym drynk it efter & with Goddes grace he sall be
delyuerd of his euyll.

An oþer. Tak playntayne, pee delion & rede nettill, & stamp
þam & drynke þe jus.

Or tak rew & wormot, of aþer ilike mekill, & stamp þam 20
& temper þam with hate water or wyn & gyff hym to
drynk fastand.

Or tak þe rute of walwort & wesche it & stamp it &
temper it with wyn or with stale ale and gyf hym to
drynke, or þe euyll tak hym, & couer hym wele in his 25
bedde & owthir sall þe euyll leue hym or he sall spewe.

A gude oyntment for alle feuers [1] Tak a handefull of lynsede & sethe it wele in water &
clence it & tak als mekill of oyle of roses & meng it togedir & anoynte þe mannes body þer-with & his fete &
his handis. 30

A gude oximell for all feuers [2] Tak þe rute of fynkell & þe rute of percell, þe rute of
ache, þe rute of loufache & þe rute of radik ana, & wesche
þam wele & schafe þam & schere þam in littill leches &
do þam in ayselle all a nyghte & temper þam on þe morne
& sethe þam in þe same aysell to þe thirde part be sothen 35
in. Clence it þan thorow a clathe. Tak þan twa
partise of þat ayselle & þe thirde part of hony & sethe
to-gedir to it be als thik als hony &, if þe man be encos-

---

[1] MS. *repeats* for alle feuers.
[2] MS. *repeats* for all feuers.

Liber de Diversis Medicinis.

tyfe, þan tak euerferne þat growes on þe ake, ij vnce or
iij, & sethe þer-with at þe begynnynge of þis oximell &
gyff þe seke man twa sponefull or iij with hate water
at morn & at euen, if nede be. Tak þe jus of rose &   [A]n en-
5 of walwort & whete branne & menge to-gedir in maner   plaster for
of a plaster & lay it on a lyn clathe & lig it to his stomak   þe feuer¹
& bynd it þer-to & it sall helpe hym sone. /

f. 306v.   Tak pulioll reall & sethe it in water & gyff hym it at   For to do
drynke þer-of, when þe hete bygynnes, & it sall sone do   awaye bryn-
10 it awaye.   nyng of þe feuer.²

Tak iij obles & write firste in ane of theym+.1.+elie   Nota. A
+sabaoth+and on þe toþer oble+adonay+alpha+ &   charme for
o+Messias+ & on þe thirde oble+pastor+agnus+   þe feuers.
fons+and gif thir thre obles to hym þat hase þe feuers   Nota bene.
15 thurgh iij dayes with haly water fastande.

Or tak iij obles & write firste in ane+Pater est Alpha+
& O+Filius+vita+Spiritus sanctus remedium+ & tak &
write in perchemyn+Agios+Otheos+Atanatos+yskiros
+ymas+eleson+Ego sum Alpha+ & O+Christus vincit
20 +Christus regnat+Christus imperat+and, when he es
hale, caste þe charme in the fire.

Tak oile of violett & woman mylk & menge to-gedir &   For hym þat
anoynt his fronte & his eres & his nese thirlles & wesche   hase þe
his fete in warme water þat þe whitte chessebolle &   feuers &
25 letouse hase bene sothen in.   may no[t]³ slepe⁴

Tak lekes & sethe þam all hale & sythen stamp þam   For þe
wele and smalle & hauyrmele grotes & schepe talghe &   gowte.
do all samen in a pott & sethe þam wele & sythen lay þam
on a cloute & lay it on þe sare.

30   Tak an owle & do of þe fethyrs & opyn it & drawe it   A gude
clene, as þu walde ette it, & salt it wele. Þan do it in a   oynement
new pott & couer it wele with a tele stane & do it in an   for all
hate owen to it be wele rostede, bot noghte al brynt.   gowttes.
Þan tak & stamp it wele with bare grese & anoynte þe
35 goute by þe fire & do so ofte & it sal es[e].

Tak brok grese & katt grese & fox grese, horse grese,   An oþer.
bare grese ana, & þe leues of cucumerbers, & stamp þam

---

¹ MS. *repeats* þe feuer.
² MS. *adds* brynnynge of þe feuer.
³ MS. no.
⁴ MS. *adds* & may not slepe.

        & tak als mekill jus þer-of als will wey agayn alle þe gresses, & welle it all to-gedir in a pan & drawe it thorow a clathe & do it in boystis and anoynte thare nede is.

An oþer. Tak brok grese & of þe raton, of þe katt, of þe fox, of þe horse, of þe bare, & tak fethirfewe & ayselle & a lyttill lynsed & stampe all to-gedir with þe grese & þan warm it hate in a scharthe and anoynte þe gowte bi þe fire and do so ofte & it will ese mekill.

Also an oþer. Tak þe rede snyles & do þam in a pott & strewe salte on þam, for þay will sone melte, & anoynte þe goute þer-with by þe fire with a fethir & it sall helpe the.

An oþer. Tak a moldwarppe & sethe it wele in wax & wryng it thorowe a clathe & do it in boystes, for euer þe langer þat it is halden, the better it is to many oþer euylls þan þe gout.

An oþer. Tak þe leues of henbayne one missomer euen & stampe þam a littill & fill a mekill pott bretfull & thirlle þe pott in þe bothome & couer it a-bown with a tele stane & make a hole depe in þe erthe / vndir þe erthe & do þat pott þer-in & sett a littill lede vndir þe pott bothome to kepe in þe oyle þat comes of þe henbayne thurgh þe pott. Fill þan þe hole all abowte þe pott with erthe & lay agayn þe erthe stanes & dyghte it at þu may mak þi fire ouer it all þe tweluemonthe, and, at þe tweluemonethe ende, þan tak vp at þu fyndys in þe lede & do it derely vp in a vesselle of glas. Þis oile es wonderly gud to þe goute & to þe rankle & to many oþer euylles, if it be ofte sythes anoynte þer-with be þe fire. Yf þu hafe noghte þis oyle, tak þat oile þat is made of þe sede of henbayne als men dose of oþer sedis & anoynte þe goute þer-with.

An oþer. Nota. Tak alde bare grese & melt it in a wele scoured pan & helle it in-till a bacyn & lat it stande to þe salt be fallen to þe grounde. Eft-sones mak clene þe pan & tak þe schire of þe bacyn & do in þe pan, bot not þe grondes, & do þer-to virgyn wax als it were þe fourt part. Þan tak rekills & mak it in poudir & teme þam thurgh a scarce & do it to þe same & to þe wax & welle þam all to-gedir a while. Þan tak þe pan fra þe fire &, alsone als þe mekill hete es [1] ouer gane, tak poudir of

---

[1] MS. *repeats* hete es.

Liber de Diversis Medicinis.

mastik, als mekill als of þe rekills, & do þer-to & ay be
stirrand with þi sclyce. &, when it is so calde þat þu may
halde þi fynger þer-in, þan tak als mekill bromstane in
powdir als þu had of rekills & mastike & do þer-to &
5 stirre ay wele with þi slyce to þu see þat it be thikke als
hony & þan gedir it vp & do it in clene boistes & anoynte
þe goute þer-with bi þe fire, & withowtten dowt it sall
mende þe mekill or all, what kynde of gout so euer
it be.

10 Tak gude bromstane & mak gud poudir þer-of & grynd   [A]n oþer.
it with oile of egges on a stane als it were vermyon. Þis
oynement is gude for alle goutis &, if a leprous man be
anoynt þer-with, it will do hym mekill gude & mekill
ese.

15 Tak ambrose & wild nept & sethe þam & stamp þam   Emplaster [for þe] gout.[1]
wele with alde grese & anoynte þe gout bi þe fire. It
will hele it wondirfully wele, & enplaster it to after þe
anoyntement.

Tak þe ȝolkis of v egges & a sponfull of vynagre & iij   [An] oþer for þe rede gout in handis & fete.
20 sponefull of barly mele & iij sponefull of henbayne sedis
& mak poudir þer-of all in samen & lay it on þe gout.

Tak þe rute of radik & whette bran & stamp all samen   An oþer. Nota bene.
& temper it with vryne & lay it on þe gout.

Tak ald chese & schafe it & tak þe floure of groundyn   An oþer.
25 leues and hony & aysell & þe whittes of egges & menge al
samen & mak a playster & lay þer-to. /

f. 307 v.   Tak auance, horshelme, whilde sauge, betoyn, sauyn,   An oþer.
centory, fenkell, herbe John, burrege rute & osmonde, of
ilkan euen porcyon. Sethe þam with water & licoresse
30 & drynk it at euen hate & at morne calde. It is gude
for þe gout in the lendis.

Tak vervayne, jubarbe, violett, whete floure & sethe   An oþer.
to þe thikknesse of a plaster & syne do þer-to þe jus of
ache & lay it þer-to.

35 Tak lynsede & sethe it in water till it be thikke sothen.   Experiment for alle gouttynes[2] rynnand and flyande.
Þan draw it & stamp it & grynd it in a clene mortere
& caste þer-to fresche schepe talghe & menge it wele
with þe jus of henbayne & herbe benett & caste þan all

---

[1] MS. repeats for þe gout.
[2] MS. adds & all gouttynes.

Liber de Diversis Medicinis.

grounden to-gedir in a pott &, when þe lynsede is sothen
in, chaufe þam wele to-gedir & lay þam on þe gout.

For þe gout artetik to chase it owt of what place þat it is in.

Tak þe grese of a bare and of a brok & of a whitt catt
with þe jus of water cresses, ij vnces, & sethe in a pott to
þay be thikk &, when þu will anoynte þe body goutes, 5
sett hym bi-twix ij fires elike & anoynt his body ouer
bot þat þu will þe gout passe owt & þat be laste anoynt.

For þe paralisi.

Þis oynement is gud for paralisi & for all oþer calde
passiouns. Begyn we firste at þe hate gummes and
sythen at þe hate spyces and sythen at þe hate rotes and 10
sythen at þe hate grisses.

Off gummes þat are hate.

Mirre, storax, olibane, mastike, opeponak, ammoniak,
bedellium, seraphin, salbanum, terrebintym, pixgreke,
pixliquidum, euphorbe, castorium, of all thies xiiij
gummes tak of ilkane ane vnce. 15

Spices þat are hate.

Clowes de golofre, nuutmugg, canell, galynga, setuale,
gynger, longe pepir, white pepir, aloes epotik, of ilkane of
thir spices tak halfe an vnce.

Off hate rotes.

Rotes of fenkalle, rotes of percell, rutes of brusk, rotes
of spourge, rutes of pyon, rutes of pappwort, rutes of 20
alysander, rotes of polipodi, rutes of gladyn, rotes of
yrislirik, rotis of louache, rutes of philipendula, of ilkan
of thies rutis tak halfe a handfull.

Herbes þat are hate.

Centory, burnett, germandre, white brissoke & rede
diptonge, gladyn, wilde sawge, cowesleppes, ȝarow, 25
alisandre, prymrolle, centurion, lauandre, cresses, rede
cale, pelleter, rewe, sawge, iarue, mynt saraȝine, puliole
montane, origane, þat is puliol realle, calamynt, calamyn,
camamil, ysope, aueroyn, auance, rede nettill, louache,
flour of gayle, pitory, herb John, þe leues of þe lorelle, 30
wormot, gronswale, smalache, sauine, ypocone, recoyn, of
ilkan of thir herbis tak a handfull. /

[Of]f sedis [þat a]re hate.

Stafiȝagre, caraway sedis, of marigolde sedis, of [f. 308r.]
mustarde sedis, white pepir sedes, of fenicrek, of lynsede,
of cresses sede, of pepill sede, of coconode, of ilkane of this 35
sedis tak halfe an vnce, of fresche schepe talghe a pounde,
of white fresche grese als mekill as may suffice, of mede
wax iiij vnces, of[1] all thies thynges mak ane oynement
for þe euyll bi-fore neuennede.

[1] MS. *adds* ilkan *crossed out.*

Saue

[He]re may þu lere for to make Saue, the wilk es a
gude drynke & ane oynment for þe woundis or þe hurtes
with-in & with-owtten of þe body of man or woman &
5 it es called Saue. And þe firste by-houes þe to gedir
theis herbis þat are here wretyn : burnette, betoyne,
pympernolle, dauk, morsus diaboli, tormentill, crois,
bugill, pigill, sinagle, herbe Robert, herb John, herb
Wauter, herb yue, cosoud maior, cosoud milnen, consoud
10 petit, crope de cambre, fenell with þe sede rouge, cholet,
waranc, mader, spourge, fawethistill, samson, gronswalle,
melice, egrymoyn, cheuerfoille, id est wodrofe, violet,
playntayne, id est waybred, launcelle, id est ryb, peluette,
id est moushere, vesche, floures de genest, id est brome,
15 herb saunce crop, ache petit, auance, crop de rouge
runcebrere, lange de cheyn, cynkfoil, milfoil, rouge vrtice,
id est nettill rede, flosere, id est strabery wyes, tansay,
id est philoga, osmonde. Of all thies herbes tak euen
porcion out-tane of madir and of auance, for of þe mader
20 tak als mekill weghte as of twa oþer bi-fore neuenned.
& stamp þam wele &, when þay are wele stamped, late
þam riste in a vessell of tre þe space of ten dayes and,
after þe x daye es passed, do to thies herbis [1] þe doubill
weghte of fresche buttre of Maye & þan sethe þam ouer
25 þe fire & late þam swa sethe to-gedir to þe buttre be halfe
wastede. Þan all warme coille þe confeccion swa
boillede thurgh a canvace & afterwarde late it kele &
sithen clence it wele with calde water to it be clere
clensede & þan afterwarde tak a galon of gude / whitte
30 wyn & a porcyon of gude vynagre & do þam ouer fire in
a clene vesselle & do þer-in þe coylett wele weschyn &
sethe þam to-gedir to þe wyn & þe vynagre be nere
wastede & þan tak þam down of þe fire & suffre þam to
kele & sythen gedir vp þat þat fletis a-bown & put it in
35 boystes for to safe & gyfe þer-of to wonded men þat hase
wondis depe & stangyng in wondis & bolnynge in wondis
& with þis sal þu safely hele þam. & gyff þam at drynk
þer-of arely at þe morne & late at euen of þe grettnes of
a mousfiche.

[1] MS. adds do to crossed out.

Liber de Diversis Medicinis.

Gratia Dei. Medcyn þat is called Gratia Dei, þat is made on þis manere : Tak litarge iiij vnces, ceruse iij vnces, roste of a belle of bras ij vnces, of vertgres ij vnces, of sarcocol iiij vnces, of mastik, galbanum, ammoniak, of ilkane iiij vnces, with encence iij vnces, of bedellium halfe ane 5 vnce, of pik greke, pik nauill, of þam ij vnces. All this bi-fore be graythede & boylled in a ponde of oyle de olyue till þay wax blake & sythen keped wele. This emplaster clenses wondis and sowdis þam to-gedir & dose owte dede flesche & newe flesche gars grewe. It is a gud 10 heler for brynnand werkes, wondis & kiles, whare so bee.

An oþer Gratia Dei þat is ane enplaster and thus sall it be made. Tak wax, rosen, turbentyn, of ilkan a pounde, of mastik iij vnces, betoyn, of pympernolle, of veruayn, of ilkan a quartron. Þan stampe thies herbis wele & sethe 15 þam wele in ij galouns of white wynne or rede vn-to þe thirde party. Afterwarde coyle þam thorow & saue wele þe [1] coylett fra filthe. Þan take þi rosen & thi wax & resolue wele in a clene dowble vessell ouer þe fire & coyl þam thorow a clathe & caste þan þat coylett of gummes 20 to þe coylett of wyne & of gresses & sethe þam to-gedir vn-to þe wastyng of þe wyne. Aftirwarde tak þat ilk confeccion saa sothen & do it in a doubill vessell ouer þe fire & do þe mastik pouder þer-in to þe mastik be resoluede & sythen afterwarde þi turbentyn & moue it sotely til it 25 be resolued &, as swithe so it be resoluede, tak þe confeccion of þe fire smertly with-owtten duellynge and poure it thurgh a clathe & suffre it to refraide & þan gedir vpe with clene handis, anoynte with oyle de olyue & safe / þi enplaster wele, for it is gude till alde wondis & *f.* 309r. to newe & to synows coruen and bristen and till junttours, 31 to hewen flesche, to dede flesche in wondis & till apostymms, of alkyn maner of kankir, festre, venyme & for helle fire, for þe emeraudes & for brokes. Þis enplaster, it wirkes, it heles, it drawes and helis mare with-in woke 35 þan all oþer enplasters dose with-in a monethe.

[F]or to remoile Gratia Dei. Tak camamyle, wormot, mellilotum.

[F]or to ripe an enpostyme. Tak brance vrcyne, wilde malue.

[F]or to opyne þam. Tak ysop, germander, smalach, percell.

[1] MS. *adds* colett *crossed out.*

Liber de Diversis Medicinis. 69

Tak wilde sauge, fymter, woraunce.   [F]or to [1] clence þam.
Tak mynt, borage, cicory, flour of oxtonge, þat is longe de beefe.

[H]ere bygynnes þe maner to mak salues & entretis &
5 drynkes & cyroyns to wondis & to all oþer hurtes of mans body and þe firste for wounde in þe heuede : Tak betoyne & stampe it with alde gres & fry þam to-gedir & sythen draw it thurgh a clathe & do it appon lyn & lay it on þe wonde & ilk a third daye lay þe white of an egge
10 þer-on & he sall waresche sone.

Tak wormot & stayncroppe ana, & bray þam & boyl   [For bone broken in þe heuede.]
þam in vynagre & do þer-to whete branne & lay to þe sare.

Tak pugill, bugill, herb Robert, auance, red cale, tansay,   [For] wondis & bolnynge in þe hede.
15 hemp croppes ana, & tak of madir als mekill as of all þe oþer herbis, & do þer-to ambros, burnet & þe crispe malue &, if þer be bane broken & þu dare noghte serche it ȝit, gyf hym þis to drynke : Tak the wort tansay, hemp croppes, horse mynt, rede nettill, brere croppes & als
20 mekill mader as of all þe oþer herbes. Stamp þam samen & sethe þam in white wyne & gyf it hym at drynk &, if it come owte at þe wounde & he caste nott, þan it is a takyn þat he sal lyfe. Þan gare serche þe wonde & schaue þe broken banes qwayntely þat þu tame nott þe
25 tay of þe harnnes &, if it blede faste, wipe softely with softe lyne & syne tak softe lyne & wympill to-gedir & lay it ouer þe wonde & tak whete flour wele boltede & strewe on þe clowte þat lygges on þe wonde. & after þat late a woman þat fedis a knafe childe, if it be a man þat is
30 woundide, mylke hir pappes softely on þe mele þat is strewed on þe cloute þer-on & strewe it with flour, as þu dide þe toþer, & of þe mylk till it be euen with þe flesche,
f. 309v. & hille þe heuede & late it / be stille til on þe morn. Þan vnhill þe hede softely &, if þu fynde þer-aboun as it were
35 a burbill þat standes on þe water when it raynnes, þan is it a sygne of dede, &, if þu see bi-fore his tay als it ware a spynnande webbe or rede, þat is taken þat þe ryme of þe hernes es broken & it is a sygne of hasty dede. &, if þer be many of thir sygnes, gyf hym ilk day twis at

[1] MS. *adds* che *crossed out.*

H

drynk, anes at morne, anoþer tym at euen. Þis drynk gars
broken banes come owte & clenses þe ryme of þe hernes
of blode & heles þe wonde, and, if it be swa broken þat
men by-houes do þer-in masere, late þan wele rounge [1]
þe broken of þe heuede als bi-fore it is said & sett þer-in 5
a pese of maser & anoynt it with þis oynement after
wretyn.

Oynement. Tak pulioll montane, baynwort, ambrose, rib, bubill,
seterib, celidoun, cheuerfoill, rede nettill, lekes, ache,
waybrede, morell, tansay, & betoyn, of ilkane ilike 10
mekill, & stamp þam wele samen with swyne gres fresche
& fre rekills, a lytill hony, vyrgyn wax, &, when all thir
thynges ere wele stampede samen, do þam in a clene
bacyne or in a pan & do þer-to white wyn & þan lat it
stande all a daye & a nyghte & on þe morne do it vn-to 15
þe fire & sethe it wele & gyf it gude walmes. Syne tak
it doune and drawe it thorowe a clathe & do it vp &,
þer-whils it is oghte sare, anoynt it þer-with & it sall hele
full wele.

An oþer for heued broken & þe bane be hale.[2] Tak a handfull of malues and a handfull of wormot & a 20
handfull of mugwort, & stamp þam samen full small, &
tak iiij vnces of þe flour of whete & iij vnces of hony &
rede wyn & tak iij vnces of galte gres & do þe hony in a
panne & scome it & do þer-in þe gres & mak it to welle
hate & syne mak it in a playster & lay it alle warme on 25
þe heuede.

An oþer salue to wonde on þe body.[3] Tak þe heuedis of lekes with alle þe fases & stampe þam
& do þe woyse in þe wonde. & tak lyne & mak a tent &
wete it in þe woyse & putt it þer-in. & tak þe substance
of þe lekes at þe jus was wrongen thurgh & lay it appon 30
& bynde it þer-to. Do þis plaster iij dayes to, bot
remowe it noghte bot ilk a daye anes, &, after þe iij day,
tak whete mele & gude wyn & do whitte sayme þer-to
& welle wele to-gedir. Þan tak a lyn clathe & do ij
falde or thre or a pece of white lethir & do þin enplaster 35
þer-on & lay it ouer þe wonde & do so ilk a daye and
gif hym at drynke / thir[4] iij gresses with a littill ale: pigill, f. 310r.

---

[1] MS. *adds* it *crossed out*.
[2] MS. *repeats* broken & þe bane be hale.
[3] MS. *adds* to woundis on þe body.
[4] MS. *repeats* and gif hym at drynke *before* thir.

Liber de Diversis Medicinis. 71

bugill & sanigle. &, when he hase dronken þam, þay
will come owt at þe wonde & clence it with-in & hele it
wele with-owtten.

Tak larde & mak sayme þer-of and tak hony & wyne & *An oþer.*
5 rye mele & sethe þam to-gedir & do þam on a clathe &
lay it þer-to & it sal clence it & hele it.

Or tak centory & mak poudir þer-of & strewe it on þe
wonde & it sal hele it.

Or take þe jus of ache & þe whitte of an egge & þe
10 flour of whete & pouder of rekills ana, & menge þam
to-gedir so þat it be thik & do it one þe wonde & remewe
it ilk daye anes.

Tak betoyn a handfull, comfory a handfull, madir, [A] gude
baynwort a handfull, of hemp sede ij vnces. Stamp all drynk [for
15 to-gedir wele & small. Tak þan a quartron of white wyn wondes.[1]
& a quartron of water & do all in a pott ouer þe fire &
sethe it into þe halfe & coyle it thurgh a clathe & drynk ilk
a day a mese at þe morne & at þe euen & lay a brere lefe
to þe wonde.

20 Tak comfery, marygolde, matfelon, millfoile, auance, [2] *An oþer.*
þe white rute of þe walwort, baynworte, cerfoil, herb
Robert, ambrose, maroȝl, pelwet, rede dok, polipodi &
celidon ana, & of mader halfe þe weghte of all þir oþer
herbis. Sethe þam in ale or in wyn & drynke þam morne
25 & euen. Do as it es said by-fore.

Tak þe rede nettill, rede cale, pympernoll, cerfoill, *An oþer.*
mynt, porret, tansay, aueroyn, bugill, sanigle, waraunce.
Now here bene þe vertus of thies herbes: Þe nettill &
þe rede cale suffers noghte þe wonde hele. Of thies
30 herbes tak a pounde. Mynt & porret, þat swages werke
in wondes. Þer-of tak halfe a pounde. Bugill & sanegle
haldes þe wondes fra perell. Þer-of tak a pound.
Pympernolle, cerfoill & waraunce ledis þe drynke in-to
þe wounde. Of þam tak halfe als mekill als of all
35 þe toþer herbes. Þan stampe þam in a mortere & mak
smalle balles of thaym, of þe mekilnes of a doufe [3] egge,
& do þam vp to drye fra þe wynde & þe sonne.

---

[1] MS. *repeats* for wondes.
[2] MS. *adds* cerpodye *crossed out.*
[3] MS. *adds* egge *crossed out.*

Liber de Diversis Medicinis.

An oþer. Tak auance, tansay, egrymoyn, hemp croppes, ony ȝone sede, rede cale croppes, ambros, matfelon & als mekill mader as of thre of theis oþer herbes, & stamp þam to-gedir & drynke þam.

An oþer. Tak auance, comfery, ȝarow, croppes of hempe, tansay, rede cale, aueroyn, & mader als mekill as halfe thies oþer herbes, / and syne stamp þam & mak þam in balles & do þam vp to drye. *f.310v.*

An oþer gud drynk for all wondes. Tak waybrede, rib, violett, auances, cropp of þe rede brere, matfelon, herb Robert, tansay, betoyn, milfoille, comfery, baynewort, of ilkane ilike mekill, & of þe rote of mader agayn all thies oþer herbes. Stampe þam all & mak pelottes of þam & dry þam in the sonne or in þe wynde & drynk þam in wynnter.

A gud syroyn when herbis failes for all wondis. Tak a pound of virgyn wax, a pounde of olibanum, a pounde of encruce of þe ere, a pound of ditayne, a pound of playntayn, a pound of jubarbe, a pound of littill consoude, a pound of milfoille & a pound of watercresses. Tak thies gresses & stampe þam ilkan by hy[m] ane & temper þam with wyn & late þam rest a nyghte & on þe morn do þam in a pott ouer þe fire & late þam welle wele & syne tak it doun & drawe it thorow a clene clathe.

An oþer. Tak herb John, herb Robert, bugill, pigill, milfoille, consoude, playntayne, auance, of all thies herbis tak þe jus, & wax & pik & a littill gres, & mak syroyn. To all kyles & wondis it is gude.

An oþer sirope for alle wondis. Tak þe firste iij dayes & lay þer-to noghte bot lyne & þe white of an egge & chaunge it morne & euen. & þan tak ix stalkes of gronswale with þe rotes & v of spourge with þe rutes & als many croppes of þe rede brere, & stampe all wele to-gedir with a sawcerfull of hony & þan wrynge owte all þe jus thurgh a clene clathe & do it in a clene pane ouer þe fire & boile it a whalme. & þan tak it doun & stop þer-in iij dices of whete brede & gif hym thase thre at euen, when he gase to his bedde. & do so with ilk a sirope & brede viij dayes or ix. And when þu sees þat þe wounde es wele rotyn & whelis [1] whitoure faire, tak þan iij stalkes of gronswalle & v of

---

[1] MS. *adds* & *above the line.*

bugill & sanigle. &, when he hase dronken þam, þay will come owt at þe wonde & clence it with-in & hele it wele with-owtten.

Tak larde & mak sayme þer-of and tak hony & wyne & *An oþer.*
5 rye mele & sethe þam to-gedir & do þam on a clathe & lay it þer-to & it sal clence it & hele it.

Or tak centory & mak poudir þer-of & strewe it on þe wonde & it sal hele it.

Or take þe jus of ache & þe whitte of an egge & þe
10 flour of whete & pouder of rekills ana, & menge þam to-gedir so þat it be thik & do it one þe wonde & remewe it ilk daye anes.

Tak betoyn a handfull, comfory a handfull, madir, [A] gude drynk [for baynwort a handfull, of hemp sede ij vnces. Stamp all wondes.[1]
15 to-gedir wele & small. Tak þan a quartron of white wyn & a quartron of water & do all in a pott ouer þe fire & sethe it into þe halfe & coyle it thurgh a clathe & drynk ilk a day a mese at þe morne & at þe euen & lay a brere lefe to þe wonde.

20   Tak comfery, marygolde, matfelon, millfoile, auance,[2] *An oþer.* þe white rute of þe walwort, baynworte, cerfoil, herb Robert, ambrose, maroʒl, pelwet, rede dok, polipodi & celidon ana, & of mader halfe þe weghte of all þir oþer herbis. Sethe þam in ale or in wyn & drynke þam morne
25 & euen. Do as it es said by-fore.

Tak þe rede nettill, rede cale, pympernoll, cerfoill, *An oþer.* mynt, porret, tansay, aueroyn, bugill, sanigle, waraunce. Now here bene þe vertus of thies herbes: Þe nettill & þe rede cale suffers noghte þe wonde hele. Of thies
30 herbes tak a pounde. Mynt & porret, þat swages werke in wondes. Þer-of tak halfe a pounde. Bugill & sanegle haldes þe wondes fra perell. Þer-of tak a pound. Pympernolle, cerfoill & waraunce ledis þe drynke in-to þe wounde. Of þam tak halfe als mekill als of all
35 þe toþer herbes. Þan stampe þam in a mortere & mak smalle balles of thaym, of þe mekilnes of a doufe [3] egge, & do þam vp to drye fra þe wynde & þe sonne.

[1] MS. *repeats* for wondes.
[2] MS. *adds* cerpodye *crossed out.*
[3] MS. *adds* egge *crossed out.*

Liber de Diversis Medicinis.

An oþer. Tak auance, tansay, egrymoyn, hemp croppes, ony3one sede, rede cale croppes, ambros, matfelon & als mekill mader as of thre of theis oþer herbes, & stamp þam to-gedir & drynke þam.

An oþer. Tak auance, comfery, 3arow, croppes of hempe, tansay, rede cale, aueroyn, & mader als mekill as halfe thies oþer herbes, / and syne stamp þam & mak þam in balles & do þam vp to drye.

An oþer gud drynk for all wondes. Tak waybrede, rib, violett, auances, cropp of þe rede brere, matfelon, herb Robert, tansay, betoyn, milfoille, comfery, baynewort, of ilkane ilike mekill, & of þe rote of mader agayn all thies oþer herbes. Stampe þam all & mak pelottes of þam & dry þam in the sonne or in þe wynde & drynk þam in wynnter.

A gud syroyn when herbis failes for all wondis. Tak a pound of virgyn wax, a pounde of olibanum, a pounde of encruce of þe ere, a pound of ditayne, a pound of playntayn, a pound of jubarbe, a pound of littill consoude, a pound of milfoille & a pound of watercresses. Tak thies gresses & stampe þam ilkan by hy[m] ane & temper þam with wyn & late þam rest a nyghte & on þe morn do þam in a pott ouer þe fire & late þam welle wele & syne tak it doun & drawe it thorow a clene clathe.

An oþer. Tak herb John, herb Robert, bugill, pigill, milfoille, consoude, playntayne, auance, of all thies herbis tak þe jus, & wax & pik & a littill gres, & mak syroyn. To all kyles & wondis it is gude.

An oþer sirope for alle wondis. Tak þe firste iij dayes & lay þer-to noghte bot lyne & þe white of an egge & chaunge it morne & euen. & þan tak ix stalkes of gronswale with þe rotes & v of spourge with þe rutes & als many croppes of þe rede brere, & stampe all wele to-gedir with a sawcerfull of hony & þan wrynge owte all þe jus thurgh a clene clathe & do it in a clene pane ouer þe fire & boile it a whalme. & þan tak it doun & stop þer-in iij dices of whete brede & gif hym thase thre at euen, when he gase to his bedde. & do so with ilk a sirope & brede viij dayes or ix. And when þu sees þat þe wounde es wele rotyn & whelis [1] whitoure faire, tak þan iij stalkes of gronswalle & v of

---

[1] MS. *adds* & *above the line.*

Liber de Diversis Medicinis.

spourge & fyue of brere croppe & stamp þam & mak thi
syrope als þu dide bi-fore & dice it with brede stoppede
þer-in morne till þat it be hale & lay not to þe wonde
bot firste smalle lyn þer-on & a brere leffe þer-on a-
5. bouen or a rede cale lefe & luk ay þat he ette no gowttous
mettes.

He þat will mak littill syrone, tak gud fresche schepe   An oþer
talghe, virgyn wax, pik nauale, galbanum. Gare þam   syroyne to wondis.
boyle welle & styrre þam softely & do a lyttill wyn
10 þer-in. Syne tak mirre & olibanum and powdir of
mastike & do þe foresaid thynges þer-in & lat þam boile
wele, bot luk þat þay be wele stirrede. Þis syroyn is
ful gude.

f. 311r. Tak a handfull of savyn & a handfull of sauge & a   [A gu]de oynment [for
15 handfull of rewe & a handfull of tansay, & stamp þam   w]ondes.
wele to-gedir & sethe þam wele in oyle of olyue & do
wax & swyn grese þer-to fresche & powder of mastik
& do all to-gedir & mak ane oynement þer-of.

Tak celydoyn rotes & of gouke flores with þe leues,   [An] oþer
20 centrum galli, wild louache, of ilkan a handefull, scabius,   gude [oyn]ment for wondis.
a handfull. Thies herbis stampe wele with a pounde of
schepe talghe & a pounde of olyue &, when þay are wele
stampede, do þam to-gedir & lat þam riste vij dayes or
viij & syne sethe þam in a vesselle ouer þe fire to þe
25 gresses falle to þe grounde & syne coyle þam thorow a
clathe & do þat ilk coylett in a caldron & do þer-to iij
vnces of wax in somer, in wynter ij vnces, &, when all
es molten, caste in-to þam pouder of olybane, mastik &
vertgrese & of ilkane halfe ane vnce. Bot, or þu do in
30 the vertgres, proue þam halfe to-gedir & loke if þay
change colour so þat it wax grene. Do it fra þe fire &
caste þer-in an vnce of aloen epatik pouderd & in oyle
resolued & menge al togedir. Þis oynement is gud for
all wondis & to gedir new flesche, & fordose dede
35 flesche.

Tak galt gres, hony, & oyle of nuttes, & do þer-to þe   [A g]ud
jus of chesseboll croppes grene with all þe sede & þe   salue [for wondis.
jus of rew & waybrede. Sethe wele þe jewses of thiese
herbis all samen & mak thi salfe wele þer-of & syne coyle
40 it & do it in boystes.

74   *Liber de Diversis Medicinis.*

[A]n oþer.   Tak pigle, bugle, sanegle, selfehale, herb John, herb Robert, herb Wawter, smalache, strabery wythes, wodbynd croppis, rib, waybred, homlok, henbayn & wormot. Stamp þam & welle þam wele in buttre & þan draw þam after thorow a clathe & do to þam wax & olybane.   5

[A p]laster for [w]ondis.   Tak þe jus of plantayn & þe jus of morell & þe jus of ache & þe jus of walleworte & whete flour, & mak it in a plaster with-owtten fire & lay it to.

[A gu]d oynement.   Tak auance, bugle, pigle, sanegle, ache, herb John, herb Wauter, herb Robert, waybrede, rib, raynwort, þe 10 leues of the rede cale, þe croppes of þe rede brere, þe white malue & wallewort. Stamp ilk an herb by it selfe & tak of ilk an herb ilik mekill jus & do it in a pan. The white malue is so fatte, & þu may gete no jus þer-of, for-þi tak þe lefes & do þer-to. & tak þan virgyn wax 15 & fresche schepe talghe / &[1] hony & May buttre & alde   f. 311v. swyn grese & wyn ana, & luk þat all thies thynges weghe als mekill als halfe þe jus of herbes. & do all thyes thynges þan in a pan & sethe þam wele & þou may wette by þe leues when þai are sothen ynowghe, when 20 þay wax ȝalowe & nessche, & do on thi naile & droppe with a sclice & late it kele þer-one &, if it wax grene, þan is it enoghe. & do þan rikills þer-to & stirre it wele & do it doun of þe fire and wrynge it thorowe a clathe in-till a clene bacyn. & when it is somdele calde, 25 do it in boystis. And, if þu may not hafe all thies herbis, tak als many als þu may fynde & do þer-to wax & sethe þam with sayme & do rikills þer-to & wrynge it thrugh a clathe & do it in boystes. If þu may noghte, tak ache, rib & waybrede & baynwort & wax. 30 Welle þam in sayme & do to rikills and [do][2] it in boystis.

An oþer.   Tak þe rote of alcea, one Englische called wymalue, fenkell, percell, ache, comfery, sporuge, osmounde, gronswalle and iij croppes of þe brere and, if þe wonde 35 be depe in þe flesche, tak þe maste of osmonde &, if þe bane be in sondre, tak þe maste of spourge &, if þe wonde be bolnede, do þan leuke þer-to &, if þu may noghte thole

---

[1] MS. *repeats* talghe *before* &.
[2] MS. *omits some such word as* do.

Liber de Diversis Medicinis. 75

  þam for bitternes, do auance þer-to & þat ilk tyme lay
a brere lefe þer-to.
  Tak buttre, oil & whete bran & wyn & menge þam An oþer for to slake þe
samen & do þam to a slawe fire & stirre þam wele & werke of wouⁿdes.
5 lay þam warme appon þe wounde & þe werke sall slake.
  Tak þe crommes of whete brede hate & þe jus of An oþer.
ache & stampe to-gedir & ¹ lay one þe wounde all hate.
  Tak þe wilde nepte & mak powdir þer-of & do þer-of An oþer for wound
in þe wounde and it sall open. sperred to-gedir or it
10 Tak strabery wythes with alle þe rute & sethe it in be hale.
water & clence it thorow a clathe & gif it hym to drynke An oþer.
& it sal opyn þe wounde with.
  Tak ache, auance, gronswalle & spourge, of ilkan a A drynk for bledynge
handfull, & sethe þam in a galon of water to appell. inwarde. Nota. Nota.
15 Þan coille it thorow a clathe & do hony þer-to till it
bere ² an egge. Þan sethe it & scome it & claryfy it &
gyf it hym at drynke, at euen warme & at morne calde.
  Tak nepte & stamp it & drynk þe jus & it sall caste To caste owt blode fro
out þe blode with-owtten any duellynge. dynt or wounde.
20 Or tak þe white malue & mak pouder þer-of & drynk
it with wyne & it sall caste out þe blode.
  Tak wodbynde & stamp it & lay on þe wond & it [To] drawe owt broken
wil draw owt wondirfully. / [b]anes of woundis.
f. 312r. Tak violett and drynke it, for it castes owt broken An oþer.
25 banes of mannes wondis lyghtly.
  Tak þe hare of an hare skyn & wynd it rounde as any Gorrynge.
appill & swalow it down & he sall be hale.
  Tak poudir of encense & mastik & tonge of dragon ana, [T]o hele wondis [to
& blende with þe white of ane egge & do it on a lyn þ]ay be sanede
30 clowte & lay it appon þe wonde þer þe synues are in
sondre & he sall be sone hale.
  Tak saundyuere or coprose, also pouder of a crak, [A po]uder to do a[way]
þat is to say, of þe heued, of þe fete, of þe bowells, brynt dede flesche.
in a new pott, also vnslokynde lyme, blake pepir,
35 orpyment, strange ayselle, hony & barly mele, euen
porcyons, & boyle þam in a newe pott to poudir. Þis
poudir is gude to sla þe ³ kankre. Also of brynt bacon

---
¹ mak powdir þer-of & do þer-of in þe wounde & it sall open *crossed out*. MS. *adds* and.
² MS. *adds* it nere *crossed out*.
³ MS. *repeats* þe.

or brynt salt beefe. Also for soure sauoure do þer-in sape & copprose & qwikke lyme blendede to-gedir. Also, for to mak a hole, do þer-on kantarydes or garleke or scottleke.

[An o]þer poudir for [ded]e flesche.

Tak wormot & þe white of an egg & scome it, & brynt salt, þe scome of brasill, white glase, of ilkan elike mekill, also poudir of sall gemme. Also tak vnslekked lyme & clere hony & do to-gedir in a basyn & do it in þe son to dry to þu may mak poudir þer-of. Also tak lange wortis, hony & rye mele & mak an enplaster and lay to þe sare & it sall amende and hele.

[A gu]de drynke [for b]lane of þe hede [bro]ken, *secundum* R. de O.
Broken ribbis.

Stamp betoyne wele & drynk þe jus þer-of & lay þe drafe appon þe wounde & it sall brynge a-way þe broken banes & hele þe wonde, and egrymoyn wil do þe same & is þe mare hastily helande.

Drynk þe jus of littill consoude & tak mekill of þe jus & als mekill swete mylke & þe flour of whete & do all to-gedir & mak a plaster and lay to the sare syde.

[A gu]d poudir to ... flesche.

Tak poudir of mastik & frank encense & canelle & corall, of ilkan euen ilike, & mak poudir þer-of.

[A] gude poudir for fest*re*, also poudir of gude grisses.

Tak a tade & a neddir & a wesill & a moldwerpe & brakans & bryn þam in a newe pott all to-gedir to poudir.

[An o]þer for þe ka*n*kir in [w]omans pappis þat ¹man ne sal noghte schere.

Tak comfery & herb Jhon & mak in poudir & caste in, for þat kankir is gud to hele wi*th* thies herbis.

Tak Wormot & þe white of an egge vt sup*ra* for poudir for dede flesche.

[For] to dry & for [to s]oude a wou*n*de [to]-gedir.

Tak þe ij p*a*rties of þe oile of rose & þe iij p*a*rty of wax & þe jus of plantayn, a gretter porcyon þan of wax. Mak þam to-gedir & anoynte þe ther-with. For wondis þat wil not hele & þat haldis open: Tak frankencense & arnement gronden al to poudir & do it in þe hole.

[For] to close a [wou]nde.

Tak turbentill & anoynte it þer-with & it sall close. /

Tak þe poudir of litarge & strewe it in þe wonde.

For to mak a wounde harde & waste þe wheto*ur* & ware.

For kankir in þe wonde: Tak sawge, rewe, cerfoile, primerolle, hondistonge, kalcroppe, bugill, sanygle & ȝarow, ana a handfull, & of bryane a handfull. Stamp þam to-gedir all thies grisses & syne boile þam in wyn & gyf þe sek iij dayes.

f. 312v.

---

¹ MS. *adds* womans pappes *before* þat.

Liber de Diversis Medicinis.

  Tak mader, tansay, radecole, auance & baynewort, euen ilike, & stamp þam in a morter & sethe all in wyne, at euen hate & at morne calde, & sethe it in a pott & dry it with dok leues.

For to hele wonde of goute or festre.

5 Tak þe galle of a swyne, iij sponefull, & tak þe jus of homeloke rute & tak iij sponefull of aysell & blende all samen, þe galle & þe jus & þe ayselle. Þan tak & do þam in a vesselle of glas to halde to þe seke man þat þu will schere & tak þer-of a sponefull & do till a galon of
10 wyne or of ale &, if þu will mak it strangere, do ij sponefull to þe galon. Þan tak a copefull þer-of & gyf hym to drynke & he sall slepe sone. Schere hym þan als þu will and he sall nott fele it. Tak vnto þe man þe galle of þe galte and to þe woman þe galle of þe gilt.

Nota istud bene : To garre a man slepe to he be schorne.

15 Þare are ij maners of festres, ane hate & anoþer calde. Þe calde es strayte & a littill hole hase, & þe hate es large & mare perilous. Now here may þu lere & here whare-of it comes þe kankir & þe festre. It commes of a wonde or of a sare þat is wrange helide & brekes owt
20 afterwarde &, if it be in þe flesche, þer rynnes of it ware &, if it be in the synues, þare commes owte als it were brown lee &, if it be in þe bane, þer commes owte als it were thik blode. & þe festre hase a narowe hole with-owtten & wyde with-in. Þe kankir hase a wyde
25 hole with-owtten & narowe with-in. Þe festre es seldome þat it ne hase ma holes þan ane. Þe kankir es euermare with a hole.

Medcyns for to knawe þe festre or þe kankir.

  Tak waybrede, white tansay, ȝarow, white malue, ache & auance & stamp ilk a grise by hym-selfe &
30 wrynge owt þe jus & luk þat þu hafe of ilk a grese ilik mekill jus & þat by weghte. Þan tak walwort & stamp it & tak als mekill jus of it als of al thies oþer gresses bi weghte.[1] Þan tak virgyn wax & fresche schepe talghe & hony & buttre of May & al[d][2] swyn gres & wyn & of
35 ilkan ilike mekill bi weghte & luk þat al thies thynges laste neuennede wey als mekill als þe jus of walwort. Þan do all thies thynges in a pan & welle þam wele, bot þe white malue salle þou sethe þer-with, for þu may nott

For þe festre. An enplaster.

---

[1] MS. *adds* whil þat all thies thynges laste *crossed out.*
[2] MS. als.

wrynge owte þe jus þer-of als of þe iij oþer, / for it is so
fatt. When it is alle wele wellide, wryng it thorow a clathe
& do it in boystis. Þan tak whete flour & do a party of
þat oynement þer-to & welle it to-gedir þat it be thikke
als growelle & wesche þe wonde morne & euen with
wyne & lay þan thi plaster þer-to. & do so ilk day till
he be hale & drynk ilk day fastand wormot and auance.

[For] to gare flesche [hel]e after kankir or festre.

Tak fresche schepe talghe & wax & poudir of olibanum
and menge all to-gedir & lay to þe kankir or þe festre.

A water for festre or kankir.

Tak alom glas, halfe a pound, & crop of mader, a gud
gopen, & a potell of rynnande water & scarlett flokkes
& boile all samen & powm garnett schelles in poudir &
a handfull of sauge & anoynte þe sare þer-with.

[Pl]aster for þe festre or þe kankir.

Tak a halupenyworthe of schepe talghe molten &
alle þe crommes of a halpeny lafe of alsome brede of
whete & a potelle of alde ale & boile all samen.

[A pou]dir for to sla [þe fe]stre or þe kankir.

Tak benes, rye, darenell, arnament & salt, of ilkan
ilike mekill, & do all in a new pott of erthe & bryn it to
þu maye ¹ stampe it, & grynde it to powdir & temce it
thorowe a sarce. & tak a stele of malue & luk þat it be
welked. Thurghe wete it & do it in þe powdir þat it
cleue þer-on all a-bowt & putt it in þe thirlle down to
þe grounde & lay thyn enplaster þer-on þat is bi-fore
saide. Þis poudir wil sla þe festre. Do þe stele with
þe poudir þer-in v dayes or viij & syne may þu do a tent
þer-in of lyne &, euer als it by-gynnes to hele, mak thi
tent schortere and ilk day wasche the wounde twyse.

An oþer.

Tak laurioll & dry it & stamp it all to poudir & þan
tak þe poudir & sethe it in hony to þu may mak tenttis
þer-ofe & þan do a tent in ilk a thirlle & couer it with
clowttes & bynd it swa þat it gaa noghte owte vn-to
þu vndo it at morn. & þan clence þe thirlles & wasche
þam with hate wyne & do so ilk daye to þu may see þe
rede blode come owte after þe tent & þan may þu hele
it vp with powdir of rikills & þe jus of waybrede.

An oþer.

Tak þe rutes of morelle & wasche þam & stamp
þam wele & lay þam to þe festre at morn & at euen &
euer clence it wele of gotours & wasche it with hate
wyne.

¹ MS. *adds* stap *crossed out.*

Liber de Diversis Medicinis.

Tak egrymonde & stampe it & lay it to þe festre twise [A]n oþer.
on þe day & wasche it [with] ¹ hate wyn.
Tak a plate of coper & wete it with vynagre & tak salt [A]n oþer.
f. 313v. & strewe þer-on / & stamp it to it be lik powdir & strewe
5 it one þe plate with vynagre þer-on & sett it on þe qwik
coles till it be wele brynt. Þan wete þi plate efte-sones
with vynagre & efte strewe salte þer-on & bryn [i]t ² on
þe coles & do so to þu hafe mekill powdir of brynt salte
in þe plate & dry it in þe sonne. Þan grynde it to it be
10 dely poudir & þan tak þe two partiese & menge with þe
thirde party of poudir of vertgrese. Þan do ilk a day of
this poudir in þe thirlles of þe festre & putt it doun to
þe grounde with a tent & do so ilk day to þu see þe flesche
by-come rede & new & clens it. Þan & do þer-to ilk a day
15 Apostolicon & do it to, to þat it be hale, for þis is full
sekir medcyn.

Tak herb Robert, auance, sanygle & bugle ana, & An oþer.
sethe þam in wyn or in welle water mengede with ale
þat is made with whete malte. Þis drynk sall þe seke
20 man drynke to he be hale & nane oþer. & sone, when he
hase dronken, hafe thi plaster redy of dede tonge, þat
is þi halfe tonge, & lay it þer-to &, ay when þu
vndose it, wasche it with hate wyn & clens it of
gotours.
25 Tak þe rute of þe wilde cucurd & dry it & schere it in
schyues & mak tentis þer-of to fande hou depe þe hole
is. Tak þe greia of þe wyne þat men fyndis in þe
tounnes þat litsters & goldsmythes vses. Stampe it in
dely poudir & sethe it in hony & mak it so thikk þat þu
30 may mak tentis þer-of & do ilk a day of þase tentis in
þe thirlles at morne & at þe euen & bynd þam to faste &,
ilk tyme þat þu vndose it, scoure it wele with tentis
made of lyn clathe & wasche it wele with hate wyne
& do so ilk day to þe festre be dede, & þat may þu wete
35 þer-by when þer commes no gotour out. And þan for
to take & hale it with frank encense & þe jews of waybrede, to do þer-to ilke daye.

Tak swyn gres & hony ana, & do it in a pan & do bene An oþer.
mele þer-to & welle a littill to-gedir & mak an emplaster

¹ MS. wele.   ² MS. brynt.

Liber de Diversis Medicinis.

& do to þe sare. It dose mekill gud bothe to festre and kankir.

An oþer. Tak salt & hempe sede & hondbayne, of ilkane ilike mekill, & bray þam & mak dely poudir of þam & do it in þe thirlles.

An oþer. Tak rede cale croppes & þe nettill croppes & þe tendrons of þe rede brere ana, & of mader als mekill als of all þe oþer herbis, & stamp þam & mak þam in smalle balles & do þam to ke[le].

An oþer. Tak þe jus of morelle & do þe wose in þe thirlles of þe festre iij dayes or iiij. & þe substance þat þe jus es wrongen out of, lay þer-to with-owtten, & þan tak arnament, pepir & nitere & of all iij elik mekill & mak poudir þer-of. Þan tak þe jus of walworte & ayselle ana, & do þer-to oyle & welle it to-gedir to it be thik als¹ oynement. Tak þan a malue stele & steke þe thirlles hou depe þay are. Þan mak thi tentis of lyne als lange als thi samplare gose depe. Wete þi tentis wele in þe oynement & put þam doun to þe grounde & anoynt it with oynement & do so ilk day till þe thirlles be clensede þat þer come na mare gotour owt. Þan mak thi tentis euer þe schortere to it be hale.

An oþer. Tak a fysche þat men calles a roche & bryn it in a newe pott & mak dely powdir þer-of. Þan tak þe jus of auaunce & helle it in þe thirlles & fill þe thirlles with þe poudir & do so ilk day to þe thirlles be dryed & þe wonde hale. & gare þe seke ilk a daye drynk þe jews of auaunce.

An oþer. Tak þe jus of fox gloues rote & stampe it with mannes vryn & wrynge it thorow a clathe & wesche þe felon ofte þer-with.

An oþer. Tak auaunce & stampe it & drynke it & do þe plaster & þe poudir of white glas & hony & anoynte it with all & syne do it þer-in iij dayes.

An oþer. Tak hempe sede & rewe sede & bryn þam to poudir & tak þe jus of ache & stamp with alle & gyf hym at drynke.

.. staunche .. festre. Tak gayte mylke & mannes fen, euen ilike, & temper þam with oile of nuttis & mak kakis þer-of & late þam dry & do to þe sare, for it is gude to stawnche þe festre.

¹ MS. *repeats* thik *before* als.

Liber de Diversis Medicinis.

  Tak þe barke of þe grenc ake & do a-waye þe vttereste. [Fo]r festre or bolnynge of legges.
Syne bryn it & sloken it in water & grynd it to poudir.
Þan menge it with ȝolkes & do it in þe hole & it sal clence
it. &, if þe hole be depe, putt þer-in a tent with glaire.
5 Tak tender stalkes of a dokane & falde it in ane of þe [For to] wiete if þat goute or festre be hate or calde.
leues & lay it in þe aymeres till it be rede ynoughe.
Þan stampe it & make an enplaster þer-of & lay it on þe
holes ij dayes & iij nyghtis &, if it auaile not, þan is it
þe gout festre hate.
10 Tak rye flour & clere hony teres & mak hard daughe [Fo]r gout festre hate.
þer-of & mak als many smale kakis als þer is thirlles & do
to ilk thirlle a kake &, when þay are wate, do þam
a-waye & do to oþer & do so to it be hale & drynk ilk
day auaunce or oþer thynge als it is by-fore saide.
15 Tak þe jus of auance & þe jus of laureaule & þe white [Fo]r gout festre calde.
of an egge, of aþer ilike mekill, & tak rye flour & knede
þer-with & do to þe thirle, als it were an enplaster, &
bynd it with a clathe & late it lygge þer-at till it falle
f. 314v. a-waye bi it-selfe / & þan do oþer to on þat ilk maner
20 & do so to þe festre be hale & ilk a day drynk þe jus
of auance.
  Tak lene bakon & bryn it & do it one þe sare, for it is An oþer.
gud for þe goute festre.
  Stampe þe rute of radik & wrynge þe jus in þe hole & For worme and kankir.
25 he sall warische. & also tak nesche sape & radik &
menge to-gedir & mak a plaster & lay þer-to.
  Tak þe heued of a storke or of a crane & þe feete & For þe kankir.
all þat is with-in þe storke bot þe body & do it all in a
pott of erthe þat was neuer vsede & do it in an owenn
30 & dry it swa þat þu may mak powdir þer-of & do of þat
powdir on þe kankir & it sall be hale with-in iij dayes.
  Tak olibanum album & dry it & mak powdir þer-of & An oþer.
do it on þe kankir to it be hale.
  Tak þe leues of flambe & morell & mak an enplaster An oþer.
35 þer-of & do to þe kankir, when þe werke is a-way.
  Tak powdir of morell þat is brynt & do þer-on & it
sall sla þe kankir & drawe þe flesche to-gedir.
  Tak vertgrese, arnament, bronstane brynt, ana weght, An oþer.
& bryn þam all to powdir & mak þer-of powdir & of þat
40 powdir strewe on þe kankir and, if þe kankir be on a

man, wesche it ilk a daye with þe pys of a knafe childe
&, if it be on a woman, wesche it ilk a day with þe pys of
a mayden childe or þe poudir be strewede per-one to þe
kankir be dede. Bot, when it is weschen, mak it dry
with hardes, or þu strew þe poudir per-on. Þe kankir 5
will be dede with-in þe firste day, & þan, when þe kankir
is dede, sall þu do on þis manere : Tak þe jus of ache &
a littill hony & senn & do þam to-gedir in a pan & lat
þam welle with a slawe fire & þan do per-to a littill of
whete mele till it be thik als growelle. & tak it þan 10
doun of þe fire &, if þer be any knottis of mele, vn-do
þam with thyn handis and menge þam wele. Tak þan
hardes with-owtten scheffes & hakk þam small & strewe
þam on þe kankir & þan lay thyn enplaster per-on ilk
day to it be hale. 15

To sla þe kankir. Tak powdir of salt nitere & hete it with aysell & do it
on þe kankir & it sall sla it.

Or mak þe powdir hate in a scarthe all dry & strewe
þe powdir on þe kankir & it sall sla it. & when it is
dede, tak þe medcyn by-fore saide & do per-to & it sal 20
sone b[e hale].[1]

An oþer. Tak arnament & bryn it & stampe it all to poudir &
do per iij poudirs to-gedir ana & þat bi weghte & do a
littill per-to & mak it hate & do it on þe kankir.

If þu may nott hele þe kankir with nane of thies 25
medcyns, schere þan þe flesche with a raysour doun to
þe bane als ferre als þe euyll lastis per-on & tak þan þe
ȝolkes of egges & oile of rose & menge to-gedir & do
per-in ix dayes per-efter. & þan tak sawge & comfery
& mirt, of ilkan a handfull, of blake benes, of nete flesche 30
brynt, of orpyment, of pyons, of ilkan ij vnces, & of all
thies thynges mak dely poudir & do on þe kankir to it be
hale.

An oþer. Tak at þe bygynnynge & wasche þe kankir with
hate water & hony & þan tak morell & stampe it & 35
wrynge þe jus on þe kankir & lay þe substance per-to
with-owtten &, if þer be dede flesche with-in, tak þe
askes of bene straa or of brynt asche & menge per-with
alde swyn grese & lay it to þe kankir.

[1] MS. *omits* -e hale.

NOTES

The following notes are intended to furnish the historical background of individual recipes. In some cases it has been necessary to supply more extended comments upon certain words than was feasible in the Glossary. In many cases, references to parallels illustrative of the history of individual recipes have been given. References have also been given to practically all the close parallels found in the Middle English texts examined. A few of the most characteristic parallels are quoted. Owing to the large number of references involved, it has been necessary to use greatly abbreviated titles of the works referred to. Wherever possible, the abbreviated title consists of the name of the medical writer, followed, in parentheses, by the name of the editor whose edition is being quoted. A complete list of the abbreviated titles is given in the Appendix.

1/1-3. Close parallels : Dawson 2; " Wo so haþ hakyng or torment in his hed mak lye of verueyne or of betayne or of fillus or of wermot & þer wiþ wasch þy hed prius in þe wyke " (Roy 12 G iv, f. 188v). Thornton seems to be closer to the correct reading than Roy 12 G iv. Other parallels differ only in connecting names of plants by *and* instead of *or* : Müller 116/36-38; Henslow B 106/4-5; Henslow D 135/1-2. Dawson, Roy 12 G iv, and Henslow have *lye* instead of the Thornton *lee*.

1/4-7. Parallels, each following a parallel to 1/1-3 : Müller 116/39-117/2; Dawson 3. *& yvęn terrestre, ache* does not appear in the parallels.

1/8-11. Parallel : *Coll. Salern.* (Renzi) IV, 193-194. Middle English parallel, following a parallel to 1/4-7 : Dawson 4.

1/12-14. Pliny (Mayhoff) xx, 152 and Galen (Kühn) XII, 529 prescribe *puliol* for headache. Parallels : Serapion (1497) *De simpl. med.* II, 165; *Romania* XXXII, 100/25-28; *Camb. Antid.* (Sigerist) 161; Dawson 8; Heinrich 124b/4-5.

1/15-17. Parallel : Marcellus (Niedermann) I, 45. Close parallels : Dawson 5, 454; Müller 117/3-5. Parallels designated as remedies for earache : Henslow A 37/8-10; Henslow B 110/6-8; Roy 12 G iv, f. 188v.

1/20-21. Parallels : *Leechbook* III (Leonhardi) 94/5-7; Larsen 203.

1/22-24. Parallels : Dawson 12; *Camb. Antid.* (Sigerist) 160. The Latin parallel, which corresponds closely in other respects, has *puleio cum flore suo*, suggesting that Thornton's *with þe jewse of þe floure* is probably a better reading than Dawson's *and pound it with floure*.

1/25-26. Parallels : Dawson 449; Henslow B 83/4-7.

1/27-28. Parallels : Dawson 10; Heinrich 124b/9-11; *Anglia* XVIII, 295/9-16; *Camb. Antid.* (Sigerist) 160; Larsen 203.

2/3-5. Many similar recipes have been found, but no exact parallels. Pliny (Mayhoff) xx, 135 and *Coll. Salern.* (Renzi) IV, 193 prescribe rue juice, oil of rose, and vinegar for headache.

2/6-7. Galen (Kühn) XII, 529, 538 prescribes the application of *puliol* mixed with honey for headache.

2/11-13. No exact parallels were found, but many similar recipes : Müller 117/8-10; Dawson 7, 453; Roy 12 G iv, f. 188v; Henslow B 106/6-9.

2/14-15. Parallel : Serapion (1497) *De simpl. med.* III, 321.

2/16-19. Close parallel : Roy 12 G iv, f. 189r. See notes to 26/3-13.

2/20-22. Parallels : Heinrich 88b/23-29, 124b/17-19. These parallels confirm the conjecture that *playlster* is an error for *playster*.

2/23-24. All parallels lack *rose* : Heinrich 81a/2-5; Müller 51/10-12, 117/

12-14. Thornton's heading, *for fantome in the heuede*, seems to be approximately equivalent to the Latin caption in Heinrich : *pro vanitate capitis*, which appears in Müller as *for vanytee in þe hed*.

2/27-28. Parallel : Avicenna (Gerard) *Canon* II, 622. For head lice, Paulus (Adams) III, 3 recommends the application of stavesacre mixed with vinegar and oil.

2/33-34. Galen (Kühn) XII, 582, 584, 585, 588, 589 prescribes stavesacre for headache, and Pliny (Mayhoff) xxiii, 18 recommends that head sores be treated with a combination of stavesacre and sandarac (*red arsenic sulphide*; cf. orpiment, *trisulphide of arsenic*).

2/35-36. Parallels : Dawson 312 ; Müller 117/15-18. Thornton's *trauellyng in slepe* is paralleled by Müller's *trawayll in his slepe or fantesyis* and Dawson's *fantñs and dwelsynge*. A longer passage in praise of betony occurs on 26/3-13. For the use of herbs as amulets, see Alexander (Puschmann) I, 567.

3/1-2. Parallels : Henslow A 68/20-21 ; Müller 98/13-15 ; Heinrich 82a/19-22 ; Roy 12 G iv, f. 189r.

3/3-4. *Sayme de/voyr* is probably a garbled form of *sandiver*. *Saundyuer*, a normal variant of *sandiver* (appearing, for example, in Heinrich 106a/10), could easily have been mistranscribed by an ignorant scribe as *saim-* or *saym-*. A variant *sandivoire* is quoted in the NED from Topsell, *Four-f. Beasts* (1607) 357. Sandiver, copperas, and verdigris appear together in another head plaster on 3/27.

3/13-19. Parallel : Dawson 778. There are also several parallels to the first portion of this recipe, in which the making and application of the plaster are described : Henslow B 106/15-18 ; Roy 12 G iv, f. 193r ; *Romania* XXXVII, 367/53. The recipes in Henslow B and *Romania* XXXVII follow the plaster with a treatment of garlic and honey instead of honey alone. The recipe in Roy 12 G iv prescribes a totally different application after the plaster. *Do it not a-wey in-to þe ix day* in Henslow B 106/17 is possibly nearer the original version than Thornton's unintelligible *do it noghte ix dayes*.

3/20-24. The juice of various plants of the genus *Allium* was prescribed by Pliny (Mayhoff) xx, 40 and by the Salernitan Petrocellus, *Peri Di* (Löweneck) 6/1-2 as a local application in the cure of scalp diseases. Parallels to 3/13-19, perhaps attempting to gain the combined effect of two originally separate cures, prescribe a subsequent application of garlic and honey.

3/32. *Blaunke alome* is probably a name for *burnt alum*, a white powder. Cf. *powder of alowme*, Müller 138/23, and *pouder of brend alym*, Heinrich 92a/4.

4/15-16. Galen (Kühn) XII, 503 prescribes meal mixed with honey-water for sore head.

4/24-25. Parallel : Roy 12 G iv, f. 193r.

4/26-29. For head scales Paulus (Adams) III, 1 recommends burning the head of a fox, adding certain herbal ingredients (not agrimony, however), and applying the mixture to the scales.

4/35. As herb bennet and hemlock were both used to designate *Conium maculatum*, L., it is possible that the sign between *herbe benett* and *homloke* is an illegible *.i.*, *vel*, or the like.

5/5-6. Parallel : Larsen 202.

5/9-10. The use of mallow, especially the cooked root, in the treatment of the hair appears in : Pliny (Mayhoff) xx, 224 ; Galen (Kühn) XII, 461-462 ; and Alexander (Puschmann) I, 449.

5/11-12. Myrtle had long been used to prevent falling hair : Pliny (Mayhoff) xxiii, 161 ; Galen (Kühn) XII, 432, 435, 436, 438 ; Avicenna (Gerard) *Canon* II, 454 ; Constantinus (1510) I, 2. Thornton's Latin quotation is found in Rhazes (1510) *Antid.* II, 271, with only a slight difference in word-order.

5/13-14. In Henslow A 70/3-8 lye of beanstraw is prescribed as a depilatory.

5/21-23. Ant eggs are prescribed in Dawson 443 to make hair grow, and in the Anglo-Saxon *Leechbook* I (Leonhardi) 46/39-47/2 to prevent hair from growing. The blood of a bat is prescribed in a compound depilatory in *Glasgow Antid.* (Sigerist) 160.

5/24-25. Parallel : Roy 12 G iv, f. 189r-189v.

Notes.

5/26–27. See note to 5/21–23.

5/29–30. Galen (Kühn) XII, 445, quoting Archigenes; Alexander (Puschmann) I, 455; Paulus (Adams) III, 2; Avicenna (Gerard) *Canon* IV, 509; Najm (Guigues) 138/11; and Lanfrank (Fleischhacker) 179/4–8 prescribe lupine water, either alone or mixed with other ingredients, for making the hair blonde.

5/31–33. Macer (1527) 18 mentions the use of *salvia* to darken hair.

5/34–6/4. These two successive Thornton recipes appear as a single recipe in Henslow D 141/18–22.

6/7–8. *Pympernoll* tempered with wine is prescribed as a drink *for þe pose in þe hed* in Henslow B 107/1–2.

6/11–14. Albertus (1555) 0, 1 says that *asphodilus* is administered to free people from demoniac or melancholic afflictions, as the presence of this herb does not permit a demon to remain in the house.

6/17–18. Parallel: Larsen 203.

6/19–22. Heinrich 81a/2–5, which is headed *Unguentum bonum pro vanitate capitis*, differs only in prescribing wax instead of incense.

6/23–30. This recipe occurs in one or another of its variant forms in practically every ME recipe collection examined. Its essential feature is the use of the fresh juice of green boughs, obtained by heating the branches and catching the juice oozing from the ends. Fresh ash sap obtained in this manner is prescribed in Marcellus (Niedermann) IX, 16: "Fraxini recentem surculum, id est umore proprio adhuc madentem, ex una parte in foco pones. Cum per aliam partem sucus ebulliet, suscipies eum diligenter et oleo addito tepefactum auribus instillabis." Similar recipes prescribing the use of fresh sap from ash boughs are found in *Camb. Antid.* (Sigerist) 167; *Leechbook* I (Leonhardi), 14/4–6; Dawson 18, 266; Heinrich 81a/6–17, 131b/19–22; Müller 91/5–11, 51/13–52/5; Schöffler 195/19–24, 25–196/7; *Anglia* XXXIV 186/852–863.

Although ash sap was the variety of sap most commonly prescribed for this purpose, there were recipes in the fourteenth and fifteenth centuries that prescribed the juice from the branches of other trees, *e.g.* hazel [Henslow B 109/12–17; Roy 12 G iv, ff. 188v, 220r], elm [Heinrich 93b/6–16], and hawthorn [7/5–8; Dawson 994]. This sap was sometimes administered alone [*Leechbook* I (Leonhardi) 14/4–6; Henslow D 133/20–23; Heinrich 131b/19–22], sometimes mixed with oil [7/5–8; Dawson 994] or honey [7/29–35 (= 13/9–18); Müller 91/5–11].

Often, as in 6/23–30, a number of other ingredients were added. The most usual of these were *senegrene* (= *jubarb*) juice, eel grease or droppings, and leek juice. These added ingredients were variously combined: leek alone [Roy 12 G iv, f. 188v]; eel and leek [Dawson 18]; eel, leek, and honey [Müller 51/13–52/5]; *senegrene* [*jubarb*] and eel [*Anglia* XXXIV, 186/852–863]; *senegrene*, black eel grease, and wine [Heinrich 93b/6–16]; *senegrene*, eel, and the milk of a woman who feeds a male child [Schöffler 195/19–24]; *senegrene*, eel, and honey [Schöffler 195/25–196/7]; *senegrene*, leek, and honey [Henslow B 109/12–17; Roy 12 G iv, f. 220r]; leek, eel, and rhubarb [Dawson 266]; eel, leek, honey, and *senecio* [Heinrich 81a/6–17]; and oil, honey, leek, and *senegrene* [6/23–30]. These added ingredients represent the reinforcement of the original recipe by the addition of other well-known curatives for the same disorder. Some of the added combinations were and had long been well known as separate recipes. Honey and leek juice had been used for disorders of the ear since the time of Alexander (Puschmann) II, 73. How easy such absorbing of two recipes into one was, may be seen from 7/5–11, where a simple recipe prescribing hawthorn juice and oil is followed by a separate recipe prescribing the application of the grease of a black eel and *senegrene* juice for ear troubles. [For parallels of the latter recipe, see note to 7/9–11.]

The curative juice, whether ash sap alone or combined with other substances, was variously applied. It was usually applied to the well ear, a practice at least as old as Pliny (Mayhoff) xxix, 136. In many recipes, including all those in the Thornton *Liber* [6/23–30, 7/5–7, 29–35, 13/9–18], the mixture was simply poured into the well ear. In others [*e.g.* Schöffler 195/25–196/7;

Heinrich 81a/6-17; and Dawson 266] it was applied with the wool of a black sheep. This practice is recorded in *Leechbook* I (Leonhardi) 14/4-6 and may have been introduced much earlier.

Few recipes illustrate better than these the typical similarities and differences existing among the various members of a closely related group of medieval recipes. As we have seen, there are four recipes belonging to this group in the Thornton MS.: 1) 7/5-7, which prescribes hawthorn branch juice; 2) and 3) 7/29-35, and its close verbal parallel, 13/9-18, which prescribe ash-branch juice and honey; and 4) 6/23-30, which prescribes ash-branch juice mixed with oil, honey, leek juice, and *senegrene* juice.

Pore leeke (l. 27) is probably a tautological compound, *porret* + *leek*, perh. influenced by M. Du. *porloc*, *poreiloc*, *poretloc*, 'leek.' Kilian (17th cent.) makes *poor-look* equivalent with *L. ascalonia*, a word usually designating the shallot.

6/31-32. Ant eggs are prescribed for ear trouble in Pliny (Mayhoff) xxix, 133; *Leechbook* I (Leonhardi) 13/23-24; and Dawson 268. A parallel to this recipe, containing oil in addition to the ant eggs and rue, appears in *Archiv Med.* II, 238.

6/33-34. Pliny (Mayhoff) xxix, 133 prescribes grease, especially goose grease, with *wormot* for hardness of hearing.

6/35-36. The gall of sheep, goats, and other animals was frequently prescribed in the treatment of deafness by the medical writers of antiquity and the early Middle Ages. Pliny prescribes the use of sheep gall with honey [Pliny (Mayhoff) xxix, 133], goat gall with woman's milk [*ibid.*, xxviii, 176], and cow's gall with sheep's or goat's urine [*ibid.*]. Alexander (Puschmann) II, 73 prescribes sheep gall and oil, and Paulus (Adams) III, 23 prescribes goat gall and urine. *Leechbook* I (Leonhardi) prescribes various kinds of gall mixed with cow's milk (13/24-25), goat's urine (13/26), oil (14/2-3), and honey (14/2-3). *Glasgow Antid.* (Sigerist) 140 prescribes the gall and urine of a she-goat.

Four other recipes against deafness prescribe a combination of gall with woman's milk : Pliny (Mayhoff) xxix, 133; Dawson 263; Larsen 207; and Thornton's 8/6-7. No other recipe specifically prescribing woman's urine for deafness has been found.

6/37-7/4. No parallels have been found to this recipe, which is ascribed to William de Excestre.

7/5-7. The relation of this recipe to a large group of similar recipes is treated in the notes to 6/23-30. Avicenna (Gruner) 376/722 prescribes boxthorn and oil for earache. Dawson 994 is a fairly close Middle English parallel.

7/9-11. *Coll. Salern.* (Renzi) V, 93 suggests the use of eel-fat for deafness. Middle English parallels : Dawson 262; Henslow B 109/18-20; Roy 12 G iv, ff. 188v, 220r/19-20.

7/12-13. Pliny (Mayhoff) xx, 146 and Rhazes (1510) *Ad Almans.* IX, 35 prescribe *mentastrum* juice for insects in the ears. *Mentastrum* mixed with wine is prescribed in *Camb. Antid.* (Sigerist) 165; Dawson 968; and *Anglia* XXXIV, 186/880-895.

7/18-19. Mint juice is prescribed for the ears in *Camb. Antid.* (Sigerist) 167 and Dawson 21. See notes to 7/12-13.

7/20-21. Pliny (Mayhoff) xx, 256 prescribes the juice of wild fennel against insects or worms in the ears.

7/26-28. This recipe is identical with 13/7-8 except for slight variations in spelling. Parallel: Müller 91/1-3. Wormwood alone is prescribed for the ears in Galen (Kühn) XII, 663; Alexander (Puschmann) II, 97; Paulus (Adams) III, 23; Constantinus (1510) II, 12; Platearius (1497) *Circum instans* 174v; *Leechbook* III (Leonhardi) 95/23-24; and Dawson 927. Rue alone is prescribed in Henslow D 136/16-18.

7/29-35. This recipe is substantially identical with 13/9-18. Its relation to a group of similar recipes is treated in the notes to 6/23-30.

7/36-38. This recipe is substantially identical with 13/19-21.

8/1-2. Coriander and woman's milk are prescribed for the ears in *Leechbook* I (Leonhardi) 13/39-40 and *Leechbook* III (Leonhardi) 95/19-20.

Notes. 87

8/3-5. The omitted word after *childes* seems to be *vryn*. Cf. Alexander (Puschmann) II, 89; Haly Abbas (Stephanus) II, 51; 17 St. John's Oxford (Singer) 149; Dawson 264.

8/6-7. Parallels are treated in the notes to 6/35-36.

8/8-9. Recipes prescribing wormwood alone are listed in the notes to 7/26-28. Woodbine alone is prescribed for the ears in *Anglia* XVIII, 298/125-132.

8/10-11. Parallels: Müller 85/15-17; 17 St. John's Oxford (Singer) 149. Pliny (Mayhoff) xxviii, 175 and Marcellus (Niedermann) IX, 104 prescribe the marrow of a fresh calf mixed with cumin for deafness. Avicenna (Gerard) *Canon* II, 492 recommends the marrow of calves for any sore on the body.

8/12-15. Parallels: Heinrich 81a/23-26; Müller 55/21-23, 110/15-17; Dawson 469; Roy 12 G iv, f. 188v.

8/16-17. *Reg. San. Salern.* (Harrington) 207/33 prescribes fennel to make the sight clear.

8/18-19. Parallels: *Coll. Salern.* (Renzi) V, 93; Dawson 513.

8/20-28. Very close parallels: Heinrich 81b/2-10; Müller 110/7-14. Parallels: Heinrich 87a/3-10; Henslow B 108/17-109/2. *Robbe hit on a whestoon in a fayre bacin* in Heinrich 81b/3-4 seems to be a better reading than *rub it on a whetstane or on a basyn* in Thornton, ll. 20-21.

Bartholomaeus Anglicus (British Museum, Additional MS. 27944 of Trevisa's translation) XVII, cxcv distinguishes two varieties of ginger, the tame and the wild:

> Gynger is the roote of an herbe and is hoote & moiste as it is yseyd in plat [? earius] and some gyngere is tame and som wilde. þe wilde is more sad and fast and nouʒt so white but it brekeþ more soone . . . and þat doþ bettre tame gynger þan wylde and þe more white it is and þe newer þe scharper it is and þe bettre.

Perh. the tame corresponds to the white scraped variety and the wild to the black unscraped variety of the dried root.

8/32-34. *Allerone* seems to be a borrowing of Old French *aileron*. Spelled *alrons*, it occurs also in the *Liber cure cocorum* [R. Morris, The Philological Society's early English volume (London, 1865), Part I, p. 49]. In the *Liber cure cocorum* it is used, as is *aileron* in modern French culinary parlance, to designate the tips of the wings of a fowl. In Thornton's recipe it seems to mean ' quill,' another sense of modern French *aileron*.

8/35-9/2. Parallel: Müller 138/6-8; Larsen 204.

9/5-6. Parallel: Avicenna (Gruner) 375/721.

9/7-8. Parallels: Dawson 24 and 494.

9/25-29. This recipe is essentially the same as 12/24-26. Marcellus (Niedermann) VIII, 25 recommends *atramentum sutorium* for sore eyes. Middle English parallels: Dawson 490; Heinrich 86a/7-10; Henslow D 136/9-11. Close Middle English parallel: Dawson 472.

In medical works, *arenement* and its Latin equivalent *attramentum* seem to have meant ' vitriol ' rather than ink. Cf. the discussion of *attramentum* in *Alphita* 17: "Attramentum, calcantum idem, quedem terra [est] in Gallia cuius due sunt species, [secundum quosdam] viz. uilior species est attramentum [et] nobilior species est uitriolum. . . . Et quando attramentum per se ponitur pro uiliori intelligitur."

9/30-10/2. *Calamynt* is probably an error for *calamine* or *calamite*, medieval equivalents of the Greek *cadmia*. Both Paulus (Adams) VII, 3 and Scribonius (Helmreich) 21 mention the use of cadmia in eye medicines. An eye recipe occurs in *Coll. Salern.* (Renzi) IV, 201 in which cadmia is similarly prepared: " Recipe lapidem calamitatem [*sic*] quem Graeci *cathmion* dicunt; ipsum lapidem in foce mite et coque per 11 dies et totidem noctes, et calidum in aceto extingue." [Cf. an Old Norse translation of this Salernitan recipe in Larsen 205.] A fairly close Middle English parallel with *calamine* instead of *calamynt* appears in Dawson 497.

10/5-6. Parallels: *Leechbook* I (Leonhardi) 10/1-2; Henslow B 109/3-5; Heinrich 81a/27-30; Dawson 507; Roy 12 G iv, f. 188v.

10/10–14. The fat from boiled red slugs is prescribed in: Dawson 476; Müller 55/17–20, 71/20–72/3; *Anglia* XVIII, 297/85–92; Henslow B 107/6–7. The ashes of snails are prescribed in: Pliny (Mayhoff) xxix, 127; Paulus (Adams) III, 22; Henslow A 32/3–4; Henslow B 107/8–9.

10/15–25. Cf. 12/18–20, which is similar in general procedure. Avicenna (Gerard) *Canon* II, 727 prescribes for the eyes the application of urine-sediment that has collected in bronze jars.

10/26–31. Paulus (Adams) VII, 3 and *Reg. San. Salern.* (Harrington) 171 recommend the use of celandine for the eyes. Middle English parallels: Müller 85/1–6; Dawson 25.

10/32–34. Parallels: 17 St. John's Oxford (Singer) 147; Larsen 205.

10/35–39. Close parallels: Henslow B 108/3–7; Roy 12 G iv, f. 192v. Avicenna (Gruner) 375/721 recommends an eye salve of May butter and cumin.

11/1–2. Parallels: Constantinus (1510) II, 3; Henslow B 104/4–6; Roy 12 G iv, f. 220r; Larsen 204. Celsus (Marx) iv, 4 prescribes ashes of swallows for the eyes. Haly Abbas (Stephanus) X, 22 recommends swallow's dung for white spots on the eyes. Avicenna (Gerard) *Canon* II, 356 says that to eat swallows will sharpen the eyesight. Contrast, however, Tobit's blindness, caused by the dropping of hot swallow's-dung upon his eyes. (Bk. Tobit II, 11.)

11/3–6. Parallels: Dawson 473, 503, 995; Heinrich 87a/26–31; Müller 112/4–8. In the parallels some of the names of ingredients have become corrupted.

11/7–14. Parallels: Schöffler 193/14–19; Heinrich 81b/11–19; Henslow B 107/18–108/2; Roy 12 G iv, f. 189r; Dawson 501. The animals from which grease is taken vary slightly in some of these parallels.

11/25. Galen several times recommends pepper for sore eyes [Galen (Kühn) XII, 728, 730–731, 734–735].

11/26–27. Parallels: Dawson 502; Heinrich 87b/1–5; Müller 112/9–11; Sextus Placitus (Sigerist) 245/74–78 [*Med. Quad.* (Cockayne I) 345/7]. Constantinus (1541) I says that the gall of a hare makes the eyes clear.

11/28–32. Dawson 496 prescribes a mixture of the gall of a swine, an eel, and a cock tempered with honey and clear water, calling it the *medecyn pat ypocras vside*. Dawson was unable to find such a recipe in the *Corpus Hippocraticum*. The present editor of the Thornton *Liber* was likewise unable to discover parallels in the *Corpus Hippocraticum* either to Dawson 496 or to the somewhat similar Thornton 11/28–32.

Animal galls seem to have been much used for the eyes. It will be remembered that fish gall restored the sight of Tobit (Bk. Tobit VI, 8–9, XI, 13). Pliny (Mayhoff) xxviii, 146 states that the gall of the smaller animals is good for the eyes. Serapion (1497) *De simpl. med.* 459; Avicenna (Gerard) *Canon* II, 255; and Averrhoes (1560) V, 49 recommend many kinds of gall for eye trouble. Najm (Guigues) 164/4 approaches the so-called Hippocratic collyrium most closely in a recipe recommending the use of cock, shad, lamb, and crane gall mixed with fennel, boxthorn juice, musk, and camphor.

The varieties of aloes were frequently distinguished in medieval lists of materia medica. A typical passage giving the characteristics of socotrine and hepatic aloes occurs in Platearius (1497) *Circum instans s. aloes*: "Optimum autem aloes est cicotrinum; et discernitur ex citrino colore . . . ex substantia clara. . . . Epaticum epatis assimilatur . . . obscuram habet substantiam: et non claram." Socotrine aloes are used in several collyriums appearing in Najm (Guigues) 161/13, 16.

11/33–35. Lines 29 and 31 are from the *Regimen sanitatis salernitanum*. In most versions of the *Regimen*, the lines occur together as a couplet:

Feniculis, verbena, rosa, celidonia, ruta,
Ex istis fit aqua quae lumina reddit acuta.
[*Reg. San. Salern.* (Harrington) 173].

In some versions of the *Regimen*, the following interpolated line appears in the midst of the couplet:

Subveniunt oculis dira caligine pressis.

[*Coll. Salern.* (Renzi) I, 509/1961]. In none of the versions of the poem examined, including some twenty early printed editions (1491–1661), does l. 34 occur between the lines of the couplet. Cf. notes to 42/9–12, treating Thornton's other quotation from the *Regimen sanitatis*.

11/36–37. Pliny (Mayhoff) xxvii, 18; Paulus (Adams) III, 22; Avicenna (Gerard) *Canon* II, 66; and Najm (Guigues) 161/13, 16 prescribe aloes for sore eyes.

11/38–39. Pliny (Mayhoff) xxv, 142 and Alexander (Puschmann) II, 67 prescribe the application of henbane boiled in wine for a sore on the eye.

12/2–3. Cf. notes to 11/26–27, 28–32.

12/9–10. Similar recipes: Henslow B 107/18–108/2; Müller 110/18–24.

12/18–20. Cf. 10/15–25, which is similar in general procedure.

12/24–26. See notes to 9/25–29, which is essentially the same recipe.

12/30–32. Parallel: Müller 85/7–10.

12/33. *Rede fenell* may have been fennel with red or reddish seeds. Cf. *fenell with þe sede rouge*, 67/10. Perhaps, with the looseness of medieval colour names, red fennel seeds may have been the dark, reddish-brown seeds of German, or Saxon, fennel, as distinguished from the green seeds of sweet, or Roman, fennel. On the other hand, it may have been the sub-variety described in Lyte transl. Dodoens *Niewe Herball* (1578), p. 269 : " There is an other sorte of this kinde of Fenell [*i.e.* true Fenell], whose leaves waxe darke, with a certayne kinde of thicke or tawny redde colour, but otherwise in all things like the first."

13/7–8. This recipe is identical with 7/26–28 except for slight variations of spelling. Cf. 7/26–28.

13/9–18. This recipe is substantially identical with 7/29–35. Its relation to a group of similar recipes is treated in the notes to 6/23–30.

13/19–21. This recipe is substantially identical with 7/36–38.

13/22–28. *Pentaphylon* appears occasionally in Latin medical works : *Pentaphyllon a numero foliorum dicta, unde eam Latini quinque folium vocant*, Isidore (Migne) XVII, ix, 38; *Pentaphylon . . . est nominatus quinque-folia*, Avicenna (Gerard) *Canon* II, 552; *Pentafilon id est quinque folium*, 17 St. John's Oxford (Singer) 134.

Dioscurides (Wellman) iv, 42, 3 and Avicenna (Gerard) *Canon* II, 552 recommend cinquefoil for sore throat. Scribonius (Helmreich) liii recommends for sore throat a gargle of cinquefoil mixed with wine. Middle English parallels : Schöffler 204/12–16, 199/16–200/3; Heinrich 81b/19–28; Henslow B 101/22–102/6; Roy 12 G iv, f. 189r.

13/29–32. Close parallel : *Camb. Antid.* (Sigerist) 165 : " Potio ad colum probata a multis medicis maxime a Marcello : Sal communis—I, ciminum—I, piper—I, omnia tunde, cerne, da ex eo cocl. I in aqua calida, mirum est."

13/33–37. Pliny (Mayhoff) xxiv, 9 prescribes an application of oak galls and vinegar for the eyes. *Strynge* (l. 37) and *strynges* (side-note 7) present difficulties. String, meaning ' eye-string,' has usually been taken to refer to muscles of the eyes, considered as breaking with loss of sight or at death. This can scarcely be the meaning here, as the recipe ends : " it [*i.e.* the application of oakgall and vinegar] sall for-do þe perle [*i.e.* the cataract] & breke þe strynge of þe eghn " (ll. 36–37).

14/3. Pliny (Mayhoff) xx, 149 and *Glasgow Antid.* (Sigerist) 154 prescribe mint juice against hoarseness. Contemporary parallel : Müller 93/17–18.

14/14. The use of the blood of a hare to remove freckles is prescribed in Sextus Placitus (Sigerist) 245/127–129; *Coll. Salern.* (Renzi) IV, 204; and Constantinus (1541) I. *Glasgow Antid.* (Sigerist) 141 recommends the blood of a hare mixed with wine for removing freckles or facial spots. Middle English parallel : Schöffler 203/5. Cf. notes to 22/17–18.

14/15–19. Parallels to ll. 15–16: Heinrich 81b/29–82a/2; Müller 111/1–3, 96/19–21; Henslow A 37/3–4; Henslow B 111/1–2, 102/7–9; Roy 12 G iv, ff. 189r, 220r. Parallels to ll. 17–19: *Romania* XXXVII, 368/61; Henslow B 79/20–80/1; Dawson 839. In Schöffler 200/4–9 these two recipes occur successively. A parallel has not been found to the intervening recipe which appears on l. 17.

14/25-26. Parallel: *Romania* XXXVII, 368/61.

14/27-31. Parallels to ll. 27-28: Henslow A 10/5-7; Heinrich 82a/5-8; Roy. 12 G iv, f. 189r; Müller 111/4-6. Parallels to ll. 27-28 followed by parallels to ll. 29-31: Dawson 837; Müller 96/22-25. Parallel to ll. 29-31; Roy 12 G iv, f. 220r. *Gayttes mylke* (l. 28) seems to be the correct reading, though Müller 111/4-6 and one MS. of Heinrich 82a/5-8 have *good mylk*(e.

14/32-33. Contemporary parallels: Müller 97/1-3; Heinrich 82a/2-5; Roy 12 G iv, ff. 189r, 220r. A Latin parallel appears in *Camb. Antid.* (Sigerist) 165: "Ad eos qui per os sanguinem uomunt: Uetonica—II et lac caprinum recens per triduum bibat." *Drink . . . thris* (l. 33) is equivalent to the more usual phrase, *drynk . . .* 111 *dayis* (Müller 97/3).

14/37-15/2. Other recipes prescribing fennel and honey for the stomach are: *Reg. San. Salern.* (Harrington) 207/33; Schöffler 230/12-18, 253/19-254/2; Heinrich 128a/24-25.

15/5. Parallels: Dawson 838; *Peri Di* (Cockayne III) 137/63.

15/10-11. Parallels: Heinrich 82a/8-9; Müller 111/7-8.

15/15. Bartholomeus Anglicus (British Museum, Additional MS. 27944 of Trevisa's translation) XVII, xli gives the following account of *safron orientale*: "Ysider [&] dias[corides] . . . spekeþ of tweye maner saffron oon is ortensis & haþ þe name of gardynes ffor he groweþ þer Inne . . . þe oþer hatte Orientalis and haþ also þe name of þe place þat he groweþ Inne and is the beste and schal nouzt be y do in medicynes and he bereþ a reed flour wiþ an heed as a violette and in þe myddil þer of þre floures oþer foure and þe beste þerof be somdel reede oþer al rede and þe whiteste schal be for sake." Cf. Thompson *Mat. Med. Painting*, pp. 184-186.

15/17-20. Parallel: Schöffler 253/12-16.

15/21-30. Fennel, anise, and mallows are prescribed for the stomach in *Reg. San. Salern.* (Harrington) 167, 168.

15/31-32. Parallels: Heinrich 82a/9-11; 92a/23-29; Schöffler 196/14-15; Henslow A 8/3-5, 68/5-6, 72/13-14; Henslow B 110/15-17, 96/1-5; Dawson 596, 623; Müller 97/4-6, 116/32-35; Roy 12 G iv, f. 189r.

15/33-34. On the basis of an entry in Halliwell's *Dictionary of archaisms and provincialisms* referring to but not quoting this recipe, Britten-Holland *Dict.* 468 includes a *throck-needle* identified as *Scandix Pecten*. Halliwell seems to have mistranscribed *thros-nedils* as *throc nedils*, as he uses this spelling for his catchword.

15/35-36. *Puliol* boiled in wine is prescribed in Schöffler 196/18 against stinking breath from the nose.

16/7-10. Parallels: Müller 97/14-98/2; Roy 12 G iv, f. 189r.

16/20-21. Except for the mention of horse marrow, 16/20-21 is substantially identical with 18/11-12. Other parallels: Henslow A 8/16-17; Müller 98/11-12; Roy 12 G iv, f. 189r.

16/24-26. Parallels: Henslow A 45/15-17; Henslow B 112/10-13; Roy 12 G iv, f. 193v.

16/30-31. Juice of leeks is prescribed for toothache in Pliny (Mayhoff) xx, 53 and Avicenna (Gerard) *Canon* II, 74.

16/32-35. Oribasius (Raeder) X, 36 recommends that pepper be put into the cavity of an aching tooth. The following works prescribe the holding of powdered pepper and warm or hot urine in the mouth as a cure for toothache: Avicenna (Gerard) *Canon* II, 556; Heinrich 87b/6-12; Schöffler 201/8-12; Roy 12 G iv, f. 189r.

17/5-6. Pliny (Mayhoff) xxiv, 77 advises that for toothache the juice of ground ivy berries should be poured into the ear on the opposite side. Parallels: Avicenna (Gerard) *Canon* II, 172; *Archiv Med.* II, 240.

17/11-18. Fumigations with henbane seed were much used both in antiquity and in the Middle Ages as a remedy for toothache. They are prescribed in Scribonius (Helmreich) liv; Galen (Kühn) XII, 869, 877, 878, XIV, 428; Marcellus (Niedermann) XII, 2; Paulus (Adams) III, 26; *Mag. Salern.*

106/80v; and Plateariua (1497) *Circum instans* 176. Two methods of fumigation seem to have been most common. In the first method, the patient inhaled the smoke of a candle made of henbane, wax, etc. In the second, the patient inhaled the fumes of henbane, incense, etc. laid on a hot stone. Fumigations of the candle type are prescribed in 18/4-7. *Reg. San. Salern.* (Harrington) 173 prescribes a fumigation of the incense-stone type with henbane seed, leek seed, and incense, similar to that of 17/11-18. Other Middle English versions of this type are: Heinrich 82a/12-19; Müller 97/7-12; Dawson 33, 912; Roy 12 G iv, f. 189r; Henslow A 8/6-10; Henslow B 95/14-20, 111/19-112/2; Henslow D 139/14.

These Middle English parallels illustrate very well the shifting similarities and dissimilarities characteristic of such recipes. The ingredients and process are essentially the same in all. *Frankincense* appears as *rekills* in some of the versions, as *stor* in Henslow B 111-112 and Roy 12 G iv, f. 189r, and as *floure* (perhaps a corruption of *stor*) in Dawson 33. The statements of method differ considerably, though the process described is clearly the same. Almost all end with a statement parallel to the Thornton: *it sal sla þe wormes & fordo þe werke.*

Thornton's *glowande tile stane* (l. 12) and *hote tile stone* (l. 15) indicate dialect mixture. This slight admixture of non-Northern forms adds interest to the forms in the parallels. All recipes which continue closely parallel through *glowande tile stane* (l. 12) have *glowing(e*, or *glowyng(e til-, tyl-, teyl-*, etc. *-ston(e,* or *stoun.* Unfortunately, no version follows ll. 14-17 closely enough to point to a parallel confirming *hote tile stone* (l. 15). None of the recipes ending with statements closely parallel to ll. 17-18 have the Northern *it sall sla*, but all have either *that wil (wol) sle(n)* or *it shall (schal) sle.* These consistently non-Northern parallels suggest that perhaps here Thornton may have been converting a recipe from a more southerly dialect into his own, lapsing into the form of the original in *hote tile stone* (l. 15).

17/19-21. Pharmaceutically this recipe is identical with 18/8-10, though differently expressed. Other parallels: Scribonius (Helmreich) liii; Plateariua (1497) *Circum instans s. iusquiamus.*

17/22-24. Parallels: Schöffler 257/11-13; Henslow B 95/21-24; *Anglia* XVIII, 299/167-170; Larsen 208. *þe taughe of a tupe* is paralleled by: *schepis talwe (Anglia)*; *schepes talgh* (Henslow B); *schepis talow* (Schöffler); *flot þat er rennur ur hruta kioti* (Larsen).

17/25-34. No parallels have been found to clarify ll. 32-33.

18/1-2. Pliny (Mayhoff) xxviii, 178; Galen (Kühn) XIV, 240; Sextus Placitus (Sigerist) 235/6-9 [as well as the Old English translation of Sextus Placitus: *Med. Quad.* (Cockayne I) 335/3]; and Avicenna (Gerard) *Canon* II, 181 prescribe burnt hart's horn ashes for toothache. Middle English parallels: Henslow B 112/14-16; Müller 98/3-5.

18/8-10. Pharmaceutically this recipe is identical with 17/19-21, though expressed differently. *Kerif* is a variant of *kerf*, 'carve,' as is indicated by the following parallel in Roy 12 G iv, f. 189r: " Take þe rote of henbane & kerf hit on peces & ley on þy toth iij nytes & hit schal sle þe wormes."

18/11-12. 18/11-12 is substantially identical with 16/20-21, except for the addition of horse marrow in the latter recipe. Other parallels are listed in the notes to 16/20-21.

18/13-30. Although no charm for toothache identical with all of this one has been found, there is some parallelism to ll. 25-28 in Müller 130/19-21 and to ll. 23-30 in Heinrich 104b/23-105a/4. How conventional are the phrases of the charm may be seen from the supplications to St. Apollonia in Gaddesden (Cholmeley) 49; *Germania* XIII, 179; *Germania* XXXII, 454; *Zeitschrift f. deutsch. Alt.* XXXVIII, 16.

19/32-33. Parallel: Paulus (Adams) III, 24. Pepper mixed with mastic is recommended to clear the head of humours in Paulus (Adams) I, 46.

19/34-35. *Centory* in hot water is prescribed for loss of appetite in *Leechbook* II (Leonhardi) 56/31. Middle English parallels: Müller 98/19-21; Henslow A 69/1-3; Heinrich 82b/6-10.

Notes.

19/36–38. Parallels: Henslow A 9/5–6; Müller 98/16–18. Cf. þou gost, in both parallels, with the Thornton þu gase.

20/1–4. Parallels: Henslow A 9/1–4; Dawson 1010. The Henslow A version is headed: *Electuarium pro illis qui non possunt comedere*; the Dawson: *To staunch þrist*.

20/5–7. This recipe is substantially identical with 25/28–31 except that, in the latter recipe, *centory* is added as an alternate for lovage root, and lukewarm white wine is specified instead of merely wine. Other parallels: Henslow A 8/18–20; Heinrich 82b/10–13; Müller 99/1–4, 111/15–17; Dawson 1008.

20/8–9. Alexander (Puschmann) II, 317 prescribes holding the feet and the finger tips in water as a remedy for hiccoughs. Dawson 1013 prescribes holding the hands of the hiccoughing patient in hot water or ale. Henslow A 69/6–7 is a fairly close parallel.

20/13–16. Parallels: Henslow A 69/4–5; Dawson 1015. Neither parallel adds the direction to the patient to hold his breath as long as he can, a detail which has lingered to modern times as a home remedy for hiccoughs.

20/17–22. No parallels have been found to this interesting recipe attributed to the Rector of Oswaldkirk. Both ȝucre (28/1) and ȝucre caffatine (20/20) occur, in the *Liber*, only in recipes attributed to the Rector of Oswaldkirk. This is one of several details seeming to connect the recipes attributed to the Rector of Oswaldkirk with a sophisticated rather than a popular vocabulary and tradition.

20/30–34. Close parallels: Henslow A 9/15–20; Dawson 550. The Thornton heading seems to be a short version of the heading which appears in the parallels: " A lectuary for many yuels for the host for the brest for rotelynge in the throte for byles for sores in the side for the myst and for the stomach " (Dawson 550). *Mylte* (l. 31 and Henslow A, l. 16) is probably a better reading than *myst* (Dawson 550).

20/35–36. Parallel: Dawson 551. Henslow A 10/1–2 prescribes sage stamped and drunk *wiþ-oute water* in a recipe immediately following a parallel to 20/30–34.

20/37. An interesting parallel appears in *Leechbook* I (Leonhardi) 18/40–41: " Wiþ driȝum hwostan eft ȝenim eolonam [i.e. *horshelm*] & ȝalluc [i.e. comfrey], ete on huniȝes teare." Middle English parallels: Dawson 191, Heinrich 82b/17–25; Müller 99/8–10; Henslow A 9/13–14; Henslow B 115/4–5. The original ingredients seem to have been *horshelm* and comfrey, although other plants are mentioned instead of these in some of the parallels, e.g. *horehounde* (Dawson), *h)orshouue* (Henslow A and B) and *consilie* (Henslow A).

As has been pointed out by previous editors of recipe collections, the *dry coghe* (side-note 12) and the *dry hoste* (side-note 11) refer to a cough caused by excessive dryness in the complexion of the patient, not a cough accompanied by little or no expectoration. See Müller 99/n.3 and Schöffler 32–33.

21/1–3. Dawson 552 is parallel except that, in it, pepper is omitted.

21/15–17. Both the *Practica Petrocelli* and its English version, the *Peri Didaxeon*, prescribe pepper, cumin, and rue mixed with honey for a sore uvula. [*Peri Di* (Cockayne III) 107/36; *Peri Di* (Löweneck) 20/31, 21/36]. Middle English parallels: Heinrich 82b/13–16; Müller 99/5–8, 111/18–21; Dawson 190; Henslow A 9/10–12, 69/11–13; Henslow B 101/5–9, 114/18–21.

21/33–34. Parallels: Henslow A 12/3–5; Schöffler 210/18–21. Heinrich 82b/26–28 prescribes *quint foile* tempered with stale ale *Pro torcione & dolore ventris*.

21/35–36. *Herb. Ap.* (Sigerist) 22/5–7 and its Old English translation, *Herb. Ap.* (Cockayne I) 81/2, prescribe warm plantain juice for the stomach.

22/1–2. Parallel: Heinrich 82b/28–29.

22/3–4. *It'* (l. 3) is apparently an abbreviation of L. *item*. Possibly this was copied verbatim from a recipe in which *item* was used to indicate that the chief or sole ingredient of the preceding recipe was likewise to be used in it. Were *rewe* substituted for *it'*, Henslow A 69/14–16 would be a fairly close parallel to 22/3–4: " Who-so hat wryngyng in hys wombe. Nyme rewe and stampe

hit wiþ stale ale or with water, and drynke hit; and hit schal do þe goud."
Another example of *it'* occurs in 22/30; see note.

22/6–7. Parallel : Roy 12 G iv, f. 220v.

22/8–10. A close early parallel occurs in *Camb. Antid.* (Sigerist) 163 : " Item [i.e. Ad tortione uentris] folia rute XV, piperis grana IX, aneti semen ut III leuent teris cum aqua, bibat." Of the two Middle English parallels, Henslow A 69/17–19 is more closely similar to the Thornton version of the recipe than Henslow A 12/6–8.

22/10–12. The drinking of rue *ad inflationem (uentris)* is prescribed in *Camb. Antid.* (Sigerist) 162. Henslow A 69/14–16 prescribes rue stamped with stale ale or water for *wryngyng in hys wombe*.

22/17–18. Sextus Placitus (Sigerist) 267/6–8 and Constantinus (1541) recommend the blood of a bull for removing facial spots. Sextus Placitus (Sigerist) 245/127–129 prescribes the blood of a hare for removing freckles. Of the Middle English versions of this recipe, one (Heinrich 87b/13–16) is closely parallel to the Thornton recipe. Another (Heinrich 132a/22–27) prescribes bull's blood washed away with bean water. Several recipes prescribe bull's blood alone for freckles or facial spots : Dawson 339; Müller 90/20–22; Henslow B 113/1–2. For recipes prescribing only hare's blood, see note to 14/14.

22/19–20. Black soap and quicksilver are prescribed *Ad morpheam* in Heinrich 145b/1–6.

22/21–23. Parallels : Henslow A 34/14–35/2 ; Roy 12 G iv, f. 192v. " Ffor þe red bleynus in þe face take þe rote of weybrode & salt & þe rote of burres stamp hem togidere with eysel & þer with wasche þy face " (Roy 12 G iv, f. 192v).

22/30–31. *It'* is apparently an abbreviation of L. *item* copied from a recipe in which it was used to indicate that the chief or sole ingredient in the preceding recipe was to be used here likewise. Cf. note on the other occurrence of *it'*, 22/3–4.

22/32–34. A potion of fennel and ache root is prescribed, *Ad stomachi inflationem*, in *Camb. Antid.* (Sigerist) 164. Middle English parallels : Henslow A 11/13–15 ; Heinrich 82b/4–6 ; Schöffler 207/28–208/1 ; Roy 12 G iv, f. 189r ; Müller 111/12–14 ; Dawson 856, 1002.

23/11–12. *Reg. San. Salern.* (Harrington) 170 and *Anglia* XVIII, 330/940–945 state that hyssop is good for the breast. Heinrich 93a/19–22 prescribes hyssop and wine *Pro pectore reumatico .i. encombered*, and Schöffler 205/1–3 hyssop and ale *for streytnesse off þe brest*. Close parallel : Dawson 1004.

23/13–17. Parallels : Schöffler 207/9–16 ; Heinrich 106a/20–28. The briefer recipe, Dawson 862, is similar, except for the substitution of *camamyll* for *calamynt*.

23/18–20. *Leechbook* I (Leonhardi) 19/6–8 prescribes rue, *averoyne*, horehound, and honey for the breast.

23/28–29. Petrocellus (Löweneck) 38/17–40/5 [*Peri Di* (Cockayne III) 129/60] prescribes rue and vinegar for various ailments of the breast and stomach.

23/33–36. Parallel : Müller 100/4–8. *It'* (l. 33) is probably *it* and not an abbreviation of L. *item*. See notes to 22/3–4, 30–31, where *it'* seems to be an abbreviation of *item*.

24/8. The glossing of *grete groun mustard* as ' coarsely ground mustard ' is suggested by such phrases as the following : *mustard grete grounden*, Roy 12 G iv, f. 220v ; *ones grounden mustard, ibid.*, f. 211v.

24/22–26. Henslow B 115/9–11 directs that brimstone be powdered, soaked in vinegar, and rubbed on the morphea.

24/27–35. Middle English parallels : Heinrich 82a/22–30 ; Henslow A 10/8–15 ; Dawson 1001. An Anglo-French parallel is given in Heinrich 148a/9–21 :

> En contre le maladie de coer & de stomak engleyme que fet homme quant il nad talent amanger Prenez centorye & quises bien en bon seruoice & stale, & quant il est bien quite, prenez les herbes hors & braies, & les metes arere en le seruoice e quises dere chief, & puys quilles perun

vne draps nete de lynge, & dunque prene3 le tierce partie de mel clarfye, & les .ij. parties de ceo, & medles ensembles & quises altre foitz tanque il soit espe, & puisse mettes en boistes, & dones les malades aboire chescun jour .iij. quoilles, & si il garra, & auera boun talent amanger et oustera tout3 le glettons en tut le quere.

24/36-38. Parallel: Müller 99/11-13.

24/39-40. In Müller 99/14-16 a potion of ache seed, cumin, and linseed is prescribed for the heart. Parallels to the Müller recipe are listed in Müller 99, n. 5.

25/3-17. Parallel: Henslow A 10/19-11/12. It is probable that both versions of this recipe have come from a common original. Neither recipe seems to give a consistently better picture of this original than the other. Henslow A has *horshouue* instead of *horsehelme* (l. 4), omits *saueray* (l. 6), and gives *centorie* twice. The Thornton recipe lists both *mogworte* and *modirworte*, both *nept* and *mynt*. *Serlange*, in Henslow A, appears as *longe de cerfe* in Thornton (ll. 4-5). Henslow A has *fairrour* instead of *fynere* (l. 14) and adds: " 3yf hit be a strong man or woman, do þer-to þe lasse licoris " before the direction to add more honey if the patient is feeble (ll. 9-10).

25/28-31. This recipe is substantially identical with 20/5-7 except that it adds centory as an alternate for lovage root and specifies lukewarm white wine instead of just wine. For parallels, see notes to 20/5-7.

25/39-40. Parallels: Dawson 748; Henslow A 17/16-18.

26/1-2. Dragance root with wine is prescribed against snake bites by Pliny (Mayhoff) xxiv, 150; *Herb. Ap.* (Sigerist) 47/1-4; *Herb. Ap.* (Cockayne I) 109/2; and *Anglia* XVIII, 324/685-688.

26/3-13. Betony is given particular prominence in a number of medical works. It is not clear whether this special emphasis existed in antiquity or was largely influenced by the *De herba vettonica* attributed to Antonius Musa and closely associated with the *Herbarium* of Apuleius and the *Liber Medicinae* of Sextus Placitus. The verse treatise on herbs in the Stockholm Medical MS. begins with betony and devotes nearly twice as many lines to it as to any other herb. Henslow A 70/18-71/21 contains a long passage headed *Here beþ þe vertues of betayne* that includes medical uses of betony, most of which are mentioned in *De herba vettonica*.

Recipes prescribing betony for *fanteme* or *trauellyng in slepe* are listed in the notes to 2/35-36. General prescriptions of betony as an antidote to poison may be found in Henslow A 71/19-20; *Anglia* XVIII, 308/37-38, 309/47-58; Roy 12 G iv f., 189r.

Musa (Sigerist) 10/158-160 prescribes: "Ad serpentiam morsus. Vettonicae dragmas III, in uini eminis III dilutum, potui datum, omnium serpentium morsus sanat." In the Anglo-Saxon translation the patient is directed to drink the weight of three *tremissis* of betony mixed with four cupfuls of wine [*Herb. Ap.* (Cockayne I) 79/22]. In *Leechbook* I (Leonhardi) 34/6-8 the weight of three pennies of betony mixed with three cups (*bollan*) of wine is prescribed as a poison antidote. A close parallel to the Thornton recipe in ll. 3-7 occurs in Roy 12 G iv, f. 189r:

> Anoþur 3if þu drunken venyme or puyson take betayn & drye hit & make poudur þer of take of poudur as miche as þu may take by twene þy iij fyngeres twyus & do þer to iij cuppe ful of wyne & Sethe hem well togedre til þe þridde parte be soden in & drynk hit fastyng.

26/16. Dawson 133 states that garlic mixed with honey destroys the poison of a dog's bite.

26/17-18. Both this recipe and that in ll. 21-22 below seem to be versions of a poison antidote prescribing a potion of hemp seed boiled in goat's milk. The following Old French version appears in *Romania* XXXVII, 363/18:

> En contre tot venim et empoisounement, cuisiez chanevieus en let de chevre, et desi a la tierce part, et pis en boive l'enferm par .iij. jorz, quer soz ciel n'a si bonne medecine fors triacle.

Henslow B 83/8–11 is a fairly close translation of the French text, with the hitherto unexplained *seede of chaune* (or *chanue*) for the French *chanevieus*.

26/24–27. Horehound with old wine is prescribed as an antidote potion in *Herb. Ap.* (Sigerist) 95/14–15 [*Herb. Ap.* (Cockayne I) 151/5].

26/31–32. Parallel: Henslow A 13/12–14.

27/7–12. A close parallel to both parts of this double recipe occurs in Roy 12 G iv, f. 193v. *Dayesye* appears in Roy 12 G iv instead of *baynwort*. This tends to confirm our tentative identification on *baynewort* as daisy, *Bellis perennis*, L.

27/13–15. Parallels: Dawson 717, 916; Roy 12 G iv, f. 193v.

27/16–17. Hemlock is recommended for this same purpose in Pliny (Mayhoff) xxv, 154; Serapion (1497) *De simpl. med.* III, 347; Avicenna (Gerard) *Canon* II, 671; *Coll. Salern.* (Renzi) IV, 38; and Macer (1527) 43.

27/17–18. Avicenna (Gerard) *Canon* II, 357 directs the anointing of women's breasts with henbayne (*hyoscyamus*). Dioscurides (Wellman) iv, 68, 4 and Pliny (Mayhoff) xxvi, 152 prescribe henbane [Medieval Latin *iusquiamus*, cf. *Sinon. Bart.* 14 and *Alphita* 20] and wine for the breasts. Perhaps *iusquiamiadi* (or *-aimadi*) is a variant of *iusquiamus*.

27/19–21. Platearius (1497) *Circum instans* 187 gives a recipe that closely parallels this, except that he uses *amoniaco* for *aromatica* (l. 19). Cf. the following from Bartholomaeus Anglicus (British Museum, Additional MS. 27944 of Trevisa's Translation) XVII, lxxviii: " Right as galbanum is þe droppyng of a certeyn tree oþer herbe and haþ anoþer name and hatte armoniacum, twigges & sprayes of þis tree men of þe lond kerueþ in somer tyme and þe droppyng þat droppeþ þer of is ycleped gutta and armoniacum also among phisicians as ysid seiþ."

27/22–24. Avicenna (Gerard) *Canon* II, 671 and Larsen 153 prescribe the use of hemlock to dry up the breasts.

27/27–28. Pliny (Mayhoff) xx, 256; Dawson 898; and Henslow A 45/18–19 prescribe vervain alone for producing milk. Ketham (Sudhoff-Singer) x prescribes fennel alone for the same purpose. Parallels: Heinrich 84b/29–31; Müller 107/20–21.

27/31–34. This recipe, attributed to the Rector of Oswaldkirk, is closely paralleled in *Camb. Antid.* (Sigerist) 162:

> Ad uentrem mouendum : Aneti semen, feniculi semen, coriandri semen, rute semen, livestici semen, petrosilini semen ana—I, sal communis—I. Ex his fac puluerem molissimum et dabis exinde plenum coclear in uno sorbili.

Except for its addition to *comyn*, Larsen 196 also contains a close parallel to this recipe.

27/36–38. Other recipes prescribe the use of fresh pork broth boiled with certain herbs as a laxative: Dawson 186, 187; Heinrich 83a/16–20; Müller 55/11–13. The Thornton recipe includes the longest list of herbs. Mallows, mercury, borage, and violet seem to be the herbs appearing most frequently in the versions of this recipe.

28/8–12. Parallel: Serapion (1497) *De simpl. med.* VII, 16. Haly Abbas (Stephanus) X, 10 prescribes white turbit, sesame, and sugar as a laxative.

28/13–15. Mallow is mentioned as a laxative in Paulus (Adams) I, 43; Macer (1527) 41/2; and *Reg. San. Salern.* (Harrington) 168. Arderne (Power) 11/26–27 prescribes mallow and swine's grease against costiveness. Parallels: Müller 100/9–12; Dawson 555 (with *hokkes* instead of *malues*); Henslow A 12/9–11 (with *mapnes* instead of *malues*).

28/19–21. This recipe and 29/30–31 are alike in prescribing the external application of bull's or ox's gall for constipation. Here it is to be applied with wool to the navel, in 29/30–31 it is to be rubbed on the anus. Serapion (1497) *De simpl. med.* 459 gives an exact parallel of 28/19–21. Larsen 196 gives a parallel of 29/30–31. Avicenna (Gruner) 373/715 prescribes the application of bull's gall to the navel without mention of the use of wool, while Sextus Placitus (Sigerist) 267/13–17 prescribes the application of bull's gall to the anus with wool. Henslow A 12/12–13 seems to belong to this group, having *ancle* erroneously for either *anus* or *navel*.

28/32-37. Similar directions for clysters are to be found in Paulus (Adams) I, 44; Dawson 188; and Arderne (Power) 29/23-32.

28/38-29/3. Polypody boiled in hen broth was prescribed as an aperient in Pliny (Mayhoff) xxix, 80; Alexander (Puschmann) II, 363; and Mesue (Platearius) 70 B. An old cock instead of a hen was recommended for use with polypody in Dioscurides (Wellman) ii, 49; Avicenna (Gerard) *Canon* II, 296; Serapion (1497) *De simpl. med.* 429. Middle English recipes resembling 28/38-29/3 are Heinrich 95b/24-96a/1; Dawson 1028; Müller 87/18-29. As *euerfernie* and *polipodi* are synonymous, so far as can be discerned, the *&* joining them probably should be regarded as an error for *id est*. In 37/34, 41/31, 61/12, and 63/1 it is the *euerfern(e* that is mentioned as growing on the oak.

29/11-13. Wallwort and honey are prescribed as a laxative in *Camb. Antid.* (Sigerist) 164 and Dawson 189.

29/16-17. Pliny (Mayhoff) xxvi, 64 prescribes tithymal as a laxative. The following parallel occurs in *Camb. Antid.* (Sigerist) 164 : " Item titimalo radice sicca ad solem et postea puluer facis, sic potes dare ubi uolueris solutionem."

29/22-23. The same recipe, differently worded, occurs in 30/6-7. The closest parallels to this twice-repeated recipe occur in *Herb. Ap.* (Sigerist) 26/5-7 [*Herb. Ap.* (Cockayne) I 87/2] and *Camb. Antid.* (Sigerist) 165. Both of these recipes specify two spoonfuls of *quinquefolium*. Among the other parallels, Roy 12 G iv, f. 193r prescribes quintfoil, not specifying the quantity; Dioscurides (Wellman) iv, 42 prescribes an unspecified quantity of quintfoil taken in wine; Schöffler 210/18-21 prescribes three spoonfuls of quintfoil taken at three separate times; and Heinrich 82b/26-28 prescribes three spoonfuls of quintfoil tempered with stale ale.

29/24-25. Both Aristotle (Forster) iii, 17 and *Reg. San. Salern.* (Harrington) 168 prescribe cale juice as an aperient.

29/26. Pliny (Mayhoff) xxviii, 58 prescribes goat's milk as a laxative.

29/27-29. Parallel : *Anglia* XVIII, 307/477-480.

29/30-31. For parallels see notes to 28/19-21.

29/37-30/5. These two recipes are paralleled by two in Roy 12 G iv, f. 193r.

30/6-7. For parallels see notes to 29/22-23.

30/8-9. *Herb. Ap.* (Sigerist) 22/5-7 [*Herb. Ap.* (Cockayne I) 83/4] prescribes waybread (*i.e.* plantain) *Ad uentris dolorem.*

30/10-11. The two parts of this recipe appear in two recipes in *Leechbook* II (Leonhardi) 69/1-2 and 71/8-9. Heinrich 826/28-29 prescribes the application of *puliol* to the navel.

30/12-14. Parallels : Dioscurides (Wellman) iii, 34; Paulus (Adams) VII, 3; Schöffler 221/1-3; Dawson 644, 376; Henslow A 70/1-2; Heinrich 83a/13-16.

30/23-25. Parallel : Henslow B 116/1-2.

30/28-29. In Sextus Placitus (Sigerist) 238/77-80, a parallel to this recipe occurs, having *natura cerui* for þe *kynd of hert*. *Natura*, in Latin, and both *nature* and *kind*, in English, frequently mean ' testicles.' The testicles of the hart were used as a materia medica. They are mentioned, for example, in an earlier recipe in Sextus Placitus (Sigerist) as *cerui testiculos* (237/45).

30/30-31. Pliny (Mayhoff) xxviii, 205 and Avicenna (Gerard) II, 126 prescribe fresh cheese in wine for the flux. A Middle English parallel occurs in Roy 12 G iv, f. 196v.

30/32-33. Pliny (Mayhoff) xxvi, 53 prescribes cinquefoil juice and milk for the flux.

30/34-31/2. Parallels : Constantinus (1510) IV, 15; Roy 12 G iv, f. 189v; Henslow A 37/11-15, 41/14-17; Henslow B 82/21-83/3, 115/15-20; Heinrich 95a/28-95b/4, 85a/2-7; Dawson 527.

31/3-5. Parallels : Dawson 308; Henslow B 115/14-15; Henslow B 115/14-15.

31/11-15. Parallel : Henslow A 12/16-19.

31/16-19. Parallel : *Camb. Antid.* (Sigerist) 166.

31/20-24. Avicenna (Gruner) 480/957 prescribes the eating of the cooked flesh of an old cock for dysentery. There are a number of Middle English parallels prescribing the flesh of a young chicken instead of that of an old cock: Dawson 309; Roy 12 G iv, f. 192r; Henslow A 36/16-18. Henslow A 13/1-6 is a fairly close parallel marked only by dialectal differences.

31/26-27. Both *Herb. Ap.* (Sigerist) 23/20-22 and *Camb. Antid.* (Sigerist) 166 prescribe the drinking of plantain cooked in vinegar for dysentery.

31/31-32. Pliny (Mayhoff) xxviii, 205; Haly Abbas (Stephanus) II, 52; and Roy 12 G iv, f. 201v prescribe burnt hart's horn for dysentery.

32/4-6. Parallel: Dawson 104.

32/22-23. Parallel: Marcellus (Niedermann) XXVII, 62. Pliny (Mayhoff) xxvi, 119 prescribes the drinking of betony with honey-sweetened wine for dropsy. Musa (Sigerist) 8/113-14 prescribes betony in warm water. In the midst of long passages on the virtues of betony, both Henslow A 71/1-2 and *Anglia* XVIII, 308/17-18 mention the use of betony and honey for the relief of dropsy.

32/24. Dioscurides (Wellman) i, 10 refers to the use of asarabacca for the relief of dropsy.

32/28-32. Aristotle (Forster) ix, 1 prescribes the application of newly flayed hides in a glutinous condition to keep down inflammation and swelling. The following Middle English recipes prescribe for the dropsy the application of a thick paste made of the boiled shavings of hides: Müller 95/28-96/4; Dawson 249 (latter part); Roy 12 G iv, f. 189v; and Sloane 393, f. 38r.

The closeness of these four Middle English parallels has influenced the glossing of *flexigines of schepe tharmes*. *Flexigines* has been interpreted as a scribal corruption of *fleshing*, ' skin scraped from hides before tanning.' The parallels have: *schauyng* (Roy 12 G iv, f. 189v); *flesshe* (Dawson 249); *fleschynge* (Müller 95/30); and *flexynghe* (Sloane 393, f. 38r). *Tharmes* seems either to have meant, in some cases, ' hides ' rather than ' entrails ' or to have been mistakenly inserted for *hides* or a word of similar meaning. For *schepe tharmes* and *nete hidis* the parallels have: *schepys skynnys* and *netis skynnis* (Müller 95/30-96/1); *shepis fellis* and *netis fellys* (Dawson 249); *schepe skynnes* and *net skynnes* (Roy 12 G iv, f. 189v); and *schepis hidis* (Sloane 393, f. 38r).

32/33-37. Parallels: Müller 107/21-25; Dawson 249. The glossing of the Thornton *birs* (l. 33) as ' bruise ' is confirmed by the occurrence of *brisse* in l. 22 of Müller 107/22-25, a fairly closely parallel recipe.

33/9. *Cald mynt* may be an error for *calamint*. Whether such an error would be due to a popular etymology of *calamint* as ' cold mint ' or to a scribal misreading of *a* as *d* has not been positively determined. The former explanation seems less likely than the latter, especially since calamint was regarded as a hot herb. It is listed as hot in 66/28 and in Galen (Kühn) XI, 883; Avicenna (Gerard) II, 157; and Chauliac (Nicaise) 643.

33/16-21. Pliny (Mayhoff) xxiv, 52 prescribes a potion composed of the roots of the elder tree boiled in wine. Middle English parallels: Schöffler 224/15-20; *Anglia* XVIII, 306/445-454.

33/37-38. Macer (1527) 46 and Gaddesden (Cholmeley) 34 recommend *spica* in the treatment of kidney diseases.

34/16-17. *Reg. San. Salern.* (Harrington) 169 mentions sage as being good for the palsy. Instructions to eat it in all foods are included in Dawson 734.

34/22. *Fel gerie* remains unexplained.

34/29. Gaddesden (1492) 83, 1 and 173, 1 gives recipes for making *claretum* or *pigmentum*. Nicaise in *Chauliac* (Nicaise) 684 defines *clare* or *clere* as a sweetened wine in which various aromatics were infused and identifies it with *bonum pigmentum* and *hippocras*.

34/37-35/2. Parallels: *Camb. Antid.* (Sigerist) 163; Henslow A 13/7-11. The disease being treated here is apparently some disease with rapidly spreading cutaneous symptoms. The heading of the Latin recipe is: " Ad sanguinem erraticum qui per membra spargitur." In the heading of the Henslow A recipe, which corresponds fairly closely to the Thornton heading, *pikelyd* is used instead of *plowkky*.

35/3-4. Macer (1527) 20 recommends a potion composed of cerfoil and wine for pain in the side.

35/5-8. Two close parallels in Roy 12 G iv, ff. 181r and 212r have the heading : " f]for þe Stiche in a monn*us* (mann*es*) Syde". For *sothen rede wirtes* (l. 5), the recipe on f. 181r has *redewortes*, that on f. 212r has *rede wortes*.

35/9-11. Parallels : Dawson 125; Henslow A 13/15-17.

35/12-14. The following recipes are parallel except for the fact that the former omits olive oil and the latter adds rosin : Henslow A 14/3-5; Dawson 126.

35/18-20. *Herb. Ap.* (Sigerist) 84/8-10 prescribes the application of a ground, cooked mixture of marsh mallow (*ibiscum*), mallow (*malua*), and fenugreek (*feno Graeco*) for all kinds of *encatisma*. The old English translation, *Herb. Ap.* (Cockayne I) 141/3, prescribes the application of a mixture of marsh mallow (*merse mealuwe*), cress (*cærsan*), linseed (*linsæde*), and meal. None of the three Middle English parallels corresponds closely in detail. Schöffler 249/17-20 adds sour dough to the mixture. Heinrich 105a/17-30 and Schöffler 218/3-15 specify a more elaborate method of preparation and direct that the mixture is to be fried in barrow's grease before it is applied.

36/30. *Apostolion* may be an error for *Apostolicon*, possibly from a misexpanded contraction. *Apostolicon* is discussed in the notes to 79/15.

Dewte was long interpreted as a variant of *deutry*, the name of a herb. It is now known to be a salve made of various herbs compounded with fats, oils, and waxes. It is also mentioned in Heinrich 114a/11, 141a/5-6 and in Müller 120/2. The following recipe for *Dewte* is given in Schöffler 254/20-255/4 :

For to make dewte. Take ij m. of mylfoyle, henbane m. j, of wyllde nepe m. iiij, ache m. ij, lyly m. iij, of weybrede m. ij, of brokyn-lempe m. j, rubarbe, ru, gayle, mercury, of euery m. j, chekyn-mete m. iij, salt grece, hengrece, may-butter, oyle de olyffe, capun-grece, ele-grece, frankynencence, vergyn-wax, of euery aleche moche, and sethe all þes to-geder and þen yt ys goode.

36/32-38. Close parallel : *Rel. Ant.* I, 51/18-24.

37/4-6. The Latin recipe in l. 6, which repeats the prescription of columbine juice for quinsy, is to be found in *Coll. Salern.* (Renzi) V, 95/3225 with *amarisci* instead of *anarisci*. Schöffler 204/12 prescribes columbine seed for sore throat.

37/7. Pliny (Mayhoff) xxiii, 75 prescribes almonds for drunkenness.

37/9. Rhazes (1510) *Ad Almans* V, 76 advises that for relief of drunkenness the head be sprinkled with tepid (not cold) water.

37/10-11. In a series of recipes for the prevention of drunkenness, Rhazes (1510) *Ad Almans* V, 76 gives three remedies closely resembling 37/9-13. The second and third recipes of Rhazes are exact parallels to 37/11-13. In the first recipe, Rhazes, advising that the hands and feet be put into cold water, uses *hands and feet* where 37/9-10 has *hyngers*. See the notes to 37/11, 12-13.

37/11. Parallel : Rhazes (1510) *Ad Almans* V, 76. Avicenna (Gruner) 413/813 prescribes the drinking of water and vinegar or whey water and junket to restore a man from inebriety.

37/12-13. Parallels : Rhazes (1510) *Ad Almans* V, 76; Avicenna (Gruner) 413/813; Gordon (1496) 72.

37/16-17. Parallel : Rhazes (1510) *Ad Almans* V, 76. Avicenna (Gruner) 413/813 prescribes that camphor be smelled to restore a man from drunkenness.

37/18-21. This recipe is similar in many ways to that which follows it (ll. 22-25). Marcellus (Niedermann) XIX, 24 prescribes *horshelm* root for leprosy. Middle English parallels : Müller 102/13-17; Heinrich 85b/23-26 ; Dawson 781; Henslow A 19/5-8.

37/22-25. This recipe is similar to that which precedes it; see notes to 37/18-21. Compare the relation of 37/26-29 to 37/30-33.

37/26-29. See notes to 37/30-33, a recipe similar in many respects. Compare the relation of 37/18-21 to 37/22-25.

37/30-33. Parallels : Dawson 782, 789; Henslow A 19/9-12; Heinrich 126a/2-5.

38/13-14. Parallels : *Herb. Ap.* (Sigerist) 186/17;. Larsen 212.

38/15. Parallel : Paulus (Adams) III, 3.

Notes. 99

38/16–20. Parallel: Henslow A 18/12–15.
38/25–28. *Reg. San. Salern.* (Harrington) 172 prescribes willow for worms. *Entres* may be a garbled loan-word from Old French *entrerus*, Latin *interruscus*, ' the layer between the outer bark and the inner core', in which case the passage gives directions to take þe *bark of wilghe þat is bitwene þe tre &* þe *vtter barke* and the middle bark (*entres*) of the root likewise. The etymology of *entrerus* is treated in *Romania* XXXVII, 119–120, 374.

38/29–30. Pliny (Mayhoff) xxviii, 59 and Heinrich 128b/1–3 prescribe ashes of burnt hartshorn against worms. Sextus Placitus (Sigerist) 236/17–19 and its Old English translation, *Med. Quad.* (Cockayne I) 335/5 prescribe hartshorn ashes mixed with water. Leechbook I (Leonhardi) 37/25–26 prescribes them mixed with honey.

39/7–10. Parallel: Schöffler 202/11–14.

39/19–41/25. Gaddesden (1492) 78/2 and Gordon (1496) 76v prescribe a similar treatment of epilepsy. In Bernard de Gordon's account of the procedure, the parents or friends of the epileptic fast three days before the patient goes to the priest for aid. At the close of the ceremony the patient is given a copy of his vow to wear about his neck for protection.

41/31–34. Parallel: Dawson 361.

42/9–12. In a form of this charm which appears in Heinrich 105b/3–12, the patient is instructed to write with the blood of the little finger of the right hand on a parchment the names: *Iasper* ⊞ *melchior* ⊞ *baltasar*. Then, putting gold, myrrh, and frankincense into the parchment, he is to close it and hang it around his neck. Gordon (1496) 76v recommends that for the relief of epilepsy one whisper into the ear of the patient : *Gasper fert myrrham, thus Melchior, Balteser aurum*. These words constitute a line from the expanded form of the *Regimen sanitatis* edited by Renzi. The line appears as the first of three, which complete the recipe :

> Gasper fert myrrham, thus Melchior, Balthasar aureum,
> Haec trea qui secum portabit nomina Regum
> Solvitur e morbo, Domini pietate, caduco.
> [*Coll. Salern.* (Renzi) V, 87]

These three lines appear in garbled form in the midst of a charm in *Antiquary* XXXIX (1903), 276. Cf. the notes to 11/33–35, treating Thornton's other quotation from the *Regimen Sanitatis*.

42/16–17. Parallel: Heinrich 105b/15 19 :

> ant 3yf hyt [the patient] be achyld, þat ys an innocent, drawe blod of þe same fynger, þat ys by fore y sayde, & wryte þe þre kyngges names in amaser wyþ þe blod, & wasche hyt wyþ ale or mylk, & let þe chyld drynke hyt, & he schal be hole.

Perhaps this is the procedure which Thornton calls " drinking written " (l. 16).

42/19–20. The use of peony as a preventive of epilepsy goes back at least as far as Galen (Kühn) XI, 859. Its use was also recommended by Serapion (1497) *De simp. med.* I, 51; Avicenna (Gerard) *Canon* II, 561; and Macer (1527) *s. de pyretro*. Haly Abbas (Stephanus) IV, 21; Gordon (1496) 266; Gaddesden (1492) 78/2; and Larsen 170, like Thornton, prescribe the use of both peony and pyrethrum.

42/28–33. Parallels : *Rel. Ant.* I, 51/25–29; Dawson 210.

42/34–43/4. Crawfurd in " The blessing of cramp rings " in Singer's *Studies in the history and method of science* (Oxford, 1917), I, 173 quotes a close parallel to this recipe from a fourteenth century manuscript in the Arundel collection, the number of which he fails to give.

42/38–43/7. Rings were worn as charms against disease at least as early as the sixth century A.D. Alexander (Puschmann) II, 377 prescribes the wearing of an iron ring carved with the words : " Flee, flee, O Gall ! The lark has sought you " and a magical sign. For colic he recommends a ring set with a stone carved to represent Hercules strangling a lion. For the medieval use of cramp

100   *Notes.*

rings see R. Crawfurd, " The blessing of cramp rings," *Studies in the history and method of science,* ed. C. Singer (Oxford, 1917), I, 165–187.

43/39. *Camelle* is perhaps an error for or variant of *camomile.* Van Wijk, I, 16, 95 lists *camil* as a synonym of *camomile* (*Anthemis nobilis,* L.) as well as of *cammock* or *milfoil* (*Achillea millefolium,* L.).

44/3–4. Pliny (Mayhoff) xxvi, 150; *Herb. Ap.* (Sigerist) 74/18–19 [*Herb. Ap.* (Cockayne I) 131/5]; and *Coll. Salern.* (Renzi) IV, 135 prescribe agrimony and vinegar for warts. Middle English parallels : Dawson 955; Müller 90/13–15; Roy 12 G iv, f. 189v.

44/5–6. Parallels : *Coll. Salern.* (Renzi) IV, 135; 17 St. John's Oxford (Singer) 149; Henslow A 45/1–2.

44/7–8. Parallels : Serapion (1497) *De simpl. med.* 453; *Coll. Salern.* (Renzi) V, 90; Henslow A 45/3–4.

44/11. Parallel. *Coll. Salern.* (Renzi) IV, 135.

44/16–17. Parallels : Heinrich 83b/16–18; Schöffler 238/5–6; Henslow A 15/4–6. Compare Thornton's " with ⟨wyth⟩ wyn " (l. 17) with Schöffler's " with wyte wyne " (l. 6) and Heinrich's " wyþ whit wyne " (l. 18).

44/18–19. A *cristallan* appears in the Old English *Lacnunga* (Cockayne III) 11/11 in a list of herbs and is identified by Cockayne as the *crystallium* of Pliny (Mayhoff) xxv, 140, which is generally identified as psyllium (*Plantago psyllium,* L.). The stone crystal seems to have been used in contemporary medical recipes [see Heinrich 85a/1–2; Dawson 621; and Henslow A 25/9–10]. An Old French manuscript of the fourteenth century gives explicit recognition of the use of both the herb and the stone *cristal.* The patient is directed to drink : " la poudre de cristal et le jus dune herb que on apelle le " (*Archiv Med.* II, 271).

44/22–25. As the Middle English parallels of this recipe are especially characteristic of the average though not the closest parallels, we shall quote them, beginning with the two most like the Thornton recipe. (1) Henslow A 15/7–9 :

   Pro illo qui non potest retinere vrinam.—Take gotes clauwys and bren hem in a newe pot al to poudre and ete þat poudre in potage. Et sine dubio habebit sanitatem.

(2) Müller 101/14–102/2 :

   For hym þat may no3t holdyn pisse. Tak gottys-clawys, and brenne hem in a newe potte all to powdir, and þanne ete þat powdir in þin potage; and withowtyn dowte þou schalt ben hooll.

(3) Heinrich 128b/3–5 :

   Qui non potest retinere vrinam. Brenne þe clowes of agoot, & gyue hym to drynke þe pouder for to wyþ stanche blod. [MS. Sloane 405 has : [Who so may not holde his pys. Bren Gotes cleyn & vse þe poudre þer of in Metes & drynkes.]

(4) Heinrich 85a/9–12 :

   Qui non potest retinere vrinam. Take þe clawes of a goot, [MS. Sloane 3153 : gotes clawes and þe clees or clawes of geet.] and brenne hem, & make poudre þer of, [MS. Sloane 3153 interpolates : but þou must brenne hem in a new pot of erthe.] and let þe seeke vse hit in his potage, asponefulle at ones and he schal be hool.

(5) Schöffler 238/1–3 :

   For hym þat may not hold hys pysche. Take þe cleys of a goote and byrne hem to poudyr and vse þat pouder euery daye a sponfull yn hys potage.

(6) Dawson 731 :

ffor hym þat may nat hold hys water. Take þe clawes of a gote & brenne hem to poudre and do þe poudere in thi potage & vse it.

(7) The recipe below, from Roy 12 G iv, f. 189v, almost certainly belongs in this group of parallels. It seems unlikely that chunks of ash to be powdered would be obtained from the burning of tallow. This fact combined with the occurrence of *goat claws* in the other parallels has led to the suggestion that *talow* is an error for *talon*, also spelled *taloun, talown* :

Who So may not holde pisse take got*us* talow & bren hit & make poud*ur* þer of & hete þe poud*ur* in potage.

These parallels suggest that Thornton's *gud clowes* is an error for *goat claws*. The eating of burnt claws and hoofs seems to have been a recognized treatment of diuresis. The powder of burnt swine's hoofs is prescribed in Pliny (Mayhoff xxviii, 215; Marcellus (Niedermann) XXVI, 85; *Leechbook* I (Leonhardi) 28/1-4; *Anglia* XVIII, 299/185-190; and Dawson 724.

44/28-30. Parallels : Dawson 730; Henslow A 15/1-3; Heinrich 83b/13-16; Roy 12 G iv, f. 220r. All the parallels have *sangwynarie*, or some variant spelling of it, except Roy 12 G iv, which has 3*arow*. This suggests that yarrow or milfoil was sometimes called sanguinary. Shepherd's purse or bursa pastoris was also called sanguinary. Cf. *Sinon. Bart.* 38 and *Alphita* 34/1-4.

44/31-33. This recipe, attributed to the Rector of Oswaldkirk, is paralleled by Müller 135/16-18.

44/34-35. Parallel : *Anglia* XVIII, 300/197-200.

44/36-39. Parallels : Henslow A 14/9-12; Ketham (Sudhoff-Singer) xix.

45/1-3. Benedicta is referred to as an electuary in Heinrich 97b/32. *Coll. Salern.* (Renzi) I, 872-873 and V, 36 recommend its use for bladder trouble. The following recipe for it is given in *L'antidot. Nicolas* (Dorveaux) 6 :

Benoite est dite, quar ceus qui la receivent la beneissent. El vaut à artetique, à poacre; el fait pisser; el purge les rains et la vessie.

Pren : esule, once .ii.; turbit, çucre, ana dragme .x.; girofle, espic, dragme .i.; safran, saxifrage, lonc poivre, amome, sal gemme, garingaut, carvi, fanoil, brusque, groumil, [ana dragme .i.]; miel sofeisant.

El soit donee au soir ou vin chaud en quantité d'une chastaine.

On *chawdpys*, cf. : "Diabetico passio immoderata urinae effusio, vel dicitur chaudepisse." *Alphita*.

45/4-5. A recipe for *Agrippa* appears in Galen (Kühn) XIII, 1030. Arderne (Power) *Lesser Writings* 110 refers to it as " ane oyntment that potecaryes sellen and it is whyte of coloure." Larsen 180 advises that the limbs be rubbed with *Agrippa* to give relief from the stone. In listing its virtues, *L'antid. Nicolas* (Dorveaux) 32 says :

Unguent agripe vaut à idropiques et à totes emfleumes. il fait uriner. Si il soit oint sus le ventre, il lasche.

The form of *Agrippa* prescribed by the Rector of Oswaldkirk was probably much like that of the following recipe in *L'antid. Nicolas* (Dorveaux) 32 :

Pren : br[i]one, livre .ii.; racine de eible, once .ii.; charduns marins, once .ii. Les racines soient lavees et soient triblé et soient mis en .iii. livre d'eule de lenti[s]c. Au tierz jor soient mis boillir jusque les racines commencent à abaisier; puis soient mis en .i. sac et praint et colé; puis soit mis sus le feu; et, com il commencera à boillir, soit i mis .xv. once de cire blanche. La cire remisse, soit mis jus et lessé fraidir.

45/6-8. Parallels : Müller 100/16-101/2; Roy 12 G iv, f. 220r; *Rel. Ant.* I, 52/1-3; Henslow A 14/13-16.

K

45/38-39. *Anglia* XVIII, 300/191-195 prescribes that cherry-stone kernels be eaten and drunk with holy water.
46/24-29. Macer (1527) 18/2 prescribes sage leaves against venom. A Middle English parallel : Müller 74/12-17.
46/30-31. Parallels : Dioscurides (Wellman) iii, 32; Isidore (Migne) XVII, 9, 29; Larsen 210; Henslow B 80/4-5; Dawson 999; Roy 12 G iv, f. 193r. Part of the word preceding -ne seems to have disappeared with the wearing away of the edge of the page. It is likely that the missing letters were þor, making the word [þor]ne. þorne is mentioned in the heading of the group of recipes to which the Henslow B parallel belongs. The Roy 12 G iv recipe is headed : " ffor þorne in fet or in hond."
47/6-11. It is perhaps significant that the one recipe attributed to *Ser Apilton* should prescribe *Diatarascos, Diachylon, Marciaton*, and *Catholicon*. These compound unguents with high-sounding names seem to occur most frequently in the bills of medicines supplied to the royal family, the army upon expeditions, and the like. See, for example, the following documents in *Records of the Exchequer, the King's Remembrancer, Accounts*, to which Mr. Salzman has called my attention in a letter of August 18, 1935 : A list of drugs for the king, 34 Edward I (368.30); a list of drugs for the Scottish Expedition, 16 Edward II (379.3); medicines for the Queen, 7 Edward II (375.11 and 12); and medicines for the Queen, 17 Richard II (402.18 and 19). The last of these, a list of medicines supplied to Anne of Bohemia in her last illness, has also been called to my attention by Miss Rickert, who kindly loaned me a rotograph of it. Only a few of the most common are mentioned in the vernacular recipe collections. Directions for making these preparations are given even less frequently in the Middle English recipe collections.

Salzman, on p. 119 of *Medieval byways* (London, 1913), says that *Diatarascos* was a plaster of the patent medicine type compounded of pitch, wax, acetic acid, and aromatics. He mentions its occurrence in a list of drugs taken on one of the Scottish expeditions. From his letter of August 18 referred to above, it is clear that he is referring to the list of drugs for the Scottish expedition, 16 Edward II, *Records of the Exchequer, the King's Remembrancer, Accounts*, 379.3. No other mention or discussion of *Diatarascos* has been found in ancient, medieval, or modern works. Special search was made for it in all works examined for parallels. It does not occur in either the Latin or the French *Antidotarium of Nicolaus*.

The following recipe for *Catholicon* appears in *Antid. Nicolai* (Platearius) 374/4F, G :

> Catholicon . . .
> Reci. sene bene mundati, casiaefi. mundae,
> tamarindorum ana. vnc. viij. reu. violarum,
> polypo. anisi ana. vnc. iiij liqui mundae, pendi.
> candi. ana. drach. iiij quatuor se. frigidorum munda.
> vnc. i. Accipe iterum lib. i. polypodii quercini, &
> tere modicum, & in aqua diutissime
> decoque, & ex colatura fac syrupum cum li. viij.
> zuccari. In parte autem colaturae distempera casiam
> & tamarindos, & in fine decoctionis syrupi pone,
> deinde confice electarium, imponendo pulueres
> aliorum.

The name *Diachylon* was applied to both a plaster and a syrup. Clearly it is the plaster which *Ser Apilton* was prescribing. Recipes for the emplaster occur in most of the important medical works from Galen (Kühn) XIII, 996-998 to Heinrich 126b/3-9. Mesue (Platearius) 163/3H-4E, 164/1B, 1D-2A; Najm (Guigues) 169/1; *Bamberger Antid*. (Sigerist) 38, 39; *Glasgow Antid*. (Sigerist) 121; Chauliac (Nicaise) 604; and Mondeville (Pagel) 526 give recipes for the *Diachylon* plaster. There were several varieties of *Diachylon*. Litharge and wax or oil seem to be the most constant ingredients. A common kind was

Notes. 103

made with the addition of ceruse and red lead [e.g. Heinrich 126b/3–9]. This kind was sometimes known as *Diachylon nigrum* or *l'emplastre noire* [see Heinrich 126b/3 and Chauliac (Nicaise) 604]. Another common variety was made with the addition of mucilaginous herbal ingredients [e.g. *Glasgow Antid.* (Sigerist) 121]. There is no indication as to which of these types the *Diachylon* prescribed by *Ser Apilton* belonged.

Oile Marciaton was another of the elaborate unguents. No other reference to it has been found in Middle English. It is listed among the drugs supplied to Anne of Bohemia in her last illness (*Exch. K. R. Accounts*, 402.18). Sigerist, *Studien* 193 shows how this unguent grew from a comparatively simple compound of seven or eight ingredients in the works of Paul of Aegina to an elaborate preparation of some fifty odd ingredients in the *Antidotarium of Nicolaus*.

47/8–9. Recipes for making oil of laurel are given in Rhazes (1510) *Antidot*. 3 and Najm (Guigues) 130.

47/12–15. Parallels: Roy 12 G iv, ff. 181v, 193v, 212v. The parallel on 193v also has *rede hertis tonge .i. cerfoil*. Each of the other parallels has *cerfoil* alone. The glossing of *hart's tongue* as *cerfoil* in two versions of this recipe presents difficulties because *hart's tongue* is usually glossed *cerlang* (*Scolopendrium vulgare*) whereas *cerfoil* is a common synonym of *chervil* (*Anthriscus Cerefolium*). *Cerefolium* is also glossed *cerlang* in *Anglia* XXIV, 434. Perhaps the confusion of *cerfoil* and *cerlang* was a fairly common error of medieval glossators. See notes to 59/15–16.

48/5–7. *Leechbook* I (Leonhardi) 45/7–9 prescribes the application of dry, powdered blood as a styptic. Müller 135/19–21 prescribes an ointment with blood which has been fried in a pan.

48/8–15. Parallels: Henslow A 29/8–15; Dawson 829.

48/16–19. Paulus (Adams) III, 24; Constantinus (1510) II, 15; Larsen 137; and *Archiv Med*. II, 226 prescribe burnt eggshells for stopping nosebleed. Middle English parallels: Dawson 627; Henslow B 110/11–12; Müller 74/8–11.

48/20–22. Parallels: Dawson 830; Henslow A 29/16–18; Müller 105/3–6.

48/23–24. Parallels: Müller 105/8–9; Henslow A 29/19–20.

48/25–27. Parallel: *Rel. Ant.* I, 53/9–11. There is a lacuna in the Halliwell MS. between the heading and the herb nettles.

48/28–30. *Brynt*, 'soot,' not recorded in the NED, is confirmed by the following parallel in *Leechbook* I (Leonhardi) 45/1–3: "Nim ceteles hrum ʒeʒnid to duste scead on þa wunde."

48/31–32. Pliny (Mayhoff) xxx, 112 and Serapion (1497) *De simpl. med.* 439 prescribe earthworms as a styptic. An Old French recipe prescribes earthworms cooked in oil (*Romania* XXXVII, 364/30).

48/36–37. Parallel: Arderne (Power) 30–31.

49/1–2. Parallels: Platearius (1497) *Circum instans s. sanguis draconis*; Schöffler 197/19–20. Serapion (1497) *De simpl. med.* III, 341 and Avicenna (Gerard) *Canon* II, 609 recommend the use of dragon's blood for stanching blood without indicating the method of applying it.

49/3–4. Arderne (Power) 66/22–23 prescribes the ashes of a burnt linen cloth as a styptic.

49/5–6. Roy 12 G iv, f. 181y prescribes "þe þoudir of felte of a blak hat þat is brenned in þe fire" as an ingredient in a more elaborate styptic recipe. Larsen 208 recommends the application of singed felt.

49/7–8. $A + G + L + A$ occurs also in Müller 80/27 and in Heinrich 103a/25, 111b/16, and 112a/15. These four letters apparently form a tetragrammaton regarded as a symbol of the Christian deity. In Heinrich 111b/16 $+ a + g + l + a + tetragrammaton$ is followed by such epithets of the Divinity as *alpha & ω, primogenitus*, and the like. Compare also the following passages from charms where *agla* is likewise used for the name of the deity:

a) " + Xristus vincit + Xristus adiuvet te + agla per hoc nomen audet nominaire."
Cod. 980. Gotha. S. 12ᵇ, *Germinia* XXXII, 45–46.

b) "Coniuro te per nomen dei sanctissimum quod est compositum hys IIII or a.g.l.a."

MS. Add. 17527, l. 17b, *Zeitschrift f. deutsch. Alt.* XXXVIII, 20.
49/9–11. Parallel : Heinrich 84a/1–5. This parallel, though not extremely close, suggests that *syndegrefe* is probably an error for *synegrene*.
49/12–16. Parallels : Henslow 16/10–12 ; *Rel. Ant.* I, 53/1–6. The extremely close parallel in *Rel. Ant.* indicates that the recipe probably should continue to give directions for removing the grease.
49/19. Paulus (Adams) III, 81 recommends copperas for leprous nails.
49/22–27. Parallels : Roy 12 G iv, f. 189v ; Henslow A 31/14–20.
50/2–3. Parallel : *Rel. Ant.* I, 52/42–44. *Rel. Ant.* has : " tak the souredock, and falde hit in a kale lefe " instead of " tak wodsoures & do in a doke lefe."
50/20–22. Close parallel : *Rel. Ant.* I, 53/16–18.
50/23–25. Parallels : Henslow A 46/1–2 ; Arderne (Power) 12/39–13/4.
50/38–51/2. Parallel : *Anglia* XVIII, 303/339–342. The form of expression in this verse parallel is not close enough to offer added proof that Thornton's *wyse* is an error for *wype*.
51/3–4. Parallel : *Coll. Salern.* (Renzi) II, 703.
51/15–54/7. This material is an abridged translation of the shorter version of the tract on the pestilence attributed in several manuscripts to John of Burgundy. Unlike most versions of the treatise, the Thornton version begins and ends without mention of its authorship. Most of these headings and colophons giving ascriptions of authorship are edited in Murray 5–11, 30 and *Archiv Med.* V, 69–73. Schöffler 175–179 contains a bibliography, with critical discussions, of the various modern works attempting to identify John of Burgundy.

The other manuscripts of both versions of this pestilence tract are listed in *Archiv Med.* V, 69–72 and Murray 5–11. Three manuscripts have been edited. The first, Murray 26–29, is a Latin version appearing in British Museum, Royal MS. 13 E.x, the Black Book of Paisley. The second, Murray 30–33, is a Scottish translation appearing in the *Liber S. Marie de Calchou*. The third, *Archiv Med.* V, 72–75, is a sixteenth century English translation occurring in Sloane MS. 2320. The two English translations do not follow closely the Latin version of MS. Royal 13 E.x. In fact, MS. Sloane 2320 differs so widely from all the other MSS. of the treatise that Murray calls it an abridged version of the longer version rather than a manuscript of the shorter version. The numerous divergences of these manuscripts from each other as well as from the Thornton text have made it seem inadvisable to make extensive search among all extant manuscripts of the treatise for the manuscript from which Thornton may have copied his text.

51/23–28. Compare : Murray 26/22–27 :

> nec vtatur balneis, nec nimium sudet, quia tunc aperti sunt pori corporis, per quos aer intrat venenosus, qui debilitat et destruit vitales spiritus corporales. Ex maxime frequentacio luxurie, quia illa naturam et poros patefacit, ita quod nequaquam aer intrare possit humanos spiritus intoxicando.

It is perhaps significant that the one Latin quotation is so very different in wording as well as in sense. It would suggest that MS. Royal 13 E.x is probably not closely similar to the Latin manuscript which Thornton may have translated. Sir William Craigie has further suggested that it is unlikely that a Northern English work would have had a Scottish source.

51/33–34. Corresponding to Thornton's *for tysayn . . . compleccion* MS. Royal 13 E.x has " (tisana), quia talis potus est valde bonus, et principaliter illis qui sunt colerice compleccionis." The Latin text adds further : " quoniam illi sunt calidi et sicci, et communiter in corpore calidi " (Murray 27/2–4).

52/2–3. The *clensying place* of the liver is described in the Latin text as " inter crura et corpus in crurium concauitatibus " (Murray 27/12).

52/8–9. Thornton's " hert þat is grounde of mannes kynde " appears in the Latin text as " Cor quod est principium et radix vite et humanam naturam " (Murray 27/16).

52/21. Thornton's " castes a man in-to an agewe " appears as " deicit hominem in febrem acutam " in the Latin text (Murray 27/29).

52/21-22. Thornton's " & makes a boche or a kille " appears as " et causat ulcus " in the Latin text (Murray 27/30).

52/24-25. Thornton's " Who so feles any prikkyng of blode or flakeryng " appears in the Latin text as " quis sentit aliquam stimulacionem uel sanguinis tremulacionem " (Murray 27/34-28/1), in Sloane 2320 as " Whoo soo falleth in this evel and feleth any pryckyng or flakeryng of blood " (*Archiv Med.* V, 74/52-53), and in MS. Kelso as "Qua felys any preking of blude or flecrying " (Murray 31/17-18).

52/30-31. For " bledyng [be]tymes o[f] vaynes þat I sall tell after," MS. Royal 13 E.x. has " sanguinis minucio de venis quas narrabo " (Murray 28/6); MS. Kelso has " bledyng betymis of the vanys that I sall tell " (Murray 31/22-23); and MS. Sloane 2320 has " bledyng by tyme on the veynes that I shal telle " (*Archiv Med.* V 74/58-59).

52/36. For *matir* the Latin MS. has *materia* (Murray 28/10); MS. Sloane 2320 has *matier* (*Archiv Med.* V, 74/63); and MS. Kelso has *meter* (Murray 31/24).

52/37-38. Thornton's " þe hert vayne þat is callede cordiaca " appears in the Latin MS. as " vena cordis que dicitur cordiaca " (Murray 28/12).

53/4-5. Thornton's " & so haste a man to his endynge " appears in the Latin MS. as " et cicius hominem ad suum interitum festinabit " (Murray 28/19-20).

53/8-9. For Thornton's "þe veyne þat is bitwix þe thomell taa & þe nexte " MS. Royal 13 E.x has : " uena que est sita inter maguum articulum et secundum articulum " (Murray 28/22-23); MS. Kelso has „ wayn betwex the the meltha and the tother than nest it " (Murray 31/38-39); and MS. Sloane 2320 has : " ye veyne bitwixt grete too and the too, that is next is " (*Archiv Med.* V, 74/76-77).

53/12-13. Thornton's " if þe boche be mare owtwarde to þe sidde " appears in the Latin MS. as " si materia sit lateri magis extrinseca " (Murray 28/26).

53/14-16. For Thornton's *blede . . . boche* the Latin manuscript has " fiat fleobothomia de vena inter cauillam pedis et calcem, vel de vena eque sub cauilla que nominatur sochena, vel aliter ventiletur super crux iuxta ulcus cum pixide uel cum cornu " (Murray 32/4-7); MS. Kelso has " bled of the vayn betwex ankleth and the hole, or on the vayn that is ewin under the ankleth that is called the sophene, or ell be the ventosyd on the the with a boist or a horne besyde the byle " (Murray 28/27-30); and MS. Sloane 2320 has " blede on the veyne bitwene the ancle and the hele or on the veyne, that is under tha ancle, that is called sophena, or ells be thou ventused on the thyes with a boxe beside the bocche " (*Archiv Med.* V, 74/82-84).

53/17-23. The Thornton version is somewhat closer to that in MS. Sloane 2320 (*Archiv Med.* V, 74/86-92) than to that in MS. Kelso (Murray 32/8-13) or to that in the Latin MS. (Murray 28/32-36). The Thornton version differs from all three other manuscripts in prescribing the bleeding of the *mediana* instead of the *cordiaca*.

54/18-20. Parallels : Henslow A 45/5-8; Roy 12 G iv, f. 192v. Instead of " ilkane illike mekill rois blende," Henslow A has " and stampe euerych on by hym-selue; and whethe ys left of ius meng," and Roy 12 G iv has " & stampe eueriche by hem self & wich so hathe left of ius meng." *Rois* would seem to be an error for *ius*.

54/26-27. Parallels : Heinrich 106a/3-6; Roy 12 G iv, ff. 181v, 212v. All parallels have *wyld(e malwe*.

54/33-40. A close parallel of this rather complicated recipe : *Rel. Ant.* I, 53/23-32. *Synagle* (l. 33) appears as *senygle* ; *gume of the sour plumtre* (l. 34) as *gumme of asoure plumtre.*

54/35. WHITE PIK : Cf. *Resina .i. pix alba, rosin*; *Resina potest appellari omnis gumma a resudo resudas, appropriatur nichilominus ad designandum gummam abietis quando simpliciter invenitur. Sinon. Bart.* 36.

55/1-16. Parallels : Roy 12 G iv, f. 189v ; Henslow A 30/18-31/13.

55/28-29. *This grene oynement sanatyfe* (ll. 29-30) is probably the *oynement þat men callen vnguentum viride* of Henslow 86b/26-27. It was probably a healing

106 Notes.

salve owing its green colour to the presence of *viridis eris*. For a Thornton recipe for a green salve of this sort see 73/19–35.

56/4. The interpretation of *lupners* as *lupines* is corroborated by Paulus (Adams) VII, 3, who says that lupine kills worms when used externally or internally.

56/6–8. This recipe with the omission of vinegar as an ingredient is given in *Coll. Salern.* (Renzi) V, 227.

56/11–18. Parallels: Kotham (Sudhoff-Singer) xi; Dawson 523; Schöffler 252/17–23; Historical Manuscripts Commission, *Report on the manuscripts of the late Reginald Rawdon Hastings* (London, 1928) I, 422. Dawson p. 15 and W. Dawson, *Magician and leech* (London, 1929), pp. 141–146 discuss the Egyptian analogues of this recipe.

56/21–24. Albertus (1555) *De secretis mulierum* 8, 12; Müller 82/13–83/2, 106/26–30.

56/24–28. Hippocrates (Jones) *Aphorisms* v, 42 says that a woman carrying a male child is of good color, one carrying a female child of bad color.

56/29–38. A similar Latin charm with many small divergences appears in Henslow A 32/5–12.

57/1–2. Gaddesden (1492) 105/2 recommends the same curious remedy with the addition of mallow leaves.

57/3–4. Avicenna (Gerard) *Canon* II, 196 and Gaddesden (1492) 105/2 recommend the use of cassia fistula for the same purpose.

57/5–7. Henslow A 32/15–17 is a parallel to this charm.

57/8–15. Parallels: Henslow A 32/18–33/5; Roy 12 G iv, f. 220r.

57/16–17.   ⟶
    SATOR ↑
 | AREPO ↑
 | TENET |
 ↓ OPERA |
    ROTAS
   ⟵

This is one of the most widespread of magic formulae. It is known to have existed as early as the fifth century A.D. in Asia Minor. From the Near East, it seems to have spread all over Europe. One of its special features is that the outer row of letters always reads *sator*, following the arrows, and, reverse-wise, *rotas*. Seligman rejects the attempts to translate the words into a Latin sentence. He connects it with the simpler Ruach-formula, in which the Hebrew word meaning 'spirit' is similarly made into a square. Cf. Seligman, "Die Satorformel," *Hessische Blätter für Volkskunde*, XIII (1914), 154–183 and "Ananisapta und Sator," *loc. cit.* XX (1921), 1–14.

57/18–19. Ketham (Sudhoff-Singer) xi recommends a drink of woman's milk and olive oil as an aid in childbirth.

57/20–22. Parallel: Gaddesden (1492) 105/2.

57/24–25. Long charms for use in childbirth frequently contain the formula 'sancta ... peperit' repeated with a variety of different holy names. This kind of charm is discussed and illustrated in *Germania* XXXII, 458.

57/26–29. Parallels: Gaddesden (1492) 105/2; Henslow A 33/6–10; Dawson 256; Müller 46/11–15.

57/30. Parallel: Müller 46/16–17.

57/34–36. Parallel: Platearius (1497) *Circum instans s. peonia*.

57/37–58/2. Parallel: *Rel. Ant.* I, 53/37–40. Bartholomaeus mentions the use of gagate water as a test of virginity (Trevisa's translation, British Museum, Additional MS. 27944, f. 201r).

58/3–5. Parallel: Henslow B 113/9–13; Heinrich 86a/11–15. The Heinrich recipe has *pouder of bayes* instead of *cokille mele*.

58/7–8. The following entry suggests that *Ispia maior* is an error for *Ippia maior* : *Ippia major, i. pimpernella cum flore rubeo, Sinon. Bart.* 25.

58/14. ORBANE : Cf. *Lacta alio nomine dicitur orobus orobonis, gumma est de qua urina et humana fit per carminum, Alphita* 93/17–19.

58/15–16. Parallel: *Anglia* XVIII, 312/199–204.

58/19–21. Parallels: Henslow A 44/13–15; *Archiv Med.* VIII, 374; Larsen, 198.

58/22–25. Parallel: Larsen 201.

58/26–28. Parallel: *Romania* XXXVII, 368/66.

Notes. 107

58/28–38. An extremely close parallel to this passage on the signs of death occurs in *Rel. Ant.* I, 54/1–11. In the *Pricke of conscience*, ed. Morris (London, 1865) ll. 816–829, there occurs a passage in which about half of these signs are listed in the same order. Discussions of the signs of death are fairly common both in ancient and medieval medical works. Hippocrates with his interest in prognosis treats them at especially great length. Among the discussions of the signs of death to be found in the works of these medical writers are the following: Hippocrates (Jones) *Prognosticon* ii, iii, iv, ix; Celsus (Marx) I, 6; Paulus (Adams) II, 4; an anonymous Latin fragment of the fifth or sixth centuries in *Archiv Med.* XXIII, 89; Averrhoes (1560) IV, 43; Avicenna (Gerard) *Cantica* I; 17 St. John's Oxford (Singer) 133; and *Coll. Salern.* (Renzi) I, 491/1396–1403; V, 61–2/2116–2151. No one of these Latin and Greek passages closely parallels the whole paragraph of signs in Thornton and *Rel. Ant.* Nevertheless, nearly every individual sign occurs in one or another of these lists. Some of the signs occur in almost every list.

In addition to these medical lists of signs of death, there are a number of Middle English religious lyrics containing lists of mortal tokens. In general, the lists are composed of different signs from those occurring in the Thornton manuscript. The lyrics are discussed as a group with some mention of their probable sources in the notes to an exemplar edited by Carleton Brown in *English lyrics of the XIIIth century* (Oxford, 1932), pp. 130, 220–222.

As no list paralleling the whole group has been found outside Middle English, it is interesting to see which signs appear most commonly in earlier medical works. Each sign of death is quoted below, followed immediately by the form in which it occurs in *Rel. Ant.* I and the *Pricke of conscience*. After these quotations, there are listed a few representative references to parallels in earlier medical works. The list of references, while representative, is by no means complete.

(*a*) Thornton: "when his browes heldes down;" *Rel. Ant.*: "Qwen his broues hildes doune;" *Pricke*: "his browes heldes doun wyth-alle;" 17 St. John's Oxford (Singer) 133; Hippocrates (Jones) *Regimen in acute diseases* xlii, 11–12.

(*b*) Thornton: "the lefte eghe es mare þan þe righte eghe;" *Rel. Ant.*: "the lefte eigh mare than the ryght ye;" *Pricke*:

þe lefte eghe of hym þan semes les,
And narower þan þe right eghe es;

17 St. John's Oxford (Singer) 133; Avicenna (Gerard) *Cantica* I, 421; Paulus (Adams) II, 4; Hippocrates (Jones) *Prognosticon* ii, 28–29.

(*c*) Thornton: "The nose ende waxes scharpe;" *Rel. Ant.*: "Neyse ende waxes sharp;" *Pricke*: "Hys nese, at þe poynt, es sharp and smalle;" *Coll. Salern.* (Renzi) I, 491/1396–1398; Avicenna (Gerard) *Cantica* I, 439; *Archiv Med.* XXIII, 89; Paulus (Adams) II, 4; Celsus (Marx) I, 6; Hippocrates (Jones) *Prognosticon* ii, 6.

(*d*) Thornton: "his eres waxes calde;" *Rel. Ant.*: "his eres waxes calde;" Avicenna (Gerard) *Cantica* I, 436; Celsus (Marx) I, 6.

(*e*) Thornton: "his eghne waxes holle;" *Rel. Ant.*: "his eighen waxes halle;" Avicenna (Gerard) *Cantica* I, 436; *Archiv Med.* XXIII, 89; Paulus (Adams) II, 4; Celsus (Marx) I, 6; Hippocrates (Jones) *Prognosticon* ii, 6.

(*f*) Thornton: "The chyn falles;" *Rel. Ant.* "the chyn falles;" *Pricke*: "þan bygynnes his chyn to falle;" *Coll. Salern.* (Renzi) I, 491/1401–1403, V, 62/2147; 17 St. John's Oxford (Singer) 133; Hippocrates (Jones) *Prognosticon* iii, 16–17.

(*g*) Thornton: "his eghne & his mouthe are opyn when he slepes bot he be wonut þerto;" *Rel. Ant.*: "his eighen and his mouth es opon; when he slepes bot he be wont tharto;" Avicenna (Gerard) *Cantica* I, 421.

(*h*) Thornton: "his ere lappes waxes hethy;" *Rel. Ant.*: "his ere-lappes waxes lethy;" *Coll. Salern.* (Renzi) I, 491/1396: "auris pulpa rigens;" *Archiv Med.* XXIII, 89: "longeaque aures;" Celsus (Marx) I, 6: "aures frigidae languidaeque."

(i) Thornton : " his fete waxes calde ; " *Rel. Ant.* : " his fete waxes calde ; " *Pricke* : " His fete waxes calde ; " *Coll. Salern.* (Renzi) I, 491/1401-1403 ; 17 St. John's Oxford (Singer) 133 ; Hippocrates (Jones) Prognosticon ix, 1-3, xv, 30 ; *Aphorisms* vii.

(j) Thornton : " þe wambe falles awaye ; " *Rel. Ant.* : " his wambe falles away ; " *Pricke* : " his bely clynges ; " *Coll. Salern.* (Renzi) V, 62/2147 ; 17 St. John's Oxford (Singer) 133.

(k) Thornton : " if he pull þe strase or þe clathes ; " *Rel. Ant.* : " if he pulle the straes or the clathes ; " cf. *Coll. Salern.* (Renzi) V, 61/2119 ; Avicenna (Gerard) *Cantica* I, 424 ; Hippocrates (Jones) *Prognosticon* iv, 5-7.

(l) Thornton : " if he pyk at his nose thirlles ; " *Rel. Ant.* : " if he pyke at his neyse thrilles."

(m) Thornton : " his forheuede waxes rede ; " *Rel. Ant.* : " his forhede waxes rede ; " *Coll. Salern.* (Renzi) V, 62/2150.

(n) Thornton : " ȝong man ay wakande, alde man ay slepande ; " *Rel. Ant.* : " yonge man ay wakang ; alde man ay slepand ; " *Pricke* :

And if nere þe dede be a yhung man,
He ay wakes, and may noght slepe þan
And an aldeman to dede drawand
May noght wake, bot es ay slepand ;

Coll. Salern. (Renzi) V, 61/2116-2117, 62/2168-2169 ; 17 St. John's Oxford (Singer) 133.

(o) Thornton : " his ij membres caldes agayn es kynde & hides þam ; " *Rel. Ant.* : " his twa membres waxes calde agayne kynde, and hydes tham ; " 17 St. John's Oxford (Singer) 133.

(p) Thornton : " if he rotell ; " *Rel. Ant.* : " if he rutills." This sign appears in several of the religious lyrics, as " þe þrote Roteletȝ," F. Furnivall *Political, religious, and love poems* (London, 1866) pp. 249-250, 253.

59/1. *Betoyn* : *vetoyn* is evidently a mistaken repetition of two common names for the same herb.

59/7-9. Parallels : Müller 92/4-8 ; Dawson 524 ; Henslow A 25/3-6.

59/10-11. Parallels : Heinrich 101a/14-16 ; Henslow A 25/7-8 ; Dawson 525.

59/15-16. Romania XXXVII, 364 ; Dawson 535 ; Müller 92/9-11. þe *ius of cerfoil & cheruell* presents difficulties because *cerfoil* and *cheruell* usually appear as synonyms. For þe *ius of cerfoil & cheruell, Romania* XXXVII has *jus de cerfuil*, Müller *serwoyle*, and Dawson *therfoile*. Dawson's *therfoile* should probably be transcribed *cherfoile*. Perhaps, in the Thornton recipe, two synonyms have been mistaken for two separate ingredients. See notes to 47/12-15, 4/35, 28/38-29/3.

59/20-25. Parallel : *Romania* XXXVII, 364.

59/26-28. Parallels : Henslow A 37/16-38/2 ; Müller 96/9-12 ; Dawson 349.

59/29-30. With *horshoue þat is called vngula caballi* compare *Farfara, i. ungula caballina, Sinon. Bart.* 20 and *Bardani, farfara, ungula equina uel ungula caballina* [*idem*], *angl. feldhoue, Alphita* 21/1-4.

60/1-6. *Herb. Ap.* (Sigerist) 24/40-42 prescribes drinking the juice of three plantain roots in wine or water for tertian fever. See notes to 60/21-30.

60/14-17. Najm (Güigues) 9 gives a recipe for rose syrup that is very similar to Thornton's. *Antid. Nicolai* (Platearius) 390/4F gives a recipe for rose syrup that differs chiefly in the addition of the beaten whites of eggs.

60/21-30. Parallels : Dawson 349 ; Henslow A 38/3-11. Parallel to ll. 25-29 : Dawson 757. It is not impossible that ll. 25-29 represent a recipe for tertian fever adapted to quartan fever by increasing the number of roots or plants from three to four. See notes to 60/1-6.

60/31-61/2. A close parallel : *Rel. Ant.* I, 54/12-20.

61/10-16. A close parallel : *Rel. Ant.* I, 54/21-27 :

For the fever lente : qwha that has the fever agu, that men calles lente evell, if the sekeman heved werkes that he may noght slepp, tak everferne

Notes. 109

that waxes on the ake, with the rote, and seth hit wele, and tak mynt, of ayther y-lik mekell, and stamp tham wele, and mak ane emplaster, and lay on the forheyd, and on the thunwanges, but enoynt hym first with popilion.

Dawson 349, which is headed "ffor þe feuer of A mannes hede that makyth the hede to Ake that he may nat slepe," is parallel except that the final anointing is with *puliol* instead of *popilion*.

61/15, 19, 33. *Populeon* is an ointment usually made of oil or grease and herbal ingredients among which poplar leaves are included. It is prescribed in *Coll. Salern.* (Renzi) I, 482. A recipe for making it is included in *L'antidot. Nicolas* (Dorveaux) 31–32. *Populeon* is among the complicated preparations with special names most frequently occurring in vernacular medical works. At least three recipes for making it occur in the Middle English recipe collections: Heinrich 109a/1–10; Henslow B 118/17–119/3; Roy 12 G iv, f. 179v–180r. Though the herbs included in each of these recipes and that in *L'antidotaire* differ quite widely except for the poplar leaves, the method of preparation is much the same. The recipe from Roy 12 G iv probably represents approximately the kind of *populeon* prescribed in the Thornton recipes:

> Un*guentum* vocatur Popileon sic debu*s* fieri
> Tak leues of popeler & endiue morel si*n*grene
> plantayne porslake ribbegra*s* gronswyly leues
> of þe lilye leues of letuse white pople .i. popy
> & smalage of all þese ilichemiche saue
> þe pepeler leues for of hem þu schalt take
> as michas all þe oþer herbes & tak oyle of
> olyue yf *per* be iij pou*n*d of herbes & iij pou*n*d
> of gres dj q*uatron* of oyle is I now & whan all
> þese ar gronden let hem stond to gidere in a
> pot a fowrtenith & afterwart melt hem
> ouer þe fuyr til hit be all molten & þen wryng
> hem þoru a cloth in to a clene vessel til hit be
> cold & put hem þen*n*e into a box & kepe hit til
> þu haue nede & þis oynement serueth for hote
> goute & hote scabbus for vnkemes for akyng of
> bresed blod & many oþer eueles.

61/20–23. Similar recipes for making syrup of violets are given in Serapion (1497) *Practica* VII, 23; Haly Abbas (Stephanus) X, 20; Platearius (1497) *Circum instans s. viola*; and Najm (Guigues) 10.

61/30. þe *fransie* may be delirium connected with *fever ague*. Compare the following from the *Book of quinte essence* (ed. F. Furnivall; London, 1866) 22/10 : *þe feuere agu haþ comounly alienacioun of witt, & schewynge of þingis of fantasy*.

62/4–8. Parallel: Henslow A 38/16–39/2. Henslow A has *hors-houue* instead of *herbe John*.

62/10–17. A close parallel : *Rel. Ant.* I, 54/28–36.

62/27–30. Both Alexander (Puschmann) I, 323 and *Glasgow Antid.* (Sigerist) 121 prescribe linseed and rose oil as a fever ointment.

62/31–63/4. In Hippocrates (Jones) II, 112 *oxymel* is a simple mixture of honey and vinegar. *L'antidot. Nicolas* (Dorveaux) 22 gives a recipe using honey, vinegar, and the roots of fennel and radish.

63/11–21. Ll. 11–15 are paralleled by Heinrich 105a/9–16; ll. 16–18 by Heinrich 86a/28–866/6. In the last of these charms the use of Greek words without regard to their meaning is interesting. The Greek words *Ayos otheos, ayos yschyros, ayos athanatos, eleyson ymas* occur in a similar Latin charm in Cod. 980 Gotha. S. 12b (*Germania* XXXII, 456).

63/24. The identification of *whitte chessebolle* is, in part, confirmed by the following passage from Bartholomaeus Anglicus (British Museum, Additional MS. 27944 of Trevisa's translation) XVII, cxxviii: " Popy ... is double, commun and wylde. Ther of comeþ Ius þat physiciens clepeþ opium oþer opion.

Of þe commune, som is whyte and . . . sum is blak & . . . som is reede and thus diuersitee of kynde is knowe by floures white purpur Reede oþer whytissh."

63/30–35. Parallels : Schöffler 234/8–14; Heinrich 85b/27–86a/2; Dawson 655; Henslow A 19/15–20/2; Henslow B 102/13–20; Müller 103/27–104/2; Sloane 393, f. 60. These parallels, containing the words *hote, stone bores, þu woldest* illustrate excellently the variety of dialectal forms to be found in parallels of the same recipe. In this case the Thornton version is consistently Northern; the others Midland or Southern.

63/37. *Cucumerbers* is perhaps an error from the confusion of *cucumer* and *cucumber*. Serapion (1497) *De simpl. med.* II, 204 includes cucumbers among the ingredients in an elaborate recipe for gout.

64/4–8. Parallel : Henslow A 20/3–9. Henslow A has the Southern *vox* where Thornton has the non-Southern *fox*.

64/9–11. A similar recipe, Heinrich 134b/3–6, names three different kinds of snails : *.iij. maner of snayles . þe yelwe . þe blake . & þe whyte horned*.

64/16–30. Parallel : Müller 37/6–14. Close parallel : *Rel. Ant.* I, 55/2–16.

65/10–11. Arderne (Power) *Lesser Writings*, 113 recommends oil of eggs for the gout. Middle English parallels : Schöffler 234/21–24; Henslow A 20/10–13. See also Schöffler 234/n. 3.

Recipes for *oil of eggs* are given in Rhazes (1510) *Antidot.* 3, Mesue (Platearius) 178/3 G, and Heinrich 145a/21–24.

65/15–18. Parallel : Dawson 280.

66/8–39. In observing the traditional elements in the recipes, it is perhaps of interest to see how consistently the herbs classed as hot in this recipe had been classed as hot since the time of Galen:

TABLE I

INGREDIENTS CLASSIFIED AS HOT BOTH IN THE LIBER AND IN PREVIOUS MEDICAL WORKS [1]

Ingredients classified as hot, 66/9–35	In Galen (Kühn) [vol. and page]	In Avicenna (Gerard), *Canon* II [page]	In Chauliac (Nicaise) [page]
mirre	XII, 81	475	651
storax	XII, 131	623	656
olibane	—	532	—
mastike	XII, 113	461	650
opeponak	XII, 94	528	652
ammoniak	—	8	640
bedellium	—	115	642
seraphin	XII, 120	637	656
salbanum (= *galbanum*)	XII, 153	319	647
terrebintym	XII, 113	690	657
pixgreke	XIII, 709	546	654
pikliquidum	XIII, 709	546	654
euphorbe	XIII, 271	236	646
castorium	I, 649	125	644
clowes de golofre	—	318	647
nuutmugg	—	502	—
canell	XII, 26	127	644
galynga	XII, 54	321	—
setuale	—	745	—

Blanks in the table indicate that the ingredient could not be identified in the text.

TABLE I (cont.).

Ingredients classified as hot, 66/9–35	In Galen (Kühn) [vol. and page]	In Avicenna (Gerard), Canon II [page]	In Chauliac (Nicaise) [page]
gynger	XI, 880	746	—
longe pepir	XII, 97	557	654
white pepir	XII, 97	556	654
aloes epotik	XI, 822	66	640
fenkalle	XII, 67	281	646
percell	XII, 99	56	—
brusk	—	—	—[1]
spourge	XII, 141	429	—
pyon	—	561	—
pappwort	XII, 128	261	—
alysander	XII, 128	56	—
polipodi	—	542	—
gladyn	—	358	—
yrislirik	—	—	—
louache	—	386	—
philipendula	—	—	—[2]
centory	XII, 19	161	664
burnett	—	—	—
germandre	XII, 153	135	—
white brissoke	XV, 179	142	644
rede diptonge	I, 682; XI, 863	468	—
gladyn	—	358	—
wilde sawge	XII, 138	—	655
cowesleppes	—	—	—
ȝarow	—	—	653
alisandre	XII, 128	56	—
prymrolle	—	—	—
centurion (= centory)	XII, 19	161	644
lauandre	—	495	—
cresses	XII, 58	509	645
rede cale	XV, 179	142	644
pelleter	XII, 110	554	654
rewe	XII, 100	578	655
sawge	XI, 871	—	655
iarue	—	—	653
mynt saraȝine	XI, 836	50	641
puliole montane	XI, 857	468	—
origine	I, 682	533	—
calamynt	XI, 883	157	643
calamyn	—	—	—
camamil	XI, 833	121	643
ysope	XII, 149	365	649
aueroyn	XI, 799	86	642
auance	—	—	—
rede nettill	XI, 817	725	652
louache	—	386	—
gayle	XII, 81	—	—
pitory (= paritory)	—	—	653

[1] *Bruscus* is classified as hot in *Coll. Salern.* (Renzi) V, 240.
[2] *Philipendula* is classified as hot in *Coll. Salern.* (Renzi) V, 249.

TABLE I (cont.).

Ingredients classified as hot, 66/9-35	In Galen (Kühn) [vol. and page]	In Avicenna (Gerard). Canon II [page]	In Chauliac [Nicaise] [page]
herb John	XII, 148	363	649
lorelle leues	XI, 863	452	—
wormot	XI, 8	—	—
gronswale	XI, 844	—	—
smalache	XII, 118	56	640
sauine	XI, 839	5	—
ypocone	XII, 148	—	—
scafiȝagre	XII, 129	622	656
caraway sedes	XII, 13	140	—
marigolde sedis	—	377	651
mustard sedis	XI, 421	683	—
white pepir sedis	XII, 97	556	654
fenicrek	XII, 141; XV, 457	251	646
lynsede	XII, 62	446	650
cresses sede	XII, 58	509	645
pepill sede	—	106	—
coconode	XIII, 568	214; 452	—

66/12. STORAX : Cf. " Storacis sunt tria genera, s. calamita que interpretatur bona gutta . . . storax quando simpliciter ponitur pro calamita intelligitur," *Alphita*, 178.

66/13. *Salbanum* is perhaps an error for *galbanum*. Like the gum resins *opeponak, ammoniak,* and *seraphium* which precede it, *galbanum* is derived from an umbelliferous plant.

The identifications of *pix greke* and *pix liquid* are based on descriptions of modern processes of producing tar and colophony. The following passage in Bartholomaeus Anglicus (British Museum, Additional MS. 27944) XVII, cxxiii implies that in some cases the names were used of the same substance, which reminds us that the medieval processes and products differed from modern ones : " Of picche is double maner of kynde þe oon hatte schippe picche . . . and picche y molte is y cleped picche liquida . . . þe harde picche is componed in oon manere and the fletynge in neissche in an oþer maner and many clepeþ þis fletyng pycche colophonia oþer pix greca, picche of grees, for in grees is mochel þer of y founde."

66/17. LONGE PEPIR : The fruit spikes from which long pepper is obtained consist of a large number of small berries packed closely around a central axis. In the Middle Ages, they were generally believed to be the flower stalks of the plant yielding white and black pepper. Cf. Dawson 694.

66/24. WHITE BRISSOKE : Cf. " The kale, that he says, not ere of garths bot of gressis, that grouys bi thaim ane in the feld, as brisokes," H. R. Bramley, *The psalter . . . with a translation . . . by Richard Rolle* (Oxford, 1884), XXXVI, 21. Van Wijk p. 89 lists *bresich* as a French name of the ordinary variety of *Brassica oleracea*.

66/27. *Mynt sarazine* is probably the *Menthe sarracénique* mentioned in Chauliac (Nicaise) 680 where it is identified as either *Achillea ptarmica*, L. or *Achillea pyrenica*, Sibth. The earliest occurrence noted in NED is in the *Grete Herball* of 1525, where it is called *Mynte romayne or sarazine* and classed as a hot herb.

66/28. *Calamyn* may be either a mistaken repetition of the preceding item or an error for *calamus*, which is listed as hot in Avicenna (Gerard) *Canon* II, 160.

Notes. 113

66/31. YPOCONE : Paulus (Adams) VII, 3 lists *hypecoon* as cold. Serapion (1497) *De simpl. med.* lists as hot a herb called *ypicone* or *ypericon*, also called *camepiteos*.

66/35. COCONODE : Cf. " laureole . . . frutex est . . . cuius semen coconidium dicitur," Platearius (1497) *Circum instans s. de laureole*; " Coconidium, .i. semen laureole," *Alphita* 43/25.

67/1-39. This is a recipe for the wound-drink *Save* which, as Schöffler points out, pp. 104-108, is neither ' salve ' nor ' sage ' but the name of a particular compound. Other recipes for *Save* are to be found in : Henslow A 55/1-56/12 ; Henslow B 117/17-118/16 ; Henslow C 126/18-127/18 ; Dawson 827 ; Müller 47/4-48/6, 9-17. As in the case of other elaborate preparations, the ingredients vary to some extent but the procedure is almost exactly the same in all versions.

67/7. CROIS : Cf. " Herba cruciata i. croyse," *Sinon. Bart.* 23.

67/10. CROPE DE CAMBRE : Dawson 872, another recipe for *Save*, includes hemp crops as an ingredient.

67/11. Perhaps *samson* is an error for *ramson* owing to a scribal misreading of *r* as *s*. *Ramson* is identified as *affodill* in Dawson 562 and *Alphita* 3/10-15. Modern English *ramson* is the broad-leaved garlic, *Allium ursinum*. NED identifies the Middle English occurrences of the word with this plant.

67/15-16. ROUGE RUNCEBRERE : *Rounce Brere* is glossed *Mures beries* in a fourteenth century document edited in M. R. James, *Catalogue of the Manuscripts in St. John's College, Cambridge* (Cambridge, 1913), p. 155. Modern French *ronce* means 'blackberry'. Medieval Latin *teneritatem runcis* is glossed by Old French *tendron de ronche*. See *Romania* XXXII, 365, 366.

67/16-17. The identification of *red nettill* is based on the following :

> The nettle hatte vrtica and haþ þat name for he brenneþ þe body þat it toucheþ and it is of fuyry kynde as macer seiþ . . . of netles is double kynde oon brenneþ and byteþ and gendreth bleynes and ycchinge and haþ scharpe leues and rowgh and somdel reede and rowe stalkes wiþ egges and brenneþ his hond þat it handeleþ and is heuy of smelle wiþ somdel bitter sauour. Anoþer maner of netle is þat hatte þe dede ouþer þe blynde nettel and haþ leues more white þan þe oþer haþ and more and roundere and byteþ nouzt hem þat it handeliþ and haþ flour now reed and now whyte wiþ ful heuy smelle and sauour and þat nettle is medicynal.

[Bartholomaeus Anglicus (British Museum Additional MS. of 27944 of Trevisa's translation) XVII, cxciii]. The following quotation suggests that *red netel* was sometimes used of the especially stinging species of *Urtica* called Grecian nettle (*U. pillulifera*, L.) : *Urtica greca, rouge urtcie, reed netel, Alphita*, 192.

67/17-18. ME. *tansay* and Med. L. *tanacetum* were applied to a wider range of plants than those comprising the modern genus *Tanacetum*. *Tanacetum album* (*Sinon. Bart.* 41) and *T. agreste* (*Alphita* 181) are glossed by ME. *gose gres*(e (?*Potentilla anserina*). *Alphita* lists a *Tanacetum* = *Athanasia* (?*Athanasia maritima*) and a *Tanacetum domesticum nel ortolanum* (?*Tanacetum vulgare*). No evidence has been found that any of the cudweeds (Linnæan genus *Filago*) were called tansays.

67/39. MOUSFICHE : Mouse pea (?*Lathyrus macrorrhizus*, Wimm.) is given as a synonym of vetch in *Sinon. Bart.* 45 and *Alphita* 131.

68/1-12. Jean Pitard's *unguentum quod vocatur gratia dei* (*Archiv Med.* II, 213) seems to be the earliest record of *Gratia Dei*. This fourteenth century recipe of Pitard's resembles more closely the *Gratia Dei* of 68/13-30. Middle English recipes similar to that of 68/1-12 are : Müller 49/5-14, 129/4-16, and Henslow A 48/23-50/15. In Müller 129/4-16 the salve is called *donum dei*. See Müller's note to 49/5-14. See notes to 68/13-30.

68/13-30. Similar recipes for *Gratia Dei :* *Archiv Med.* II, 213 ; Müller 136/18-137/18 ; Henslow A 48/1-22 ; Henslow B 86/4-20 ; Heinrich 122a/20-122b/10 ; Dawson 301 ; Ketham (Sudhoff-Singer) xx. See notes to 68/1-12.

68/38. Platearius (1497) *Circum instans* III, 9 uses *branca vrsina* with old swine grease instead of with mallows for apostyms.

69/4-9. Parallels : Heinrich 142b/15-17 ; *Anglia* XVIII, 302/290-292.

69/14–70/19. Parallels : Dawson 92–93; Henslow A 50/16–51/5; Roy 12 G iv, f. 190r. Like the Thornton recipe, Dawson 92–93 has two separate herbal recipes, one a plaster, the other a drink. Henslow A and Roy 12 G iv have instead a single recipe, containing many of the same ingredients, which may be used either as a plaster or a drink. The directions which follow the herbal recipes (or recipe) furnish a striking illustration of fairly close verbal similarity throughout a long passage :

Dawson 93	Henslow A51/6–52/7	Roy 12 G iv, f. 190r
And iff it com nat owt ne he kest nat than itt is a tokyne off lyve than do serch the wound and chaufe þe brokyne bones sotelly and slely that þou ne tame the tay of the breyne and if it be bled fast wyþ hyme softly with soft lynnen cloth And afterward take soft lynnen cloth & wrape and wymple it togeder and lay it ouer þe wound and take whete floure wele bultyde and straw on the clowt that lyeth on the wound full softly and afterward lat a woman that fedith a knawe childe if it be a man that is wounditt mylke her papp softly on the floure that is strawed on the clowt & afterward lay another cloute þer vpon and straw it with floure as þu didest þat othir and of the mylke til it be evyn with þe flesshe and hyll þe hed and latt it be still till on þe morow then on þe morow vnhill the hede softly and iff þu se þer aboue as it was bloburs lyke to that þat standith on water when it raynyth then it is signe of deth And iff thou se before the tay as it wer a spynnynge webb or reede that is tokynge that þe reme of þe brayne if brokyn then this is sygne of hasty deth opynly provyd And if þer non of thies signes be geven hyme ech day	ȝif hyt comyt out at þe wounde and saue þe brokyn quatliche hit loke þat þou touche noȝt þe tay of þe brayn; and ȝif hit blede faste wype hit with a lynne clout and þenne tak a lynne clout þat ys werid and softe ley on þe wounde and whete-mele þat ys wel y-boutyd, and strowe vppon þe clout fayre and sotele; and þenne let a womman þat fedyþ a knaue child ȝif hit be a man lete his heite melke þeron on þe flour and after ley an ouþer cloþ þer-vpon and flour and melle þer-vpon with-oute by-fore þe wounde by-hynde þe flech and hele hys heuyd softly and ȝif þou se þer abou[e] as hit were a borbel þat stondiþ on þe water whanne hit ys y-remeuyd þanne ys signe of deþ; and ȝif þou se by-fore hys teyþ as hit were a blod spume web þat ys tokenyng þat þe veyne of his arme ys brokyn and þat ys signe of hastely deþ; and ȝef þer be non of þese sygnes ȝef hym eche day ones at morwe and ones at eue þys drynke to make þe brokyn bones come out; and clense þe rewme of þe bran of þe bloud þat helyþ þe webbe; and ȝef þyn heuyd be brokyn to-fore þanne þat man by-houuyþ do þer-on maser lete hym remuy wel þe broken of þe wounde as	ȝif hit come oute at þe wonde serche þe wonde & saue þe broken bon coyntelich þat þu tame not þe teye of þe brayn & ȝif hit blede fast wype hit softe with a lynnen cloth werut & þan take a lynnen cloth wered & softe ley vpon þe wonde & take wete floure þat is wel bultud & straw vpon þe cloth fayre & softly & þen let a wommon þat fedes a knaue childe ȝif hit be a mon þat his hurted meke herted mylken vpon þe flour & aftur ley on an oþer cloute þer vpon & floure & mylke als he dud by fore til þe wonde be euen wiþ þe flesch & hulle þe hed & let hym be tille þe morn & þen vnhulle þe hed softly ȝif þu se þer on aboue as hit were a burbel þat stondes on þe water when hit rennes þat is signe of deth & ȝif þu se byfore is tye as hit were a blo spinant webbe red þat is tokene þat þe reme of þe brayne is broken & þat his signe of hasty deth & ȝif þer be non of þese signes þen ȝif hym eueri day to drynk twyes ones at þe morn a noþur at euen þis drynk þat makeþ þe broken bonus to comen oute & clense þe reume of þe hed brayn of blod & heles þe wounde & ȝif þe hed be broken be fore þat men behouet to þe þer in a maser

Notes.

Dawson 93 (continued)	Henslow A51/6–52/7 (continued)	Roy 12 G iv, f. 190r (continued)
twyse drynke onys at morow a noþer tyme at eve this drynke ffor it makyth broken bonys to com owte & it clensith þe reme of the breyne of blode and helith the wound And iff it was so broke that hit behovyth to do þer in a pece of masere let well than ronge the broken of the hede as hit is before sayd and sett þerin a pece of maser and enoynt it with this oyntement her after ywriten	he by-fore sayd and set þer-in maser with þys oynement	let hym remeue wel þe broken of þe hed as hit is byfore seyd & set þer yn a maser & gres þe wonde with þis oynement

70/4, 6. MASER: Mace is mentioned as being highly astringent in Paulus (Adams) VII, 3 s. Μάκηρ; Avicenna (Gerard) *Canon* II, 456; and Serapion (1497) *De simpl. med.* II, 2.

70/4. Note that parallel to *rounge*, Dawson has *ronge*, Henslow *remuy*, and Roy 12 G iv *remeue*.

70/8. BAYNWORT: Two fairly close parallels have *bonwort* (Henslow A 52/7) and *bomwort* (Roy 12 G iv, f. 190r). Dawson 94 has, like the Thornton version, *baynwort*. BUBILL: As all three parallels have *bugle*, it seems likely that *bubill* is an error for *bugill*.

70/20–26. Parallel: Dawson 97.

70/27–71/3. Parallels: Müller 104/6–20; Henslow A 25/13–26/8. Parallels to 70/27–31: Henslow A 39/9–11; Müller 54/11–15; Heinrich 142a/12–14; Roy 12 G iv, f. 192v.

70/34–35. For Thornton's " tak a lyn clathe & do ij falde or thre or a pece of white lethir," Müller 104/14–15 has " take ⟨a⟩ lynen cloth, and make it two-fold or thre, or take flax or whit ledir " while Henslow A 26/3 has " take a lynne cloþ and do hit to fold oþer with leþer ".

71/4–6. Parallels: Müller 92/12–14 and *Romania* XXXVII, 366. For Thornton's " Take lard & mak sayme þer-of," the Old French recipe has " Fetes saim de lart " and Müller has " Take þe grees of þe fleyer ".

71/7–8. Parallels: *Herb. Ap.* (Sigerist) 77/8–10 [OE: *Herb. Ap.* (Cockayne I) 135]; *Camb. Antid.* (Sigerist) 167; *Romania* XXXVII, 366; Henslow A 26/13–14, 21—22, 28/9–10.

71/9–12. Parallel: Henslow A 26/9–12. Henslow A also has: *remeue hit eche day onys.*

71/20–25. Parallel: *Rel. Ant.* I, 55/17–23. For Thornton's *maroȝl*, *Rel. Ant.* has *maroile*; for Thornton's *bayneworte*, *Rel. Ant.* has *baywort*.

72/15–23. Parallel: Dawson 685. Dawson has *lard* and *pich rosen* instead of *entruce of þe ere.*

72/24–27. Parallel: Dawson 686. The Dawson recipe has the following heading: " An oþer enoyn to wound." It ends: " make this enoyn to all kyles and to all woundes."

73/7–13. Parallel: Heinrich 105b/19–106a/2.

73/14–18. Parallel: Dawson 656.

73/19–35. Parallels: Heinrich 107b/17–108a/12; Henslow B 87/19–88/7. The *grene oynement* referred to in 55/29 was probably a salve very similar to this one. In the parallels this recipe is called *Unguentum viride*. The heading as it appears in Henslow B continues: " A goud oynement grene, which clenseth wondis and norischith good flesche in wondes olde and freteth Iuel flesche withoute violence and is best."

73/22. For *olyue*, Henslow B 88/1 has *oyle dolyue* and Heinrich 107b/21 has *oyle de olyfe*.

74/9-32. Parallels : Roy 12 G iv, f. 189v; Henslow A 27/1-19. Similar recipes : Heinrich 98a/29-98b/13, 143a/24-143b/7; Dawson 654.

74/33-75/2. Parallel : Heinrich 142b/2-15.

75/8-9. Parallels : Henslow A 26/18-20, 28/7-9. Cf. notes to 75/18-19.

75/18-19. Parallels : Dawson 222; Henslow A 30/6-9. Cf. notes to 75/8-9.

75/20-21. Parallel : Henslow A 30/10-11.

75/22-23. Parallel : Arderne (Power) 89/4-6.

75/24-25. Parallel : Henslow A 28/20-21.

75/26-27. Parallel : *Rel. Ant.* I, 55/24-26. The parallel in *Rel. Ant.* is headed *For hym that is gorwounded*.

75/28. Perhaps *tonge of dragon* is a garbled form of *dragagantum*, a gum similar to *incense* and *mastik*. Cf. *diptonge* for *dittany*, 66/25, and *dede tonge þat is þi halfe tonge*, 79/21-22.

75/32-76/2. Parallel : Dawson 706-708.

76/9-10. Cf. *lange wortys de chare* in MS. Harleian 279 (ed. Austin *Two fifteenth century cookery books*, EETS 91) : " Take fayre worts . . . and parboyle hem . . . þan take hem vp of þe water . . . an cut þe leuys a-to or a-þre, and caste hem in-to þe beff." Cf. also Mn. Sc. *lang kail*, cabbage, esp. when boiled without being mashed or much cut up (Wright EDD and Jamieson).

76/12-14. The application of betony juice to draw broken bones from a wound is included among the recipes in : Petrocellus (Löweneck) 6/5-6 [Old English translation : *Peri Di* (Cockayne III) 87/3], *Leechbook* I (Leonhardi) 8/3-5, and *Leechbook* III (Leonhardi) 100/10-11.

76/19-20. Parallel : Dawson 710.

76/21-22. Parallel : Dawson 710. Dawson has *buke rafen* instead of *brakans*.

76/29-32. Parallel : Roy 12 G iv, f. 193r.

76/34. Parallels : Dawson 85; Arderne (Power) 27/34-39.

77/5-14. Parallels : Dawson 852 and Henslow B 90/9-91/2. This sleeping potion is called *dwale* in Henslow B.

77/15-26. Similar passages occur in other texts giving the symptoms of hot and cold festers, of *kankirs* and festers, etc. None of these contain all of the facts given here. The longest, Dawson 545, parallels all but ll. 16-17. Other shorter passages occur in : Heinrich 104a/21-28; Schöffler 235/12-15; Sloane 393, f. 60; Henslow A 20/14-18.

77/28-78/7. Parallels : Schöffler 235/16-236/9; Henslow A 20/19-21/16. For Thornton's " þe white malue sall þou sethe þer-with, for þu may nott wrynge owte þe jus þer-of als of þe iij oþer, for it is so fatt," Henslow A has " þe white malew þou schalt boyle þer-with al hol, for þou myȝt noȝt wryng the wos out þer-of as þou doust of þe ouþer grase, for hit ys so fat." The Schöffler recipe does not include this comment on the mallow. For the *wyte tansey* (*white tansay*) of Thornton's and Schöffler's version, Henslow A has *wilde tansi*. Cf. *Tanacetum album i. gose grese, Sinon Barth* 41 and *Tanacetum agreste . . . anglice gose gres, Alphita* 181.

78/17-27. Parallel : Henslow A 21/17-22/6.

78/28-35. Parallel: Henslow A 22/7-14.

79/1-2. *Herb. Ap.* (Sigerist) 73/8-11 prescribes the application of agrimony *Ad uulnera et canceromata* [Old English : *Herb. Ap.* (Cockayne I) 131]. Middle English parallel : *Anglia* XVIII, 327/807-808.

79/15. *Apostolicon* is a white unguent made of olive oil, vinegar, and a variety of other drugs. It seems to have derived its name from the fact that it was originally made of drugs besides oil and vinegar to the number of twelve, the number of the Apostles. Cf. Mondeville (Pagel) 544. Recipes for *Apostolicon* are found in many medieval works : *L'antidot. Nicolas* (Dorveaux) 17; *St. Gall Antid.* (Sigerist) 82; Lanfrank (Fleischacker) 342/1-8; Heinrich 121b/11-122a/19; Müller 63/27-64/3; Ketham (Sudhoff-Singer) xx.

79/21-22. Possibly " *dede tonge þat is þi halfe tonge* " is a corruption of or a play upon the word *ditany* from L. *diptamnus*. Cf. *diptonge*, 66/25, and *tonge of dragon*, 75/28.

79/25–27. The following passage from Bartholomaeus Anglicus (British Museum, Additional MS. 27944 of Trevisa's translation) tends to confirm the identification of *wilde cucurd* as *Citrullus colocynthis*:

> Plinius seiþ þer is a wilde Cucurbita as gret as a fynger and groweþ in stony place & helpiþ moche þe stomak and guttis . . . . Isider seiþ þat a wilde cucurbyta is þe same þat is colequintida, a manere weþe wynde, a wel bitter herbe and springeþ in spray toward þe grounde as cucurbita doþ and haþ grete leues wiþ heuy smyl as cucurbita haþ . . . . it seemeþ þat þe firste maner cucurbita beriþ goordis and þat þe worste manere Cucumer bereþ pynopyns.

80/17. Perhaps *to see* has been omitted after *thirlles*.

80/23–27. Middle English parallel: Schöffler 235/5–11. Dioscorides (Wellman) ii, 28; Oribasius (Raeder) II, 49; and *Archiv Med*. II, 49 likewise prescribe burnt fish for gout fester.

81/5–9. Parallels: Roy 12 G iv, f. 192v; Henslow A 33/14–19.
81/10–14. Parallels: Henslow B 103/15–18; Henslow A 22/22–23/4: *Anglia* XVIII, 301/237–242.
81/15–19. Parallel: Henslow A 22/16–21.
81/22–23. Parallel: *Anglia* XVIII, 301/251–254.
81/27–31. Parallels: *Romania* XXXVII, 362/1; Larsen 213.
81/34–37. Parallel: Henslow A 23/5–9.
81/38–82/4. Parallels: Henslow A 23/10–16; Dawson 219.
82/4–15. Parallel: Henslow A 23/16–24/3.
82/22–27. Parallel: Henslow A 24/4–9.

GLOSSARY

Wherever possible, the names of plants have been identified at least tentatively. In few cases are the identifications incontestable, and, in many, the scanty and sometimes contradictory nature of the material precludes positive identification. It was felt that, in most cases, the suggestion of a probable identification would at least serve as a point of departure for further study.

Abown, *adv.* above,—said of vomiting as opposed to evacuation. 15/24, 26/15, 28/4, 29/13.
Ache (1), *n.* ? wound, ? buttock, 59/14. ? OE. *aece* or ? OF. *nache*.
Ache (2), *n.* ? smallage, *Apium graveolens*, L., 11/16, 22/32, 32/8, 47/27, 48/30, etc.; **ache sedes,** 24/39; **ache rute,** 32/12. OF. *ache*. Cf. **Smalach(e.**
Ache petit = smalach(e, 67/15.
Affadill, *n.* ? asphodel, ? a plant of the genus *Asphodelus*, 6/12. Med. L. *affodillus*.
Agewe, *n.* = **feuer agew(e,** 52/21. OF. *ague*.
A + G + L + A, a tetragramaton, 49/8. *See note.*
Agnayls, *n. pl.* ? corns, 49/side-note 7. OE. *angnaezl*.
Agrippa, *n.* an ointment, 45/4. *See note.*
Ay, *adv.* ever, 17/31.
Ayer(e, *n.* air, 19/21, 21/30.
Aymers, *n. pl.* embers, 27/2. ON. *eimyrja*.
Aysell(e, *n.* vinegar, 5/22, 11/3. OF. *aisil*.
Ayther, *pron.* each (of two), 21/1 ; **aþer,** 3/14.
Ake, *n.* oak, 81/1.
Ake appills, oak galls, 13/34, 27/7.
Album, *see* **Olibanum.**
Alcea, *n.* the marsh mallow, *Althaea officinalis*, L., 74/33.
Ald(e, *a.* old, 4/18, 21/5.
Alisandre, *n.* alexanders, *Smyrnium olusatrum*, L., 66/26; **alysandre,** 45/33; **alysander,** 66/21; **alisaundir,** 32/24. OF. *alisaundre*.
All(e, *a.* all, 4/side-note 1, 72/side-note 6; **al,** 59/34.

All(e, *adv.* entirely, 2/1, 3/17 ; **al,** 6/2.
Allerone, *n.* probably quill, possibly pinion, 8/33. F. *aileron*. *See note.*
Almaste, *adv.* almost, 31/23.
Alme, *n.* elm, 61/7; **almebarke,** 5/17. ON. *álmr*.
Almondes, *n. pl.* almonds, 25/22.
Aloe cicotrine, a highly prized dark, transparent form of aloes obtained from the plant *Aloe socotrina*, Lam., 11/31. Med. L. *aloe cicotrina*. *See note.* Cf. **Aloes epotik.**
Aloes, *n. pl.* a purgative drug made from the juice of plants of the genus *Aloe*, 11/36.
Aloes epotik, an inferior opaque, liver-coloured, crystalline form of aloes, obtained from the plant *Aloe socotrina*, Lam., *pl.*, 66/17 ; **aloen epatik,** 73/32. Cf. **Aloe cicotrine.**
Alome, *see* **Blaunke alome.**
Alom glas(e, crystallized alum, 9/17, 19, 78/10.
Also, *adv.* also, 2/25, etc.; **alswa,** 38/26.
Alsome, *a.* ? wholesome, 78/15.
Ambre orientale, ? the fossil resin amber, 58/13.
Ambrose, *n.* ? wood sage, *Teucrium Scorodonia*, L., 23/3, 25/19, 62/4, 65/15; **ambros,** 3/25, 44/28, 69/16; **ambros leues,** 34/20. OF. *ambroise*.
Amend(e, *v.* recover from illness, 19/31, 42/27.
Ammoniak, *n.* gum ammoniac, a gum resin obtained from the ammoniac plant, *Dorema ammoniacum*, D. Don., 66/12, 68/4. OF. *ammoniac*, L. *ammoniacum*,

119

Ampull, *n.* a small bottle or flask, 8/24.
Ana, *adv.* ana, equal amounts of each of the preceding, 3/4, 12/13, 22/39, 23/3, 25/39, *etc.*; **ana weght,** 81/38; **ana & þat bi weghte,** 82/23. Med. L. *ana,* Gr. ἀνά.
Ande, *n.* breath, 15/26. ON. *ande.*
Ane, *adv.* alone, 32/16, 33/25, 72/20.
An(e, *num.* one, 17/30, 63/11.
Anes, *adv.* once, 1/9.
Anete, *n.* dill, *Anetum graveolens,* L., 15/12, 25/19; **anete sede,** 34/27. OF. *anet.*
Anewe, *v.* renew, 10/36.
Angell brede, a purgative cake, 28/5.
Anger, *n.* pain, inflammation, 61/16.
Ankill, *n.* ankle, 53/14.
Annys, *n.* anise, *Pimpinella anisum,* L., 3/8, 6/38, 15/27; **anys,** 27/32, 43/39; **annys sede,** 50/29. OF. *anis.*
Anoyntement, *n.* ointment, 65/18.
An oþer, another; —like L. *item,* used in introducing an additional recipe for the same disease, 1/side-note 1, *etc.*
Apostym, *n.* cyst, abscess, 35/side-note 8, 36/side-note 3; **apostymms,** *pl.*, 35/side-note 5. Cf. **Appostym, Enpostyme.**
Apostolicon, *n.* an unguent, 79/15. *See note.*
Apostolion, *n.* ? = apostolicon, 36/30. *See note.*
Appell, ? error for a **pottell,** 75/14.
Appill, *n.* apple, 75/27. Cf. **Ake appills.**
Appostym, *n.* = apostym, 35/22.
Araby, Arabike, *see* **Gomme araby.**
Arage, *n.* orach, a plant of the genus *Atriplex,* 27/36; **areges,** *gen. s.*, 15/12.
Archangelica, *n.* blind or dead nettle, a plant of the genus *Lamium,* 14/24. Cf. **Rede nettill.**
Areges, *see* **Arage.**
Arely, *adv.* early, 67/38.
Arenement, *n.* = arnement, 9/25, 28/30.
Aristotill, *n.* ? 58/6.
Arnement, *n.* vitriol, a sulphate, probably of iron, 12/24, 26/14, 58/14, 76/31; **arnament,** 78/17, 81/38, 82/22. Cf. **Arenement.** *See note to* 9/25.
Aromatica, *n.* = galbanum, 27/19. *See note.*
Artetik, *a.* arthritic, 66/side-note 1. OF. *artetique.*
Asafetida, *n.* asafoetida, an alliaceous-smelling gum-resin from the juice of certain species of *Ferula,* 27/19.
Asche, *n.* the ash-tree, 6/23; **ashes,** *pl.*, 34/2; **þe scho asche,** 61/6–7; **esche,** 7/29.
Ashe, *n.* ash, 5/31; **askes,** *pl.*, 1/19.
At, *prep.* at, 3/11; to; -introducing an infinitive of purpose, 6/5.
At, *conj.* that, 47/22; *rel. pron.* what, 64/25; which, 70/30..
Aþer, *pron.* = ayther, 3/14.
Auaile, *v.* avail, 81/8.
Auance, *n.* herb bennet, *Geum urbanum,* L., 21/24, 43/27, *etc.*; **avance,** 4/17, 54/33, 55/32; **auaunce,** 80/31; **auances,** 72/9; **auance sede,** 33/1. OF. *avence.*
Aueroyn(e, *n.* averoyne, *Artemisia abrotanum,* L., 1/27, 2/8, 37, 66/29, 71/27, 72/6; **aueroyn,** *vel sowthrenwode,* 34/3; **aueron,** 61/6. OF. *averoine.*
Awen, *pron.* own, 28/28; **awenn,** 34/2.
Axes, *n.* attack (of fever), 59/31, 60/20.
Aȝarabackara, *n.* asarabacca, *Asarum europaeum,* L., 32/24. L. *assarum bacca.*

Bayes, *n. pl.* berries (of the ivy), 46/10.
Baynewort(e, *n.* bonewort, ? daisy, *Bellis perennis,* L. (*See note to* 27/9), 9/16, 16/17, 38/8, 54/8, 72/11, 77/1; **baynwort(e,** 27/9, 59/4, 70/8, 71/14, 21, 74/30. OE. *bānwyrt.* Cf. **Raynwort.**
Bak(ke, *n.* bat, 5/21, 27. Cf. ODan. *nath-bakkae,* OSwed. *nattbacka,* night bat.
Balloke, *n.* testicle, 37/1; **ballokesȝ** *pl.*, 37/14, 48/36.
Bane, *n.* bone, 69/17, *etc.*; **banes,** *pl.*, 39/12, *etc.* Cf. **Bone.**
Bare, *n.* boar, 4/34; **bare gres(e,** 39/7, 63/37.
Barke, *n.* bark, 15/12; bark (of a root), 21/8, 38/39; husk (of a

Glossary.

nut), 55/19; **barke duste,** 54/29-30.
Bathe, *a.* both, 20/8, *etc.* Cf. **Bothe.**
Bathe, *adv.* both, 28/4. Cf. **Bothe.**
Bawme, *n.* balm, an aromatic substance obtained from various trees of the genus *Balsamodendron,* 11/19.
Be, *v.* be, 47/19, *etc.*; *pr.* 2 *s.,* **arte,** 15/25; *pr.* 3 *s.,* **is,** 1/17, *etc.*; **es,** 5/7, *etc.*; *pr. pl.,* **are,** 12/side-note 5, *etc.*; **bene,** 71/28; **er,** 37/39, 42/35; *pa.,* **was,** 4/13, *etc.*; *pr. subj.,* **be,** 1/16, 12/37, *etc.*; *pa. subj.,* **were,** 34/6, 21/12, *etc.*; **ware,** 51/32; *p. p.,* **bene,** 5/30, *etc.*
Bedde, *n.* bed, 28/36, *etc.*; a bed of herbs upon which the patient is to lie, 32/33; a bed (of growing plants), 18/32.
Bedellium, *n.* bdellium, a gum-resin resembling myrrh, obtained from shrubs of the genus *Commiphora,* 66/13, 68/5.
Beke, *v.* to suffuse pleasantly with warmth, 55/37.
Bene, *n.* bean; —a measure of quantity, 19/11; **bene mele,** 27/14; **bene straa,** 50/5.
Benedicta, *n.* an electuary, 45/1. *See note.* Not in NED.
Benett, *see* **Herbe benet(t.**
Bere, *v.* carry, 42/37; give birth to, 56/37; support by viscosity, 75/16.
Betoyn(e, *n.* betony, *Stachys betonica,* Benth., 21/24, 26/3, 32/22, 33/1, 23, 58/7, 59/1 (*See note*), 65/27, *etc.* OF. *betoine.* Cf. **Botoyne, Vetoyn(e.**
Bygynnes, *v.* begin, *pr.* 3 *pl.,* 51/14, *etc.*
By-houes, *v.* behove, *pr.* 3 *s.,* 67/5.
Birs, *v.* = **brysse,** 32/33.
Blaynes, *n. pl.* blains, inflammatory swellings, 22/side-note 8.
Blak, *a.* pale, 56/27. OE. *blāc.*
Blak(e, *a.* black, 6/1, 15/31. OE. *blaec.*
Blake pepir, black pepper, pepper from the dried unripe berries of *Piper nigrum,* 75/34.
Blak slaes, the fruit of the blackthorn, *Prunus spinosa,* 11/4.
Blake snyles, black snails, 9/23. Cf. **Rede snyle.** *See note to* 64/9-11.

Blak mynt, peppermint, *Mentha piperita,* L., 15/31. Cf. Schöffler 84.
Blaunke alome, ? burnt alum, a white powder, 3/32. *See note.*
Blawe, *v.* blow, 61/39; (with ellipsis) 62/2.
Bledder, *n.* the bladder (of the human body), 44/38; the bladder (of an animal, esp. one prepared for use as a container) **bleddir,** 19/10, 28/34; **bledder,** 28/35.
Blede, *v.* bleed, 5/3.
Bledyng, *vbl. n.* bleeding, haemorrhage, 47/side-note 6, 48/33; letting of blood, 52/30.
Blered, *ppl. a.* bleared, 9/side-note 8.
Blode, *n.* blood, 5/21; **blode latynge,** 47/26, side-note 7, 52/20. Cf. **Blude.**
Blomes, *n. pl.* blossoms, 45/17.
Blude, *n.* = **blode,** 31/14.
Bludy, *a.* bloody, 32/side-note 1.
Boche, *n.* botch, boil, ulcer, 52/21, 53/5, 10, 12, 16.
Boef, *see* **Lange de beefe.**
Boyste, *n.* a box for ointments, *pl.,* **boystes,** 4/10; **boistes,** 37/23; a cupping-glass, **boyste,** 53/15; **boystes,** *pl.,* 53/23. OF. *boiste.*
Bolnede, *p. p.* swelled, 74/38.
Bolnyng, *vbl. n.* swelling, 22/side-note 4.
Bolo armonico, bole armeniac, an astringent earth, 53/40.
Boltede, *p. p.* sifted, 69/27.
Bone, *n.* = **bane,** 69/side-note 2; **bones,** *pl.,* 54/side-note 6.
Borage, *n.* borage, *Borago officinalis,* L., 23/37, 27/36, 69/2; **burrege rute,** 65/28. OF. *borreche, bourrache,* Med. L. *borrago.*
Bothe, *a.* = **bathe,** 61/1.
Bothe, *adv.* = **bathe,** 53/29, 80/1.
Botoyne, *n.* = **betoyn(e,** 26/8, 10, 12.
Bowells, *n. pl.* bowels, 75/33.
Bray, *v.* crush to powder, 1/18. OF. *breier.*
Brakans, *n. pl.* brakens, large ferns, 76/22. *See note.*
Brance vrcyne, ? sea-dock, *Acanthus mollis,* L., 68/38.
Brandreth(e, *n.* gridiron, 7/29, 13/9-10. ON. *brand-reid.*
Brasill, *n.* a red dye-stuff made from the wood of one of the species of *Caesalpina,* 76/6. Cf.

Thompson, *Mat. Med. Painting*, pp. 116–121.

Brere, *n.* brier, 72/10; **brere croppe**, 27/4; **brere lefe**, 51/11.

Breste, *n.* the front of the body, 19/35, *etc.*; the *mamma*, 27/28; **brest**, 23/side-note 6.

Bretfull, *a.* brimful, 64/17.

Bryane, *n.* bryony, ? *Bryonia dioica*, Jacq. 76/37. OF. *bryone*, L. *bryonia*.

Bryn, *v.* burn, 10/3; **brynnand**, *ppl. a.*, 68/11.

Brynnynge, *vbl. n.* burning, 50/38.

Brynt, *n.* ? residue of burnt material clinging to the sides and bottom of a pot, 48/28. See note. Not in NED.

Brysse, *v.* bruise, 39/11, *etc.*; **bryssede**, *p. p.*, 23/23; **bryssed**, *ppl. a.*, 55/side-note 1. Cf. **Birs**.

Brissoke, *see* **White brissoke**.

Brissour, *n.* brusure, 47/15; **bryssour**, 47/side-note 1.

Bryste, *v.* burst, 6/13; *p. p.* **brostyn**, 36/19; **brustyn**, 36/26; *ppl. a.*, **bristen**, 68/31.

Brok, *n.* badger, 66/3; **brok grese**, 63/36, 64/4.

Brokes, *n. pl.* breakings of the skin, 68/34.

Brome, *n.* broom, a shrub of the genus *Genista*, 32/38, 45/17, 67/14; **brome stalke**, 48/20.

Bromstane, *n.* brimstone, 3/30, *etc.*; **bronstane**, 81/38.

Broo, *n.* liquid (of broth), 29/8.

Browes, *n. pl.* eyebrows, 58/28.

Brusk, *n.* ? butcher's broom, *Ruscus aculeatus*, L. (= Med. L. *bruscus*) or ? teasel, *Dipsacus sylvestris*, Mill. (called brushes in some Mn. dialects), 66/19.

Bubill, *n.* = **bugill**, 70/8. See note.

Bugill, *n.* bugle, probably *Ajuga reptans*, L., 67/8, 69/14, 71/1, 27, 31, 72/24, 76/36; **bugle**, 54/33, 59/4, 23, 74/1, 9, 79/17. OF. *bugle*.

Burbill, *n.* bubble, 69/35.

Burnett(e, *n.* ? the salad burnet, *Poterium sanguisorba*, L. or ? the great burnet, *Sanguisorba officinalis*, L., 29/35, 46/19, 66/24, 67/6; **burnet**, 69/16. Cf. **Littill burnett**.

Burre, *n.* a plant producing burs, perhaps the burdock, 22/21.

Burrege = borage; **burrege rute**, 65/28.

Bursa pastoris, *n.* shepherd's purse, *Capsella bursa-pastoris*, L., 22/24. Not in NED.

Burtre, *n.* the elder tree, *Sambucus nigra*, L., 15/12, 23/37, 30/15.

Buttre, *n.* butter, 3/30; **buttre of May(e** = **Maye buttre**, 4/38, 67/24, 77/34.

Caffatine, *see* ȝucre **caffatine**.

Cake, *n.* any compressed mixture of materials, 43/11. NED: 1528, in this sense.

Calamyn ? 66/28.

Calamynt (1) *n.* ? calamine, an ore of zinc, 9/30. See note. OF. *calamine*.

Calamynt (2) *n.* a plant of the genus *Calamintha*, 22/38, 23/13, 58/6, 66/28. Several species were distinguished. (Cf. *Sinon. Bart.* 14, *Alphita* 27, 148, and Barth. *De Prop. Rerum* XVII, xxxiv.) It is not clear which species was meant when no qualifying word was used. OF. *calament*, Med. L. *calamentum*.

Calde, *a.* cold;—caused by a lack of heat in the complexion of the patient,—said of a disease, 32/side-note 7, 33/side-note 3, 66/8, 77/16, 81/side-note 2; for the correction of excessive heat;—said of a remedy, 53/25.

Caldes, *v.* become cold, *pr.* 3 *pl.*, 58/37.

Cald mynt, *n.* ? error for **calamint (2)**, 33/9. See note.

Cale, *n.* kale, a plant of the genus *Brassica*, probably a variety of *Brassica oleracea*, L., 27/37; a soup of kale and other vegetables, 27/side-note 9 (NED: 1470, in this sense); **cale lefe**, 51/9; **cale stokes**, 43/7. Cf. **Kalcroppe**, **Red(e cale**.

Calles, *v.* call, *pr.* 3 *pl.*, 3/29, *etc.*; **callis**, 38/18.

Camamyll, *n.* camomile, *Anthemis nobilis*, L., 35/29, 34; **camamill**, 22/38; **camamil**, 66/29; **camamyle**, 68/37. OF. *camomille*.

Cambre, *see* **Crop de cambre**.

Camelle, *n.* = **camamyll**, 43/39. See note.

Camfire, *n.* camphor, 11/31. Cf. **Caumfere.** OF. *camfre,* Med. L. *camphora.*
Canell(e, *n.* cinnamon, the inner bark of the tree *Cinnamomum zeylanicum,* Nees, and possibly also the inferior bark of *Cinnamomum cassia,* Blume, 33/6 66/16, 76/19. OF. *canele.*
Caraway, *n.* = **carui,** 26/17; caraway (-eaway) **sede(s,** 50/30, 66/33.
Carui, *n.* caraway, *Carum carui,* L., 3/7; **caruy,** 7/1; **carwy,** 22/5. Med. L. *carui.*
Cassia fastula, the laxative pulp obtained from the pods of *Cassia fistula,* L., 57/3.
Caste, *v.* vomit, 15/24, 59/2.
Castorium, *n.* castoreum, a substance secreted by glands of the beaver, 66/14. OF. and L. *castoreum.*
Catholicon, *n.* an electuary, 47/7. See note. NED : 1611.
Caufe, *v.* warm, 14/25. OF. *chaufer.* Cf. **Chaufe.**
Caumfere, *n.* = **camfire,** 37/17.
Celidon(e, *n.* ? the greater celandine, *Chelidonium maius,* L., 9/22, 10/7, *etc.*; **celidoyne,** 2/11; **celydoyne,** 4/17; **celidoun,** 70/9; **celydoyn rotes,** 73/19. Med. L. *celidonia maior.*
Centory(e, *n.* ? one of two plants : 1. ? the yellow centaury (Med. L. *centaurea maior*) ; 2. ? the lesser centaury (Med. L. *centaurea minor*), 8/29, 12/11, 19/36, 20/32, 25/28, *etc.*; **centorie,** 21/24, 23/6, 24/4, *etc.* Med. L. *centaurea.*
Centurion, *n.* = **centory(e,** 66/26. Gr. κενταύρειον.
Centrum galli = **slaream,** 73/20, *centrum galli. i. slaream,* 14/7-8.
Cephalica, *n.* the cephalic vein, 53/19.
Cerfe, *see* **Longe de cerfe.**
Cerfoil(e, *n.* probably chervil, *Anthriscus cerefolium,* Hoffm., 45/33, 59/15, 71/21, 76/35; **cerfoill,** 71/26; **cerefoill,** 35/30. *See notes to* 47/12 *and* 59/15. Cf. **Charwelle, Cheruell, Cheuerfoill(e, Hertistonge.**
Cermoyntayne, *n.* sermountaine, *Laserpitium siler,* L., 6/38. OF. *sermontain.*

Ceruse, *n.* = **white lede,** 68/2.
Charbocle, *n.* carbuncle, 11/side-note 10. ONF. *carboucle.*
Charme, *n.* charm, 18/side-note 5, 56/side-note 5, 57/side-notes 2, 3, 63/side-note 3.
Charwelle, *n.* ? a variant form of cerfoil(e, 50/16. Cf. **Cerfoil(e, cheruell.**
Chaufe, *v.* = **caufe,** 66/2.
Chawdpys, *n.* ? some urinary or venereal disease, strangury, 45/ side-note 1. *See note.*
Cheyn, *see* **Lange de cheyn.**
Chepes, *n.* sheep, *gen. s.,* 4/30.
Cherestane kyrnells, cherry stone kernels, 45/38, 50/31; **cherestankirnells,** 45/7.
Cheruell, *n.* ? a variant form of cerfoil(e : ⟨*cheuerell*⟩ *cheruell,* 35/3; *pe jus of cerfoil & cheruell,* 59/15. Cf. **Cerfoil(e, Cheuerfoill(e.** *See note to* 59/15.
Chesseboll croppes, the tops of the opium poppy, *Papaver somniferum,* L., 73/37. Cf. **Whitte chessebolle.**
Cheuerfoill(e, *n.* probably woodbine, *Lonicera periclymenum,* L., 67/12, 70/9. The identification as *wodrofe* in 67/12 is probably an error. Cf. identification as *woodbynde,* Müller, 115/2, 36, note 2. Cf. **Cerfoil(e.**
Childe, *n.* a foetus, a newly born infant, 9/20, 56/21, 27, 57/side-note 4, *etc.*; **childre,** *pl.,* 56/18.
Childynge, *n.* delivery, 57/side-note 6.
Cholet, *n.* shallot, *Allium ascalonicum,* L., 67/10. NED: 1400 only.
Cicory, *n.* chicory, *Cichorium intybus,* L., 69/2.
Cicotrine, *see* **Aloe cicotrine.**
Cifoil, *n.* ? 29/14.
Cynkfoil, *n.* cinquefoil, *Potentilla reptans,* L., 67/16. Cf. **Pentafilon, Fiuelefe, Quintfoil(e.**
Cyroyns, *n. pl.* = **syroyn(e,** 69/5.
Claye, *n.* clay, 21/30. Cf. **Cle vrynall.**
Clarett, *n.* wine sweetened and infused with aromatic herbs, 34/29. *See notes.*
Clathe, *n.* cloth, 1/6; **clathes,** *pl.,* bed-clothes, 58/34.
Cle vrynall, clay urinal, 10/22. Cf. **Claye.**
Clefe, *v.* cleave, 18/8. Cf. **Cleue.**

Clere, *a.* used as *n.* the upper, clearer portion of a mixture which has been allowed to settle, 9/38. Cf. **Schire**.
Cleue, *v.* cleave, 6/1. Cf. **Clefe**.
Clister, *n.* enema, 28/side-note 9.
Cloue, *n.* a small bulb, forming part of the compound bulb (of the garlic), 3/20.
Clowes, *n. pl.* clove, the dried flower-bud of *Caryophyllus aromaticus*, L., 33/6, 44/22.
Clowes de golofre = clowes, 66/16. OF. *clou de gilofre (girofle)*, Gr. καρυόφυλλον.
Clusteryng, *vbl. n.* ? 27/side-note 4.
Cobills stanes, cobble stones, 19/5.
Coconode, *n.* seed of the spurge laurel, *Daphne Gnidium*, L., 66/35. Cl. L. *coccum gnidium*, Med. L. *cocognidium, coconidium*. Not in NED. *See note*.
Coghe, *n.* cough, 19/15; **dry coghe**, 20/side-note 12; **perilous coghe**, 21/side-note 4. Cf. **Dry ; Perilous coghe**.
Coile, *v.* strain, 36/11; **coille**, 67/26, 75/15; **coyl(e**, 11/20, 12/32, 68/17, 19, 71/17, 73/25, 39. Cf. *coulez le jus parmi un drap*, Romania XXXVII, 362/9. Not in NED.
Coylett, *n.* the residue of straining, 67/31, 68/20, 73/26; ⟨colett⟩ **coylett**, 68/18; **coilett**, 36/11. Cf. **Coile**.
Cokille mele, meal made from the cockle, *Lychnis githago*, Lam. or from darnell, *Lolium temulentum*, L., 58/4.
Colery3en, *n.* a person of choleric complexion, 47/21. Cf. **Colorik**.
Colyandre, *n.* coriander, *Coriandrum sativum*, L., 8/2; **Coliandre sede**, 60/18. OF. *coliandre*.
Colorye, *n.* collyrie, an eye-salve, 9/34, 10/side-note 4; **colore**, 11/32. L. *collyrium*.
Colorik, *a.* choleric, 51/34. Cf. **Colery3en**.
Columbyne, *n.* a plant of the genus *Aquilegia*, probably *Aquilegia vulgaris*, L., 24/18, 51/11; **colombyne**, 37/4.
Com(e, *v.* come, 7/15, 20/16; *pr.* 3 *s.*, **comes**, 51/35; **commes**, 79/35.
Comfery, *n.* comfrey, *Symphytum officinale*, L., 20/37, 47/16, 50/17, 71/20, 72/5, 11, 74/34, 76/23, 82/29; **comfory**, 71/13.
Comyn, *n.* cumin, the seed of *Cummin cyminum*, L., 6/38, 10/35, 11/15, 13/29, 21/1, 15, 22/39, 24/39, 48/2, 50/29.
Compleccion, *n.* complexion, the combination of humours in the body, 51/34.
Confeccion, *n.* a medicinal preparation, 32/19, 39/5, 67/26, 68/23, 26–27.
Consoude, *n.* ? = **comfery**, 72/25. Cf. **Cosoud maior, Cosoud milnen, Littill consoud(e**.
Consoud petit, ? the daisy, *Bellis perennis*, L., 67/9–10. OF. *consoude petite*, equivalent to Med. L. *consolida minor*. Cf. **Littill consoud(e**.
Contrarius, *a.* refractory (of hair), 5/side-note 6.
Coperose, *see* **Coprose**.
Coprose, *n.* copperas, 50/9, 75/32; **copprose**, 76/2; **coperose**, 3/3, 27, 49/19.
Corall, *n.* coral, 76/20.
Cordiaca, *n.* the cardiac vein, 52/38. Cf. **Hert veyne**.
Cornes, *n. pl.* seeds (of pepper), 2/12, 16/13, 22/8, 60/19.
Coruen (1), *p. p.* severed, 68/31.
Coruen (2), *p. p.* ? bent, 56/26, 27.
Cosoud maior ? = **comfrey**, 67/9. Med. L. *consoud maior*. Cf. **Consoude**.
Cosoud milnen, ? bugle, *Ajuga reptans*, L., 67/9. Med. L. *consoud media*. Cf. **Consoude**.
Cotidiane, *see* **Feuer cotidiane**.
Cotom(e. *n.* raw cotton, esp. for applying medicaments, 9/1, 12/28; cotton (thread) **cotome**, 56/9.
Couch, *v.* couch, put in horizontal layers, 33/10.
Couchede, *ppl. a.* hidden, 55/28.
Cowesleppes, *n. pl.* cowslip, *Primula veris*, L., 66/25.
Crak, *n.* crake, crow, 75/32.
Cramp(e, *n.* cramp, 42/side-note 5, 43/6.
Crane, *n.* crane, the bird, 81/27.
Cress(e, *n.* cress, a plant of the mustard family (*Cruciferae*), 36/7; **cresses**, *pl.*, 39/7, 58/7, 66/26; **cresses sede**, 66/35. Cf. **Garthe cresse sede, Water cresse, Wellecresse**.

Glossary. 125

Crispe malue, crisp mallow, *Malva crispa,* L., 69/16–17.
Cristallanus, *n.* ? psyllium, *Plantago psyllium,* L., 44/18. Med. L. *cristallium. See note.*
Crois, *n.* crosswort, *Galium cruciata,* Scop., 67/7. *See note.*
Crommes, *n. pl.* crumbs, 75/6.
Crope de cambre, ? hemp top, 67/10. OF. *canvre,* var. of *chanvre,* L. *cannabis* ; cf. Romania XXXVII, 365. *See note.*
Croppe, *n.* the top (of an herb), 27/1, *etc.* ; **crop(e,** 67/10, 15 ; **cropp,** 72/9 ; *pl.* **croppes,** 16/13 ; **croppis,** 74/3.
Crown, *see* **Preste crown.**
Cucumerbers, *n. pl.* cucumber, *Cucumis sativis,* L., 63/37. *See note.*
Cucurd, *see* **Wilde cucurd.**

Daysies, *n. pl.* daisy, *Bellis perennis,* L., 12/7. OE. *daeȝes eage.*
Darenell, *n.* darnel, *Lolium temulentum,* L., 78/17.
Date stanes, date stones, 16/27.
Dauk, *n.* the wild carrot, *Daucus carota,* L., 67/7. L. *daucus.*
Dede, *n.* death, 58/38, 69/36.
Dede, *a.* dead, 30/14, *etc.*; dead (of flesh), 50/2, *etc.*; dead (of a fester or canker), 79/34, *etc.* ; ? 79/21. *See note to* 79/21.
Defaute, *n.* deficiency, 51/21, 56/14.
Defenes, *n.* 7/side-note 1.
Deflede, *p. p.* dissolved, 30/26.
Degre, *n.* gradation of intensity of one of the four elementary qualities, 2/27.
Dely poudir, ? a very finely ground sort of powder, 79/10, 29, 80/4, 24, 82/32.
Deliuer, *v.* throw off (poison, rheum, *etc.*) ;—said of the body, 26/15 ; **delyuer,** 59/10 ; *refl.* relieve by vomiting or evacuation, 28/37, 29/12 ; relieve by causing evacuation ;—said of a laxative medicine, 28/21, 29/15 ; relieve (of a foetus), 57/side-note 4 ; *p. p.* released from disease, cured, **delyuerde,** 41/29.
Deliuerance, *n.* relief by vomiting or evacuation, 28/4.
Dentdelyon, *n.* dandelion, *Leontodon taraxacum,* L., 29/32. OF. *dent de lion,* corresp. to L. *dens lionis.* NED : 1513.

Depart, *v.* separate, 58/28 ; **departede,** *p. p.,* 51/16.
Derely, *adv.* ? securely, 64/25.
Detony, *n.* = **dytoyn(e,** 53/27, 39.
Dewte, *n.* a salve, 36/30. *See note.*
Diacolon, *n.* diachylon, an ointment, 47/7. *See note.*
Diatarascos, *n.* an ointment, 47/6. *See note.* Not in NED.
Dice, *v.* cut into cubes, 73/2.
Dices, *n. pl.* small cubes, 72/35.
Dietide, *p. p.* dieted, 53/31.
Dietynge, *vbl. n.* feeding, regulation of diet, 51/21.
Dille, *n.* dill, *Anethum graveolens,* L., 25/25 ; **dile,** 22/9. OE. *dille.*
Dynt, *n.* the cavity of a wound, 75/side-note 6.
Diptonge, *see* **Rede diptonge.**
Distemper, *v.* mix with a liquid, 4/18, 10/30.
Distourbance, *n.* disturbance, 2/side-note 9. *See* **Distourbes.**
Distourbes, *v. pr.* 3 *s.* irritates, 2/30.
Distroy(e, *v.* destroy, 38/side-note 3, 52/9.
Dytoyn(e, *n.* ? dittany of Crete, *Origanum dictamnus,* L. or ? fraxinella, white or bastard dittany, *Dictamnus albus,* L., 14/22, 21/23 ; **ditayne,** 72/16 ; **dytane,** 46/30. Cf. **Detony, Rede diptonge.**
Do, *v.* do, put, 1/6, *etc.* ; do ; —used as a substitute for a previous verb, 1/10, *etc.* ; **doo,** 10/3 ; **dose,** *pr.* 2 *s.,* 5/6, *etc.* ; **dose,** *pr.* 3 *s.,* 7/13, *etc.* ; gives (a man great ease), 2/32 ; **dide,** *pa.* 2 *s.,* 69/32, 73/2 ; **did,** *pa.* 2 *s.,* 43/3 ; **done,** *p. p.,* performed, 58/2 ; finished, 52/29.
Dokane, *n.* ? = **dok(e,** 81/5.
Dok(e, *n.* dock, ? *Rumex obtusifolius,* L., **dok(e lefe (leues),** 50/3, 38, 77/4 ; **doke rotes,** 4/17. Cf. **Dokane, Rede dok(e.**
Doufe, *n.* dove, **doufe fen,** 44/7 ; **doufe egge,** 71/36.
Draffe, *n.* dregs, lees, 35/22 ; **drafe,** 38/36.
Dragans, *n.* dragonwort, *Dracunculus vulgaris,* Schott, 25/39, 26/1, 34/32. OF. *dragance* (NED : dragons).
Draghte, *n.* draught, dose, 25/37.
Dragie, ? a candy in the centre of which is a nut, a grain of spice,

or a small quantity of a medicinal substance, 50/33; **dragy,** 50/ side-note 6. OF. *dragie.*
Dragon, *see* **Tonge of dragon.**
Drame, *n.* ? an apothecaries' dram, an eighth of an ounce, 59/26.
Draw(e, *v.* draw, pull, 36/33, *etc.*; draw out the guts (of a fowl), 39/11, 63/30; strain, 4/37, 13/1, *etc.*; promote suppuration, 9/29, 10/27, 12/14.
Dredis, *v. pr.* 3 *s.* dreads, 54/4.
Dry, *a.* dry, 30/3, *etc.*; caused by a lack of moisture in the complexion of the patient;—said of the cough, 20/side-notes 11, 12; possessing the elementary quality of dryness, opposite of moisture; —said of an herb, 2/27. *See note to* 20/37.
Dryfe, *v.* = **dryve,** 10/33, *etc.*
Dryve, *v.* drive, 46/side-note 8. Cf. **Dryfe.**
Droppe, *n.* drop, 56/22.
Dropsy, *n.* dropsy, 32/side-notes 2, 7, 33/side-note 3, *etc.*
Duellynge, *n.* delay, 68/27.

Efte, *adv.* afterward, 9/31.
Egge schelleful(l, *n.* eggshellful, 9/36, 22/36; **egschelfull,** 6/25.
Eghe, *n.* eye, 8/13, *etc.*; *pl.* **eghn(e,** 8/30, side-note 6; **eghene,** 12/23; **eghnen,** 12/side-note 3.
Egremoyn(e, *n.* agrimony, *Agrimonia eupatoria,* L., 2/9, 4/28, 35/9, *etc.*; **egremon(e,** 8/35, 12/27; **egrimoyn(e,** 17/3, 45/18 54/21; **egrymoyn(e,** 2/21, 67/12, 72/1, 76/14; **egrymonde,** 79/1. OF. *eigremoine.*
Ele skynnes, eel skins, 48/33. NED: 1562.
Elena campana, elecampane, horsheal, *Inula helenium,* L., *horsell pat some men calles elena campana,* 3/29. Med. L. *elena campana,* var. of *enula campana* (NED: elecampane).
Ellern, *n.* the common elder, *Sambucus nigra,* L., 14/5; **ellere tree,** 33/17. OE. *ellaern.*
Emerawdes, *n. pl.* haemorrhoids, 43/side-note 8; **emeraudes,** 68/34.
Emplaster, *n.* plaster, 79/39; emplaister, 22/side-note 14. Cf. **Enplaster.**
Emplaster, *v.* plaster, 1/13, 2/6, 47/28. Cf. **Enplaster.**

Encheson, *n.* cause, 52/6.
Encostyfe, *a.* costive, 61/19, 62/38–63/1. Not in NED.
Encostyfenesse, *n.* costiveness, 27/35, side-note 8; **encostyfnesse,** 26/23. Not in NED.
Encruce, *n.* ? 72/16.
Endynge, *vbl. n.* death, 53/5.
Englewe, *n.* bird-lime, 32/30.
Enoynte, *v.* anoint, 2/10.
Enplaster, *n.* = **emplaster,** 33/side-note 1, 68/side-note 2, *etc.*; **enplayster,** 49/side-note 9.
Enplaster, *v.* = **emplaster,** 38/35, 57/1; **enplayster,** 50/27.
Enpostyme, *n.* = **apostym,** 68/side-note 4.
Entres, *n.* ? the layer immediately under the outer bark of the trunk, branches, or root of a tree, 38/26. ? OF. *entrerus,* L. *interruscus, see* Romania, XXXVII, 119–120, 374.
Entret(e, *n.* a plaster or salve, 54/17, 55/39, side-note 1; **entretis,** *pl.,* 69/4. OF. *entrait.*
Envenomed, *ppl. a.* poisoned, 46/26–27, 53/1; **envenymede,** 26/side-note 3.
Epatik, epotik, *see* **Aloes epotik.**
Epworte, *n.* ? 6/15. Not in NED.
Erbe, *n.* = herb(e, 30/10; **erbes,** *pl.,* 33/10.
Ere, *n.* ear, 6/10, 7/3, *etc.*; **erre,** 7/side-note 4; **ere lappes,** lobes of the ear, *pl.,*58/32–33. Cf. **Here.**
Erthe yven = **yven terrestre,** 17/5; **erthe yven leues,** 34/20.
Es, *pron.* his, 58/37.
Esche, *n.* = asche, 7/29.
Ett(e, *v.* eat, 19/15, 20/37, 24/33, *etc.*; **ete,** 2/19; *pr.* 3 *pl.,* **ettes,** 18/side-note 2; **ettis,** 9/side-note 9; corrode, **ete,** 49/20.
Euerfern(e, *n.* a fern of the genus *Polypodium,* ? the common polypody, *Polypodium vulgare,* L., 37/34, 41/31, 61/12, 63/1; **euerfernie,** 28/38. *See note to* 28/38–29/3. OE. *eofor fearn.*
Euyll(e, *n.* disease, diseased condition, 2/side-note 9, 6/14, 30/7, *etc.*; esp. attacks of recurrent diseases, as epilepsy and tertian fever, 42/7, 14, 60/6, 29, *etc.*
Euyll, *a.* diseased, 9/28.
Euphorbe, *n.* euphorbium, an acrid gum resin obtained from *Euphorbia resinifera,* Berg. and

similar species of *Euphorbia*, 66/14. OF. *euforbe*.
Ewe, *n.* yew, *Taxus baccata*, L., 11/19.
Ewfrase, *n.* euphrasy, *Euphrasia officinalis*, L., 12/9, 10, 13, 33; **ewfrace,** 9/22; **ewefrase,** 8/18. OF. *eufrase*.
Experiment, *n.* remedy, 65/side-note 8.

Faces, *n. pl.* white rootlets (of the leek), 6/27. Cf. **Fases**.
Failes, *v. pr.* 3 *pl.* fails, 72/side-note 4.
Falde ? *n. pl.* folds, or ? *adv.* (ij) fold, 70/35. See note.
Fald(e, *v.* fold, 27/1, 81/5.
Falland euyll, falling sickness, epilepsy, 42/14. Cf. L. *morbus caducus*.
Fande, *v.* prove, find out, 79/26.
Fanteme, *n.* lightness of the head, esp. of a delirious sort, 26/9; **fantome,** 2/side-note 8. See note to 2/23-24.
Farse, *v.* stuff (an animal with grease, herbs, *etc.*), 28/40, 36/36; **farses,** *pr.* 2 *s.*, 36/37.
Fases, *n. pl.* = **faces,** 34/22, 70/27.
Fastula, see **Cassia fastula.**
Fatt, *a.* fat, 36/33; ? mucilaginous, ? juicy, 78/2; **fatte,** 74/14.
Fawte, *n.* lack, 53/3.
Fawthistyll, *n.* one of two plants: 1. teasel ? *Dipsacus fullonum,* L. or ? *Dipsacus sylvestris*, Mill. or 2. sowthistle, a plant of the genus *Sonchus*, 32/39; **fawthistill,** 43/39; **fawethistill,** 67/11; **fawethistills,** 32/24; **fawthistyll sede,** 50/32. Double initial *f*'s in 32/24, 67/11 confirm the evidence of the other instances that the scribe of this MS. intended the initial letter to be *f* rather than *s*.
Febles, *v. pr.* 3 *s.* makes feeble, 51/25.
Fedis, *v. pr.* 3 *s.* feeds, 10/38.
Felon, *n.* boil, abscess, 54/15, 16, side-notes, 1, 2, 6, 80/29.
Felten, *ppl. a.* made of felt, 43/14; **feltyn,** 49/5.
Femygreke, *n.* = **fenygreke,** 35/18, 36/35, 49/31.
Fen, *n.* excrement, 44/7, 49/17, 50/13, 80/37.
Fenell(e *n.* fennel, *Foeniculum vulgare*, Mill., 10/6, 7, 25, 11/31, 12/30, 14/37, 15/27, 20/1, *etc.*; **fenell sede,** 11/15-16. Cf. **Fenkell, Rede fenell.** OE. *finuȝl, finul* ; ult. fr. L. *foeniculum.*
Fenygreke, *n.* fenugreek, *Trigonella foenumgraecum*, L., 49/28; **fenicrek,** 66/34. OE. *fenograecum.* Cf. **Femygreke.**
Fenkell, *n.* = **fenell,** 9/21, 12/5, *etc.*; **fenkall(e,** 27/32, 32/7, 44/36; **fenkell rute,** 32/11; **fenkell sede,** 43/40, 45/35. L. *foeniculum.* Cf. **Rede fenkell.**
Ferntikills, *n. pl.* freckles, 14/side-note 6.
Festen, *v.* fasten, 5/side-note 3; **festyn,** 5/foot-note 4. OE. *faestnian.*
Festre, *n.* fistula, an ulcer with a narrow opening, 50/12, 77/side-note 1, 78/24, side-note 1, 79/12, 80/39, 81/side-note 2, *etc.* Cf. **Goute** (2), **Gout(e festre.**
Festres, *v. pr.* 3 *s.* ulcerate, putrify, 52/20.
Fethirfewe, *n.* = **feuerfew,** 29/14, 64/5.
Feuelefe, *n.* = **fluelefe,** 21/33.
Feuer agew(e, ague, a malarial fever with regularly occurring paroxysms, each paroxysm having successive stages of chill, fever, and sweating, 25/side-note 7, 53/31, *þe feuer agewe þat men calles lente euyll*, 61/10.
Feuer cotidiane, an ague with paroxysms recurring daily, 59/side-note 4.
Feuer duble tercyane, an ague with a double set of paroxysms, each recurring every other day, 60/side-note 2.
Feuerfew, *n.* feverfew, *Pyrethrum parthenium*, L., 25/1. Cf. **Fethirfewe.**
Feuer lente, a slow fever, a kind of ague, 61/side-note 3. OF. *fievre lente.* Cf. **Feuer agew(e.**
Feuer quartane, an ague with paroxysms recurring every third day, 60/37-38, 61/5. Cf. *þe feuer þat is callede þe quartane takes a man or a woman ilk thirde day*, 60/21-22.
Feuer tercyane, an ague with paroxysms recurring every other day, 59/38-39, side-note 5, 60/side-note 2.

Glossary.

Fyall, *n.* phial, 11/20. OF. *fiole*, fr. L. *phiala*.
Fiche, *n.* the small bean-like fruit of the vetch, a plant of the genus *Vicia*; a measure of quantity, 9/13. Cf. **Bene, Vesche.**
Fifleues, *n.* = **fluelefe**, *pl.*, 25/6.
Filage, *n.* ? common cudweed, *Filago germanicus*, L. (*Gnaphilium germanicum*, Willd.) or ? field cudweed, *Filago arvensis*, L. (*Gnaphilium arvense*, Willd.), 9/21. Cf. **Philoga.**
Filles, *n. pl.* leaves, 1/1. OF. *fueille, foille*. Cf. ME. *foil*, leaf (of a plant). *See note*.
Filth(e, *n.* dirt, 68/18; pus, 54/16; excrement, 16/37.
Fymter, *n.* fumitory, ? *Fumaria officinalis*, L., 35/27, 69/1. OF. *fumeterre*.
Fynkell, *n.* = **fenkell**, = **fenell**, 21/4, 62/31; **fynkall**, 32/38.
Fiuelefe, *n.* cinquefoil, *Potentilla reptans*, L., 30/6. Cf. **Feuelefe, Fifleues, Pentafilon, Quintfoil(e.**
Fla, *v.* flay, 34/9.
Flakeryng, *vbl. n.* fluttering, throbbing, 52/25.
Flambe, *n.* ? spearwort, *Ranunculus flammula*, L., 81/34. Cf. *Sinon. Bart.* 21 and *Alphita* 63/10–14, note 5. OF. *flambe*.
Flete, *v.* float, 56/23. OE. *flēotan*.
Fleumatik, *n.* a person of phlegmatic complexion, 47/20. OF. *fleumatique*.
Flewme, *n.* mucus of the nasal passage, 2/25, side-note 9.
Flexigines, *n. pl.* ? 'fleschinges,' flesh scraped from the flesh-side of a hide about to be tanned, 32/28. *See note*.
Flyande, *ppl. a.* moving rapidly from limb to limb,—said of gout, 65/side-note 8. Cf. *gout erraunt*, Schöffler 54.
Flyes, *v. pr.* 3 *s.* puts to flight, 52/9.
Flyk, *n.* flitch, 55/1, 58/22.
Flix, *n.* = **flux**, 30/18, 29, side-notes 7, 11. OF. *flux*.
Flokkes, *see* **Scarlett flokkes.**
Florence weghte, the weight of a gold florin, 57/3. OF. *florence*.
Flores, *n.* = **flour(e** (2), *pl.*, 60/36, 73/19.
Floresche, *v.* flourish, 60/35.
Flosere, *n.* **strabery wyes**, identified in 67/17. Cf. *fraser*, a Latin name for the strawberry, *Sinon. Bart.* 22.
Flour(e (1), *n.* flour, 17/36, 47/27.
Flour(e (2), *n.* flower, 1/22, 6/12; *pl.* **floures**, 9/21, *etc.*; **flours**, 25/8. Cf. **Flores.**
Floures de genest, broom, a plant of the genus *Genista*, *floures de genest .i. brome*, 67/14.
Flux, *n.* flux, probably dysentery, 29/5. OF. *flux*, L. *fluxus*. Cf. **Flix.**
Folous, *v. pr.* 3 *pl.* follow, 52/38.
Forhyngrede, ? 50/7–8.
Founce, *n.* bottom, 46/13. AF. *founz*.
Fox gloues, *n.* foxglove, *Digitalis purpurea*, L., *gen.*, 80/28.
Fra, *prep.* = **from**, 17/32, 21/13, *etc.*
Frankencens(e, *n.* frankincense, 16/25, 79/36, *etc.*
Fransie, *n.* frenzy, ? delirium, 61/30. *See note*.
Fre rekills, frankincense, 70/12.
Frekles, *n. pl.* freckles, 22/side-notes 5, 8.
Fresche, *a.* fresh, 28/17; not artificially preserved, 27/38, 38/6; not salted,—said of butter, 4/38, 20/24; fresh as opposed to salt (water), 53/33.
Frete, *v.* rub, 5/23. Cf. **Frote.**
Frying pan, frying pan, 47/37.
Fro, *prep.* = **from**, 7/6, 53/13, 54/4, 75/side-note 6.
Froyte, *n.* = **fruyte**, 51/28.
From, *prep.* from, 18/33. Cf. **Fra, Fro.**
Fronte, *n.* forehead, 1/21. OF. *front*.
Frote, *v.* rub, 16/11, 29. OF. *froter*. Cf. **Frete.**
Fruyte, *n.* fruit, 47/24. Cf. **Froyte.**
Fundament, *n.* anus, 29/19, 31/35; **fundement**, 28/28.
Fute, *n.* foot, 53/8; *pl.*, **fete**, 34/9, *etc.*; **feete**, 81/27.

Ga, *v.* go, 13/36; *pr.* 2 *s.*, **gase**, 2/1; *pr.* 3 *s.*, **gase**, 31/15, 72/36; *pr. subj.* 3 *s.*, **ga**, 59/8, 62/12; **gaa**, 78/31. Cf. **Gange, Go, Ouer-gane.**
Gagate, *n.* jet, 57/37.
Gayle, *n.* bog myrtle, *Myrica gale*, L., 66/30. OE. *gaʒel*.
Gayte, *n.* goat, 5/27, *etc.*; **gayte mylke**, 4/28–29, *etc.*; **gayttes mylke**, 14/28.

Glossary. 129

Galbanum, *n.* galbanum, an aromatic gum resin obtained from the juice of certain species of *Ferula,* 68/4, 73/8. Cf. **Salbanum.**
Galte, *n.* hog, boar, 10/16, 77/14; **galt(e gres(e,** 11/8-9, 24/20-21, 73/36. ON. *galte.*
Ganers, *n.* gander, *gen.,* 49/17.
Gange, *v.* = **ga,** *pr. subj.,* 10/17, 58/27. Cf. **Ga, Go.**
Gape, *v.* gape, open the mouth wide, 19/20. ON. *gapa.*
Gare, *v.* cause, 4/11, side-note 1; **garre,** 77/side-note 2. Cf. **Gere.**
Garleke, *n.* garlic, *Allium sativum,* L., 3/20, *etc.*; **gareleke,** 47/31; **garleke heddes,** 24/11.
Garsynge, *vbl. n.* scarification, 47/side-note 7. See illustration in Singer, ' Figures of the Bristol Guy de Chauliac MS.,' *Proc. Roy. Soc. Med.* X (1917), 75.
Garthe cresse sede, the sede of garden cress, *Lepidum sativum,* L., 30/35.
Gedir, *v.* gather, 10/11, *etc.*; suppurate, 49/27, 36.
Gemme, *see* **Sall gemme.**
Gencyane sede, the seed of the gentian, ? *Gentiana lutea,* L., 5/34.
Genest, *see* **Floures de genest.**
Gere, *v.* = **gare,** 3/13.
Germander, *n.* germander, ? *Teucrium chamaedrys,* L., 68/39; **germandre,** 66/24; **germaunder,** 58/9.
Gesarn, *n.* = **gyssarn,** 61/3.
Getyn, *p. p.* gathered, 48/26.
Gif, *v.* give, 6/13; **giff(e,** 32/5, 38/27; **gyf(e,** 14/26, 32/35; **gyff(e,** 5/34, 13/30; **gyffes,** *pr.* 3 *s.,* 27/20.
Gilt, *n.* a young female pig, 77/14. ON. *gyltr.*
Gynger, *n.* ginger, the root of *Zinziber officinale,* Rosc., 8/20, 9/16, *etc.* Cf. **White gynger.**
Gyssarn, *n.* gizzard, 15/3. Cf. **Gesarn.**
Gladyn, *n.* gladdon, ? *Iris pseudacorus,* L., 16/1, 25/39, 66/21, 25.
Glair(e, *n.* white of egg, ? specially prepared, as by whipping, and used as an adhesive, 12/13, 81/4; **glare,** 12/24. OF. *glaire.* Cf. Thompson, *Mat. Med. Painting,* pp. 50-52.

Glaunders, *n.* a contagious disease in horses, communicable to man, 43/side-note 1. NED: 1523, in this sense.
Glett, *n.* phlegm collected in the stomach, 15/2, 24/34. OF. *glette.*
Gnawyng, *vbl. n.* ? aching, 47/side-note 2.
Go, *v.* go, 33/27; *pr.* 2 *s.,* **gose,** 9/39, 10/23, 15/38, 45/32, *pr.* 3 *s.,* **gose,** 19/12; *pr. subj.,* **goo,** 19/21. Cf. **Ga.**
Gode, *a.* good, 18/12. Cf. **Gud(e.**
Goyng owt of þe sete, diarrhoea, 43/side-note 4.
Golofre, *see* **Clowes de golofre.**
Gomme araby, gum-arabic, a gum from certain species of *Acacia* or a substitute from a native tree, 15/15; **gome arabike,** 21/7; **gomme of araby,** 30/26. Cf. Thompson, *Mat. Med. Painting,* pp. 57-58. Cf. **Gumme.**
Gommes, *n. pl.* gums of the mouth, 16/29.
Gopen, *n.* gowpen, a double handful, 78/11. ON. *gaupn.* NED: gowpen, 1325... 1536.
Gorrynge, *vbl. n.* ? 75/side-note 9. See note to 75/26-27.
Gose grese (1), goose grease, 11/9.
Gose grese (2), goose grass, ? silverweed, *Potentilla anserina,* L., 3/25. Cf. **Grese.**
Gotour, *n.* matter, pus, 79/35, 80/21; **gotours,** *pl.,* 78/38, 79/24. OF. *goutture,* ' ce qui dégoutte.'
Gouke flores, *n.* ? cuckoo flower, *Cardamine pratensis,* L., *pl.,* 73/19.
Gout artetik, gout affecting the joints, 66/side-note 1. Cf. **Goute** (2).
Gout(e (1), *n.* one of the various manifestations of gout, or a disease with similar symptoms, 63/35, side-note 5, 65/8, 31, side-note 3; *pl.* **goutes,** 66/5; **gowttes,** 63/side-note 6. The variety of senses of **gout(e** is due in part to the variety of meanings of Med. L. *gutta,* and in part to the number of forms in which the disease may appear, and, hence, the number of diseases with which it may be confused. In its various forms, gout appears with cutaneous,

apoplectic, and anginal symptoms. *See* New Sydenham Lexicon, gout; Dictionnaire encyclopedique, **goutte**. Cf. **Rede goute**.

Goute (2), *n.* = **gout (e festre**, fistula, 64/27, 77/side-note 1, 81/side-note 2; **gowte**, 54/side-note 6. DuCange, **gutta**, quotes Domnizo, a Canossan monk of the twelfth century: *Gutta, quam dicunt fistulam, generante, putredo quaedam assidue stillabat*. Cf. **Gutt**.

Gout(e festre, fistula, 81/9, 23, side-notes 3, 4. Godefroy, **festre**, cites from *Des XIII manieres de vilanie*: *Toutes vilainnes et vilain Aient toute le mal Saint Gillain Et goute feske* (= festre) *et goute arthique*. Cf. **Goute (2)**.

Gouttynes, *n.* gout, 65/side-note 8.

Gowttous, *a.* apt to bring on attacks of **gout artetik**, 73/5.

Graythede, *p. p.* prepared, 68/7.

Gratia dei, an emplaster for cleansing and healing wounds, 68/1, side-notes 1, 2, 3.

Graue, *v.* ? 42/7.

Grauelle, *n.* a mass of urinary crystals (in the bladder), 50/side-note 6.

Greia, *n.* ? wine-stone, 79/27.

Greke, *see* **Pix greke**.

Grene, *a.* fresh, not dried, 6/23, 50/6.

Grene oynement, a green-coloured salve, the green colour usually being caused by the presence of verdigris or *viridis eris*, 55/29. *See note*.

Grese, *n.* herb, 28/40, 77/30; *pl.* **gresis**, 23/14; **gresses**, 25/16, 20, *etc*. Cf. **Gose grese (2)**, **Grisse**.

Grete, weep, 58/16.

Gret flesche, coarse, probably boiled, meat, 53/32.

Grete salt, coarse salt, 4/4.

Grete groun mustard, coarsely ground mustard, 24/8. *See note*.

Grete mustarde, coarsely ground mustard, 14/17.

Grewe, *v.* = **growe**, 4/25, 50/12.

Grynd(e, *v.* grind, 6/15, 56/4; *ppl. a.* **grounden**, 66/1; **grownden**, 12/25; **gronden**, 76/31; **groun(e**, 24/8, 50/34; **gron**, 49/31.

Gryndyng, *vbl. n.* pain, 29/side-note 10.

Grisse, *n.* = **grese**, 38/18; **grise**, 23/11; **gryse**, 41/38; *pl.* **grisses**, 59/22, *etc.*; **grysses**, 55/32.

Gromelle, *n.* gromelle, a plant of the genus *Lithospermum*, 44/12, 16, 45/6, 19, 33, 46/19; **gromelle sede**, 50/30. OF. *gromil*.

Gron, *see* **Grynd(e**.

Grond, *see* **Growe**.

Gronswalle, *n.* groundsel, ? *Senecio vulgaris*, L., 54/26, 67/11, 72/39, 74/35, 75/13; **gronswall**, 20/32, 49/37; **gronswale**, 66/31, 72/30; **gronswell**, 36/24. OE. *grundswylize*.

Grotis, *n. pl.* groats, 32/10, 33/2.

Grounde, *n.* bottom, 49/20, *etc.*; **gronde**, 55/2; **grounde** fundamental principle, 52/8; **grondes**, *pl.*, 64/35.

Growe, *v.* grow, 4/side-note 4; **growen**, *p. p.*, 29/side-note 9; **grond**, *pr. ppl.*, 11/side-note 10. Cf. **Grewe**.

Growell(e, *n.* thin porridge with chopped meat cooked in it, 28/3, 78/5. OF. *gruel*.

Gud(e, *a.* = **gode**, 1/17, 5/side-note 3, *etc*.

Gude, *n.* good, 16/35.

Gumme, *n.* the inspissated juice of certain herbs, (*of wobbynde*), 36/35; **gvmme** (*of yven*), 5/21; the secretion from certain trees, **gume** (*of the sour plumtre*), 54/34; **gummes**, *pl.* gums, resins, gum-resins, 66/9, 15, 68/20; **goummes**, 66/side-note 3. Cf. **Gomme araby**.

Gundy, *a.* full of water;—said of the eyes, 9/side-note 8, 12/side-note 3.

Gutt, *n.* = **gout(e festre**, 50/12.

Hafe, *v.* have, 6/6, *etc.*; **hase**, *pr.* 2 *s.*, 8/21, *etc.*; *pr.* 3 *s.*, 2/35, *etc.*; *pr. pl.*, 48/17; **had**, *pa. s.*, 31/11, 65/4; **hadde**, *p. p.*, 52/28. Cf. **Haue**.

Hayrefe, *n.* hairif, *Galium aparine*, L., 58/9.

Hakk, *v.* chop up, cut into pieces, 82/13.

Hald(e, *v.* hold, 1/12, 20/14, *etc.*; **haldis**, *pr.* 3 *s.*, 14/side-note 17; **halden**, *p. p.*, 64/14. Cf. **Holde**.

Hale, *a.* well, in good health, 3/6; whole, 41/28.

Glossary. 131

Hale, *v.* heal, 79/36; **hales,** *pr.* 3 *s.*, 17/8.
Haly, *a.* holy, 34/24.
Hande, *n.* hand, 6/12; *pl.* **handes,** 16/11; **handis,** 6/11.
Happe, *v.* cover for warmth, 34/5.
Harde herand, deaf, 6/side-note 12.
Hardes, *n. pl.* hards, the coarse residue of heckling flax or hemp, 10/26, *etc.* Cf. **Herdes.**
Hardyn, *v.* become hard, 37/32.
Harede, *see* **White harede.**
Harhone, *n.* horehound, *Marrubium vulgare,* L., 36/7; **harehone,** 26/24. Cf. **Horshoue, Harofe, Harune.**
Harnes, *n. pl.* brains, 51/38; **harnnes,** 69/25. Cf. **Hernes, Herenes.**
Harofe, *n.* = **harhone,** 8/8.
Harune, *n.* ? = **harhone,** 35/34, 36/14.
Hasenes(se, *n.* hoarseness, 13/12, 14/side-note 1. OE. *hasnes.*
Haste, *v.* cause to move quickly, drive, 53/5.
Hate, *a.* hot, 1/23, *etc.*; caused by an excess of heat in the complexion of the patient;—said of a disease, 33/side-note 3; possessing the elementary quality of heat;—said of materia medica, 2/27, 66/9, side-notes 3, 4, 5, 6, 7. Cf. **Hote.**
Haue, *v.* = **hafe,** 28/4, 38/16.
Hauyr, *n.* oats, 29/37; **hauyr(e cake,** 7/36, 13/19; **hauyre straa,** 5/13.
Hauyrmele, *n.* oatmeal, 16/7, 28/16, 49/9; **hauyrmele grotes,** 36/18, 63/27; **hauyrmele grotis,** 32/9-10, 33/2. NED: 1785.
Haw, *n.* an excrescence in the eye, 12/side-note 9.
Hawthorne, *n.* hawthorn, 7/5.
Heddes, *n. pl.* the compound bulbs (of garlic), 24/11.
Hed werke, headache, 3/side-note 2; **heued werke,** 2/side-note 4.
Heldes, *v. pr. pl.* bend (downward), 58/28.
Heler, *n.* healer;—said of an ointment, 68/11.
Helle, *v.* pour, 6/28, 34/32, 64/32.
Helle fire, St. Anthony's fire, erysipelas, 68/33-34.

Helpe, *v.* help, 8/30; **helpede,** *p. p.*, 54/6.
Hemp(e, *n.* hemp, *Cannabis sativa,* L., 43/17, 72/5; **hemp croppes,** 69/15; **hemp(e sede,** 11/15, 80/3.
Henbayn(e, *n.* henbane, *Hyoscyamus niger,* L., 16/22, 17/11, 19/18, 35/24, 54/34, 61/26, 64/16, *etc.*; **henebayne,** 11/38; **henbayne sedis,** 34/31.
Henbell(e, *n.* henbane, *Hyoscyamus niger,* L., 18/4, 8.
Herb(e, *n.* herb, 15/33, 74/12. Cf. **Erbe.**
Herbe benet(t, herb bennet, ? *Geum urbanum,* L. or ? *Conium maculatum,* L., 35/29, 65/38; probably *Conium maculatum,* L., *herbe benett* ? *and homoloke,* 4/35. See note.
Herb(e John, St.-John's-wort, *Hypericum perforatum,* L., 58/6, 62/4, 65/28, 66/30, 67/8, 74/1, 9; herb Jhon, 76/23.
Herb(e yue, ? ground pine, *Ajuga chamaepitys,* Schreb., 58/9, 67/9.
Herb(e Robert, herb Robert, *Geranium Robertianum,* L., 38/8, 54/28, 67/8, 69/14, 71/21-22, 72/10, 24, 74/1-2, 10, 79/17.
Herb saunce crop, ? 67/15.
Herb Wauter, woodruff, *Asperula odorata,* L., 67/8-9, 74/10; **herb Wawter,** 74/2.
Herdes, *n. pl.* = **hardes,** 9/26, 28.
Here, *n.* = **ere,** 6/29, 13/17.
Herenes, *n. pl.* = **harnes,** 1/sidenote 7.
Heryng, *vbl. n.* hearing, 6/9.
Hernes, *n. pl.* = **harnes,** 34/10, *etc.*
Hert, *n.* hart, 30/28, 54/36; **hert horne,** 31/31, 38/29; **herte merghe,** 5/7.
Hert(e, *n.* heart, 4/30; stomach, 24/34; **nexte thy herte,** on an empty stomach, fasting, 45/31. NED: 1542, sense 4.
Hert bryne, heartburn, cardialgy, 25/side-note 3.
Hertis horne, the horn of a hart, 18/1.
Hertistonge, ? hart's tongue fern, *Scolopendrium vulgare,* Sm., 47/29; *hertis tonge .i. cerfoil,* 47/12. Cf. **Cerfoil(e, Hyndestong.**
Hert veyne = *cordiaca,* 52/37.

Hesill, *n.* hazel, *Corylus avellana,* L., 11/22. OE. *haesel.*
Hethy, *a.* ? error for *lethy,* ' supple,' 58/33. See note.
Heued, *n.* the bulb of a leek, 6/27.
Heued vayne, head vein, 53/17.
Hewen, *ppl. a.* injured, cut, 68/32.
Hides, *v. pr. pl.,* 58/37.
Highe, *adv.* loudly, 14/side-note 2 ; **hye,** 13/13.
Hille, *v.* cover, 69/33.
Hyndestong, *n.* hart's tongue, *Scolopendrium vulgare,* Sm., 20/26. Cf. **Hertistonge.**
Hir, *pron.* her, *gen.,* 56/25 ; *dat.,* 27/3 ; *acc.,* 58/4. Cf. **Scho.**
Holde, *v.* = **hald(e,** 19/13.
Holle, *a.* hollow (of the eyes), 58/31.
Holyoke, *n.* marsh mallow, *Althaea officinalis,* L., 49/24.
Homlok(e, *n.* hemlock, *Conium maculatum,* L., 4/35, 74/3 ; **homlokes,** *pl.,* 27/22 ; **homeloke rute,** 77/6. Cf. **Herbe benet(t.**
Hondbayne, *n.* ? dogbane, ? *Mercurialis perennis,* L., 80/3.
Hondistonge, *n.* hound's tongue, *Cynoglossum officinale,* L., 24/1, 76/36 ; **hondestonge,** 8/29 ; **hond tonge,** 59/20.
Horsell, *n.* horsheal, *Inula helenium,* L., *horsell pat some men calles elena campana,* 3/29. OE. *horselene.* Cf. **Horshelme.**
Horse mynt, a wild mint, ? *Mentha sylvestris,* L., 69/19.
Horshelme, *n.* = **horsell,** 14/34, 20/37, 65/27 ; **horsehelme,** 24/15, 25/4, 37/18 ; **horshelne,** 39/4 ; **horslne,** 37/22 ; **horshelme rutes,** 23/21-22.
Horshoue, *n.* horsehoof, *Tussilago farfara,* L., 7/28, 13/7, 20/31, 23/3, 6, 18, 24/36, *horshoue pat is called vngula caballi,* 59/29 ; **horshofe,** 38/8 ; **horsehoue,** 20/23.
Host(e, *n.* cough, 19/15, 20/30, side-notes 7, 10. ON. *hoste.*
Hote, *a.* = **hate,** 17/15, 19/16, 20.
Houseles, *a.* without a shell,— said of a snail, 10/10.
Humour, *n.* humour, 25/side-note 5 ; **humours,** *pl.,* 8/4, 10/33.
Hurte, *a.* injured,—said of the eyes, 8/35.
Hurtes, *n. pl.* injuries, 67/3, 69/5.

Iarue, *n.* yarrow, *Achillea millefolium,* L., 66/27. Cf. **Ʒarow(e.**
Iewse, *n.* 11/8, *etc.* ; **jews,** 79/36 ; **jeuse,** 1/22, *etc.* Cf. **Ius.**
Ilk(e, each, 3/5, 7/33 ; **Ilk(e** same, 15/10, 68/22.
Ilkan(e, *pron.* each, 3/27, 7/1.
Ill, *a.* pernicious, 25/side-note 5.
Ymelle, *prep.* among, 19/6.
In-til(l, *prep.* into, 17/17, 21/27.
In-to, *prep.* into, 7/27.
Ypocone, *n.* horned cumin, *Hypecoun procumbens,* L., 66/31. F. *hypécoon.*
Yrislirik, *n.* Illyrian iris, ? *Iris germanica,* L., from which orrisroot was obtained, 66/22.
Ysels, *n. pl.* embers, ashes, 4/13. OE. *ysel.*
Isope, *n.* hyssop, *Hyssopus officinalis,* L., 36/8 ; **ysop(e,** 20/23, 23/6, 33/1, 66/29, 68/39 ; **ysoppe,** 21/23, 57/31. OF. *ysop.*
Ispia maior, ? error for **ippia maior,** ? = **pympernoll,** 58/7-8. See note.
Item, same, 22/3. See note.
Iubarb(e, *n.* houseleek, *Sempervivum tectorum,* L., 58/10, 60/8, 9, 18, 65/32, 72/17.
Yue, *see* **Herb(e yue.**
Iuniper, *n.* juniper, *Juniperus communis,* L., 5/5, 34/21.
Iunttours, *n. pl.* joints, 68/31.
Ius, *n.* = **jewse,** 15/20, *etc.*
Yven, *n.* ivy, ? *Hedera helix,* L., 5/22, 11/16, 17/7, 46/10 ; **yven leues,** 5/15 ; **yven beries,** 45/9.
Yven terrestre, ground ivy, ? *Nepeta glechoma,* Benth., 1/4, 2/8, 12/30. Cf. L. *hedera terrestris.* Cf. **Erthe yven.**

Kalcroppe, *n.* the crop of the cale, 76/36. Cf. **Cale.**
Kankir, *n.* an ulcer or rankling sore, 68/33 [An explicit statement of its symptoms is given, 77/17-27, and receipts for its cure are listed, 76/35-82/39] ; **kankire,** 50/12; **kankre,** 75/37 ; possibly cancer, 76/side-note 6.
Kantarydes, *n.* the dried beetle, *Cantharis vesicatoria,* 76/3.
Kele, *v.* cool, 11/12.
Kerif, *v.* carve, 18/8. See note. Cf. **Coruen** (1).
Kile, *n.* ulcer, boil, 49/27, 54/25, *etc.* ; **kyle,** 49/36, *etc.* ; **kille,** 52/22. ON. *kyli.*

Glossary. 133

Kynde, *n.* class, sort, 65/8; nature, 52/8; **kynd**, ? testicle, 30/28. See note to 30/28.
Kyndely, *adv.* naturally, 52/9.
Kirkes, *n. pl.* churches, 42/35.
Kirnells, *n. pl.* kernels, 55/19. Cf. **Cherestane kyrnells.**
Knafe childe, a male child, 56/23, *etc.*; **knaue childe**, 9/20.
Knawe, *v.* know, 77/side-note 3.
Knottis, *n. pl.* lumps, 82/11.

Lactifer, *see* **Philadelphia lactifer.**
Lafe, *n.* loaf, 30/20.
Lamede, *ppl. a.* lamed, crippled, 12/side-note 10.
Lange, *a.* long, 76/9; **lengare**, *comp.*, 19/30. Cf. **Longe pepir.**
Lange, *adv.* long, for a long time, 13/35; **langer**, *comp.*, 11/5.
Lange de beefe, bugloss, a boraginaceous plant, ? esp. a plant of the genera *Lycopsis* and *Anchusa*, ? *Echium vulgare*, L., 59/17–18. OF. *langue de boeuf*, Med. L. *lingua bovis*. Cf. **Longe de beefe.**
Lange de cheyn, hound's tongue, ? *Cynoglossum officinale*, L. 67/16. AF. *langue de chein*, Med. L. *lingua canis*. Cf. **Hondistonge.**
Lange wortis, ? cabbage boiled whole and then chopped very coarsely, 76/9–10. See note.
Lappes, *see* **Ere.**
Lard(e, *n.* cured pork fat, 10/16, 29/18. OF. *lard*, 'salt pork,' 'bacon.'
Lat(e, *v.* let, allow, 1/9, 7/32; **latte**, 10/19; cause, *followed directly by inf.*, 6/3; let (blood, in phlebotomy), 9/3; **latis**, *pr. pl.*, 48/38; **laten**, *p. p.*, 47/19.
Latynge, *see* **Blode.**
Laton, *n.* a gold-coloured alloy of copper identical with or resembling brass, 43/5.
Lauandre, *n.* lavender, ? *Lavandula vera*, DC., 21/22, 33/9, 66/26.
Lauerwort, *n.* ? 20/26. Not in NED.
Launcelle, *n.* ribwort *Plantago lanceolata*, L., *launcelle .i. ryb*, 67/13. OF. *lancele.*
Laureall, *n.* ? spurge laurel, *Daphne laureola*; 15/10; **laureaule**, 81/15; **laurioll**, 78/28. Cf. **Lorell(e.**
Leches, *n. pl.* physicians, 10/side-note 4. OE. *laece.*

Leches, *n. pl.* leaches, strips, 62/33. OF. *lesche.*
Lectuarie, *n.* = **letuarye**, 20/30.
Lede, *n.* lead, 5/23, 64/20. Cf. **White lede.**
Ledis, *v. pr. pl.* lead, 71/33.
Lee, *n.* lye, 1/18, 4/13; a detergent, 4/22, 49/12–14; water infused with herbal juices, 1/2. See note to 1/1–3.
Leese, *v.* loosen, 48/13; deliver (from an epileptic fit), lesid, *p. p.*, 42/13.
Lefe, *n.* leaf, 8/12, *etc.*; **leffe**, 73/4; **lefes**, *pl.*, 4/17, *etc.*; **leues**, 2/21, *etc.*
Leke, *v.* leek, *Allium porrum*, L., *pl.*, **lekes**, 17/11, 43/35; **lekis** 16/30; **leke blades**, 57/29; **leke fases**, the white rootlets of the leek, 34/22. Cf. **Scottleke.**
Lely, *n.* ? the madonna lily, *Lilium candidum*, L., 22/13, 29, 54/33; **lely rutes**, 54/19.
Lendis, *n. pl.* loins, 65/31.
Lente euyll, a slow fever, þe *feuer agewe þat men calles lente euyll*, 61/10. Cf. **Feuer lente.**
Lentes sede = **lynsed**(e, 26/28. ? Nthn. ME. (Sc.) *lint*, flaxplant, + *sede.*
Leper, *a.* leprous, 39/side-note 2.
Leprous, *a.* leprous, 65/12.
Lere, *v.* learn, 67/2, 77/17.
Lethir, *n.* leather, tanned skin, 70/35; an appliance made of leather, 47/10; **lether**, 28/35; **lethyre**, 42/25; a whit(t)e lethir, 50/15, 55/12–13.
Letouse, *n.* ? cultivated lettuce, *Lactuca sativa*, L. or wild lettuce, *Lactuca scariola* or a similar or related genus, 63/25; **letuce**3, *pl.*, 59/10.
Lett(e, hinder, 20/9, 15; **lett ... to** (inf.) prevent ... from (*vbl. n.*), 5/side-note 3.
Letuarye, *n.* electuary, 20/side-note 1; **letuaryse**, *pl.*, 53/26. Cf. **Lectuarie.**
Leuer, *n.* liver, 15/1. Cf. **Lyuer.**
Lew, *a.* lukewarm, 21/12. Cf. **Lewk(e.**
Lewk, *v.* make lukewarm, 34/32.
Lewk(e, *a.* lukewarm, 7/13, 30/37. Cf. **Lew.**
Licorice of ynde, ? Indian licorice, the root of *Abrus precatorius*, L., 21/7.

M

Licorise, *n.* licorice, the root of *Glycyrrhiza glabra,* L., 21/8, 23/7, 23; **licorice,** 39/5; licores(e,23/38, 24/2; **licorece,** 25/9; **licoresse,** 19/9, 65/29; licoresche, 46/8; **lycoryse,** 50/32. Cf. **Liquorice.**

Licour, *n.* liquor, a liquid, 35/37; likour, 47/33.

Ly(e, *v.* lie, 7/32, 13/15, 19/12; **lyes,** *pr. pl.*, 19/19. Cf. **Lygg(e.**

Lyes, *n.* = **lisse,** *pl.*, 2/26, etc.

Lyfe, *v.* live, 31/1, etc.; **lyffe,** 34/7; **liffe,** 30/34.

Lygg(e, *v.* = **ly(e,** 3/22, 36/22, etc.; **lygges,** *pr.* 3 *s.*, 69/28; lay (*tr.*), **lig,** 63/6.

Lym(e, *n.* lime, calcium oxide, 5/17, 48/8, etc.; a sticky substance, bird lime, **lyme,** 32/30.

Lyn clathe, a piece of linen cloth, 12/13, 15/9, etc.; **lyn clothe,** 33/34; **lyn clowte,** 24/23; **lyn cloute,** 28/27, 49/3.

Lyn(e, *n.* a plant of the genus *Linum,* esp. the cultivated flax plant, *Linum usitatissimum,* L., 27/37, 35/19; lint or linen cloth, 10/36, etc.

Lynsed(e, *n.* linseed, the seeds of flax, 28/22, 49/23, 54/23, 64/6, 65/35. Cf. **Lentes sede.**

Liquid, *see* **Pix liquid.**

Liquorice, *n.* = **licorise,** 21/6.

Lyppis, *n. pl.* lips (of a fox), 4/26.

Lisse, *n. pl.* lice, 38/foot-note 1; **lysse,** 38/side-note 3. Cf. **Lyes.**

Litage, *n.* litharge, a yellow or brownish-red compound of lead (lead monoxide), much used in certain kinds of medicinal preparation, 61/34; **litarge,** 76/34.

Litsters, *n. pl.* dyers, 79/28.

Littill burnett, ? salad burnet, *Poterium sanguisorba,* L., 3/26.

Littill consoud(e = consoud petit, 72/17–18, 76/16.

Littill morell, black nightshade, *Solanum nigrum,* L., 58/10–11. Cf. NED: petty morel, *s. v.* morel.

Lyuer, *n.* = **leuer,** 29/25, etc.

Liuerwort, *n.* a plant having leaves or similar parts believed to resemble the liver in shape or to be effective in curing diseases of the liver, ? liverwort, *Marchantia polymorpha,* L. or ? the hepatica, *Hepatica triloba,* Chaix, 24/2; **lyuerworte,** 25/5.

Lofage, *n.* = **louache,** 27/32.

Loke, *n.* lock (of wool), 28/19.

Longe de beefe = lange de beefe, 69/2–3; **longedeboef,** 27/36.

Longe de cerfe, hart's tongue fern, *Scolopendrium vulgare,* Sm., 25/4–5.

Longe pepir, pepper obtained from the fruit-spikes of *Piper longum,* L. or related species, 66/17. *See note.*

Lorell(e, *n.* ? laurel, *Laurus nobilis,* L., 2/4, 38/5, 47/9, 66/30; **lorell lefe,** 16/5. Cf. **Laureall.**

Louache, *n.* lovage, *Levisticum officinale,* Koch, 20/5, 25/28, 66/22, 29; **loufache,** 62/32; **loueache,** 4/36, 22/13. Cf. **Lofage, Wild louache.**

Luk(e, *v.* look, take care, 23/26, 47/22.

Luppines, *n.* lupine, ? the white lupine, *Lupinus albus,* L., *pl.*, 5/29.

Lupners, *n. pl.* ? lupines, 56/4.

Ma, *a.* more, 77/26; **mare,** 25/10, *etc*; **maste,** most, 74/37. Cf. **More.**

Mader, *n.* ? the wild madder, *Rubia peregrina,* L., native in England or ? dyer's madder, *Rubia tinctorum,* L., cultivated in Southern Europe during the Middle Ages, 67/11, 69/20, 71/23, 77/1, 80/7; **madir,** 27/5, 59/1, 71/13. Cf. Thompson, *Mat. Med. Painting,* pp. 121–122. OE. *maedere.*

Maydenhare, a kind of fern, ? *Adiantum capillus-Veneris,* L. or ? *Asplenium trichomanes,* L., 20/26, 24/2.

May(e buttre, butter churned in May, 3/30, 5/33, 9/7. Cf. **Buttre of May(e.**

Maile, *n.* a film growing over the eye, 11/side-note 5. OF. *maille, maile.* NED: 1601, in this sense.

Maynflour, *n.* flour of the finest quality, 43/34.

Maythes, *n.* stinking camomile, ? *Anthemis cotula,* L., 43/15. OE. *maʒoþe, maeʒþa.*

Mak(e, *v.* make, 1/1, 3/16, etc.; **makes,** *pr.* 2 *s.*, 5/31; *pr.* 3 *s.*, 27/21, 52/21; *pr. pl.*, 51/25; **made,** *p. p.* 19/16, *etc.*

Malady, *n.* so.e, diseased part of the body, 55/25.
Malecolyn, *n.* a person of melancholy complexion, 47/21.
Malue, *n.* a variety of mallow, ? *Malva sylvestris*, L., 23/37, 35/18, 78/20; **malues**, *pl.*, 5/9, 15/28, 27/36, 35/29, 50/23, 61/26. Cf. **Crispe malue, Rede malue, White malue, Wymalue**.
Maluestri, *n.* ? a plant resembling mallow, 15/21. Cf. *-astrum* in such words as *mentastrum, marubastrum* (*Alphita* 109), *pipastrum* (*Alphita* 146).
Maner(e, *n.* method of action, 47/side-note 5, 68/2; kind, 47/side-note 1, 50/22.
Marciaton, *n.* a salve for pains in the joints, 47/8. *See note.*
Mare, *adv.* more, 68/35. Cf. **Ma**.
Marygolde, *n.* marigold, *Calendula officinalis*, L., 6/17, 71/20; **marygoldes**, *pl.*, 44/5, 54/18; **marigolde sedis**, 66/33.
Maro₃l, *n.* maroil, probably horehound, *Marrubium vulgare*, L., 71/22. OF. *maroil*. Not in NED.
Maser(e, *n.* ? mace, the external covering of the nutmeg, 70/4, 6. *See note.*
Mastik(e, *n.* mastic, a resin obtained from the mastic tree, *Pistacia lentiscus*, L., 55/7, 66/12, 73/11, etc.; **mastyk(e**, 2/29, 55/10; **mastik(e powdir (pouder)**, 28/6, 68/24. OF. *mastic*.
Matfelon, *n.* knapweed, ? *Centaurea nigra*, L., 32/39, 71/20, 72/2, 10; **matefelon**, 54/18, 59/1. OF. *matefelon*.
Matir, *n.* humour, 52/30, 32, 36, 53/10; **mater(e**, 52/10, 53/7, 16.
Maturatif(e, *n.* a medicament causing the formation of pus, 36/side-notes 3, 7; **maturatyfe**, 36/32.
Mawen, *p. p.* mown, 4/14.
Medcyn(e, *n.* remedy, medicament, 5/side-note 3, 8/15, 26/18, 51/19.
Medcynable, *a.* having curative properties, 20/22.
Mede wax, ? virgin wax, 66/37-38. *See E. St.* LV, 135.
Mediana, *n.* = **myd veyn**, 53/20. *See note.*
Mekil(l, *a.* much, 21/14, 46/2; large, 64/17.

Mekill, *adv.* much, 20/4.
Mekilnes, *n.* size, 71/36.
Melice, *n.* melissa, ? *Melissa officinalis*, L., 67/12. OF. *melisse*.
Melle, *v.* mix, 28/27.
Mellilotum, *n.* melilot, *Melilotus officinalis*, Lam., 68/37. Med. L. *melilotum*, Late L. *melilotos*.
Membre, *n.* bodily organ, 53/24; **membres**, *pl.*, 51/37; testicles, 58/36.
Mend(e, *v.* improve in health, 6/22, 23/1; cause to improve in health, 9/14, 65/8.
Meng(e, *v.* mix, 1/8, 62/28; **menged**, *p. p.*, 52/7.
Menyson, *n.* dysentery, 15/24, 29/5, 30/29, 32/side-note 1.
Mentastrum, *n.* horsemint, ? *Mentha sylvestris*, L., 7/12. Not in NED.
Mercury, *n.* quicksilver, 22/19.
Mercuriale, *n.* mercury, ? *Chenopodium Bonus-Henricus*, L., 41/39; **mercuryale**, 27/36. OF. *mercuriel*. NED: 1607, in this sense.
Merghe, *n.* marrow, 16/20.
Mese, *n.* portion, 71/18.
Messynge, *n.* a kind of brass, 28/32. NED: maslin.
Mete, *n.* food, esp. in contrast with drink, 18/3, 26/27; animal flesh used as food, **metis**, *pl.*, 21/14.
Metigatyfe, *n.* mitigative, a soothing remedy, 43/33. L. *mitigativus*.
Myddes barke, the first layer immediately under the outer bark, 15/12. Cf. **Entres**.
Myd veyn, the median vein of the arm, 53/19. *See note.* Cf. **Mediana**.
Mye, *v.* crumble, 23/15, 36/36. OF. *mier*.
Milfoille, *n.* yarrow, *Achillea millefolium*, L., 72/10, 18, 24; **milfoil**, 67/16; **mill(e)foile**, 43/27, 71/20; **mylfoil**, 14/34, 15/5.
Mylte, *n.* spleen, 20/31.
Mynt, *n.* mint, a plant of the genus *Mentha*, 7/18, 12/1, 66/27; **mynt sede**, 50/31.
Myrknes, *n.* dimness of sight, 12/side-note 12.
Mirre, *n.* myrrh, a gum-resin from the tree *Commiphora abyssinica*, L., 73/10. OF. *mirre*.

Mirt, *n.* the berry of the myrtle tree, ? *Myrta communis,* L., 82/30. OF. *mirta.*

Modirworte, *n.* ? = **mogwort(e,** 25/5.

Mogwort(e, *n.* mugwort, *Artemisia vulgaris,* L., 25/5, 35/9, 57/32, 58/17; **mogewort,** 35/1. OE. *mugwyrt.* Cf. **Mugwort(e.**

Moldwerpe, *n.* mole, 76/21; **moldwarppe,** 64/12.

Montenance, *n.* amount, 9/13; **montenaunce,** 18/36; **mountenance,** 33/35.

More, *a.* used as *n.* more, 51/2. Cf. **Ma.**

Morell(e, *n.* nightshade, esp. black nightshade, *Solanum nigrum,* L., 27/9, 61/18, 78/36, 81/34, 36; **moreoles,** 37/34. OF. *morele.* Cf. **Littill morell.**

Morfewe, *n.* morphew, a leprous or scurfy eruption, 24/24, side-note 6. OF. *morphée,* L. *morphea.*

Mormaile, *n.* mormal, an inflamed sore, esp. on the leg, 58/side-note 3. OF. *mortmal,* Med. L. *mortuum malum.*

Morsus diaboli, devil's bit, *Scabiosa succisa,* L., 67/7.

Mosse, *n.* moss, a plant of the class *Musci,* 50/36.

Moure egges, larvae of ants, 5/21, 6/31.

Mousfiche, *n.* ? a kind of vetch, 67/39. *See note.* Cf. **Vesche.**

Moushere, *n.* mouse-ear, *Hieracium pilosella,* L., 34/21, 35/21, 67/14.

Mow, *v.* be able, 12/12.

Mugwort(e, *n.* = **mogwort(e,** 43/17, 57/30, 70/21.

Mukke, *n.* dung, 50/20.

Mustarde, *n.* mustard, a plant of the mustard family (Cruciferae) ? black mustard, *Brassica sinapioides,* Roth. or ? white mustard, *Brassica alba,* Boiss., 14/17, 24/8; **mustard sede,** 61/34.

Na, *a.* not any, 31/11, 56/16; **no** 26/18, 26/27, *etc.*

Na, *adv.* no, not, 80/21; **no,** 19/15.

Nane, *a.* not any, 79/20. Cf. **Non(e.**

Narowe, *a.* narrow, 17/13.

Nauale, *see* **Pik nauale.**

Navill, *n.* navel, 33/8; **nauyll,** 22/1; **nauelle,** 57/27.

Neddir, *n.* adder, 43/9.

Nedis, *adv.* necessarily, 53/38.

Nept(e, *n.* cat-mint, *Nepeta cataria,* L., 20/33, 22/6, 25/6, 30/12, 36/7, 56/19. OE. *nepte.*

Nepta, *n.* = **nept(e,** 47/18. Med. L. *nepta.*

Nesche, *a.* soft, 38/23, *etc.*; **nessche,** 74/21.

Nese, *n.* = **nose,** 37/17, *etc.*; **nese thirlles,** 15/32, 63/23.

Nesyng, *vbl. n.* sneezing, 18/3. OE. *fneosung.*

Net(e, *a.* belonging to neat, 28/34, 32/29, 50/7, 82/30.

Nettill, *n.* nettle, a plant of the genus *Urtica,* 27/37, 48/26; **nettyll,** 45/33; **nettills,** *pl.,* 39/7; **nettill croppes,** 80/6; **nettill sede3,** 5/24. Cf. **Rede nettill.**

New, *v.* renew, 36/23, 54/17.

Nitere, *n.* = **salt nitere,** 80/13.

No, *see* **Na.**

Noye, *v.* harm, 26/26.

Non(e, *a.* not any, 10/24, 19/21, 21/30, *etc.* Cf. **Nane.**

Nowhare, *adv.* nowhere, 52/17.

Nose, *n.* nose, 61/39; **nosse bledyng,** 48/33, side-note 9; **nose ende,** 58/29–30; **nose thirlles,** 16/18, *etc.* Cf. **Nese.**

Nott, *n.* = **nutte,** 26/29.

Nutte, *n.* nut, **nuttes,** *pl.,* 5/6; **nutte kirnells,** 55/19. Cf. **Nott, Oile of nuttis.**

Nuutmugg, *n.* nutmeg, a seed obtained from the fruit of the tree *Myristica fragrans,* Houtt., 66/16.

Oble, *n.* wafer, 63/12; **obles,** *pl.,* 28/7, 63/11; **oble yryns,** wafer-irons, 28/3. OF. *oublee.*

Obletes, *n. pl.* wafers, 28/4. Med. L. *obleta.*

Oil(e, *n.* oil, probably olive oil, 22/30, 75/3; **oyl(e,** 1/20, 6/34; oil pressed or distilled from herbs, 64/26, 29. Cf. *Alphita* 129/8–9.

Oil(e de olife = **oile of olyfe,** 35/13, 36/14; **oile de olyfe,** 43/37; **oyle de olyue,** 4/4, *etc.*

Oile of egges, egg oil, oil extracted from the yolks of eggs, 65/11. *See note.*

Oile of nuttis, oil extracted from nuts, 80/38; **oyle of nuttes,** 73/36. Cf. Arderne (Power) 95/22–34; Müller 46/5–10.

Oile of olyfe, olive oil, 57/19; **oyle of olyue,** 6/26, *etc.* Cf. **Oil(e de olife.**

Oile of rose, an oil obtained from a mixture of rose petals and olive oil which has been heated gently, strained, and allowed to stand for several weeks, 76/27; **oyle of rose,** 27/7; **oil of roses,** 37/12; **oyle of roses,** 1/8–9, *etc.* Cf. Rhazes (1510) Antidot. 3; Arderne (Power) 92/23–93/17.

Oile of violett, an oil obtained from a mixture of violet flowers and olive oil, made as **oile of rose,** 63/22. Cf. Rhazes (1510) Antidot. 3; Arderne (Power) 93/18–20.

Oil of lorell, an oil obtained from laurel berries, 47/8–9. Cf. Müller, 37/15–17.

Oynement, *n.* ointment, 2/side-note 8; **oynment,** 73/side-note 2; **oyntement,** 4/side-note 1; **oyntment,** 62/side-note 3.

Olibane, *n.* = **olibanum,** 66/12; **olybane,** 73/28, 74/5. OF. *oliban.*

Olibanum, *n.* olibanum, frank-incense, a fragrant gum resin obtained from trees of the genus *Boswellia,* 72/15, 73/10, 78/8; **olibanum album,** ? olibanum changed to a whitish pulp by being treated with water, 81/32.

Olyue, *n.* ? = **oile of olyfe,** 73/22. *See note.*

On, *num.* one, 18/33. Cf. **An(e.**

Ony3one, *n.* onion, *Allium cepa,* L. *pl.* **oyne3ouns,** 36/29; **oyneons,** 61/37; **ony3one sede,** 72/1–2. Cf. **Rede vnyon.**

Onkome, *n.* boil, 24/side-note 5, 49/22. NED: 13.. —1570.

Opeponak, *n.* opopanax, a gum resin from the root of *Opopanax chironium,* Koch, 66/12. L. *opopanax.*

Opyn(e, *v.* open, 63/30, 68/side-note 5, 75/12.

Or, *prep.* before;—said of time, 48/12.

Or, *conj..* before;—said of time, 41/38, 42/16, 59/35, 82/5.

Orbane, *n.* gum-lac, a variety of lac produced by a scale insect, 58/14. Med. L. *orobo, orobonis. See note.*

Orientale, *a. see* **Ambre orientale, Safron orientale.**

Origane, *n* pennyroyal, *Mentha pulegium,* L., 66/28. OF. *origane.*

Origanum, *n.* = **origane,** 25/19. Cf. Wright Wülcker 557/20. L. *origanum.*

Orpiment, *n.* yellow arsenic, tri-sulphide of arsenic, found in nature as a bright yellow mineral and valued for its resemblance to gold, 5/17; **orpyment,** 2/33, 5/22, 75/35, 82/31. OF. *orpi-ment,* fr. L. *auripigmentum.*

Orpyn, *n.* orpine, *Sedum telephium,* L., 54/11. OF. *orpin.*

Osmonde, *n.* osmond, a kind of fern, 65/28, 67/18, 74/36; **osmounde,** 74/34. AF. *osmunde.*

Ouer, *a.* outer, 33/17.

Ouer-gane, *p. p.* passed, 55/6.

Owen, *n.* oven, 31/37; **owenn,** 81/29; **owun,** 30/20.

Oximell, *n.* a medicinal drink of vinegar, honey, and herbal juices, 62/side-note 4, 63/2.

Oxtonge, *n.* = **lange de beefe,** *oxtonge þat is longe de beefe,* 69/2.

Payne, *n.* difficulty, 50/11.

Pape, *n.* nipple, 57/38; *pl.* **pappes,** 26/side-note 9; **pappis,** 27/side-note 1.

Papwort(e, *n.* = **mercuriale,** 45/34, 46/4, 19, 50/30; **papewort,** 46/1; **pappwort,** 66/20.

Paralisi, *n.* palsy, 66/8, side-note 2. OF. *paralisie.* Cf. **Parlsy.**

Parche, *v.* parch, 29/37.

Parchynge, *vbl. n.* parching, 29/38.

Parytory, *n.* pellitory, *Parietaria officinalis,* L., 33/9. Cf. **Pitory.**

Parlsy, *n.* = **paralisi,** 34/side-note 2. OF. *paralisie.*

Passion, *n.* a fit of intermittent fever, 59/35; **passiouns,** *pl.,* diseases, 66/9.

Pecherfull, *n. pl.* pitcherfuls, 26/5. Cf. OF. *pechier.* NED: 1693.

Pee delion, *n.* ? ladies' mantle, *Alchemilla vulgaris,* L. 62/18.

Pelleter, *n.* pellitory of Spain, *Anacyclus pyrethrum,* DC. or a plant resembling it, 4/33, 14/21, 36/10, 45/17, 66/27; **peleter,** 38/37; **pelleter barke,** 38/39. OF. *peletre.*

Pellotes, *n. pl.* pellets, 72/13. OF. *pelote.*

Pelwet, *n.* = **moushere,** 71/22; **peluette** *.i. moushere,* 67/13.

Pentafilon, *n.* = **cynkfoil,** 54/21; **pentafoyloyn** *.i.* **quintfoyle,** 13/22. *See note to* 13/22. Med. L. *pentafilon.* Cf. **Quintfoil(e, Fiue-lefe.**

Pepble stones, pebble-stones, 33/11–12.
Pepir, *n.* pepper, 2/12; **pepir cornes,** dried berries of *Piper nigrum,* L., 16/13. Cf. **Blake pepir, White pepir, Longe pepir.**
Peple, *n.* ? darnell, *Lolium temulentum,* L. or ? a kind of mallow, 26/36; **pepills,** 17/1; **pepill sede,** 66/35. Cf. Wright Wülcker 601/45, 715/22; Cath. Angl.286; Rel. Ant. I, 53; Arderne (Power) Lesser Writings, 109–110; NED: popple.
Percell(e *n.* parsley, *Petroselinum sativum,* Hoffm., 24/1, 25/3, 44/20, 46/21; **percill,** 44/36; **percell rute,** 32/11; **percell(e sede,** 31/9, 50/29. OF. *persil.* Cf. **Persell.**
Perel, *n.* a kind of cataract of the eye, 8/side-note 10, 11/side-note 2; **perill,** 13/side-note 7. Cf. Med. L. *perula,* Du Cange. Cf. **Perle** (2).
Perell, *n.* danger, 71/32.
Perilous coghe, ? consumption, 21/side-note 4.
Perle (1), *n.* pearl, 13/5.
Perle (2), *n.* = **perel,** 13/37.
Persell, *n.* = **percell(e,** 21/23.
Peruynge, *n.* periwinkle, a plant of the genus *Vinca,* 59/17. OE. *peruince,* AF. *perwenke.*
Pestilence, *n.* pestilence, 51/15; **pestylence,** 51/31.
Philadelphia lactifer, ? 53/39–40.
Philipendula, *n.* dropwort, *Spiraea filipendula,* L., 45/34, 50/30, 66/22.
Philoga, *n.*? *tansay .i .philoga,* 67/18.
Phiseke, *n.* medical science, 51/39.
Pigill, *n.* stitchwort, *Stellaria holostea,* L., 67/8, 70/37, 72/24; **pigle,** 74/1, 9. Cf. **Pugill.**
Pik, *n.* = **pik nauale,** 3/36, 72/26; **pyk(e,** 3/14, 50/13. Cf. *Picis multa sunt genera sed quando simpliciter de navali intelligitur. Sinon. Bart.* 34.
Pik album = white pik, 54/35.
Pik greke, *see* **Pix greke.**
Pik nauale, *Pix navalis,* the residuum of the distillation of *Pix liquida,* 73/8; **pik nauill,** 68/6. Cf. **Pik.**
Pilial reall = puliol reall, 14/25.
Piliol, *n.* = **puliol,** 14/29, 15/35.
Pille, *v.* peel, 17/28.

Pympernoll(e, *n.* pimpernel, *Anagallis arvensis,* L., 6/7, 9/21, 12/33, 18/4, 59/23, 67/7; **pympernol(e,** 14/1, 22/27, 53/28; **pympernell,** 53/40. OF. *pimpernelle.*
Pion, *n.* a plant of the genus *Paeonia,* 34/26, 57/34; **pyon,** 66/20; **pyons,** *pl.,* 50/31, 82/31.
Pyssyng(e, *vbl. n.* urine, 3/3, 35/32, 38/1.
Pitory, *n.* = **parytory,** 66/30. Cf. MS. Brit. Mus. Royal 12 G iv f. 194r, pitorie.
Pixgreke, colophony, the resin remaining from distillation of crude turpentine with water, 66/13; **pik greke,** 68/6. Cf. *Pix greca, i. colofonia, Sinon. Bart.* 34. See note to 66/13.
Pixliquid, tar, the insoluble residuum of destructive distillation of the wood of certain conifers, 4/4, 6; **pixliquidum,** 66/14. See note to 66/13. Cf. *Pix liquida* \ *idem, terpiche, Sinon Picula* / *Bart.* 34. Cf. **Pik.**
Playntayn(e, *n.* = **plantayn,** *playntayn .i. waybred,* 17/22, 44/26, 62/18, 67/13, 72/17, 25.
Playster, *n.* = **plaster,** 3/28, *etc.*
Plantayn, *n.* plantain, *Plantago major,* L., 74/6, 76/28. Cf. **Playntayn(e.**
Plaster, *n.* plaster, 3/16. Cf. **Playster.**
Plowkky, *a.* pimpled, 34/38.
Plumtre, *n.* plum tree, 54/34.
Pnyger, *n.* ? 48/38.
Poyson, *n.* poison, 25/side-note 9. Cf. **Puyson.**
Pokett, *n.* a small bag worn on the person, 29/38, 33/7.
Polipodi(e, *n.* a fern of the genus *Polypodium,* ? the common polypody, *Polypodium vulgare,* L., 28/38, 57/1, 66/21, 71/22. *Polipodi þat waxes on þe ake* (28/38, etc.) is the English equivalent óf Med. L. *Polypodium quercinum.*
Popilion, *n.* populeon, an ointment in which poplar leaves are the most prominent herbal ingredient, 61/15, 19, 33. See note to 61/15. OF. *populeon, popelion.*
Porcalane, *n.* purslane, *Portulaca oleracea,* L., 23/30. OF. *porcelaine.*
Porcyon, *n.* portion, 7/1; **porcyoun,** 9/10; **porcion(e,** 9/17, 20/20; **porcioun,** 4/5.

Glossary. 139

Pore leeke ? = porret, or ? the shallot *Allium ascalonium*, 6/27. *See note.*
Pores, *n. pl.* pores, 52/5.
Porret, *n.* a young leek or onion, 71/27, 30; **porrett,** *.i. lekes*, 43/35.
Posenett, *n.* a small metal pot or similar vessel having three legs and a handle, 13/24, 31/18; **possenet,** 62/11. OF. *poconnet.* NED: posnet.
Potage, *n.* soup, 14/6, 27/38, 44/23, 46/2, 53/34.
Pouderd, *ppl. a.* powdered, 73/32. NED: 1591, in this sense.
Pound(e, *n.* pound, 58/10, 11; **pond(e,** 15/16, 68/7; **pownd(e,** 23/23, 39/13.
Powdir, *n.* powder, 8/21, *etc.*; **powder(e,** 2/18, 4/27; **powdre,** 4/30; **poudir,** 16/28; **pouder,** 49/19.
Powdir, *v.* powder, 29/18; **powdere,** 5/3. NED: 15.., in this sense. Cf. **Pouderd.**
Powm garnett schelles, the rinds of pomegranate, the fruit of the tree *Punica granatum*, L., 78/12.
Preste crown, *n.* dandelion, *Leontodon taraxacum*, L., 59/37. NED: 1483.
Preue, *n.* privy, 12/19.
Preue thynge, genitals, 53/7, 13.
Primerolle, *n.* primerole, ? *Primula veris*, L. or ? *Bellis perennis*, L., 76/36; **prymrolle,** 66/26.
Primerose, *n.* primrose, *Primula veris*, L., 14/15.
Pugill, *n.* = pigill, 69/14.
Puyson, *n.* = poyson, 2/17.
Puliol(e, *n.* ? pennyroyal, *Mentha pulegium*, L. or wild thyme, *Thymus serpyllum*, L., 1/12, 2/20, 20/33, 22/1, 24/36, 25/6, 19, 30/10, 35/12; **pulioll,** 36/7, 60/34; **pulyol,** 21/1. Cf. **Pilial reall, Piliol.**
Puliol montayne, ? wild thyme, *Thymus serpyllum*, L., 22/39; **puliole montane,** 66/27-28; **pulioll montane,** 70/8; **puliol de montayne,** 21/22-23.
Puliol reall, ? pennyroyal, *Mentha pulegium*, L., 2/6, 22/38; **puliollreall,** 63/8; *origane, pat is* **puliolrealle,** 66/28; **puliolryall,** 1/20; **puliol(le rialle,** 8/17, 21/22; **pulioll royalle,** 60/32.
Pure, *v.* make pure, strain, 34/13.

Quartane, *n.* = feuer quartane, 60/21, side-note 5.
Quartron, *n.* a quarter, probably a quarter of a pound, 68/15, 71/15, 16.
Quintfoil(e, *n.* = cynkfoil, 29/22, 30/32; *pentafoyloyn* .i. **quintfoyle,** 13/22. Cf. **Pentafilon, Fiuelefe.**
Qwayntely, *adv.* skillfully, 69/24.
Qwete flour, wheat flour, 24/19.
Qwik(e, *a.* alive, 13/18, 57/2; **qwikke,** 13/21; **qwyke,** 7/15; burning;—said of coals, 79/5.
Qwikke lyme, unslaked lime, 76/2.
Qwik siluer, the metal mercury, 3/31, 38/8-9, 56/3; **qwyk siluer,** 4/39.

Radecole, *n.* horseradish, *Armoracia rusticana*, Rupp., 77/1.
Radik, *n.* radish, ? *Raphanus sativus*, L., 38/21, 23, 50/31; **radik rute,** 33/1. OE. *rædic.*
Raynwort, *n.* ? error for **baynwort(e,** 74/10. Cf. **Baynewort(e.**
Raysynges, *n. pl.*, raisins, 36/35.
Raysour, *n.* razor, 82/26. OF. *rasour.*
Rankill, *n.* ulcer, festering sore, 49/side-note 9, 50/side-note 1; **rankle,** 64/27.
Raton, *n.* rat, 64/4. OF. *raton.*
Recoyn, ? 66/31.
Rede brere, ? rose brier, *Rosa canina*, L., 72/9-10, 74/11, 80/7.
Red(e cale, red kale, ? *Brassica rubra*, L., a red variety of *Brassica oleracea*, L., 29/24, 69/14; **red cale lefe,** 8/12; **rede cale croppes,** 72/2. Cf. **Cale.**
Rede diptonge, ? the pink-flowered dittany of Crete, *Origanum dictamnus*, L., perhaps in contrast with the native fraxinella or white dittany, *Dictamnus albus*, L., 66/24-25. Cf. Med. L. *diptamnus,* OF. *diptam, diptame.* Cf. **Dytoyn(e.**
Rede dok(e, red dock, *Rumex sanguineus*, L., 4/36, 27/1; **rede doke rute,** 37/26; **rede doke rote,** 3/30. Cf. **Dok(e.**
Rede fenell, ? a variety of fennel bearing red or reddish seeds or ? a variety of fennel having reddish leaves, not now distinguished as a separate species, 12/33. *See note.* Cf. **Fenell(e.**

Rede fenkell = rede fenell, 21/24, 34/3-4.
Rede gout, probably the common form of arthritic gout, of which red, swollen joints are a symptom, 65/side-note 3. Cf. **Gout(e (1).**
Rede malue, ? a variety of *Malva alcea,* L. having deep rose-coloured flowers, 26/19. Cf. **Malue.**
Rede mynt, ? horsemint, *Mentha aquatica,* L. or ? red mint, *Mentha gentilis,* L., 26/14. Cf. **Mynt.**
Rede nettill, ? the true or stinging nettle (one of the species of *Urtica*) as opposed to the dead or blind nettle (one of the species of *Lamium,* called **archangelica** in this text), 45/6, 62/18, 66/29, 67/17; **rede nettills,** 4/35, 44/12; **rede nettills croppes,** 16/13. *See note to* 67/16–17. Cf. **nettill.**
Rede snyle, a slug of the *Limacidae,* ? *Limax subrufus,* 10/10; **rede snyles,** *pl.,* 64/9. *See note to* 64/9. Cf. **Blake snyles.**
Rede vnyon, red onion, a red-bulbed variety of *Allium cepa,* L., 46/35. Cf. **Onyzone.**
Rede wirtes, ? red cabbage, a red-leaved variety of *Brassica oleracea,* L., 35/5; **rede wortes,** 11/22. Cf. **Wort.**
Redkne, *n.* water pepper, *Polygonum hydropiper,* L., 3/25. NED: 1597 (red knees).
Refraide, *v.* cool, 68/28. AF. *refraider.*
Rekills, *n.* incense, 54/38, 64/36; **rekylls,** 55/4. Cf. **Rikills.**
Reme, *n.* rheum, 2/25; **remme,** 2/side-note 9.
Remewe, *v.* = remowe, 71/11.
Remoile, *v.* ? make soft, 68/side-note 3. Cf. Arderne (Power) 93/22.
Remowe, *v.* remove, 70/32. Cf. **Remewe.**
Rescheyue, *v.* ? 28/12.
Resolue, *v.* melt, 68/19; **resoluede,** *p. p.,* 68/24.
Rest, *v.* rest, 72/20. Cf. **Riste.**
Rew(e, *n.* rue, ? *Ruta graveolens,* L., 1/25, 2/3, 13/7, 15/6, 62/20, 66/27, 73/15, *etc.*; **rewe sede,** 11/15.
Rib, *n.* = rybwort, 9/9, 58/9, 70/8, 72/9, 74/3; **ryb,** 4/36, 10/7; *launcelle .i. ryb,* 67/13.
Rybwort, *n.* ribwort, *Plantago lanceolata,* L., 41/31.

Rye, *n.* rye, 25/35; **riebrede,** 22/40; **rye flour,** 81/10; **ry(e mele,** 36/39–40, 50/17.
Right(e, *adv.* very, 1/17, 21/32; **ryghte,** 23/1.
Rikills, *n.* = rekills, 74/23; **rykills,** 41/32; **rykils,** 1/5; **rycles,** 2/23.
Ryme, *n.* rim, membrane, 69/37, 70/2.
Rynde, *n.* rind, 48/20.
Ryne, *v.* run, 28/35; **rynnes,** *pr.* 3 *s.,* 13/11; **rynnand(e,** *ppl. a.,* running;—said of water, 3/6, 34/1.
Ryng worme, ringworm (the skin disease), 50/side-note 7.
Ripe, *v.* ripen, 68/side-note 4.
Ryse mele, rice meal, 36/29.
Riste, *v.* = rest, 52/18.
Robert, *see* **Herb(e Robert.**
Roche, *n.* roach, a small fresh-water fish, 80/23.
Rois, *n.* ? 54/19. *See note.*
Rose, *n.* a shrub of the genus *Rosa,* 2/23, 45/2, 63/4; **roses,** *pl.,* 22/39, 30/3, 60/14; **rose floures,** 9/21. Cf. **Oile of rose.**
Rose, *n.* a syrup, 60/side-note 3.
Rose maryn, *n.* rosemary, *Rosmarinus officinalis,* L., 7/23, 21/22. OF. *rosmarin.*
Rosen, *n.* the solid residue from the distillation of crude turpentine with water, 39/21, 68/13; **rosyn,** 3/36.
Roste, *n.* rust, 68/2. Cf. **Ruste.**
Rote, *n.* root, 1/4; *pl.,* **rotes,** 66/19, *etc.*; **rotis,** 66/22. Cf. **Rute.**
Rote, *v.* rot, 12/37; **rotyn,** *p. p.,* 72/38.
Rotell, *v.* make a rattling noise in the throat, 58/37.
Rouge, *a.* red, 67/10.
Rouge runcebrere, ? blackberry, *Rubus fruticosus,* L., 67/15–16. *See note.*
Rouge vrtice = rede nettill, 67/16. Cf. *le rouge vrtye,* Heinrich 234/9.
Rouelle, *v.* roll, 27/2.
Rounge, *v.* ? 70/4.
Rubarbe, *n.* rhubarb, the rootstock of certain species of *Rheum,* 23/30, 51/6, 59/33.
Runcebrere, *see* **Rouge runcebrere.**
Ruste, *n.* rust, 30/24. Cf. **Roste.**

Glossary. 141

Rute, *n.* root, 12/5; *pl.*, **rutes,** 16/17, *etc.*; **rutis,** 34/26. Cf. **Rote.**

Sa, *adv.* so, 11/26, 55/8, 61/36, 62/12; **saa,** 68/23. Cf. **So, Swa.**
Safe, *prep.* except, 33/27. Cf. **Saue,** *n.*
Safe, *v.* save, keep, 67/35.
Safron, *n.* saffron, the dried stigmas of various species of *Crocus,* esp. the autumn-flowering *Crocus sativus,* L., 10/37.
Safron orientale, a highly prized variety of saffron imported from the East, 15/15. *See note.*
Sayme, *n.* grease, 37/23, 70/33, 71/4.
Sayme devoyr, ? error for **saundeuer,** 3/4. *See note.*
Salbanum, *n.* ? = **galbanum,** 66/13. *See note.*
Salfe, *n.* salve, ointment, 73/39; **salue,** 73/side-note 4. Contrast **Saue,** *n.*
Sall, *v.* shall, *pr.* 2 *s.*, 2/18, *etc.*; *pr.* 3 *s.*, 1/11, *etc.*; **sal,** 3/6, 4/25, *etc.*; **schal**(l, 4/13, 16/6, 10, 27/23; *pa.*, **scholde,** 52/26; **schuld**(e, 52/26, 53/25, 30, 32; **shuld,** 42/6.
Sall gemme, rock salt, 29/19, 76/7.
Sal maritimum, ? salt evaporated from ocean water, 11/16. Cf. Med. L. *sal marinus.*
Salt nitere, salt nitre, ? salt petre, 82/16. Med. L. *sal nitri.* Cf. **Nitere.**
Salue, *n.* = **salfe,** 70/side-note 3.
Samplare, *n.* a probe;—said of a mallow stalk, 80/18.
Samson, *n.* ? error for ramson, *Allium ursinum,* L., 67/11. *See note.*
Sanatyfe, *a.* healing, 55/30.
Sanegle, *n.* sanicle, *Sanicula europaea,* L., 71/31, 74/1, 9; **sanigle,** 71/1, 27; **sanygle,** 79/17. OF. *sanicle.* Cf. **Senigle, Sinagle.**
Sange dragon, dragon's blood, a deep brownish-red gum resin from *Dracaena draco,* L. and related shrubs, 49/1. OF. *sang dragon, sanc de dragon.* Cf. Thompson, *Mat. Med. Painting,* pp. 124–126.
Sangrede, *n.* = **senegrene,** 45/33.

Sanguyen, *n.* a person of sanguine complexion, 47/19.
Sangwynarie, *n.* a plant with pronounced styptic properties, ? shepherd's purse, *Capsella bursa-pastoris,* L. or ? milfoil, *Achillea millefolium,* L., 44/28. *See note.*
Sape, *n.* soap, 3/23; **nesche sape,** soft soap, potash soap, 38/23; **sape of spayn,** castile soap, 22/19.
Sara3ine, *n.* ? sarazine, birthwort, *Aristolochia clematitis,* L. or ? (mynt) sarazine, saracen mint, *Achillea ptarmica,* L., 66/27. *See note.*
Sarce, *n.* searce, sieve, 78/20. OF. *saas.* Cf. **Scarce.**
Sarcocol, *n.* sarcocolla, a gum which exudes from a Persian tree, probably a species of *Penaea* or *Astragalus,* 68/3. Cf. Schöffler 193, note 1.
Sare, *n.* sore, esp. a festering sore, 20/30.
Sare, *a.* sore, 9/2, 44/side-note 10.
Sattill, *v.* settle, 9/37.
Saucerfull, *n.* saucerful, 3/11; **sawcerfull,** 33/35, 45/30, 54/8, 72/32. NED: 1860.
Saue, *n.* an elaborately compounded wound-drink, 67/1, 2. Contrast **Salfe.** *See note.*
Saue, *prep.* = **safe,** *prep.*, 26/22.
Saue, *v.* = **safe,** *v.*, 26/29.
Saueray(e, *n.* savory, a plant of the genus *Satureia,* 23/33, 34, 25/6, 36/8. Ult. fr. L. *satureia.*
Sauine, *n.* savin, *Juniperus sabina,* L., 66/31; **sauyn**(e, 1/8, 2/8, 17/9, 62/5, 65/27; **savyn,** 73/14. OF. *savine.*
Saundeuer, *n.* a liquid saline matter floating over the glass after vitrification, glass gall, 49/19; **saundyuere,** 75/32; **sawndeuere,** 5/4; **sawndyuer,** 4/38–39; **sawnder,** 3/27. OF. *sandiver.* Cf. **Sayme devoyr.**
Sawge, *n.* sage, *Salvia officinalis,* L., 5/31, 6/17, 18/32, 42/32, 61/25, 66/27; **sauge,** 2/37, 14/15, 73/14; **sawge leues,** 34/19.
Sawsefleme, *n.* saucefleme, inflammation and swelling of the face, 72/side-note 10.
Saxifrage, *n.* saxifrage, a plant of the genus *Saxifraga,* 33/23.
Scabbe, *n.* a cutaneous disease,

37/24; **scabbes**, *pl.*, 37/side-note 4, 38/6.
Scabbid, *p. p.* scabbed (of animals), 37/39.
Scabious, *n.* scabious, a plant of the genus *Scabiosa*, 47/16; **scabyous**, 53/28; **scabius**, 73/20.
Scalde, *v.* scald, 28/40; **skaldand**, *pr. p.*, 21/13. Cf. **Schalde**, **Schaldynge**.
Scalled(e, *ppl. a.* scaly, 3/13, 4/11.
Scarce, *n.* ? = **sarce**, 31/32, 64/37.
Scarce, *v.* ? searce, sift, 31/32.
Scarlett flokkes, ? 78/11.
Scarthe, *n.* shard, 37/38, 48/23, 82/18; **scharthe**, 64/7.
Scathe, *n.* injury, 57/29.
Schafe (1), *v.* shave, 3/13, 4/2, 5/2, *etc.* Cf. **Schaue** (1).
Schafe (2), *v.* chafe, rub, 61/29. Cf. **Schaue** (2).
Schalde, *v.* scald, 57/26. Cf. **Scalde**.
Schaldynge, *vbl. n.* scalding, 50/side-note 9.
Schall, *v. see* **Sall**.
Schaue (1), *v.* = **schafe** (1), 4/12, 31; **Schawes**, *pr. pl.*, 32/28.
Schaue (2), *v.* = **schafe** (2), 69/24.
Scheffes, *n. pl.* the woody parts of hemp or flax, 82/13.
Schelles, *n. pl.*, egg shells, 27/10, *etc.*; rinds (of pomegranates), 78/12.
Schepe, *n.* sheep, 8/6; **schepe hede**, 34/9; **schepe talghe**, 36/20; **schepe tharmes**, 32/28; **schepe triddils**, 50/20. Cf. **Chepes**.
Schepelouse, *n.* a louse which infests sheep's wool, 7/37, side-notes 4, 6, 13/side-note 1.
Schere, *v.* cut with a sharp instrument, 17/19, 23/22, 62/33, *etc.*,; shave hair esp. from the head or face, 77/9, 12; **schorne**, *p. p.*, cut, 47/side-note 7; shaved, 77/side-note 2.
Scheryng, *vbl. n.* cutting ? of gallstones, 29/side-note 10.
Schyfe, *n.* slice, 17/19; **schyues**, *pl.*, 79/26. Cf. W. Flem. *schif*.
Schire, *n.* the upper, clearer portion of a mixture which has been allowed to settle, 55/3, 64/34. Cf. **Clere**.
Scho, *pron.* she, 25/9, *etc.* Cf. **Hir**.

Scho asche, a variety of ash tree regarded as female, 61/7.
Scholde, *v. see* **Sall**.
Schort(e, *a.* short, 6/30, 24/13. Cf. **Scorte**.
Schuld(e, *v. see* **Sall**.
Schuldres, *n. pl.* shoulders, 53/22.
Sclary, *n.* = **slaream**, 23/7.
Sclice, *n.* spatula, 74/22; **sclyce**, 4/9, 65/2; **sklisce**, 3/16. Cf. **slyce**.
Scom(e, *v.* scum, 24/31, 33/31; **scomme**, 45/22; **scum**, 33/32.
Scorte, *a.* = **schort(e**, 7/4.
Scottleke, *n.* ? Scottish asphodel, ? *Lofeldia calyculata*, Wahlenb. or ? *Lofeldia palustris*, Huds., 76/4.
Sede, *n.* seed, 5/34, *etc.*; **seede**, 1/15, 2/28; *pl.*, **sedis**, 8/17, *etc.*; **sedes**, 6/38; **sede**3, 5/24.
Segge rutes, the roots of some rush- or iris-like plant, 16/17.
Seke, *a.* sick, 33/20, *etc.*; used as *n.*, 13/36.
Sekenes, *n.* sickness, 51/22; **seknes**, 52/5.
Sekir, *a.* certain, 32/32.
Sekirly, *adv.* surely, 3/19.
Selfehale, *n.* self-heal, ? *Prunella vulgaris*, L., ? *Sanicula europaea*, L., or *Pimpinella saxifraga*, L., 74/1.
Senegrene, *n.* houseleek, *Sempervivum tectorum*, L., 6/25. Cf. **Sangrede**, **Synegrene**, **Sygrym**, **Syndegrefe**.
Senigle, *n.* = **sanegle**, 43/17.
Senn, *n.* ? senna, the dried leaves of one of the species of *Cassia*, 82/8.
Seraphin, *n.* ? sagapenum, a gum resin, probably from the juice of the plant *Ferula persica*, Willd., 66/13. NED: 1583.
Sete, *n.* anus, 43/side-note 4.
Seterib, *n.* ? 70/9.
Sethe, *v.* boil, 1/12, 14/4, *etc.*; **seeth**, 1/20; **sothen**, *p. p.*, 29/2.
Setuale, *n.* setwall, the root of *Cucurma zedoaria*, Rosc., 66/16. OF. *zedeuale*, *citoual*, ult. fr. Arab. *zedwar*.
Sew, *n.* broth, 34/18. OE. *sēaw*.
Shuld, *v. see* **Sall**.
Sifull, *n.* probably houseleek, *Sempervivum tectorum*, L., 3/34; **syfull**, 54/21. NED: cyphel, 1674.
Sygrym, *n.* ? = **senegrene**, 24/18.

Glossary.

Sile, *v.* strain, 24/18, 32/14, 46/12; **syle**, 3/10, 23/25.
Syndirs, *n. pl.* cinders, 17/28.
Sinagle, *n.* = **sanegle**, 67/8; **synagle**, 54/33; **synegle**, 26/31, 59/23. Cf. **Sanegle, Senigle**.
Syndegrefe, *n.* ? = **senegrene**, 49/9. Cf. MDu. *sindegroen*.
Syne, *adv.* afterward, 1/9.
Synegrene, *n.* = **senegrene**, 7/9. OE. *singrēne*.
Syons, *n. pl.* scions, twigs, 33/16.
Syroyn(e, *n.* a type of medicament of a consistency between that of an unguent and that of an emplaster, 72/26, side-note 4, 73/12, side-note 1; **syrone**, 73/7; **cyroyns**, *pl.* 69/5. Cf. Godefroy, cyroisne; Guy de Chauliac (Nicaise) 674.
Sirop(e, *n.* sirup, a thick, viscid liquid made esp. from herbs boiled with sugar, 61/side-note 5, 72/37; **syrop(e**, 60/side-note 2, 61/20, 73/2.
Sithen, *adv.* afterward, 5/1; **sythen**, 3/10.
Sythes, *n. pl.* times, 45/2.
Skafiȝagre, see **Stafiȝagre**.
Sla, *v.* slay, 2/25, etc.; **slaa**, 7/ side-notes 3, 5.
Slaes, see **Blak slaes**.
Slake, *v.* slake, diminish, 75/side-note 1. Cf. **Slekkes**.
Slaream, *n.* clary, *Salvia verbenaca*, L., *centrum galli .i. slaream*, 14/8. Med. L. *sclarea*. Cf. **Sclary, Centrum galli**.
Slawe, *a.* slow, 75/4.
Slekkes, *v.* slake, quench, *pr. 3 s.*, 47/2. Cf. **Slake**.
Slyce, *n.* = **sclice**, 65/5.
Slyke, *a.* such, 51/29.
Sloken, *v.* slake, 9/31, 81/2; **slokened**, *p. p.*, 56/6. NED: slocken.
Smalach(e, *n.* smallage, ? *Apium graveolens*, L., 17/35, 18/4, 32/24, 54/13, 66/31, 68/39; **smalle ache**, 32/40. Cf. **Ache petit**.
Smalle salte, finely powdered salt, 17/26.
Smedes, *n. pl.* fine powder, 61/26. NED: smeddum.
Snyle, see **Blake snyles, Rede snyle**.
So, *adv.* = **sa**, 1/10, etc.
Solsekill, *n.* ? marigold, *Calendula officinalis*, L., 8/30, 20/32, 41/32, 59/37; **solsikill**, 62/4. OF. *solsecle* fr. L. *solsequium*.
Soluble, *a.* free from costiveness, 28/15; **solubill**, 29/26.
Sone, *adv.* soon, 2/18.
Soppes, *n. pl.* sops, 30/21, 34/24; **sopes**, 20/10.
Sothe, *n.* truth, 6/4.
Soupe, *v.* sup, take supper, 13/24; **souppe**, 20/10. Cf. **Suppe**.
Sourdokes, *n. pl.* sorrel, *Rumex acetoza*, L., 43/10.
Sowdis, *v.* solder, unite closely, *pr. 3 s.*, 68/9.
Sowthrenwode, *n.* southernwood, *Artemisia abrotanum*, L., 34/3.
Sperred(e, *p. p.*, closed securely, 52/11, 17.
Sperwort(e, *n.* spearwort, either *Ranunculus flammula*, L. or *Ranunculus lingua*, L., 3/25, 7/14, 15/16, 37.
Spete, *n.* spit, broach, 31/22.
Spewe, *v.* spew, 2/18.
Spice, *n.* spice; **spices**, *pl.*, 66/18; **spyce**, 49/1; ? a specific remedy, **spice**, 18/side-note 6; **spyce**, 18/31.
Spicaray, *n.* spicery, a spicy preparation, 33/37.
Spik, *n.* ? true lavender, *Lavandula vera*, L. or ? French lavender, *Lavandula spica*, Cav., 60/9.
Spynnande, *ppl. a.* gushing,—said of blood, 69/37.
Spourge, *n.* spurge, a plant of the genus *Euphorbia*, 3/25, 15/13, 28/1, 29/14, 50/13, 66/20, 73/1; **sporuge**, 74/34; **spourges**, *pl.*, 15/20; **spourge leues**, 38/5; **spourge sede**, 15/21.
Spourge, *v.* purify, purge, 25/side-note 5, 32/36. OF. *espurgier*.
Sprenkill, *v.* sprinkle, 33/12.
Sqwarede, *ppl. a.* squared, 18/32.
Stafiȝagre, *n.* stavesacre, *Delphinium staphisagria*, L., 2/33, 56/3, 6, 66/33; **skafiȝagre**, *it is þe seede of a wilde vyne*, 2/27.
Stayncroppe, *n.* stonecrop, *Sedum acre*, L., 69/11. OE. *stāncrop*.
Stake, *n.* stitch (in the side), 35/side-note 2. See notes to 35/3-4, 5-8.
Stale, *v.* urinate, 56/12.
Stalynge, *vbl. n.* urine, 34/2, 36/4.
Stalworthe, *a.* strong (of vinegar), 13/33, 38/35.
Stamp(e, *v.* stamp, pound, beat to pulp or powder, 1/25, 49/13.

Stanche, *v.* stanch, 48/19, *etc.*;
stawnche, 31/1, *etc.*; **staunche,**
80/side-note 8; **stawnce,** 30/29;
staunce, 48/side-note 3.
Stane, *n.* a piece of rock, 17/12,
etc.; gall stone, 44/39, *etc.*;
stanes, *pl.*, pieces of rock, 19/5,
etc.; gall stones, 46/13; seeds
(of dates), 16/27. Cf. **Stone.**
Stangyng, *vbl. sb.* throbbing, aching, 67/36.
Stede, *n.* place, 49/23.
Steke, *v.* stab, pierce, 80/16.
Stele, *n.* stalk (of a plant), 78/20, 24, 80/16.
Stepe, *v.* steep, 32/26; **stepide,**
p. p., 24/24. Cf. **Stop(e.**
Stewe, *n.* vapor, 17/16.
Stewe, *v.* bathe in hot vapor,
13/24; **stewed(e,** *p. p.*, 19/27, 28, 30.
Stilled, *p. p.*, distilled, 53/27.
Stone, *n.* = **stane,** 17/15, 18/37,
19/16, 19, 20, 26; **stones,** *pl.*,
18/35, 19/6, 33/12, 43/12.
Stop(e, *v.* = **stepe,** 20/27, 72/35;
stoppede, 73/2.
Stoppe, *v.* stopper, 21/29;
stoppid, *p. p.*, obstructed, 3/side-note 3.
Stoppyng, *vbl. n.* obstruction, 23/side note 6.
Stor, *n.* incensé, 18/5.
Storax, *n.* storax, a resin probably
obtained from the tree *Styrax
officinalis*, L., 66/12. L. *storax.
See note.*
Straa, *n.* straw (of oats), 5/13;
straw (of beans), 82/38; **strase,**
pl., bedding, 58/34.
Straberye wyse, the strawberry
plant, of the genus *Fragaria*,
16/11; *flosere .i.* **strabery wyes,**
67/17; **strabery wythes,** 74/2, 75/10.
Strayte, *a.* narrow, 77/16.
Strakes, *n. pl.* ? injuries due to
blows, 46/side-note 9. Cf. *For
suelling of a stroke,* Henslow
45/20.
Strange, *a.* strong, 1/25;
strangere, *comp.*, 77/10.
Streynȝour, *n.* strainer, 34/13.
Streken, *p. p.* cut, severed, 52/34.
Strene, *v.* bind, 31/14.
Strenghe, *n.* force, 48/14.
Strenghes, *v.* strengthen, *pr.* 3 *s.*, 30/29.
Strenkill, *v.* sprinkle, 29/37.

Strynge, *n.* eyestring, 13/37;
strynges, *pl.*, 13/side-note 7.
Stroye, *v.* destroy, 56/side-note 1.
Substance, *n.* substance, esp. the
solid residue of a strained herbal
decoction, 1/13, 70/29, 80/11.
Suffre, *v.* allow, 5/28, *etc.*; **suffers,**
pr. 3 *pl.*, 71/29; **suffred(e,**
p. p., 38/33, 55/25.
Suger, *n.* sugar, 28/9, *etc.*; **sugour,**
39/2. Cf. **ȝucre.**
Superflueties, *n. pl.*, superflueties,
51/39.
Suppe, *v.* = **soupe,** 29/36.
Swa, *adv.* = **sa,** 7/33, 13/16, *etc.*
Swage, *v.* assuage, 50/25. OF.
suager.
Swalange, *adv.* so long; of time, 32/29.
Swalow birdis, swallows, 11/1.
Swalow(e, *v.* swallow, 41/28, 75/27.
Swellis, *v.* swell, *pr.* 3 *s.*, 50/side note 1.
Swellyng, *vbl. n.* swelling, 49/22.
Swete milke, milk which is not
sour, 55/17.
Swynacy, *n.* quinsy, 37/1.
Swyn(e, *n.* pig, 54/36; **swyn fen,**
50/13; **swyn flyk,** 55/1; **swyn
grese,** 6/19; **swyn mukke,**
50/20; **swyne sayme,** 37/23.
Swithe, *adv.* quickly, 68/26.
Swythynge, *vbl. n.* smarting, 55/26.

Taa, *n.* toe, 53/9.
Tade, *n.* toad, 76/21.
Tay, *n.* the outer membrane of the
brain, 69/25, 36. Cf. F. *teie
dure.* NED: 1568, in this sense.
Tak(e, *v.* take, 1/1, 12, *etc.*; **takes,**
pr. 3 *s.*, 41/26; **taken,** *p. p.*, 62/8.
Taken, *n.* token, sign, 56/23;
takyn, 69/23.
Takenynge, *vbl. n.* sign, 52/25;
takynynges, *pl.*, 56/17.
Talent, *n.* appetite, 24/35.
Talghe, *n.* tallow, 36/20, *etc.* Cf.
Taughe.
Tame, *v.* pierce, 69/24.
Tansay, *n.* tansay, *Tanacetum
vulgare*, L., 2/8, 27/4, 45/18,
69/18, *etc.*; *tansay .i. philoga*,
67/17-18. *See note.* Cf. **White
tansay, Philoga.**
Tary, *v.* tarry, 52/29.
Taughe, *n.* = **talghe,** 17/22.
Tele stane, a tile, 62/12, *etc.*;

Glossary.

tele stones, *pl.,* 43/12. Cf. **Tile stane.**
Temce, *v.* sift, 78/19.
Teme, *v.* ? empty, or ? = **temce,** sift, 64/36.
Tendrons, *n. pl.* tendrons, 80/7.
Tent, *n.* a roll of linen or similar material for insertion into a wound, 50/1, 70/28, 78/25, 79/13, 81/4; *pl.,* **tentis,** 79/26, 80/17, 22; **tenttis,** 78/29.
Tercyane, *see* **Feuer tercyane.**
Teres, *n. pl.* drops, 81/10.
Terrebintym, *n.* = **turbentyn,** 66/13. OF. *terebentine.*
Terrestre, *see* **Yven terrestre.**
Tewe, *v.* work into proper consistency, 47/7.
þai, *pron.* they, 74/20; **þay,** 7/2, *etc.* Cf. **þam, þaire, Theym, þem.**
þaire, *pron.* their, 26/10. Cf. **þai.**
þam, *pron.* them, 1/5, *etc.;* **tham,** 45/38; **thaym,** 19/side-note 3. Cf. **þai, Theym, þem.**
þare, *adv.* there, 9/29, 53/10, 77/15, 21; **thare,** 49/39; **þer,** 55/4.
Thare, *conj.* where, 64/3; **þer,** 5/7.
Tharmes, *n.* ? entrails, ? hide, 32/28. *See note.*
þase, *a. pl.* those, 79/30; **thase,** 72/36. Cf. **þose.**
Thee, *n.* thigh, 52/3; **thees,** *pl.,* 49/14.
Theym, *pron.* = **þam,** 13/10.
Theis, *a. pl.* these, 67/6, 72/3. Cf. **Thies(e, þir.**
þem, *pron.* = **þam,** 5/5.
Ther-fra, *adv.* therefrom, 53/29.
þer-till, *adv.* thereto, 51/9; **þer-to,** 3/3, *etc.;* **ther-to,** 11/39; **þer-too,** 10/3.
þi, *poss. a.* thy, 1/2; **thi,** 1/9.
Thies(e, *a. pl.* = **theis,** 17/12, 25/20; **thyes,** 74/18.
þir, *a. pl.* = **theis,** 4/5, *etc.;* **thir,** 42/10, *etc.;* **their,** 11/28.
Thirlle, *v.* pierce, 64/17.
Thirlle, *n.* hole, 78/22, *etc.;* **thirle,** 81/17.
þis, *a.* this, 7/24, *etc.;* **this,** 10/23, *etc.;* **this(e,** *a. pl.,* these, 62/6, 66/35; **þise,** 33/27, 59/22.
Thole, *v.* endure, 17/34.
Thombe, *n.* thumb, 53/21.
Thomell taa, the great toe, 53/9. ON. *þumal-tá.*

Thonwanges, *n. pl.* temples (of the head), 61/14-15; **thonnwanges,** 1/21.
Thorgh, *prep.* through, 12/13; **thorow(e,** 3/10, 4/10, *etc.* Cf. **Thrugh, Thurgh.**
Thorow, *adv.* through, 68/17.
Thornes, *see* **White thornes.**
þose, *a. pl.* = **þase,** 49/14.
Thou, *pron.* thou, 29/36; **þou,** 11/18, *etc.* Cf. **þu.**
Thryngyng, *vbl. n.* pressure, 22/side-note 2.
Thros nedils possibly shepherd's needle, *Scandix pecten,* L., 15/33.
Throte, *n.* throat, 20/14; **throtte,** 19/24.
Thrugh, *prep.* = **thorgh,** 74/29.
þu, *pron.* = **thou,** 2/17, *etc.*
Thurgh, *prep.* = **thorgh,** 13/2, 54/6.
Tile stane, = **tele stane,** 17/12; **tile stone,** 17/15, *etc.;* **tyle stones,** *pl.,* 18/35.
Til(l, *conj.* until, 5/2, 9/30, *etc.*
Till, *prep.* to, 68/32, 77/9.
Tyme, *n.* thyme, *Thymus serpillum,* L., 32/25.
Tyne, *v.* be destroyed, 34/33.
Tysayn, *n.* a medicinal drink made of barley-water, 51/33. OF. *tisane.*
Titimale, *n.* spurge, a plant of the genus *Euphorbia,* 29/16; **titmeus,** ?, 39/21.
Tome, *a.* empty;—of a deliriously 'light' head, 2/20, side-note 7. OE. *tōm,* ON. *tómr.*
Tonge, *n.* tongue, 2/30, *etc.* Cf. **Tunge, Townge.**
Tonge of dragon, ? a popularly etymologized form of *Dragantum,* gum tragacanth, a gum from certain species of *Astragalus,* 75/28. *See note.*
Tormentill, *n.* tormentil, *Potentilla tormentilla,* Neck, 10/7, 31/6, 53/28, 67/7; **tormentile,** 1/18. OF. *tormentille.*
Tothe, *n.* tooth, 16/37, *etc.;* **touthe,** 16/12; **tethe** *pl.,* 16/15, *etc.*
Tothwerk(e, *n.* toothache, 19/11, 15; **tothewerke,** 17/33; **touthewerke,** 16/7.
Tounnes, *n. pl.* large casks or barrels for liquids, 79/28.
Towelle, *n.* tewel, anus, 29/30. OF. *tuel.*
Townge, *n.* = **tonge,** 16/6.

Trayfoil, *n*. trefoil, a plant of the genus *Trifolium*, 59/12. AF. *trifoil*, OF. *trefeuil*.
Trauellyng, *vbl. n.* labour (of childbirth), 56/side-note 5; ? torment (in sleep), a nightmare, 2/side-note 11, 26/10.
Tre, *n*. tree, 38/25; wood, 28/32, 67/22.
Treacle, *n*. a medicinal salve, used as a poison antidote, 26/22. OF. *triacle*.
Triddils, *n. pl.* pellets of sheep or goat dung, 27/25, 50/20. OF. *tyrdel*.
Tried, *ppl. a.* purified, 46/8.
Trow, *v*. believe, 49/23.
Tunge, *n*. = **tonge**, 14/17.
Tupe, *n*. ram, 17/22.
Turbit(t, see **Whitt turbit(t**.
Turbentyn, *n*. turpentine, either the resin of the terebinth tree, *Pistacia terebinthus*, L. or the oleoresin extracted from various coniferous trees, 68/13, 25; **turbentill**, 76/33; **turmentyn(e**, 50/34, 54/31. OF. *tourbentine*, fr. L. *terbentina*, fr. G. τερμινθίνη
Twa, *num*. two, 3/30, etc.; two, 18/35, 19/3, 79/10.

Initial *v*, followed by a consonant.

Vndron, *n*. undern, 47/20.
Vngula caballi, horsehoof, *Tussilago farfara*, L., *horshoue þat is called vnguli caballi*, 59/29. See note.
Vnhill, *v*. uncover, 69/34.
Vnyon, see **Rede vnyon**.
Vnkyndely, *a*. unnatural, 51/30.
Vnslekked, *ppl. a.* unslacked (of lime), 5/17, 76/7; **vnslokynde**, 43/29, 75/34.
Vntil(l, *prep*. until, 23/24, 24/25.
Vrcheon, *n*. hedgehog, 36/34. OF. *hericun*. Cf. Picard, *vrichon*.
Vrcyne, see **Brance vrcyne**.
Vrynall, *n*. a glass vessel used to hold urine for medical examination, 10/22. OF. *urinal*.
Vryn(e, *n*. urine, 6/35, 46/12.
Vrtice, see **Rouge vrtice**.
Vtter, *a*. outer, 15/18; **vttereste**, outermost, 81/1.

Initial *v*, followed by a vowel.

Vayn(e, *n*. = **veyne**, 47/26, 48/18.
Vanytee, *n*. lightness of the head, esp. of a delirious sort, 1/heading.

Veyne, *n*. vein, 53/8. Cf. **Vayn(e, Myd veyn**.
Venym(e, *n*. venom, 2/17, 26/12; **venom**, 53/4.
Venom, *v*. poison with venom, 53/4; **venomed**, *p. p.*, 54/2.
Ventosite, *n*. flatulency, 43/side-note 11.
Ventousynge, *vbl. n.* the drawing of blood with a cupping-glass, 47/side-note 7.
Ventoused(e, *p. p.*, bled with a cupping-glass, 53/15, 22.
Vergeous, *n*. verjuice, a liquor made from the juice of unripe grapes or other sour fruit, 23/31. OF. *verjus*.
Vermyon, *n*. ? cinnabar, the native red sulphide of mercury or ? the same compound manufactured from mercury and sulphur, 65/11. OF. *vermeillon*. Cf. Thompson, *Mat. Med. Painting*, pp. 102–104.
Vertgres(e, *n*. a poisonous drug and pigment, green to greenish-blue in colour, resembling or identical with modern verdigris, obtained by submitting copper to the action of vinegar, marc, or a similar substance containing acetic acid, 3/3, 68/3; **vertegrese**, 3/27. OF. *vert de Grice, vert de Grece*. Cf. Thompson, *Mat. Med. Painting*, pp. 163–165.
Vertue, *n*. efficacy in curing diseases, 26/13; *pl*., **vertous**, 26/9; **vertus**, 71/28.
Veruayn(e, *n*. vervain, *Verbena officinalis*, L., 1/1, 12/33, 27/27, 57/31, 68/14, etc. OF. *verveine*.
Vesage, *n*. visage, 22/18.
Vesche, *n*. vetch, a plant of the genus *Vicia*, 67/14. AF. *vesche*. Cf. **Fiche**.
Vetoyn(e, *n*. = **betoyn(e**, 1/1, 2/9, 10/32, 12/5, 14/32, 62/4, etc.; **vetoyne leues**, 34/19.
Violet(t, *n*. violet, a plant of the genus *Viola*, 23/37, 25/8, 27/37, 45/6, 54/12, 33, 55/31, 67/12, etc.
Virgyn wax(e, virgin wax, new beeswax, 3/14, 36, 18/4, etc.; **vyrgyn wax**, 70/12.
Votoyn, *n*. = **vetoyn(e, betoyn(e**, 14/27.

Waybrede, *n*. plantain, *Plantago major*, L., 4/35, 9/9, 21/35,

Glossary.

30/8, **51**/11, **60**/26, **74**/30, etc. ; *playntayn(e .i.* **waybred,** 17/22, 67/13 ; **wayebrede,** 2/12, 4/ 17–18.

Wayte, *v.* observe constantly, 55/ 36. OF. *waitier.*

Walde, *v.* would, 19/26, 63/31. Cf. **Wil(l.**

Walmes, *n. pl. see* **Whalme,** 70/16.

Walnot tre, walnut tree, 15/17.

Walwort(e, *n.* dwarf elder, *Sambucus ebulus,* L., 2/23, 6/19, 22/ 35, 32/33, 62/23, 71/21, etc. ; **wallworte,** 29/11 ; **wallewort(e,** 74/7, 12 ; **walworthe,** 2/12, 26/36. OE. *wealhwyrt.*

Wambe, *n.* abdomen, 22/side-note 4, 29/28, 32/31, 57/27, 58/33, *etc.* ; bowels, 28/15, 36, 29/25. Cf. **Wombe.**

Warantise, *n.* guarantee, 34/8.

Waraunce, *n.* = **mader,** 71/27, 33; **waranc,** 67/11. Cf. *Alphita* 155/30-31. Cf. **Woraunce.**

Ware, *n.* pus, 76/side-note 9, 77/ 20.

Warische, *v.* recover from illness, 38/22 ; **waresche,** 29/10.

Waste, *v.* corrode, be consumed, 44/4, *etc.*; cause to be consumed, 76/side-note 9.

Wastyng, *vbl. n.* evaporation, 68/ 22.

Wate, *a.* wet, 81/12.

Water, *n.* water, 1/16, **watyr,** 56/21 ; an aqueous infusion, 25/24, 37/32.

Waterand, *ppl. a.* (of the eyes) filling with tears, 8/side-note 6.

Water cresse, water-cress, *Nasturtium officinalis,* R. Br., 20/17 ; **water cresses,** *pl.*, 66/4, 72/18.

Waterles, *a.* dry, 31/17. OE. *waterleás.*

Waters, *v.* secrete saliva ;—said of the mouth, *pr.* 3 *s.,* 19/24.

Wates, *v.* know, *pr.* 2 *s.,* 59/28. Cf. **Wiet(e.**

Wauter, *see* **Herb Wauter.**

Wax(e, *n.* beeswax, 1/5, 2/23.

We, *pron.* we, 66/9.

Webe, *n.* a film growing over the eye, 8/side-note 10, 11/side-note 2 ; **webbe,** 69/37.

Wedir, *n.* wether, castrated ram, 6/35.

Wey, *v.* weigh, 64/1, 77/36 ; **weghe,** 74/17.

Weit, *v.* know, 41/28. Cf. **Wete.**

Weke *n.* week, 1/3. Cf. **Woke.**

Welked, *p. p.,* wilted, 78/21.

Welle, *v.* boil, 1/9 ; *p. p.,* **welled(e,** 9/11, 13/23 ; **wellid(e,** 7/2, 33/3.

Wellecresse, *n.* = **water cresse,** 33/22, 46/1, 4.

Welowe lefes, willow leaves, 4/24. Cf. **Wilghe.**

Wemme, *n.* blemish, 60/2.

Wenge, *n.* wing, 8/33, 12/22.

Werke, *n.* pain, 1/11.

Werkes, *v.* ache, *pr.* 3 *s.*, 16/19, *etc.* ; **wirkes,** 68/35.

Werkyng(e, *vbl. n.* aching, 16/38, 50/28.

Wete, *v.* = **wiet(e,** 30/34, 79/34 ; **wette,** 74/20.

Whalme, *n.* a bubbling of water, esp. boiling water, a ' wallop,' 72/34 ; **walmes,** *pl.*, 70/16.

Whare, *adv.* where, 30/1, *etc.* Cf. **Where.**

Whare so, *adv.* wheresoever, 50/side-note 3.

What, *pron.* what, 10/20.

What, *a.* what, 51/19.

Whelynge, *vbl. n.* suppuration, 47/side-note 7.

Whelis, *v.* suppurate, *pr.* 3 *s.*, 72/38.

Whelm(e, *v.* turn upside down, 10/18, 12/19.

Where, *adv.* = **whare,** 47/10.

Whetour, *n.* pus, 76/side-note 9 ; **whettour,** 9/28. Cf. **Whitoure.**

Whetstane, *n.* whetstone, 8/20.

Whilde, *see* **Wilde sauge.**

While, *n.* while, 28/37 ; þe **whils,** 41/39. Cf. **Whils.**

Whilk(e, *rel. pron.* which, 46/side-note 7, 35/25. Cf. **Wilk.**

Whils, *conj.* while, 53/30.

Whit(e, *n.* albumen, 4/21, 31/34, *etc.* ; **whitt(e,** 9/24, 16/24 ; **whittes,** *pl.*, 65/25.

Whit(e, *a.* white, 50/15, 54/11, *etc.* ; **whitt(e,** 55/12, 66/3 ; **whyte,** 24/23 ; **wite,** 22/33.

White brissoke, ? a variety of *Brassica oleracea,* L., 66/24. *See note.* Not in NED.

White gynger, ? white ginger, the dried scraped root of *Zinziber officinalis,* Rosc., 8/20. *See note.*

White harede, white haired, *i.e.* covered with mold, 12/37.

White lede, ? white lead (a compound of carbonate and hydroxide of lead) or a similar white-coloured lead compound, 39/17. Cf.

148 *Glossary.*

Thompson, *Mat. Med. Painting*, pp. 90–94. Cf. **Ceruse.**

White malue, ? a variety of marsh mallow, *Althaea officinalis*, L. with white or nearly white blossoms, 49/12, 74/12, 75/20, 77/28, 38.

White pepir, pepper from the dried nearly ripe berries of *Piper nigrum*, L., 44/13, 66/17; **white pepir sedis,** the dried ripe berries of *Piper nigrum*, L., 66/34.

White pik, white pitch, *Pix burgundica*, L., the resinous juice of the *Pinus abies*, L., 54/35. Cf. **Pik album.** *See note.*

White tansay, ? silverweed, *Potentilla anserina*, L., 77/28. *See note.* Cf. **Gose grese** (2).

White thornes, hawthorn, *Crataegus oxycantha*, L., 9/5.

Whitoure, *n.* = **whetour,** 72/39.

Whitt turbit(t, turpeth, a drug from the root of *Ipomoea turpethum*, R. Br., 28/8, 10.

Whitte chessebolle, a variety of opium poppy with white blossoms, *Papaver somniferum*, var. *album*, L., 63/24. *See note.* Cf. **Chesseboll croppes.**

Who so, *rel. pron.* whoso, 8/side-note 8.

Wiet(e, *v.* know, 41/27, 56/side-note 2, 57/38. Cf. **Wete, Wates.**

Wilde cucurd, ? the bitter gourd, *Citrullus colocynthis*, Schrad., 79/25. Cf. OF. *cougourde*, fr. L. *cucurbita*. *See note.* Not in NED.

Wilde malue, wild mallow, ? *Malva sylvestris*, L., 35/24, 68/38.

Wilde sauge, ambrose, *Teucrium scorodonia*, L., 69/1; **wilde sawge,** 66/25; **whilde sauge,** 65/27. Cf. *Alphita* 8/16–19, 161/4–6.

Wild louache, wild lovage, ? *Levisticum officinale*, Koch, 73/20.

Wild(e **nept**(e, briony, ? *Bryonia dioica*, Jacq., 65/15, 75/8.

Wilghe, *n.* willow, 38/25. Cf. **Wylken leues.**

Wilk, *rel. pron.* = **whilk**(e, 67/2.

Wylken leues = welowe lefes, 39/16. Cf. **Wilghe.**

Wil(l, *v.* will, 4/11, 5/28, *etc.*; **walde,** would, 19/26, 63/31.

Wymalue, *n.* the marsh mallow, *Althaea officinalis*, L., 54/26, *altea one Englische called wymalue*, 74/33. AF. *wimave, widmalve.*

Wynagre, *n.* vinegar, 38/30.

Wyn(e, *n.* wine, 2/38, 14/2, *etc.*; **wynne,** 68/16.

Wyse, *n.* stalk (of a plant), 1/18. Cf. **Straberye wyse.**

Wythes, *see* **Strabery wyse.**

Wodbynde, *n.* probably honey-suckle, *Lonicera periclymenum*, L., 9/9, 44/9, 75/22; **woddbynde,** 5/19; **wodebynde,** 8/8; **wobbynde,** 36/35; **wodbynd croppis,** 74/2–3; **wodbynd leues,** 34/19–20.

Wode, *a.* insane, 5/side-note 13.

Wodnes, *n.* insanity, 6/9.

Wodrofe, *n.* woodruff, *Asperula odorata*, L., 44/34, 57/32; **woderofe,** 38/19; ? *cheuerfoille .i.* **wodrofe,** 67/12. Cf. **Cheuerfoill**(e.

Wodsoures, *n.* woodsorrel, *Oxalis acetosella*, L., pl., 50/2.

Woyse, *n.* juice, 6/26, 8/29, *etc.* Cf. **Wose.**

Woke, *n.* = **weke,** 4/22.

Wolle, *n.* wool, 28/19.

Wollelok, *n.* a tuft of wool, 47/33.

Wombe, *n.* = **wambe,** 26/20.

Wonut, *p. p.,* accustomed, 58/32.

Woraunce, *n.* = **warance, mader,** 69/1.

Wormot, *n.* wormwood, *Artemisia absinthium*, L., 34/3, 35/27, 46/15, *etc.*; **wormod**(e, 1/1, 29, 2/8, 6/33, 7/27, *etc.*

Wort, *n.* herb, 69/18; **wortes,** *pl.,* cabbage, 37/8. Cf. **Rede wirtes, Rede wortes, Lange wortis.**

Wose, *n.* = **woyse,** 13/10, *etc.*

Wretyn, *vbl. n.* something written, 42/16. *See note.* Cf. **Write.**

Writ, *n.* written document, 42/15.

Write, *v.* write, 42/14, *etc.*; **wryte,** 42/10; **wretyn,** *p. p.,* 67/6, 70/7.

Ʒalowe, *a.* yellow, 74/21.

Ʒarow(e, yarrow, *Achillea millefolium*, L. 31/3, 28, 32/4, 66/25, *etc.* Cf. **Iarue.**

Ʒerde, *n.* penis, 44/side-note 10.

Ʒerdis, *n. pl.* twigs, 7/5, 6.

Ʒhiskyng(e, *vbl. n.* hiccuping, 19/15, 20/9, 16. Cf. **Ʒiskes.**

Glossary. 149

ȝiskes, *v.* hiccup, *pr.* 3 *s.*, 20/sidenote 3. Cf. Ȝhiskyng(e.
ȝit, *adv.* yet, 69/18.
ȝokynge, *vbl. n.* ? itching, 55/26. Cf. NED: yuke.
ȝole, *n.* yule, 60/33 ; ȝole nyghte, 60/34.

ȝolke, *n.* yolk (of an egg), 18/36.
ȝour, *pron.* your, *pl.*, 61/1.
ȝucre, *n.* = suger, 28/1.
ȝucre caffatine, one of the better kinds of lump sugar, 20/20. Cf. Shöffler 18-20.

BIBLIOGRAPHY

Aiken, Pauline. "Vincent of Beauvais and Dame Pertelote's knowledge of medicine," Speculum, X (1935), 280–287.
Albertus Magnus. Alberti cognomento Magni de secretis mulierum libellus. Eiusdem de virtutibus herbarum, lapidum, et animalium quorundam libellus. Item de mirabilibus mundi. Lyons, 1555.
Albertus Magnus. B. Alberti Magni opera omnia. Edited by Augustus Borgnet. Vol. X. Paris: Vives, 1891.
Albucasis. La chirurgie d'Abulcasis al Zahrāwī. Translated by Lucien Leclerc. Paris: Baillière, 1861.
Albacasis. Omnium humani corporis, interiorum et exteriorum, morbis medendi ratio methodica. Et omnem curandi usum idoneorum instrumentorum graphica depictae effigies, auctore Albucase, lib. III. Anon. trans. Basle, 1541.
Albucasis. Cyrurgia parua Guidonis. Cyrurgia Albucasis cum cauterijs & alijs instrumentis. Tractatus de oculis Jesu hali. Tractatus de oculis Canamusali. Venice: B. Locatellus, 1500.
Alexander Trallianus. Alexander von Tralles. Original-text und Uebersetzung nebst einer einleitenden Abhandlung. Ein Beitrag zur Geschichte der Medicin. Edited by Theodor Puschmann. 2 vols. Vienna: Braumüller, 1878.
Allen, Hope Emily. Writings ascribed to Richard Rolle, hermit of Hampole and materials for his biography. New York and London: D. C. Heath and Co. and Oxford University Press, 1927.
Alphita. A medico-botanical glossary from the Bodleian Manuscript, Selden B. 35. Edited by J. L. G. Mowat. Anecdota oxoniensia, Medieval and Modern Series, Vol. I, Part II. Oxford: Clarendon Press, 1882.
Anglo-Saxon and Old English vocabularies. Edited by Thomas Wright and Richard Wülcker. 2 vols. London: Trübner, 1883–84.
Apuleius Barbarus. Das Herbarium Apuleii nach einer früh-mittelenglischen Fassung. Anglistische Forschungen, Heft 5. Heidelberg: Winter, 1902.
Apuleius Barbarus. The herbal of Apuleius Barbarus. Edited by Robert T. Gunther. Oxford: Printed for presentation to members of the Roxburgh Club, 1925.
Apuleius Barbarus, etc. Antonii Musae de herba vettonica liber Pseudoapulei herbarius Antonymi de taxone liber Sexti Placiti liber medicinae ex animalibus. Edited by Henry Sigerist and Ernest Howald. Corpus medicorum latinorum, No. IV. Leipzig: Teubner, 1927.
Arderne, John. De arte phisicali et de cirurgia of Master John Arderne, surgeon of Newark, dated 1412. Edited by D'Arcy Power. London: Bale and Danielsson, 1922.
Arderne, John. Treatises of fistula in ano, haemorrhoids, and clysters by John Arderne from an early fifteenth-century manuscript translation. Edited by D'Arcy Power. Early English Text Society, Original Series, No. 139. London: Oxford University Press, 1910.
Aristotle. The works of Aristotle. Edited by W. D. Ross. Vol. VII, Problemata. Translated by E. S. Forster. Oxford: Clarendon Press, 1927.
Armitage-Smith, Sydney. John of Gaunt. London: A. Constable, 1904.
Averrhoes. Averrhoes liber de medicina. Anon. trans. Venice, 1560.
Avicenna. Avicennae liber canonis, de medicinis cordialibus, cantica. Translated by Gerard of Cremona and Andrea Alpagus. Venice: Juntae, 1555.

Bibliography.

Bentham, George. Handbook of the British flora. 2 vols. London: Reeve, 1865.
Bentley, Robert, and Trimen, H. Medicinal plants. 4 vols. London: Churchill, 1880.
Bernard Gordonius. Tabula practica Bernardi Gordonii dicta lilium medicine. Venice: Gregoriis, 1496.
The book of quinte essence. Edited by Frederick Furnivall. Early English Text Society, Original Series, No. 17. London: Trübner, 1866.
Bratley, George. The power of gems and charms. London: Gay and Bird, 1907.
British Museum, Additional Manuscripts, 27944. Rotograph owned by the Middle English Dictionary.
British Museum, Royal Manuscripts, 12 G. iv. Rotograph owned by the Middle English Dictionary.
British Museum, Sloane Manuscripts, 393. Rotograph owned by Professor Edith Rickert.
Britten, James, and Holland, Robert. A dictionary of English plant names. "English Dialect Society Publications." London: Trübner, 1886.
Brown, William. "On the heraldry at Thirst," Yorkshire archaeological journal, XXII (1912–13), 215.
Brunner, Karl. "Hs. British Museum Additional 31042," Archiv, CXXXII (1914), 316–327.
Burgundy, John of. John de Burdeus or John de Burgundia otherwise Sir John de Mandeville and the pestilence. Edited by David Murray. London: Gardner, 1891.

Calendar of the Close Rolls, Henry VI. Vol. I (1422–29). "Publications of the Public Records Office of Great Britain." London: H.M. Stationery Office, 1933.
Calendar of the Patent Rolls, 1396–99, 1436–41. "Publications of the Public Record Office of Great Britain." London: H.M. Stationery Office, 1909, 1911.
Catholicon Anglicum, an English-Latin wordbook, dated 1483. Edited by Sidney Herrtage. Early English Text Society, Original Series, No. 75. London: Trübner, 1881.
Campbell, Donald. Arabian medicine and its influence on the Middle Ages. 2 vols. London: Kegan Paul, Trench, Trübner, 1926.
Celsus, A. Cornelius. A. Cornelii Celsi quae supersunt. Edited by F. Marx. Corpus medicorum latinorum, Vol. I. Leipzig: Teubner, 1915.
Chauliac, Guy de. La grande chirurgie de Guy de Chauliac. Edited by Edouard Nicaise. Paris: Ballière, 1890.
Cholmeley, Henry. John of Gaddesden and the Rosa medicinae. Oxford: Clarendon Press, 1912.
Collectio salernitana ossia documenti inediti. Edited by G. E. T. Henschel, C. Daremberg, and Salvatore de Renzi. 5 vols. Naples: Filiatre-Sebezio, 1852–59.
Constantinus Africanus. Incipit breuiarium Constantini dictum viaticum. Lyons: Villiers, 1510.
Crawfurd, Raymond. "The blessing of cramp-rings," Studies in the history and method of science, ed. Charles Singer (Oxford: Clarendon Press, 1917), I, 165–187.
Crawfurd, Raymond. The king's evil. Oxford: Clarendon Press, 1911.
Creighton, Charles. A history of epidemics in Britain. 2 vols. Cambridge: University Press, 1891–94.
Cumston, Charles. An introduction to the history of medicine, from the time of the pharaohs to the end of the XVIIIth century. London: Kegan Paul, Trench, Trübner, 1926.

Dawson, Warren. Magician and leech. A study in the beginnings of medicine with special reference to ancient Egypt. London: Methuen, 1929.

Bibliography. 153

Dictionnaire encyclopédique des sciences médicales. 100 vols. Paris : Asselin, Masson, 1868–89.
Dioscurides, Pedanius. Pedanii Dioscuridis Anazarbei de materia medica libri quinque. Edited by M. Wellman. 3 vols. Berlin : Weidmann, 1907–14.

Earle, John. English plant names from the tenth to the fifteenth century. Oxford : Clarendon Press, 1880.
The Edwin Smith Surgical Papyrus. Edited by James Breasted. 2 vols. Chicago : University of Chicago Press, 1930.
English lyrics of the XIIIth century. Edited by Carleton Brown. Oxford : Clarendon Press, 1932.

Feet of fines of the Tudor period. Yorkshire archaeological and topographical association, Record series, Vol. V, Part II. [Dewsbury], 1888.
Flückiger, Friedrich, and Hanbury, Daniel. Pharmacographia. A history of the principal drugs of vegetable origin, met with in Great Britain and India. 2d ed. London : Flückiger, 1879.
Förster, Max. " Die altenglische Glossenhandschrift Plantinus 32 (Antwerpen) und Additional 32246 (London)," Anglia, XLI (1917), 94–161.
Förster, Max. " Mittelenglische Pflanzenglossen (um 1300)," Anglia, XLII (1918), 156–162.
Förster, Max. " Mittelenglische Rätsel und Verwandtes (15. jh.)," Anglia, XLII (1918), 206–217.
Fox-Davies, Arthur. Armorial families. Edinburgh : Jack, 1895.

Gaddesden, John of. Rosa anglica. Pavia : Birreta, 1492.
Galen, Claudius. Claudii Galeni opera omnia. Edited and translated by Karl Kühn. 20 vols. Leipzig : Teubner, 1826–33.
Gallée, J. H. " Segensprüche," Germania. XXXII (1887), 452–460.
Garrett, Robert. " Middle English rimed medical treatise," Anglia, XXXIV (1911), 163–193.
Garrison, Fielding. An introduction to the history of medicine. Philadelphia : Saunders, 1914.
Goldberg, Ada, and Saye, Hymen. " An index to medieval French medical receipts," Bulletin of the Institute of the History of Medicine of the Johns Hopkins Hospital. Supplement, I (1933), 433–466.
Green, Edward. Landmarks of botanical history. Part I. Prior to 1562 A.D. Smithsonian Institution Publication, No. 1870. Washington : Smithsonian Institution, 1909.
Green, Joseph. A history of botany. London : Dent, 1914.
Grendon, Felix. " The Anglo-Saxon charms," Journal of American Folk-lore, XXII (1909), 105–237.
Gruner, O. C. A treatise on the canon of medicine of Avicenna incorporating a translation of the first book. London : Luzac, 1930.

Haeser, Heinrich. Lehrbuch der Geschichte der Medizin und der epidemischen Krankheiten. Vol. I, Geschichte der Medicin im Alterthum und Mittelalter. 3d ed. Jena : Dufft, 1875.
Halliwell, James Orchard. Dictionary of archaisms and provincialisms. 2 vols. London : J. R. Smith, 1860.
Hardy, Thomas. Syllabus (in English) of the documents relating to England and other kingdoms contained in the collection known as " Rymer's Foedera." Vol. II, 1377–1654. London : Longmans, 1873.
Hippocrates. Hippocrates with an English translation. Edited and translated by W. H. S. Jones. 4 vols. " Loeb Classical Library." New York : Putnam, 1923.
Historical Manuscripts Commission. Report on the manuscripts of the late Reginald Rawdon Hastings. Vol. I. London : H.M. Stationery Office, 1928.

Holthausen, Ferdinand. "Medicinische Gedichte aus einer stockholmer Handschrift," Anglia, XVIII (1896), 293–331.
Holthausen, Ferdinand. "Kleine Mitteilungen. De spermate hominys." Archiv, XCVII (1897), 401–408.
Holthausen, Ferdinand. "Kleine Mitteilungen. Mittelenglische und altfranzösische Pflanzenglossen," Archiv, C (1898), 158–163.
Holthausen, Ferdinand. "Rezepte, Segen und Zaubersprüche aus zwei stockholmer Handschriften," Anglia, XIX (1897), 75–88.
Holthausen, Ferdinand. "Zur altenglischen Literatur. 22. Ein frühmittelenglischer Zauberspruch," Beiblatt zur Anglia, XIX (1908), 213–215.

Inquisitions and assessments relating to feudal aids. Vol. VI, 1264–1431. York and Additions. "Publications of the Public Record Office of Great Britain." London : H.M. Stationery Office, 1920.
Isidore of Seville. Sancti Isidori etymologiarum libri XX. Edited by J. P. Migne. Patrologia latina, No. 82. Paris : Migne, 1878.

Jesu Haly. Haly Filius Abbas. Liber totius medicine. Edited by Stephanus. Lyons, 1523.
John of Gaunt's register. Edited by Sydney Armitage-Smith. Camden Society, 3d series, No. XX. London : Royal Historical Society, 1911.
Jordan, Richard. Handbuch der mittelenglischen Grammatik. Heidelberg : Winter, 1925.
Joret, Charles. "Comptes-rendus. Anecdota oxoniensia," Romania, XVI (1887), 598–602.
Joret Charles. "Recettes médicales en français publiée d'après le manuscrit 23 d'Evreux," Romania, XVIII (1889), 571–582.

Ketham, John of. The fasciculus medicinae of Johannes de Ketham alemanus. Edited by Karl Sudhoff and Charles Singer. Monumenta medica, Vol. I. Milan : Lier, 1924.
Kirk, R. E. G. Life records of Chaucer, Part IV. Publications of the Chaucer Society, No. 47. London : Kegan Paul, Trench, Trübner, 1900.
Kleinere angelsächsische Denkmäler. Edited by G. Leonhardi. Bibliothek der angelsächsischen Prosa. Edited by C. Grein and P. Wülker. Vol. VI. Hamburg : Grand, 1905.
Köhler, Reinhold. "Segensprüche," Germania, XIII (1868), 178–188.
Kunz, George. The magic of jewels and charms. Philadelphia : Lippincott, 1915.

Lanfranchus. Lanfrank's "Science of cirurgie." Edited by Robert Fleischhacker. Early English Text Society, Original Series, No. 102. London : Kegan Paul, Trench, Trübner, 1894.
Largus, Scribonius. Scribonii Largi conpositiones. Edited by Georg Helmreich. Leipzig : Teubner, 1887.
Leclerc, Lucien. Histoire de la médecine arabe, exposé complet des traductions du Grec. Paris : Leroux, 1876.
A leechbook or collection of medical recipes of the fifteenth century. The text of MS. No. 130 of the Medical Society of London. Edited by Warren Dawson. London : Macmillan, 1934.
Leechdoms, wortcunning, and starcraft of early England. Edited by Oswald Cockayne. 3 vols. Rerum britannicarum medii aevi scriptores, No. 35. London : Longmans, Green, 1864–66.
"Liber cure cocorum, ab. 1440 A.D.," Philological Society's Early English volume. Edited by Richard Morris. London : Asher, 1865.
Lincolnshire pedigrees. Edited by A. R. Maddison. Publications of the Harleian Society, No. 52. London : Harleian Society, 1904.
Luddington, Florence. "A medieval charm," Antiquary, XXXIX (1903), 274–277.

Bibliography. 155

Macer Floridus. De herbarum virtutibus. Basle, 1527.
Magistri salernitani nondum editi. Edited by Piero Giacosa. Turin : Bocca, 1901.
Manitius, Max. " Angelsächsische Glossen in dresdner Handschriften," Anglia, XXIV (1901), 428–435.
Marcellus Empiricus. Marcelli de medicamentis liber. Edited by Max Niedermann. Corpus medicorum latinorum, No. V. Leipzig : Teubner, 1916.
Matthes, H. C. " Zur Textkritik der stockholmer Medizinhandschrift X. 90," Englische Studien, LXX (1935), 110–116.
McBryde, John. " Some medieval charms," Sewanee Review, XXV (1917), 11–14.
Medical works of the fourteenth century together with a list of plants recorded in contemporary writings, with their identifications. Edited by G. Henslow. London : Chapman and Hall, 1899.
Medicina de quadrupedibus, an early Middle English version. Edited by Joseph Delcourt. Anglistische Forschungen, Heft 40. Heidelberg : Winter, 1914.
Mesue. Mesvae graecorum ac arabvm clarissima medici opera quae extant omnia. Translated by Andreas Marinus. Venice : Valgrisius, 1562.
Meyer, Paul. " Les manuscrits français de Cambridge," Romania, XXXII (1903), 18–120.
Meyer, Paul. " Manuscrits médicaux en français," Romania, XLIV (1915), 161–214.
Meyer, Paul. " Notice du ms. Bodley 57," Romania, XXXV (1906), 579–581.
Meyer, Paul. " Notice du ms. Sloane 1611 du musée britannique," Romania, XL (1911), 532–585.
Meyer, Paul. " Recettes médicales en Provençal d'après le ms. R. 14. 30 de Trinity College (Cambridge)," Romania, XXXII (1903), 268–299.
Meyer, Paul. " Recettes médicales en Français publiées d'après le ms. B. N. Lat. 8654 B," Romania, XXXVII (1908), 358–377.
Die mittelenglische Versroman über Richard Löwenherz. Edited by Karl Brunner. Vienna : Braumüller, 1913.
Ein mittelenglisches Medizinbuch. Edited by Fritz Heinrich. Halle : Niemeyer, 1896.
Aus mittelenglischen Medizintexten die Prosarezepte des stockholmer Miszellankodex X. 90. Edited by Gottfried Müller. Kölner anglistische Arbeiten, Band X. Leipzig : Tauchnitz, 1929.
Mondeville, Henry of. Chirurgie de maître Henri de Mondeville composée de 1306 à 1320. Edited by Édouard Nicaise. Paris : Alcan, 1893.
Mondeville, Henry of. Die Chirurgie des Heinrich von Mondeville. Edited by Julius Pagel. Berlin : Hirschwald, 1892.
Moore, Norman. " The Schola Salernitana : its history and the date of its introduction into the British Isles," Glasgow medical journal, LXIX (1908), 241–268.
Moore, Samuel, Meech, S. B., and Whitehall, H. B. " Middle English dialect characteristics and dialect boundaries : preliminary report of an investigation based exclusively on localized texts and documents," Essays and studies in English and Comparative Literature by members of the English Department of the University of Michigan. Ann Arbor : University of Michigan, 1935.
Müller, Gottfried. " Wortkundliches aus mittelenglischen Medizinbüchern," Britannica. Leipzig : Tauchnitz, 1929.

Najm ad-dyn Mahmud. Le livre de l'art du traitement de Najm ad-dyn Mahmoud. Translated by P. Guigues. Beyrouth : Guigues, 1903.
Neuburger, Max. History of medicine. Translated by Ernest Playfair. 2 vols. London : Frowde, 1910–25.
New Palaeographical Society. Facsimiles of ancient manuscripts. 2d series. Vol. I. London : Hart, 1913.

156   Bibliography.

Nicolaus Praepositus. Nicolai praepositi antidotarium paruum. With glosses by Platearius. Venice: Valgrisius, 1562.
Nicolaus Praepositus. L'antidotaire Nicolas. Deux traductions françaises de l'antidotarium Nicolai. Edited by Paul Dorveaux. Paris: Welter, 1896.
An Old Icelandic medical miscellany, MS. Royal Irish Academy 23. D. 43 with supplement from MS. Trinity College (Dublin) L. 2. 27. Edited and translated by Henning Larsen. Oslo: Dybwad, 1931.
Oribasius. Oribasii collectionum medicarum reliquiae. Edited by Johann Raeder. 4 vols. Corpus medicorum graecorum, No. VI. Leipzig: Teubner, 1928–31.

Page, William. The Victoria history of the county of York, North Riding. Vol. I. London: Constable, 1914.
Palladius. The Middle-English translation of Palladius " De re rustica." Edited by Mark Liddel. Part I. Berlin: Ebering, 1896.
Palladius. Palladius on husbondrie. From the unique MS. of about 1420 A.D. in Colchester Castle. Edited by Barton Lodge and Sidney Herrtage. Early English Text Society, Original Series, No. 52. London: Trübner, 1879.
The Papyrus Ebers. Translated by Cyril Bryan. London: Bles, 1930.
Paulus Aegineta. The seven books of Paulus Aegineta. Translated by Francis Adams. 3 vols. London: Sydenham Society, 1854–57.
Payne, Joseph. English medicine in the Anglo-Saxon times. Oxford: Clarendon Press, 1904.
Peri Didaxeon, eine Sammlung von Rezepten in englischer Sprache aus dem 11./12. Jahrhundert. Edited by Max Löweneck. Erlanger Beitrage zur englischen Philologie, Bd. III, Heft XII. Erlangen: Junge, 1896.
Platearius Johannes. Liber de simplici medicina dictus circum instans. Practica Platearij. Anon. trans. Venice: B. Locatellus, 1497.
Plinius, Caius. C. Plini Secundi naturalis historiae libri XXXVII. Edited by Karl Mayhoff. 6 vols. Leipzig: Teubner, 1870–98.
Political, religious, and love poems from the Archbishop of Canterbury's Lambeth MS. No. 306 and other sources. Edited by Frederick Furnivall. Early English Text Society, Original Series, No. 15. London: Kegan Paul, Trench, Trübner, 1866.
Power, D'Arcy. "The lesser writings of John Arderne." XVIIth International Congress of Medicine, Section XXIII, pp. 107–133. London: Frowde, 1914.
Power, D'Arcy, and Thompson, Charles. Chronologica medica. A handlist of persons, periods, and events in the history of medicine. London: Bale and Danielsson, 1923.
Power, Henry, and Sedgwick, Leonard. The New Sydenham Society's lexicon of medicine and the allied sciences. 5 vols. London: New Sydenham Society, 1879–99.
" The pricke of conscience," The Philological Society's Early English volume. Edited by Richard Morris. London: Asher, 1865.
Priebsch, Robert. " Segen aus Londoner HSS." Zeitschrift für deutsches Altertum und deutsche Litteratur, Band XXXVIII, neue Folge, Band XXVI (1894), 14–21.
Promptorium parvulorum. The first English-Latin dictionary. Edited by Anthony Mayhew. Early English Text Society, Extra Series, No. CII. London: Kegan Paul, Trench, and Trübner, 1908.
Promptorium parvulorum sive clericorum, lexicon anglo-latinum. Edited by Albert Way. Camden Society Publications, Nos. XXV (1843), LIV (1853), LXXXIX (1865). London: Camden Society, 1843–65.
The prose life of Alexander from the Thornton MS. Edited by J. S. Westlake. Early English Text Society, Original Series, No. 143. London: Kegan Paul, Trench, Trübner, 1913.

The Psalter or Psalms of David and certain Canticles with a translation and exposition in English by Richard Rolle of Hampole. Edited by H. R. Bramley. Oxford: Clarendon Press, 1884.

Quarter sessions records. Edited by John Atkinson. Vol. I. London: North Riding Record Society, 1884.

Religious pieces in prose and verse. Edited by George Perry. Early English Text Society, Original Series, No. 26. London: Trübner, 1867.

Reliquiae antiquae. Edited by Thomas Wright and James Halliwell. 2 vols. London: J. R. Smith, 1845.

Renzi, Salvatore de. Storia della medicina italiana. Naples: Filatre-Sebezio, 1845.

Rhazes. Opera parua Abubetri. Liber ad Almansorem. Tractatus de egritudinibus iuncturarum. De morbis puerorum. Aphorismata. Paruum antidotarium. Translated by Gerard of Cremona. Lyons: Villiers, 1510.

Rhazes. A treatise on the small-pox and measles by Abú Becr Mohammed Ibn Zacaríyá Ar-rázi (commonly called Rhazes). Translated by William Greenhill. London: Sydenham Society, 1848.

Salzmann, Louis. Mediaeval byways. London: Constable, 1913.

Schöffler, Herbert. Beitrage zur mittelenglischen Medizinliteratur. Sächsische Forschungsinstitute in Leipzig, anglistische Abteilung, Heft I. Halle: Niemeyer, 1919.

Schöffler, Herbert. "Gedruckte mittelenglisch-medizinische Texte," Archiv für Geschichte der Medizin, XI (1918), 107–109.

Schöffler, Herbert. "ME. medewax und polenwax," Englische studien, LV (1921), 134–136.

The school of Salernum. Regimen sanitatis salernitanum. Edited and translated by J. Harrington, F. Packard, and F. Garrison. New York: Hoeber, 1920.

The sege of Melayne. Edited by Sidney Herrtage. Early English Text Society, Extra Series, No. XXXIV, Part 2. London: Trübner, 1879.

Serapion, Johannes. Practica Jo. Serapionis dicta breuiarium. Liber Serapionis de simplici medicina. Anon. trans. Venice: B. Locatellus, 1497.

Sigerist, Henry. "Fragment einer unbekannten lateinischen Uebersetzung des hippokratischen Prognostikon," Archiv für geschichte der Medizin, XXIII (1930), 87–90.

Sigerist, Henry. "Studien und Texte zur frühmittelalterlichen Rezeptliteratur," Studien zur Geschichte der Medizin, Heft 13 (1923), 1–160.

Singer, Charles. "Early English magic and medicine," Proceedings of the British Academy, IX (1920), 1–34.

Singer, Charles. "A review of the medical literature of the Dark Ages, with a new text of about 1110," Proceedings of the Royal Society of Medicine, X (1916–17), Section of the history of medicine, 107–160.

Singer, Dorothea. "Some plague tractates (fourteenth and fifteenth centuries)," Proceedings of the Royal Society of Medicine, IX (1915–16), Section of the history of medicine, 159–212.

Singer, Dorothea. "Survey of medical manuscripts in the British Isles dating from before the sixteenth century," Proceedings of the Royal Society of Medicine XIII (1919), Section of the history of medicine, 96–107.

Singer, Dorothea, and Levy, Reuben. "Plague tractates," Annals of medical history, I (1917), 394–411.

Sinonoma Bartholomei. Edited by J. L. G. Mowat. Anecdota oxoniensia, Medieval and Modern Series, Vol. I, Part I. Oxford: Clarendon Press, 1882.

Skeat, Walter. "A fifteenth century charm," Modern language quarterly, IV (1901), 6–7.

Sudhoff, Karl. "Ein chirurgisches Manual des Jean Pitard, Wundarztes König

Bibliography.

Philipps des Schönen von Frankreich," Archiv für Geschichte der Medizin, II (1909), 189–278.
Sudhoff, Karl. "Die gedruckten mittelalterlichen medizinischen Texte in germanischen Sprachen," Archiv für Geschichte der Medizin, III (1909), 273–303.
Sudhoff, Karl. "Pestschriften aus den ersten 150 Jahren nach der Epidemie des 'schwarzen Todes' 1348," Archiv für Geschichte der Medizin, V (1911), 36–87.
Sudhoff, Karl. "Zur Todesprognostik," Archiv für Geschichte der Medizin, VIII (1915), 374–376.

Testamenta eboracensia. Edited by James Raine. Part II. Publications of the Surtees Society, No. 30. Durham : Surtees Society, 1854.
Thomas, A. "Notes etymologiques et lexicographiques," Romania, XXXVII (1908), 111–139.
Thompson, Charles. The mysteries and secrets of magic. Philadelphia : Lippincott, 1928.
Thompson, Daniel V. The materials of medieval painting. New Haven : Yale University Press, 1936.
Thorndike, Lynn. A history of magic and experimental science during the first thirteen centuries of our era. 2 vols. New York : Macmillan, 1923.
Thorndike, Lynn. Science and thought in the fifteenth century. New York : Columbia University Press, 1929.
Theophrastus. Enquiry into plants and minor works on odours and weather signs. Translated by Arthur Hort. 2 vols. "Loeb Classical Library." New York : Putnam, 1916.
Thornton, Mrs. Alice. The autobiography of Mrs. Alice Thornton of East Newton, co. York. Edited by Charles Jackson. Surtees Society Publications, No. 62. London : Surtees Society, 1875.
The Thornton romances. Edited by James O. Halliwell. Camden Society Publications, No. XXX. London : Camden Society, 1844.
Tschirch, Alexander. Handbuch der Pharmakognosie. 3 vols. Leipzig : Tauchnitz, 1909–25.
Tschirch, Alexander. Handbuch der Pharmakognosie. Bd. I, Lfg. 1–4. 2d. ed. Leipzig : Tauchnitz, 1930–34.

Vaccaro, Leopold. "The school of Salerno," Medical life, XXXVI (1929), 271–284.
Van Wijk, H. Gerth. A dictionary of plantnames. 2 vols. The Hague : Nijhoff, 1911–16.
The visitation of Yorkshire 1563, 1564. Edited by Charles Norcliffe. Publications of the Harleian Society, No. 16. London : Harleian Society, 1881.
Visitations of religious houses in the diocese of Lincoln. Edited by A. Hamilton Thompson. Publications of the Lincoln Record Society, No. 7. Horncastle : Lincoln Record Society, 1914.
A volume of vocabularies. Edited by Thomas Wright. 2 vols. London : Wright, 1857–73.

Whitehall, Harold. "A note on a North-West Midland spelling," Philological quarterly, IX (1930), 1–6.
Woolley, Reginald. Catalogue of the manuscripts of Lincoln Cathedral Chapter Library. London : Oxford University Press, 1927.

Yorkshire writers : Richard Rolle of Hampole and his followers. Edited by Carl Horstman. 2 vols. "Library of Early English." New York : Macmillan, 1895–96.

Zupitza, Julius. "Ein Zauberspruch," Zeitschrift für deutsches Alterthum und deutsche Litteratur, XXXI (1887), 45–52.

APPENDIX

A List of Abbreviated Titles used in the Notes and Glossary

In the list which follows, the abbreviated title of each complete book or article is followed by a cross reference to the entry in the Bibliography. Each cross reference includes enough of the entry to enable the reader to find the full title in the Bibliography. Where the abbreviated title refers to part of a book or article, the page numbers, or the volume and page numbers, follow the cross reference in parentheses.

Albertus (Borgnet). See Albertus Magnus. . . . Edited by Augustus Borgnet.
Albertus (1555). See Albertus Magnus . . . de secretis mulierum libellus.
Alexander (Puschmann). See Alexander Trallianus.
Alphita. See Alphita.
Anglia XVIII. See Holthausen, Ferdinand.
Anglia XXIV. See Manitius, Max.
Anglia XXXIV. See Garrett, Robert.
Antid. Nicolai (Platearius). See Nicolaus Praepositus. . . . With glossess by Platearius.
Archiv Med. II, V, VIII. See Sudhoff, Karl.
Archiv Med. XXIII. See Sigerist, Henry.
Arderne (Power). See Arderne, John. Treatises of fistula in ano.
Aristotle (Forster). See Aristotle.
Averrhoes (1560). See Averrhoes.
Avicenna (Gerard) *Canon*. See Avicenna. . . . Translated by Gerard of Cremona.
Avicenna (Gerard) *Cantica*. See Avicenna. . . . Translated by Gerard of Cremona.
Avicenna (Gruner). See Gruner, O. C.

Bamberger Antid. (Sigerist). See Sigerist, Henry. " Studien und Texte " (pp. 21–39).
Britten-Holland *Dict*. See Britten, James and Holland, Robert.

Camb. Antid. (Sigerist). See Sigerist, Henry. " Studien und Texte " (pp. 160–167).
Celsus (Marx). See Celsus, A. Cornelius.

Chauliac (Nicaise). See Chauliac, Guy de.
Cockayne. See Leechdoms, wortcunning, and starcraft of early England.
Coll. Salern. (Renzi). See Collectio Salernitana.
Constantinus (1510). See Constantinus Africanus.
Constantinus (1541). See Albucasis. Omnium humani corporis (pp. 322–334).

Dawson. See A leechbook.
Dict. Encyclopéd. See Dictionnaire encyclopédique.
Dioscurides (Wellman). See Dioscurides, Pedanius.

Gaddesden (1492). See Gaddesden, John of.
Galen (Kühn). See Galen, Claudius.
Germania XIII. See Köhler, Reinhold.
Germania XXXII. See Gallée, J. H.
Glasgow Antid. (Sigerist). See Sigerist, Henry. " Studien und Texte," pp. 99–160.
Gordon (1496). See Bernard Gordonius.

Haly Abbas (Stephanus). See Jesu Haly.
Heinrich. See Ein mittelenglisches Medizinbuch.
Henslow A. See Medical works of the fourteenth century (pp. 1–73).
Henslow B. See Medical works of the fourteenth century (pp. 74–122).
Henslow C. See Medical works of the fourteenth century (pp. 123–131).
Henslow D. See Medical works of the fourteenth century (pp. 132–145).

Appendix.

Herb. Ap. (Cockayne I). See Leechdoms, wortcunning, and starcraft (I, 1–247).
Herb. Ap. (Sigerist). See Apuleius Barbarus, etc. (pp. 15–225).
Hippocrates (Jones). See Hippocrates.
Isidore (Migne). See Isidore of Seville.
Ketham (Sudhoff-Singer). See Ketham, John of.
Lanfrank (Fleischhacker). See Lanfranchus.
L'antidot. Nicolas (Dorveaux). See Nicolaus Praepositus. . . . Edited by Paul Dorveaux.
Larsen. See An Old Icelandic medical miscellany.
Leechbook (Leonhardi). See Kleinere . . . Denkmäler. Edited by G. Leonhardi.

Macer (1527). See Macer Floridus.
Mag. Salern. See Magistri salernitani.
Marcellus (Niedermann). See Marcellus Empiricus.
Med. Quad. (Cockayne I). See Leechdoms, wortcunning, and starcraft (I, 326–375).
Mesue (Marinus). See Mesue.
Mondeville (Pagel). See Mondeville, Henry of. . . . Edited by Julius Pagel.
Müller. See Müller, Gottfried.
Murray. See Burgundy, John of.
Musa (Sigerist). See Apuleius Barbarus, etc. (pp. 3–11).

Najm (Guigues). See Najm ad-dyn Mahmud.
New Sydenham Lexicon. See Power, Henry and Sedgwick, Leonard.

Oribasius (Raeder). See Oribasius.

Paulus (Adams). See Paulus Aegineta.
Pliny (Mayhoff). See Plinius, Caius.
Peri Di. (Cockayne III). See Leechdoms, wortcunning, and starcraft (III, 81–143).

Peri Di. (Löweneck). See Peri Didaxeon.
Petrocellus (Löweneck). See Peri Didaxeon.
Platearius (1497). See Platearius, Johannes.
Reg. San. Salern. (Harrington). See The school of Salernum.

Rel. Ant. See Reliquiae antiquae.
Rhazes (1510) *Ad Almans.* See Rhazes. . . . Translated by Gerard of Cremona (ff. 1–217).
Rhazes (1510) *Antid.* See Rhazes. . . . Translated by Gerard of Cremona (ff. 268–278).
Romania XXXII. See Meyer, Paul.
Romania XXXVII, 358–377. See Meyer, Paul.
Romania XXXVII, 111–139. See Thomas, A.
Roy 12 G iv. See British Museum, Royal Manuscripts, 12 G iv.

Schöffler. See Schöffler, Herbert.
Scribonius (Helmreich). See Largus, Scribonius.
Serapion (1497) *De simpl. med.* See Serapion, Johannes (pp. 92–168).
Serapion (1497) *Practica.* See Serapion, Johannes (pp. 1–91).
St. Gall Antid. (Sigerist). See Sigerist, Henry, " Studien und Texte " (pp. 78–99).
17 St. John's Oxford (Singer). See Singer, Charles. " A review of medical literature."
Sextus Placitus (Sigerist). See Apuleius Barbarus, etc. (pp. 229–286).
Sinon. Bart. See Sinonoma Bartholomei.
Sloane 393. See British Museum, Sloane Manuscripts, 393.

Van Wijk. See Van Wijk, H. Gerth.

Wright Wülcker. See Anglo-Saxon . . . vocabularies. Edited by Thomas Wright and Richard Wülcker.

Zeitschrift f. deutsch. Alt. XXXVIII. See Priebsch, Robert.

ADDENDA 1969

The glossary supplement presents a selection of entries, some for words omitted in the 1938 glossary and others for words which can now be better glossed. Many other words in the *Liber* can be understood more fully in the light of the abundant evidence presented in the *Middle English Dictionary* (ed. Kurath and Kuhn, Ann Arbor: University of Michigan, 1952–).

affadill *n.* ? ramsons, *Allium ursinum* L. or daffodil, *Narcissus pseudo-narcissus* L. 6/12 [ML. *asphodelus, affodillus*].

allerone *n.* wing-tip, pinion 8/33 [OF. *aleron*].

ambre orientale ambergris 58/13.

anoyntement *n.* anointing 65/18.

apostym *n.* inflammation, gathering, abscess 36/31 . . .

aromatica *n.* prob. an aromatic gum resin, ? ammoniac or galbanum 27/19.

bawme *n.* ? a kind of mint, perh. balm, *Melissa officinalis* L., or an aromatic balsamic resin 11/19.

boche *n.* bubo (of the plague) 52/21 . . .

broken *pp.* as *n.* broken bones 70/5.

broo *n.* broth 29/8, 33/26.

cerfoil(e . . . 35/30; ? hart's-tongue fern, *Phyllitis scolopendrium* Newm. 47/12 . . . [OF. *cerfoil*].

charwelle = **cheruell** 50/16.

cheruell *n.* chervil 35/3, 59/15 [OE. *cer-felle*].

clusteryng *vbl. n.* coagulation, congestion 27/side-note 5.

coylett *n.* product of straining, strained liquid . . .

coruen *pp.* severed 68/31; ∼ **about** ? cut around, ? decayed 56/27–8.

dynt *n.* ? wound from a blow 75/side-note 6.

es in **agaynes** 58/37 (*see revised text*).

galynga *n.* galingale 33/6 [ML. *galanga*].

glett *n.* phlegm congested within the body . . .

gundy *adj.* bleared with matter . . .

hynge *v.* hang 2/35, 42/15.

hyngers *n. pl.* testicles 37/10 (*see* MED. **hongere**).

lede *n.* lead 5/23; cooking vessel, pot 64/20, 25.

litage *n.* lethargy, coma 61/34.

litarge *n.* litharge, lead monoxide 76/34.

maser(e *n.* hard-wood used for mazers 70/4, 6 (*see revised note*).

modirworte *n.* prob. = **mogwort(é**; or perh. red lamium, *Lamium purpureum* L. or motherwort, *Leonurus cardiaca* L. 25/5.

norwhare *adv.* nowhere 52/17.

162 Addenda 1969.

pokett n. small bag (for applying medicines locally) 29/38, 33/7.
reme n. in **mylke** ∼ cream 12/18–19 [OE. *rēam*].
rescheyue v. receive, take in by mouth 28/12.
ryme n. enveloping membrane (of the brain) 69/37, 70/2.
roungé v. pare or scrape (broken bones) 70/4 [cf. OF. *rongeour*, Mondeville, *Chirurgie*, ed. Bos, ii, 319].
sayme de voyr = saundeuer 3/4 [OF. *saim(e de voirre)*].
sanede pp. healed 75/side-note 10.
saxifrage n. ? burnet saxifrage, *Pimpinella saxifraga* L., greater burnet saxifrage, *P. magna* L. or saxifrage (*Saxifraga* spp.) 33/23.
scalles n. pl. scaly crusts from skin disease of the scalp 3/17, 4/side-note 1, 5/4, **skalles** 4/3.
schedde n. topmost part of the head 6/16.
schire n. clarified grease 55/3, 64/34.
serche v. probe (a wound) 69/17, 23.
teme v. pour, pour out 64/36.
wympill v. ? fold 69/26 (*see* Dawson 93, *quoted p. 114*).

NOTES

p. 84, note to 5/11–12: This Latin sentence corresponds verbatim to a recipe in Gerard of Cremona's translation of Rasis' *Antidotarium* (ed. Venice, 1497, f. 99va), except that Rasis' recipe begins *Dixit di.*, attributing it to an earlier writer, while the Thornton recipe begins *Viaticum dicit*. *Viaticum* is the title of Constantine of Africa's translation of the *Zād al-musāfir* of Ibn al-Jazzār, who died seventy-five years after Rasis.

p. 98, note to 37/10–11: The manuscript reading *hyngers* is correct. Another recipe to avoid drunkenness (ll. 14–15) advises washing the hands and *ballokes* in cold water. A recipe for staunching nose-bleed (48/36–37) uses the phrase *lay thi ballokes in* [cold water].

p. 115, note to 70/4, 6: *Maser* is probably mazer-wood, perhaps a piece of a broken mazer, used to replace the bone removed in shaving and scraping away splinters and jagged edges. Guy de Chauliac comments on this practice:

> Neuerþelatter olde men laide þerto þe pece of a cuppe, and it was but a iape, for þat tho men þat were aboute ham þe whiche were not at þe secounde removynge schulde byleue þat it schulde abyde þere in stede of the bone þat was loste [III. ii. 1, B.N.P. MS. anglais 25, f. 73v].

BIBLIOGRAPHY

Agnus Castus: A Middle English Herbal, ed. G. Brodin (Upsala, 1950).

A Middle English Translation of Macer Floridus De Viribus Herbarum, ed. G. Frisk (Upsala, 1949).

Bodman, H. L., Jun., "The *Sator*-Formula: an Evaluation", James Sprunt Studies, XLVI (1964), 131-141 [supplements note to p. 56 ll. 16-17].

Bower, R. H., "A Middle English Mnemonic Plague Tract", Southern Folklore Quarterly, XX (1956), 118-125.

Bühler, C. F., "A Middle English Medical Manuscript from Norwich", Studies in Medieval Literature in Honor of Professor Baugh (Philadelphia, 1961), 285-298.

Mayer, C. F., "A Medieval English Leechbook and its 14th Century Poem on Bloodletting", Bulletin of the History of Medicine, VII (1939), 381-391.

Nichols, R. E., "Medical Lore from *Sidrak and Bokkus*: A Miscellany in Middle English Verse", Journal of the History of Medicine, XXIII (1968), 167-172.

Riddle, J. M. "Pomum ambræ; Amber and Ambergris in Plague Remedies", Sudhoffs Archiv für Geschichte der Medizin, XLVIII (1964), 111-122.

Stannard, J., "A Fifteenth-century Botanical Glossary", Isis, LV (1964), 353-367.

Talbot, C. H., and Hammond, E. A., The Medical Practitioners in Medieval England (London, 1965), 382-383 (William of Appleton), 292-293 (William of Excestre).

Temkin, O., The Falling Sickness (Baltimore, 1945), 100-113.

Trease, G. E., "The Spicers and Apothecaries of the Royal Household in the Reigns of Henry II, Edward I, and Edward II", Nottingham Medieval Studies, III (1959), 19-52.

Trease, G. E., and Hodson, J. H., "The Inventory of John Hexham, a Fifteenth-Century Apothecary", Medical History, IX (1965), 76-81.

Whytlaw-Gray, A., "John Lelamour's Translation of Macer's Herbal" (Univ. of Leeds M.A. thesis).

www.ingramcontent.com/pod-product-compliance
Ingram Content Group UK Ltd.
Pitfield, Milton Keynes, MK11 3LW, UK
UKHW021050260426
12049UKWH00034B/34